MAKING ETHICAL DECISIONS

MAKING ETHICAL DECISIONS

Norman E. Bowie
University of Delaware

McGRAW-HILL BOOK COMPANY

New York   St. Louis   San Francisco   Auckland   Bogotá
Hamburg   Johannesburg   London   Madrid   Mexico   Montreal   New Delhi
Panama   Paris   São Paulo   Singapore   Sydney   Tokyo   Toronto

This book was set in Times Roman by J. M. Post Graphics, Corp.
The editors were Emily G. Barrosse and Barry Benjamin;
the production supervisor was Charles Hess.
The cover was designed by John Hite.
Halliday Lithograph Corporation was printer and binder.

MAKING ETHICAL DECISIONS

1 2 3 4 5 6 7 8 9 0 HALHAL 8 9 8 7 6 5 4

ISBN 0-07-006744-9

Library of Congress Cataloging in Publication Data
Main entry under title:

Making ethical decisions.

    Bibliography: p.
    Includes index.
    1. Ethics—Addresses, essays, lectures. I. Bowie,
Norman E., date
BJ1025.M24 1984   170   84-15422
ISBN 0-07-006744-9

CONTENTS

PREFACE

Making Ethical Decisions is significantly different from other texts for first courses in ethics. Most texts are either organized historically, with each philosopher appearing in chronological order, or organized on the basis of the distinction between metaethics and normative ethics, with the bulk of the normative ethics selections focusing on two theories—utilitarianism and a version of deontology.

Making Ethical Decisions addresses four overreaching issues which arise from the concerns and questions of students: Is ethics possible? What is the scope of ethics? What does it take to be a moral person? What are my responsibilities to other moral persons? Most of the classic historical figures do appear in this text, but they do not appear in chronological order. Plato, Aristotle, Kant, Bentham, and Mill all make an appearance. So do such figures as Bradley, Royce, Sartre, and Rawls. However, all of these historical figures appear in the chapters where the topic focuses on their most important philosophical contribution.

There is a chapter on utilitarianism. There is no one single chapter on deontology as such, but nearly all the concepts found in various deontological writers appear in this anthology; rules, respect for persons, rights, virtues, and justice constitute entire chapters. This text is ideally constructed so that the traditional ethical theories and the fundamental ethical concepts can be taught together in a unified whole. The reasons for this departure from the two-theory approach are both philosophical and pedagogical. Several important ethical concepts, like virtue, do not fall neatly under either of the two traditional theories. Some pedagogical research indicates that general principles may not be the most effective means for introducing ethics. For example, in its report to the National Endowment for the Humanities, the Committee for Education in Business Ethics recommended that any business ethics text provide extensive coverage of such central ethical concepts as rights, equality, and virtue. The committee's recommendation was based on the following observation:

> Since our own experimental course indicated that traditional ethical theories were unsuccessful as pedagogical devices for achieving the aims of the course, ethical theory should be introduced relatively late in the course. Best results are obtained by introducing students to central moral concepts like justice, honesty, and autonomy early in the course.

Finally, you won't see chapters devoted to naturalism, intuitionism, emotivism, noncognitivism, etc. Students don't see the point of all these "isms." However, representatives of most of these schools are included in the text. Moreover, several new areas of ethical research are included here. There are generous selections from MacIntyre's *After Virtue,* Alan Donagan's *The Theory of Morality,* and Charles Fried's *Right and Wrong.* I trust that the organization of the text will make it easier to teach a course in ethics, that enough familiar names and topics are included so that instructors will be comfortable with the text, and that enough new material is included so that instructors can feel confident that students are at least introduced to contemporary ethical research.

ACKNOWLEDGMENTS

The publication of any book or anthology requires the cooperation of a number of persons, only some of whom can be acknowledged explicitly. There are anonymous reviewers, various editors, and support persons at McGraw-Hill who are unknown to me.

Explicit and special appreciation is due to Barry Benjamin, editor at McGraw-Hill, and to my two secretaries, Sandy Manno and Pat Orendorf, who kept track of the permissions and did the necessary duplicating, typing, and proofreading.

The source of each article is identified by the person's name at the bottom of the page on which the article begins.

Norman E. Bowie

GENERAL INTRODUCTION

As members of the human community, each of us faces ethical issues. Is it morally wrong to gamble? to choose a dangerous career, such as smoke jumping? How much, if any, of my income should I give to the poor? Do I have a moral obligation to report cheating? to come forward as a witness when I have observed an automobile accident? Do I "owe" my country two years of my life either in the armed services or in something like a domestic peace corps?

These few examples provide some hint at the richness of issues which call for ethical decisions. On what basis should these decisions be made? People can decide such questions on the basis of feelings—"I just wouldn't feel right if I gambled." People can decide such questions on the basis of authority, either religious or parental—"My religion doesn't permit gambling." Some people try to avoid making difficult ethical decisions, but that just postpones the decisions, and besides, postponing a decision is a decision in its own right. Is it right to postpone ethical decisions?

A book on ethics provides the tools for making ethical decisions on the basis of knowledge about right and wrong. A book on ethics should explain what a theory about ethics is; it should provide some of the traditional understandings of central ethical concepts; it should provide a representative sample of well-known ethical theories. By using these concepts and theories, and by having an appreciation of what constitutes an ethical question, people can make decisions on the basis of reason.

To make decisions on the basis of ethical concepts and theories does not mean that everyone who uses ethical knowledge will make the same ethical decisions. We may use different theories; for example, some of us might use duty theories but not utilitarian ones to justify a charitable act. We may disagree on what the implications of a given ethical principle are; for example, whether the principle of respect for persons forbids abortions under all circumstances. We may also disagree as to how virtues should be weighted; for example, deciding which virtue, courage or love, should weigh most in considering whether or not to register for selective service. However, all these disagreements take place within the framework of ethics. They are very different in kind from the disagreements that occur when one religion forbids abortion and another permits it, or when one father encourages his son to join the armed services and another father discourages his son from joining. A course in ethics does not eliminate disagreements on ethical questions. Since ethical decisions should be made on the basis of reason rather than authority, however, the scope of the disagreements can be narrowed.

Discussions of disagreements in ethics are complicated by the fact that most ethical decisions involve questions of fact as well as questions of right and wrong. Suppose the decision up for discussion is whether or not one should accept a job in a nuclear power plant. One important element in making that decision is the facts about the risks of working in a nuclear power plant. If one person argues that morality forbids working in a nuclear power plant, while another argues that morality permits working there, their disagreement might be a factual one rather than a moral one—a disagreement, that is, about the risks of working in nuclear power plants. Nearly all disputes about nuclear arms policy are factual rather than moral. Presumably, nearly everyone agrees that nuclear war is immoral; the issue that divides us is a factual one: How can nuclear war be prevented? The discussions in this book are limited to ethical issues; factual issues are largely ignored. However, readers must not forget that a determination of the facts is crucial for making ethical decisions.

Although ethical decisions are among the most important that we make, many people wonder whether genuine ethical decisions are really possible. Sometimes this question is phrased as, "Is there a discipline of ethics at all?" or put somewhat differently, "Does ethics exist in its own right?" Now, few textbooks begin in this rather strange way. Chemistry books don't begin by discussing whether chemistry is really a science or with a discussion of how chemistry can be distinguished from alchemy. However, while most students don't doubt the scientific nature of chemistry, many students do have serious doubts about the status of ethics. These doubts may not be articulately expressed, but as any ethics professor can confirm, they exist nonetheless. The early chapters of this book address the most common doubts that students, as well as nonstudents, have about the status of ethics. These doubts are given names, explained in some detail, and then addressed by philosophers who believe they can rationally be put to rest. Of course, not everyone is convinced by these philosophical responses, and you may not be convinced either.

Chapter 1 asks what reasons can be given for behaving morally. One answer to the "why be moral" question is to reduce moral issues to prudential ones. We should make decisions on moral grounds when it is in our interest to do so. Why should I choose the career of doctor? Because I can make a lot of money curing the sick. Why should I avoid lying? Because one lie leads to another, and sooner or later I will get caught. Again this type of attitude is sufficiently persuasive to be given a name—egoism. Some egoists have been inspired by studies of human nature, and they believe people always behave egoistically. Everything they do is in terms of their perceived best interests. That's just the way people are. Egoism causes difficulties for ethical theory. Since part of what most philosophers mean by an ethical decision is that it is a decision which takes the interests of others into account, egoism would rule out ethics. The interest of another is only taken into account when, at least in theory, the interest of another can override your own interest. In other words, ethics requires that on occasion you put the interests of others ahead of your own interest. But egoists say either that you can't or that you shouldn't.

Chapter 2 considers whether or not the basis for ethical decisions is to be found in one's culture. Social scientists, particularly anthropologists, have discovered that ethical practices differ sharply from culture to culture. Given this variety among cultures, why not simply claim that what constitutes an ethical decision is a function of the culture one lives in and then urge every culture to be tolerant of every other culture. This view, called "relativism," would take account of the anthropological information on so-called primitive cultures and would eliminate the historically harsh moral judgments made about the behavior of primitive people. But, paradoxically, cultural rel-

include a principle or principles of equality. Chapter 10 provides some discussion of the various theories of justice, equality, and the relation that exists between justice and equality. If justice is to be done, in some respects the interests of each person are to count equally.

Theories of justice also provide an alternative for finding the correct moral answer to every moral question—a task which many philosophers agree is impossible. In the political context, democratic government might serve as a just means for adjudicating political disputes. After all you can't get complete consensus on every issue. Perhaps a set of procedures for settling some disputes is the best you can do. Chapter 10 considers that question as well.

But perhaps the ultimate goal of an ethical decision should be the public interest, or the interest of everyone. Chapter 11 considers that goal under the rubric of utilitarianism. Utilitarians believe that people ought to maximize good consequences. Utilitarians differ on their theories of what counts as good consequences and on the most desirable means to achieve them. Some utilitarians believe that only pleasure is good; they are called "hedonists." Others include a wider array of goods, such as beauty, truth, and justice—as well as pleasure. Utilitarians treat ethics as future-looking. To determine what is right or wrong, look ahead to what will be achieved (what will result). They analyze certain central notions of ethics, such as promise-keeping or justice, in terms of their contribution to the good. Promise-keeping, for example, leads either to good consequences or to the good (pleasure for hedonists; virtue or some other good for nonhedonists).

But many philosophers (nonconsequentialists) find the utilitarian account of justice and promise-keeping to be inadequate. Nearly all nonconsequentialists agree that achieving the good or bringing about good consequences is often the right thing to do *but not always*. The right cannot be defined in terms of the good. Ethics must also be past-looking rather than simply future-looking. When making an ethical decision it is not sufficient to simply see what good will result; you must consider your present and past circumstances and treat them as relevant to your ethical decision. Do you stand in a special relationship to anyone your decision will affect? For example, mother/daughter, teacher/student, physician/patient? Do you occupy a job, profession, or role which places special moral obligations upon you? The duty to respect privacy and confidentiality is especially binding on lawyers and priests. The police ought to be especially scrupulous in respecting the law. What are your motives? Are you trying to bring about good results because you genuinely respect your fellow human beings, or are you trying to become Rotarian of the year? Did you make a promise? Most nonconsequentialists think that a promise is morally binding even if it doesn't lead to good consequences. There is something special about promises, contracts, oaths of loyalty, etc. In general when making ethical decisions, nonconsequentialists treat desert, or giving people their due, very seriously.

Perhaps correct ethical decision-making should limit its perspective. Rather than focus on the abstract notion of the "public good," as the utilitarians suggest, it should focus on the roles, e.g., parent, employee, that we play in society and the organizations to which we belong. Students don't have an obligation of loyalty to every college; they have an obligation of loyalty to the college they attend. These role-related ob-

ativism may have implications which undercut the value of tolerance. If relativism were true, how could you have a theory which provided rational grounds for settling ethical disputes between cultures? If what really is right or wrong depends on a person's culture, isn't that the end of the matter, and doesn't further discussion end? Even the most casual observer of the world scene realizes that disagreements among cultures on matters of right and wrong are often settled by force of arms. Doesn't relativism lend credence to those who advocate settling ethical disputes by force of arms? By eliminating the possibility of reasons for an ethical decision other than the reason that the culture forbids, permits, or requires the action, the traditional account of ethics would be emaciated.

Yet another roadblock for ethics occurs when you can't do what you ought to do. In making a decision you make a choice; you are aware of alternative possibilities for action, and after deliberation of some sort you choose one action over another. That consideration of alternatives and the ultimate selection of one alternative is a decision. You usually don't decide to get sick (unless you make yourself very drunk at a party). Getting sick is not normally a decision. Getting sick is also not something for which you receive moral blame. A common slogan in ethics is "ought implies can." What that slogan means is that you can only say a person ought to do something—help a neighbor, for example—if in fact he or she can help the neighbor. It makes no sense for me to tell you that you ought to give your neighbor $100 if you don't have $100 to give. All this seems obvious enough. But how do you know what you can do? Right now most of us can't do 100 push-ups, but we could if we exercised regularly. Losing weight is hard. Studying philosophy is hard. But when does an ethical decision cease being hard and start to be impossible? Complete answers to that question lead to another branch of philosophy called "metaphysics."

Some might argue that this issue is not really an ethical issue at all. However, even if someone takes that stand—and you need not, Sartre doesn't—considerations of the nature and scope of human freedom help determine the scope of ethical theory. From this perspective, Chapter 3 can be joined with the first two chapters to constitute a unit which discusses the conditions which make genuinely ethical decisions possible.

The second section of the book considers the scope of ethics. What are the kinds of things you need to consider when you are making an ethical decision? Many people argue that you should behave morally because God demands it, and others maintain that moral behavior is required by law. But if either of these responses constituted the whole story, then ethics would be reduced to a branch of theology or a branch of the law. Chapter 4 presents some possible ways for distinguishing ethics from law and religion.

One of the more heated recent controversies in ethics is the following. Does every decision that a person makes have ethical consequences that ought to be taken into account when the decision is made? Many people would answer unhesitatingly in the affirmative. But wouldn't that make ethics impossibly burdensome? (Remember the "ought implies can" slogan.) An alternative approach is to limit the ethical consequences that ought to be considered in any decision to intended consequences that cause avoidable harm to others. Other consequences—unintended ones or consequences that bestow benefits—can be ignored. But this approach has obvious problems as well.

What about duties to oneself? Many people believe they have a moral duty to be temperate or to develop their minds to the highest extent possible. Are these duties illusory—not really moral duties at all? Or are they genuine moral obligations, but moral obligations which are less stringent than moral obligations to avoid causing harm? And what about moral heroes—people who perform moral acts at extreme personal costs to themselves? Consider whistle-blowers in government and business who warn the public of waste or dangerous products and place their jobs in jeopardy in the bargain. Should we urge our children to be moral heroes?

Another issue which falls under the "nature and scope of ethics" heading is the extent to which ethics is a matter of rules. Most of the ethical theory we learn first comes to us as rules. The Ten Commandments are a good example. But surely there's more to ethics than learning a set of rules. After all, rules can become outdated. A moral rule develops in a social context. Part of that context includes beliefs about the way the world is (facts about the world). But some of our beliefs are mistaken. The world isn't the way we thought it was. Other beliefs are incomplete. We learn more about the world. Finally the world changes. Part of ethics involves a reflection of how our ethical rules fit with the facts about the world as we know it. Rules also need interpretation. There's almost always an area of ambiguity or lack of clarity which must be settled. There are ethical and unethical ways of interpreting rules. Rules can be abused; they can serve as an alleged justification for an immoral decision. Chapter 6 considers the uses and limitations of rules in ethical decision-making. It also considers whether there is one fundamental ethical rule or whether there are several, and it considers whether moral rules are all of the same kind.

Chapters 4 to 6 address some of the more important issues about the nature and scope of ethics. However, these chapters don't propose ethical theories per se or develop ethical concepts per se. Those tasks occupy us in the remaining six chapters of the book.

Until recently most texts on ethics focused on two basic ethical theories—some version of Kantianism (anticonsequentialism) and utilitarianism (consequentialism). But in the past few years several important books have appeared which move ethics in new directions. No longer can ethical theory be divided into Kantianism and utilitarianism. For example, Alasdair MacIntyre's book *After Virtue,* a selection from which is included in Chapter 9, does not fall neatly into the standard division. With its focus on virtue and its emphasis on history and culture as the proper context for studying ethical theory, it is neither Kantian nor utilitarian. Since no text in ethics would be complete without discussions of Kantianism and utilitarianism, generous selections from both theories are found in the text. But non-Kantian and nonutilitarian theories are included as well.

Rather than divide the remaining chapters into Kantian ethics and utilitarian ethics, I have chosen to consider the three fundamental principles or concepts that any individual must consider when making an ethical decision. Hence, the chapters on respect for persons, rights, and virtue constitute a separate section. The last section focuses on how the individual might apply these principles and concepts—as well as others— in a social context.

If I had to identify one principle as the fundamental principle of ethical making, it would be the principle of respect for persons. Although many ph would deny that a principle of respect for persons could serve as the sole pi ethical decision-making, and although philosophers disagree among themse the proper formulation of a principle of respect for persons, almost every pl agrees that respect for persons is one of our fundamental duties. Chapter both Immanuel Kant's classic defense of his version of the principle of re persons and the contemporary philosopher Alan Donagan's attempt to show th for persons is the common underlying principle of Jewish and Christian th ethics. Moreover, one of the persons who deserves our respect is ourself many philosophers and psychologists agree that a sense of self-respect is for human development, including human moral development.

The remaining two chapters in this section contribute to the discussion respect. Chapter 8 shows how the principle of respect for persons can se justification for a theory of human rights. For example, some selections in the argue that we can't be full members of the human community unless we hav To make an ethical decision we have to have self-respect, and to have self-res must have rights.

As an ethical decision-maker, characterized as one who respects both hin others, how will I behave? First, I will respect the rights of others. Secon behave virtuously. Virtue is a topic which nearly disappeared from ethics te the past quarter of a century. The concept of virtue was just not considered mental moral concept. However, Alasdair MacIntyre's *After Virtue* raised ou consciousness. One of the more exciting areas of discussion and research in the concept of virtue. Some old problems are being reconsidered. For exampl asked why people who knew what they ought to do sometimes wouldn't do it. answer was, "Ignorance." People who didn't do what they ought to do, didn' know what they ought to do. Otherwise, they would do it. But many philos didn't accept Plato's answer. They think people have "weakness of will." One suggestions for overcoming weakness of will is virtuous habits. Chapter 9 is d to some of the contributions that the concept of virtue can make to ethical de making.

Since the essential characteristic of an ethical decision is the willingness to into account the interests of others, ethical decision-making most prominently o when we interact with others. The arguments in Chapters 7 and 8 tell us to re the rights of others. But how? The injunction to respect the rights of others is hopel abstract and of little help when the interests of others are so in conflict that what our decision, some person's interest is denied or ignored. What makes a moral deci so difficult is precisely the fact that interests compete. When I, as an ethical decis maker, confront a situation where my interests compete with those of others, or w my decision affects the interests of some positively and the interests of others ne tively, I need some principles for making that decision.

Theories of justice are intended to provide such principles. Such theories are signed to tell us what it means to give others their due. Theories of justice usua

ligations and the demands of loyalty they create are discussed in the final chapter. Also discussed is the chief problem with role-related obligations. Sometimes there is an apparent conflict between the role obligations we have and other moral obligations. For example, lawyers have an obligation to defend their clients in the most vigorous manner possible. To honor that obligation, lawyers might have to browbeat a witness. Would such browbeating be a correct moral decision?

Suppose a group makes an immoral decision. Even though an individual member of the group votes against the decision, or in other ways expresses disapproval of it, should the individual be held morally responsible (in whole or in part) for the group's decision? As might be expected, not all philosophers agree on the answer to this question.

However, the purpose of a text on ethics is not to give answers to difficult ethical questions. The central goal of this book is to provide the reader with the tools for making ethical decisions—with ethical concepts and ethical theories; it is not to show that every ethical theory has its critics and that any ethical concept has its limitations. That will become obvious. By covering the whole range of ethical theories and concepts, this book provides you, the reader, with a full toolbox. You will know the strengths and weaknesses of each tool. But the quality of the work, the quality of the ethical decisions you make, will be your own.

PART ONE

THE POSSIBILITY OF MORALITY

CHAPTER 1

WHY BE ETHICAL?

One of the first lessons in ethics that parents give their children is that children shouldn't be selfish. The child is told to share her toys, to play ball with his sister, to pick up things when finished with them. It's no accident that the obligation not to be selfish is at the center of a child's training in ethics. The shift from securing our own interests to sacrificing, at least on occasion, our interests on behalf of the interests of others is the essential part of what we mean by "making ethical decisions." The selfish person by definition cannot habitually make moral decisions. Such is the tradition—both in childrearing and in ethical theory.

In the general introduction I argued that one of the features of taking the moral point of view was a willingness to take into account the interests and desires of others. If you should ask why we should take account of the interests and desires of others, you are asking for a justification of one of the central features of morality itself. Such a request for justification is precisely the question a moral philosopher should be asking, and it is precisely the question that a moral philosopher should be able to answer.

Well, why should anyone take account of the interests and desires of others? Why shouldn't you just look out for your own interests and desires? It might be tempting to reply, "You should take account of the interests and desires of others because then they will take into account your interests and desires. Moreover you can only fulfill your interests and desires if other people take them into account." This is precisely the kind of reply that many parents make to their children when their children ask this kind of "why" question. "Why should I share my toys with Johnny?" "Because if you don't share your toys with Johnny, he won't share his toys with you," your mother replies. Such replies teach a valuable lesson; our interests are tied up with the interests of others. We are better able to get what we want if we help others get what they want.

However, this answer will not succeed in all situations. It works fine for the average child, but would the answer convince a bully? It certainly doesn't seem as if it would. A bully doesn't need to share. He can keep his own toys and take those of the other children. The bully does not need to help others fulfill their desires in order to fulfill his own.

This challenge to morality is raised in the selection by Plato, one of the earliest western philosophers. In the famous dialogue *The Republic,* Plato has Glaucon relate the myth of Gyges. Essentially this is the story of a shepherd who has discovered a ring which when rubbed makes the wearer invisible. Why should the owner of such a ring take the interests of others into account? Why should such a person take the point of view of morality? After all the owner of such a ring has the power to fulfill his own interests without worrying about fulfilling the interests of others. Indeed, the ring's owner could fulfill his interests at the expense of the interests of others.

One attempt to answer this question begins with an appeal to the world as it is. We are reminded that the story of Gyges is just that—a story. There aren't any magic rings. In the real world the bully has to remember that there are bigger bullies around the block or that there are teachers and police officers or even that a group of weaklings is stronger than a bully. As in the child's game "king of the mountain," the reign of the king is unstable and often short.

Many philosophers have argued that immorality really isn't in our interest. Plato makes this point with respect to the shepherd's magic ring. Plato believed that a human being is essentially composed of appetites, will, and reason, and that a happy and productive person is one whose reason controls his or her appetite and will. Plato then tries to prove that the immoral person is a person whose reason has lost control. Such a person would have a disordered soul and would be unhappy. Having a magic ring wouldn't change that fact. Hence Plato tries to argue that immorality is ultimately self-defeating. Whether or not Plato is right depends on psychological fact. Some tyrants certainly give the impression that they are happy and that their happiness is not short-lived but rather long-lasting. At the very least they would claim to be happier than the purely moral person.

These are people who reject the notion that one of the essential features of making ethical decisions is that we take into account the interests and desires of others. Some of these people are egoists. One version of egoism is an empirical theory about human behavior. It describes and explains human action. The traditional name for this type of egoism is "psychological egoism." It maintains that people are *always* motivated to act in their *perceived* best interest. As an empirical theory of human behavior, psychological egoism is not an ethical theory at all. It doesn't tell us how people ought to behave, it tells us how people do in fact behave. However, whether or not psychological egoism is true is of great interest to ethical theorists. The other version of egoism is a genuine ethical theory. Traditionally named "ethical egoism," it maintains that people *ought* to act in their *perceived* best interest. This is not a theory of how people behave in fact; the theory recognizes that people sometimes do act contrary to their perceived best interests. However an ethical egoist argues that people should not act in that way.

Before we evaluate these two versions of egoism in some depth, a few preliminary points are in order. First, although philosophers are usually careful about distinguishing the two versions of egoism, other writers and the average person are not. Those who extoll the virtues of self-interest over morality sometimes use the arguments of psychological egoism and at other times the arguments of ethical egoism. However, since psychological egoism cannot be used to support ethical egoism, it is important that the student of ethics keep the two versions distinct.

Second, don't confuse egoism with egotism. An egotist is a person who is stuck on himself, and such people make poor egoists. After all, being stuck on yourself is hardly conducive to your self-interest, and ethical egoists would surely condemn it. Marking the distinction between egoism and egotism contributes to an important point. Egoistic behavior need not be and usually is not antisocial behavior, for the simple reason that antisocial behavior is almost always detrimental to your interests.

Students of political science or economics may be familiar with the theories of two of the best-known egoists on this matter. The English philosopher Thomas Hobbes believed that people pursue their own interests in terms of seeking what they are attracted to and avoiding what repels them. But of course the interests of individuals come into conflict, and since we are all roughly equal (gunpowder is a great equalizer), no one can gain a permanent advantage over the other. It is "the war of all against all." Hence for Hobbes the fact that people act egoistically leads to chaos. However, our reason and the fact that the strongest motive of human behavior is self-preservation save the day. Rather than live in the state of perpetual war, our reason tells us that we should give up our freedom to seek our own ends as we please to a central absolute authority (the state). Only in this way can the war of all against all be ended and our ultimate self-interest be preserved.

The political economist Adam Smith started with a theory of psychological egoism very much like that of Hobbes; however Adam Smith came to a very different view about what life would look like in an egoistic world. He agreed with Hobbes that people generally behaved in terms of attempting to achieve their best perceived self-interest. (In his moral philosophy, Smith did have a place for altruistic sentiments.) The world of the competitive market best captured Smith's conception of egoism. In the marketplace we all try to buy cheap and sell dear. In that way we will maximize our own resources. However, the world of the competitive market is not like Hobbes's war of all against all. It is both orderly and productive of a high level of social good. For Adam Smith the egoistic behavior of individuals seems to be guided by an invisible hand, so that social good results. Hence the individual need not surrender very much power to the state. The state is more like a disinterested umpire than an absolute central sovereign.

This dispute between Hobbes and Smith contains a number of lessons. First, neither Hobbes nor Smith clearly distinguishes psychological egoism from ethical egoism. If I had to place my bets I would classify Hobbes as a psychological egoist and Smith as an ethical egoist. Hobbes has a mechanistic theory of human motivation, and it is easy to see how the rise of the absolute sovereign would be inevitable given Hobbes's postulates about human motivation and human reason. Yet Hobbes sometimes seems to go beyond merely describing and predicting. He seems to be urging us to accept the authority of the state. Smith doesn't have such a well-developed theory of human motivation. He more clearly seems to be saying that people ought to behave egoistically so that the benefits of market capitalism might come about. Yet at other times you get the feeling that Smith is trying to describe the world. People actually behave as they would behave in a market model.

This tension provides the clue to why psychological and ethical egoism don't support one another. If psychological egoism is true, there is no need for ethical egoism. Since psychological egoism maintains that people *are* motivated to act in their perceived best interest, then ethical egoism is useless. There is no sense in telling people how they ought to behave if they are going to behave that way anyway. The truth of psychological egoism makes ethical egoism redundant. (By the way, the truth of psychological egoism would make any other ethical theory futile; there's no sense in telling people they ought to act contrary to self-interest if they can only act in terms of self-interest.) The fact that there are elements of both description and moral exhortation in both Hobbes and Smith accounts for the tension previously noted.

Of course in saying that the truth of psychological egoism makes ethical egoism redundant, I am not saying that the psychological egoist has no place for advice in matters of ethics. Our perceptions of what is in our self-interest can be factually mistaken. Egotists are so mistaken. However, that advice is not moral advice, it doesn't give you advice about how to balance the demands of self-interest and the demands imposed on you by the interests of others. Rather it simply gives factual advice about how to obtain your own interest.

The second lesson the dispute between Hobbes and Smith teaches is that whether egoistic behavior leads to an antisocial, chaotic society or to a rather efficient, benevolent society is a matter of great controversy. The selection by Rand and Branden defends the view that the practice of ethical egoism alone is consonant with the requirements of human life and therefore, as a secondary consequence, leads to a better society.

Let's turn our attention away from the dispute between Hobbes and Smith concerning the consequences of adopting egoism as a practice and focus on the adequacy of the two versions of egoism. Since psychological egoism is a theory about human behavior, the appropriate question to ask here is, "Is psychological egoism true?" At first glance it seems that in some cases psychological egoism is clearly false. A mother rushes to save her child despite great danger to herself. An employee blows the whistle on an employer to protect the public and is fired as a result. Don't these examples undercut psychological egoism? No, the psychological egoist responds. Both the mother and the whistle-blower would have had great pangs of guilt if they had acted otherwise. In popular parlance, they couldn't have lived with themselves. This response has some plausibility—particularly in the case of the mother. It's not unreasonable to think that a mother wouldn't be able to live with herself if she didn't try to rescue her child— regardless of the magnitude of the danger to her. But what about the man who initially survived a plane crash in the Potomac River but consistently handed the rope to other passengers until he drowned? The other passengers were strangers, and he had a wife and children of his own. How was his act in his perceived best interest? No matter how altruistic the example, the psychological egoist will usually postulate some deeper motive (even an unconscious motive) of self-interest. At this point many philosophers think the psychological egoist is defeated. What looked like an empirical theory about human behavior now looks like a matter of faith. The psychological egoist will let nothing count against the theory, and hence has no empirical theory at all. After all, a scientist will submit a theory to testing and will give up the theory if the tests continually go against it.

What about ethical egoism? One of the traditional criticisms of ethical egoism is that it is contradictory or incoherent. Brian Medlin takes that approach in the selection included here. The basic strategy of this criticism is to show the paradoxes that result when you take seriously the ethical thesis that we all ought to act in our own perceived best interest. To take one example, suppose two of your friends, Jim and Jane, ask you for moral advice. Jim asks whether he should pursue his interest at the expense of Jane. Jane asks whether she should pursue her interest at the expense of Jim. Surely the ethical egoist must answer yes to both questions. The controversy enters with the critic's assertion that a yes answer to both questions gives paradoxical if not contradictory advice.

In the final selection, Kurt Baier challenges egoism by trying to show why moral reasons which take into account the interests of others are superior to reasons of self-interest. In the real world we can only achieve our aims if we agree to a set of rules which sets limits on the means individuals can use to achieve their aims. Many social scientists, especially economists, define rationality as seeking the most efficient means to achieve a given end. Baier argues that morality is the device that rational persons would use to promote their ends. Morality so conceived is, as Baier puts it, "in the interests of everyone."

Baier asks us to conduct a thought experiment. Consider two worlds—one where moral reasons are treated as superior and one where they aren't. Everyone would agree that the world where moral reasons are treated as superior is the better world. It is better because it is the world with the better quality of life, and since it is a better world it is rational to prefer it to the other.

But suppose someone wants to know why we should be rational about such things. To raise this question is to ask the question, "Why be rational?" Baier then points out that the questioner who asks for a reason for being rational is talking nonsense. In asking for a reason, one is accepting the legitimacy of reason.

Baier also considers other interpretations of the "why be rational" question. It might be interpreted, for example, as "Why should I follow reason as opposed to authority?" Baier's answer is that you need a reason for accepting this authority rather than some other authority or your own reasoning. It is fair to add that if a choice for authority is not made on reason, it must be made on a whim. In any case such a choice couldn't be justified, because an appeal to justification is an appeal to reason.

Baier's arguments and similar ones developed by other philosophers may not have persuaded everyone, but they have had an important impact on ethical theory. Any discussion of this issue must confront Baier's analysis. Let us consider a common objection to Baier's argument.

First, there is a difference between saying that morality is in the best interest of everyone including me and that following morality in this particular case is in my best interest. Just because it is in my interest that society have a rule against lying, it doesn't follow that it is in my interest not to lie in this particular case. In fact what is really in my best interest is that everyone else not lie but that I lie whenever I can get away with it. Why should I follow morality in such cases and not lie?

Philosophers do not answer this challenge with a unanimous voice. Here is one plausible response. I either did or did not agree to lie. If I did agree to tell the truth in circumstances where it was not in my interest to do so, and now I don't, I am contradicting myself. I both did and did not agree to tell the truth in circumstances where it was not in my interest. On the other hand, if I didn't agree not to lie when it was in my best interest to do so, others would not agree not to lie to me when it was in their best interest not to do so. Hence, in this set of circumstances the opportunity to lie when I am assured that no one else would lie would never arise. Since no one would agree not to lie, that world would resemble the one described by Hobbes, but that is just the world morality is designed to prevent. Hence lying in circumstances when you can get away with it is either contradictory or self-defeating. The adequacy of this response will receive further analysis in a later chapter.

The Myth of Gyges

Plato

First, I will state what is commonly held about the nature of justice and its origin; secondly, I shall maintain that it is always practised with reluctance, not as good in itself, but as a thing one cannot do without; and thirdly, that this reluctance is reasonable, because the life of injustice is much the better life of the two—so people say. . . . Accordingly, I shall set you an example by glorifying the life of injustice with all the energy that I hope you will show later in denouncing it and exalting justice in its stead. Will that plan suit you?

Nothing could be better, I replied. Of all subjects this is one on which a sensible man must always be glad to exchange ideas.

Good, said Glaucon. Listen then, and I will begin with my first point: the nature and origin of justice.

What people say is that to do wrong is, in itself, a desirable thing; on the other hand, it is not at all desirable to suffer wrong, and the harm to the sufferer outweighs the advantage to the doer. Consequently, when men have had a taste of both, those who have not the power to seize the advantage and escape the harm decide that they would be better off if they made a compact neither to do wrong nor to suffer it. Hence they began to make laws and covenants with one another; and whatever the law prescribed they called lawful and right. That is what right or justice is and how it came into existence; it stands half-way between the best thing of all—to do wrong with impunity—and the worst, which is to suffer wrong without the power to retaliate. So justice is accepted as a compromise, and valued, not as good in itself, but for lack of power to do wrong; no man worthy of the name, who had that power, would ever enter into such a compact with anyone; he would be mad if he did. That, Socrates, is the nature of justice according to this account, and such the circumstances in which it arose.

The next point is that men practise it against the grain, for lack of power to do wrong. How true that is, we shall best see if we imagine two men, one just, the other unjust, given full licence to do whatever they like, and then follow them to observe where each will be led by his desires. We shall catch the just man taking the same road as the unjust; he will be moved by self-interest, the end which it is natural to every creature to pursue as good, until forcibly turned aside by law and custom to respect the principle of equality.

Now, the easiest way to give them that complete liberty of action would be to imagine them possessed of the talisman found by Gyges, the ancestor of the famous Lydian. The story tells how he was a shepherd in the King's service. One day there was a great storm, and the ground where his flock was feeding was rent by an

From *The Republic of Plato,* translated by F. M. Cornford, 1941. Reprinted by permission of Oxford University Press.

earthquake. Astonished at the sight, he went down into the chasm and saw, among other wonders of which the story tells, a brazen horse, hollow, with windows in its sides. Peering in, he saw a dead body, which seemed to be of more than human size. It was naked save for a gold ring, which he took from the finger and made his way out. When the shepherds met, as they did every month, to send an account to the King of the state of his flocks, Gyges came wearing the ring. As he was sitting with the others, he happened to turn the bezel of the ring inside his hand. At once he became invisible, and his companions, to his surprise, began to speak of him as if he had left them. Then, as he was fingering the ring, he turned the bezel outwards and became visible again. With that, he set about testing the ring to see if it really had this power, and always with the same result: according as he turned the bezel inside or out he vanished and reappeared. After this discovery he contrived to be one of the messengers sent to the court. There he seduced the Queen, and with her help murdered the King and seized the throne.

Now suppose there were two such magic rings, and one were given to the just man, the other to the unjust. No one, it is commonly believed, would have such iron strength of mind as to stand fast in doing right or keep his hands off other men's goods, when he could go to the market-place and fearlessly help himself to anything he wanted, enter houses and sleep with any woman he chose, set prisoners free and kill men at his pleasure, and in a word go about among men with the powers of a god. He would behave no better than the other; both would take the same course. Surely this would be strong proof that men do right only under compulsion; no individual thinks of it as good for him personally, since he does wrong whenever he finds he has the power. Every man believes that wrongdoing pays him personally much better, and, according to this theory, that is the truth. Granted full licence to do as he liked, people would think him a miserable fool if they found him refusing to wrong his neighbours or to touch their belongings, though in public they would keep up a pretence of praising his conduct, for fear of being wronged themselves. So much for that. . . .

The Virtue of Selfishness

Ayn Rand
Nathaniel Branden

I

The Objectivist Ethics

Ayn Rand

The standard of value of the Objectivist ethics—the standard by which one judges what is good or evil—is *man's life,* or: that which is required for man's survival *qua* man.

Since reason is man's basic means of survival, that which is proper to the life of a rational being is the good; that which negates, opposes or destroys it is the evil.

Since everything man needs has to be discovered by his own mind and produced by his own effort, the two essentials of the method of survival proper to a rational being are: thinking and productive work.

If some men do not choose to think, but survive by imitating and repeating, like trained animals, the routine of sounds and motions they learned from others, never making an effort to understand their own work, it still remains true that their survival is made possible only by those who did choose to think and to discover the motions they are repeating. The survival of such mental parasites depends on blind chance; their unfocused minds are unable to know *whom* to imitate, *whose* motions it is safe to follow. *They* are the men who march into the abyss, trailing after any destroyer who promises them to assume the responsibility they evade: the responsibility of being conscious.

If some men attempt to survive by means of brute force or fraud, by looting, robbing, cheating or enslaving the men who produce, it still remains true that their survival is made possible only by their victims, only by the men who choose to think and to produce the goods which they, the looters, are seizing. Such looters are parasites incapable of survival, who exist by destroying those who *are* capable, those who are pursuing a course of action proper to man.

The men who attempt to survive, not by means of reason, but by means of force, are attempting to survive by the method of animals. But just as animals would not be able to survive by attempting the method of plants, by rejecting locomotion and waiting for the soil to feed them—so men cannot survive by attempting the method of animals, by rejecting reason and counting on productive *men* to serve as their prey. Such looters may achieve their goals for the range of a moment, at the price of destruction: the destruction of their victims and their own. As evidence, I offer you any criminal or any dictatorship. . . .

The Objectivist ethics holds man's life as the *standard* of value—and *his own life* as the ethical *purpose* of every individual man.

The difference between "standard" and "purpose" in this context is as follows: a "standard" is an abstract principle that serves as a measurement or gauge to guide a man's choices in the achievement of a concrete, specific purpose. "That which is required for the survival of man *qua* man" is an abstract principle that applies to every individual man. The task of applying this principle to a concrete, specific purpose— the purpose of living a life proper to a rational being—belongs to every individual man, and the life he has to live is his own.

Man must choose his actions, values and goals by the standard of that which is proper to man—in order to achieve, maintain, fulfill and enjoy that ultimate value, that end in itself, which is his own life.

Value is that which one acts to gain and/or keep—*virtue* is the act by which one gains and/or keeps it. The three cardinal values of the Objectivist ethics—the three values which, together, are the means to and the realization of one's ultimate value, one's own life—are: Reason, Purpose, Self-Esteem, with their three corresponding virtues: Rationality, Productiveness, Pride.

Productive work is the central *purpose* of a rational man's life, the central value that integrates and determines the hierarchy of all his other values. Reason is the source, the precondition of his productive work—pride is the result.

Rationality is man's basic virtue, the source of all his other virtues. Man's basic vice, the source of all his evils, is the act of unfocusing his mind, the suspension of his consciousness, which is not blindness, but the refusal to see, not ignorance, but the refusal to know. Irrationality is the rejection of man's means of survival and, therefore, a commitment to a course of blind destruction; that which is anti-mind, is anti-life. . . .

The basic *social* principle of the Objectivist ethics is that just as life is an end in itself, so every living human being is an end in himself, not the means to the ends or the welfare of others—and, therefore, that man must live for his own sake, neither sacrificing himself to others nor sacrificing others to himself. To live for his own sake means that *the achievement of his own happiness is man's highest moral purpose.* . . .

The Objectivist ethics proudly advocates and upholds *rational selfishness*—which means: the values required for man's survival *qua* man—which means: the values required for *human* survival—not the values produced by the desires, the emotions, the "aspirations," the feelings, the whims or the needs of irrational brutes, who have never outgrown the primordial practice of human sacrifices, have never discovered an industrial society and can conceive of no self-interest but that of grabbing the loot of the moment. . . .

II

Isn't Everyone Selfish?

Nathaniel Branden

The issue of selfishness versus self-sacrifice arises in an *ethical* context. Ethics is a code of values to guide man's choices and actions—the choices and actions that determine the purpose and course of his life. In choosing his actions and goals, man faces constant alternatives. In order to choose, he requires a standard of value—a purpose which his actions are to serve or at which they are to aim. " 'Value' presupposes an answer to the question: of value to whom and for what?" *(Atlas Shrugged.)* What is to be the goal or purpose of a man's actions? Who is to be the intended *beneficiary* of his actions? Is he to hold, as his primary moral purpose, the achievement of *his own* life and happiness—or should his primary moral purpose be to serve the wishes and needs of *others?*

The clash between egoism and altruism lies in their conflicting answers to these questions. Egoism holds that man is an end in himself; altruism holds that man is a means to the ends of others. Egoism holds that, morally, the beneficiary of an action should be the person who acts; altruism holds that, morally, the beneficiary of an action should be someone *other* than the person who acts.

To be selfish is to be motivated by concern for one's self-interest. This requires that one consider what constitutes one's self-interest and how to achieve it—what values and goals to pursue, what principles and policies to adopt. If a man were not concerned with this question, he could not be said objectively to be concerned with or to desire his self-interest; one cannot be concerned with or desire that of which one has no knowledge.

Selfishness entails: (a) a hierarchy of values set by the standard of one's self-interest, and (b) the refusal to sacrifice a higher value to a lower one or to a nonvalue.

A genuinely selfish man knows that only reason can determine what is, in fact, to his self-interest, that to pursue contradictions or attempt to act in defiance of the facts of reality is self-destructive—and self-destruction is not to his self-interest. . . .

Because a genuinely selfish man chooses his goals by the guidance of reason—and because the interests of rational men do not clash—other men may often benefit from his actions. But the benefit of other men is not his primary purpose or goal; his *own* benefit is his primary purpose and the conscious goal directing his actions.

To make this principle fully clear, let us consider an extreme example of an action which, in fact, is selfish, but which conventionally might be called *self*-sacrificial: a man's willingness to die to save the life of the woman he loves. In what way would such a man be the beneficiary of his action?

The answer is given in *Atlas Shrugged*—in the scene when Galt, knowing he is about to be arrested, tells Dagny: "If they get the slightest suspicion of what we are to each other, they will have you on a torture rack—I mean, physical torture—before my eyes, in less than a week. I am not going to wait for that. At the first mention of a threat to you, I will kill myself and stop them right there. . . . I don't have to tell you that if I do it, it won't be an act of self-sacrifice. I do not care to live on their terms. I do not care to obey them and I do not care to see you enduring a drawn-out murder. There will be no values for me to seek after that—and I do not care to exist without values." If a man loves a woman so much that he does not wish to survive her death, if life can have nothing more to offer him at that price, then his dying to save her is not a sacrifice.

The same principle applies to a man, caught in a dictatorship, who willingly risks death to achieve freedom. To call his act a "self-sacrifice," one would have to assume that he *preferred* to live as a slave. The selfishness of a man who is willing to die, if necessary, fighting for his freedom, lies in the fact that he is unwilling to go on living in a world where he is no longer able to act on his own judgment—that is, a world where *human* conditions of existence are no longer possible to him.

The selfishness or unselfishness of an action is to be determined objectively: it is not determined by the *feelings* of the person who acts. Just as feelings are not a tool of cognition, *so they are not a criterion in ethics*.

Obviously, in order to act, one has to be moved by *some* personal motive; one has to "want," in *some* sense, to perform the action. The issue of an action's selfishness or unselfishness depends, not on whether or not one wants to perform it, but on *why* one wants to perform it. By what standard was the action chosen? To achieve what goal?

If a man proclaimed that he *felt* he would best benefit others by robbing and murdering them, men would not be willing to grant that his actions were altruistic. By the same logic and for the same reasons, if a man pursues a course of blind self-destruction, his *feeling* that he has something to gain by it does not establish his actions as selfish.

If, motivated solely by a sense of charity, compassion, duty or altruism, a person renounces a value, desire or goal in favor of the pleasure, wishes or needs of another person whom he values less than the thing he renounced—*that* is an act of self-sacrifice. The fact that a person may feel that he "wants" to do it, does not make his action selfish or establish objectively that he is its beneficiary.

Suppose, for example, that a son chooses the career he wants by rational standards, but then renounces it in order to please his mother who prefers that he pursue a different career, one that will have more prestige in the eyes of the neighbors. The boy accedes to his mother's wish because he has accepted that such is his moral duty: he believes that his duty as a son consists of placing his mother's happiness above his own, even if he knows that his mother's demand is irrational and even if he knows that he is sentencing himself to a life of misery and frustration. It is absurd for the advocates of the "everyone is selfish" doctrine to assert that since the boy is motivated by the desire to be "virtuous" or to avoid guilt, no self-sacrifice is involved and his action is really selfish. What is evaded is the question of *why* the boy feels and desires as he does. Emotions and desires are not causeless, irreducible primaries: they are the product of the premises one has accepted. The boy "wants" to renounce his career only because he has accepted the ethics of altruism; he believes that it is immoral to act for his self-interest. *That* is the principle directing his actions.

Advocates of the "everyone is selfish" doctrine do not deny that, under the pressure of the altruist ethics, men can knowingly act against their own long-range happiness. They merely assert that in some higher, undefinable sense such men are still acting "selfishly." A definition of "selfishness" that includes or permits the possibility of knowingly acting against one's long-range happiness, is a contradiction in terms.

It is only the legacy of mysticism that permits men to imagine that they are still speaking meaningfully when they declare that one can seek one's happiness in the renunciation of one's happiness.

The basic fallacy in the "everyone is selfish" argument consists of an extraordinarily crude equivocation. It is a psychological truism—a tautology—that all purposeful behavior is motivated. But to equate *"motivated* behavior" with *"selfish* behavior" is to blank out the distinction between an elementary fact of human psychology and the phenomenon of *ethical choice*. It is to evade the central *problem* of ethics, namely: by *what* is man to be motivated?

A genuine selfishness—that is: a genuine concern with discovering what is to one's self-interest, an acceptance of the responsibility of achieving it, a refusal ever to betray it by acting on the blind whim, mood, impulse or feeling of the moment, an uncompromising loyalty to one's judgment, convictions and values—represents a profound moral achievement. Those who assert that "everyone is selfish" commonly intend their statement as an expression of cynicism and contempt. But the truth is that their statement pays mankind a compliment it does not deserve.

Ultimate Principles and Ethical Egoism

Brian Medlin

. . . There are evil opinions abroad, as anyone who walks abroad knows. The one we meet with most often, whether in pub or parlour, is the doctrine that everyone should look after himself. However refreshing he may find it after the high-minded pomposities of this morning's editorial, the good fellow knows this doctrine is wrong and he wants to knock it down. But while he believes that moral language is used to make statements either true or false, the best he can do is to claim that what the egoist says is false. Unfortunately, the egoist can claim that it's true. . . . The egoist's word seems as reliable as their own. Some begin half to believe that perhaps it is possible to supply an egoistic basis for conventional morality, some that it may be impossible to supply any other basis. I'm not going to try to prop up our conventional morality, which I

By permission. *Australasian Journal of Philosophy,* vol. 35, 1957.

fear to be a task beyond my strength, but in what follows I do want to refute the doctrine of ethical egoism. I want to resolve this disagreement by showing that what the egoist says is inconsistent. It is true that there are moral disagreements which can never be resolved, but this isn't one of them. The proper objection to the man who says 'Everyone should look after his own interests regardless of the interests of others' is not that he isn't speaking the truth, but simply that he isn't speaking.

We should first make two distinctions. This done, ethical egoism will lose much of its plausibility.

I UNIVERSAL AND INDIVIDUAL EGOISM

Universal egoism maintains that everyone (including the speaker) ought to look after his own interests and to disregard those of other people except in so far as their interests contribute towards his own.

Individual egoism is the attitude that the egoist is going to look after himself and no one else. The egoist cannot promulgate that he is going to look after himself. He can't even preach that he *should* look after himself and preach this alone. When he tries to convince me that he should look after himself, he is attempting so to dispose me that I shall approve when he drinks my beer and steals Tom's wife. I cannot approve of his looking after himself and himself alone without so far approving of his achieving his happiness, regardless of the happiness of myself and others. So that when he sets out to persuade me that he should look after himself regardless of others, he must also set out to persuade me that I should look after him regardless of myself and others. Very small chance he has! And if the individual egoist cannot promulgate his doctrine without enlarging it, what he has is no doctrine at all. . . .

2 CATEGORICAL AND HYPOTHETICAL EGOISM

Categorical egoism is the doctrine that we all ought to observe our own interests, *because that is what we ought to do*. For the categorical egoist the egoistic dogma is the ultimate principle in ethics.

The hypothetical egoist, on the other hand, maintains that we all ought to observe our own interests, because. . . . If we want such and such an end, we must do so and so (look after ourselves). The hypothetical egoist is not a real egoist at all. He is very likely an unwitting utilitarian who believes mistakenly that the general happiness will be increased if each man looks wisely to his own. . . .

An ethical egoist will have to maintain the doctrine in both its universal and categorical forms. Should he retreat to hypothetical egoism he is no longer an egoist. Should he retreat to individual egoism his doctrine, while logically impregnable, is no longer ethical, no longer even a doctrine. He may wish to quarrel with this and if so, I submit peacefully. Let him call himself what he will, it makes no difference. I'm a philosopher, not a rat-catcher, and I don't see it as my job to dig vermin out of such burrows as individual egoism.

Obviously something strange goes on as soon as the ethical egoist tries to promulgate his doctrine. What is he doing when he urges upon his audience that they should each observe his own interests and those interests alone? Is he not acting contrary to the egoistic principle? It cannot be to his advantage to convince them, for seizing always their own advantage they will impair his. Surely if he does believe what he says, he should try to persuade them otherwise. Not perhaps that they should devote themselves to his interests, for they'd hardly swallow that; but that everyone should devote himself to the service of others. But is not to believe that someone should act in a certain way to try to persuade him to do so? Of course, we don't always try to persuade people to act as we think they should act. We may be lazy, for instance. But in so far as we believe that Tom should do so and so, we have a tendency to induce him to do so and so. Does it make sense to say: "Of course you should do this, but for goodness' sake don't"? Only where we mean: "You should do this for certain reasons, but here are even more persuasive reasons for not doing it." If the egoist believes ultimately that others should mind themselves alone, then, he must persuade them accordingly. If he doesn't persuade them, he is no universal egoist. It certainly makes sense to say: "I know very well that Tom should act in such and such a way. But I know also that it's not to my advantage that he should so act. So I'd better dissuade him from it." And this is just what the egoist must say, if he is to consider his own advantage and disregard everyone else's. That is, he must behave as an individual egoist, if he is to be an egoist at all. . . .

Remembering that the principle is meant to be both universal and categorical, let us ask what kind of attitude the egoist is expressing. Wouldn't that attitude be equally well expressed by the conjunction of an infinite number of avowals thus?—

I want myself to come out on top	and	I don't care about Tom, Dick, Harry . . .
and		and
I want Tom to come out on top	and	I don't care about myself, Dick, Harry . . .
and		and
I want Dick to come out on top	and	I don't care about myself, Tom, Harry . .
and		and
I want Harry to come out on top	and	I don't care about myself, Dick, Tom . . .
etc.		etc.

From this analysis it is obvious that the principle expressing such an attitude must be inconsistent.

But now the egoist may claim that he hasn't been properly understood. When he says 'Everyone should look after himself and himself alone', he means 'Let each man do what he wants regardless of what anyone else wants'. The egoist may claim that what he values is merely that he and Tom and Dick and Harry should each do what he wants and not care about what anyone else may want and that this doesn't involve his principle in any inconsistency. Nor need it. But even if it doesn't, he's no better off. Just what does he value? Is it the well-being of himself, Tom, Dick and Harry or merely their going on in a certain way regardless of whether or not this is going to promote their well-being? When he urges Tom, say, to do what he wants, is he appealing to Tom's self-interest? If so, his attitude can be expressed thus:

I want myself to be happy   I want myself not to care
          and   and   about Tom, Dick,
I want Tom to be happy   Harry . . .

We need go no further to see that the principle expressing such an attitude must be inconsistent. I have made this kind of move already. What concerns me now is the alternative position the egoist must take up to be safe from it. If the egoist values merely that people should go on in a certain way, regardless of whether or not this is going to promote their well-being, then he is not appealing to the self-interest of his audience when he urges them to regard their own interests. If Tom has any regard for himself at all, the egoist's blandishments will leave him cold. Further, the egoist doesn't even have his own interest in mind when he says that, like everyone else, he should look after himself. A funny kind of egoism this turns out to be.

Perhaps now, claiming that he is indeed appealing to the self-interest of his audience, the egoist may attempt to counter the objection of the previous paragraph. He may move into "Let each man do what he wants and let each man disregard what others want when their desires clash with his own". Now his attitude may be expressed thus:

I want everyone to be   I want everyone to dis-
   happy   and   regard the happiness
                         of others when their
                         happiness clashes with
                         his own.

The egoist may claim justly that a man can have such an attitude and also that in a certain kind of world such a man could get what he wanted. Our objection to the egoist has been that his desires are incompatible. And this is still so. If he and Tom and Dick and Harry did go on as he recommends by saying 'Let each man disregard the happiness of others, when their happiness conflicts with his own', then assuredly they'd all be completely miserable. Yet he wants them to be happy. He is attempting to counter this by saying that it is merely a fact about the world that they'd make one another miserable by going on as he recommends. The world could conceivably have been different. For this reason, he says, this principle is not inconsistent. This argument may not seem very compelling, but I advance it on the egoist's behalf because I'm interested in the reply to it. For now we don't even need to tell him that the world isn't in fact like that. (What it's like makes no difference.) Now we can point out to him that he is arguing not as an egoist but as a utilitarian. He has slipped into hypothetical egoism to save his principle from inconsistency. If the world were such that we always made ourselves and others happy by doing one another down, then we could find good utilitarian reasons for urging that we should do one another down.

If, then, he is to save his principle, the egoist must do one of two things. He must give up the claim that he is appealing to the self-interest of his audience, that he has even his own interest in mind. Or he must admit that, in the conjunction on p. 26, although 'I want everyone to be happy' refers to ends, nevertheless 'I want everyone to disregard the happiness of others when their happiness conflicts with his own' can refer only to means. That is, his so-called ultimate principle is really compounded of a principle and a moral rule subordinate to that principle. That is, he is really a utilitarian who is urging everyone to go on in a certain way so that everyone may be happy. A utilitarian, what's more, who is ludicrously mistaken about the nature of the world. Things being as they are, his moral rule is a very bad one. Things being as they are, it can only be deduced from his principle by means of an empirical premiss which is manifestly false. Good fellows don't need to fear him. They may rest easy that the world is and must be on their side and the best thing they can do is be good. . . .

The Supremacy of Moral Reasons
Kurt Baier

Are moral reasons really superior to reasons of self-interest as we all believe? Do we really have reason on our side when we follow moral reasons against self-interest? What reasons could there be for being moral? Can we really give an answer to 'Why should we be moral?' It is obvious that all these questions come to the same thing. When we ask, 'Should we be moral?' or 'Why should we be moral?' or 'Are moral reasons superior to all others?' we ask to be given a reason for regarding moral reasons as superior to all others. What is this reason?

Let us begin with a state of affairs in which reasons of self-interest are supreme. In such a state everyone keeps his impulses and inclinations in check when and only when they would lead him into behavior detrimental to his own interest. Everyone who follows reason will discipline himself to rise early, to do his exercises, to refrain from excessive drinking and smoking, to keep good company, to marry the right sort of girl, to work and study hard in order to get on, and so on. However, it will often happen that people's interests conflict. In such a case, they will have to resort to ruses or force to get their own way. As this becomes known, men will become suspicious, for they will regard one another as scheming competitors for the good things in life. The universal supremacy of the rules of self-interest must lead to what Hobbes called the state of nature. At the same time, it will be clear to everyone that universal obedience to certain rules overriding self-interest would produce a state of affairs which serves everyone's interest much better than his unaided pursuit of it in a state where everyone does the same. Moral rules are universal rules designed to override those of self-interest when following the latter is harmful to others. 'Thou shalt not kill,' 'Thou shalt not lie,' 'Thou shalt not steal' are rules which forbid the inflicting of harm on someone else even when this might be in one's interest.

The very *raison d'être* of a morality is to yield reasons which overrule the reasons of self-interest in those cases when everyone's following self-interest would be harmful to everyone. Hence moral reasons are superior to all others.

"But what does this mean?" it might be objected. "If it merely means that we do so regard them, then you are of course right, but your contention is useless, a mere point of usage. And how could it mean any more? If it means that we not only do so regard them, but *ought* so to regard them, then there must be *reasons* for saying this. But there could not be any reasons for it. If you offer reasons of self-interest, you are arguing in a circle. Moreover, it cannot be true that it is always in my interest to treat moral reasons as superior to reasons of self-interest. If it were, self-interest and morality could never conflict, but they notoriously do. It is equally circular to argue that there are moral reasons for saying that one ought to treat moral reasons as superior to reasons of self-interest. And what other reasons are there?"

The answer is that we are now looking at the world from the point of view of *anyone*. We are not examining particular alternative courses of action before this or that person; we are examining two alternative worlds, one in which moral reasons are always treated by everyone as superior to reasons of self-interest and one in which the reverse is the practice. And we can see that the first world is the better world, because we can see that the second world would be the sort which Hobbes describes as the state of nature.

This shows that I ought to be moral, for when I ask the question 'What ought I to do?' I am asking, 'Which is the course of action supported by the best reasons?' But since it has just been shown that moral reasons are superior to reasons of self-interest, I have been given a reason for being moral, for following moral reasons rather than any other, namely, they are better reasons than any other. . . .

Moralities are systems of principles whose acceptance by everyone as overruling the dictates of self-interest is in the interest of everyone alike, though following the rules of a morality is not of course identical with following self-interest. If it were, there could be no conflict between a morality and self-interest and no point in having moral rules overriding self-interest. . . .

The answer to our question 'Why should we be moral?' is therefore as follows. We should be moral because being moral is following rules designed to overrule reasons of self-interest whenever it is in the interest of everyone alike that such rules should be generally followed. This will be the case when the needs and wants and aspirations of individual agents conflict with one another and when, in the absence of such overriding rules, the pursuit of their ends by all concerned would lead to the attempt to eliminate those who are in the way. Since such rules will always require one of the rivals to abandon his pursuit in favor of the other, they will tend to be broken. Since, ex hypothesi it is in everyone's interest that they should be followed, it will be in everyone's interest that they should not only be taught as "superior to" other reasons but also adequately enforced, in order to reduce the temptation to break them. A person instructed in these rules can acknowledge that such reasons are superior to reasons of self-interest without having to admit that he is always or indeed ever attracted or moved by them.

But is it not self-contradictory to say that it is in a person's interest to do what is contrary to his interest? It certainly would be if the two expressions were used in exactly the same way. But they are not. . . . Moral rules are not designed to serve the agent's interest directly. Hence it would be quite inappropriate for him to break them whenever he discovers that they do not serve his interest. They are designed to adjudicate primarily in cases where there is a conflict of interests so that from their very nature they are bound to be contrary to the interest of one of the persons affected. However, they are also bound to serve the interest of the other person, hence his interest in the other's observing them. It is on the assumption of the likelihood of a reversal of roles that the universal observation of the rule will serve everyone's interest. The principle of justice and other principles which we employ in improving the moral rules of a given society help to bring existing moralities closer to the ideal which is in the interest of everyone alike. . . .

So following the rules of morality is in everyone's interest only if the assumptions underlying it are correct, that is, if the moral rules come close to being true and are generally observed. Even then, to say that following them is in the interest of everyone alike means only that it is better for everyone that there should be a morality generally observed than that the principle of self-interest should be acknowledged as supreme. It does not of course mean that a person will not do better for himself by following self-interest than by doing what is morally right, when others are doing what is right. But of course such a person cannot *claim* that he is following a superior reason.

It must be added to this, however, that such a system of rules has the support of reason only where people live in societies, that is, in conditions in which there are established common ways of behavior. Outside society, people have no reason for following such rules, that is, for being moral. In other words, outside society, the very distinction between right and wrong vanishes. . . .

But someone might now ask whether and why he should follow reason itself. He may admit that moral reasons are superior to all others, but doubt whether he ought to follow reason. He may claim that this will have to be proved first, for if it is not true that he ought to follow reason, then it is not true that he ought to follow the strongest reason either. . . .

During the last hundred years or so, reason has had a very bad press. Many thinkers have sneered at it and have recommended other guides, such as the instincts, the unconscious, the voice of the blood, inspiration, charisma, and the like. They have advocated that one should not follow reason but be guided by these other forces.

. . . In the most obvious sense of the question 'Should I follow reason?' this is a tautological question like 'Is a circle a circle?'; hence the advice 'You should not follow reason' is as nonsensical as the claim 'A circle is not a circle.' Hence the question 'Why should I follow reason?' is as silly as 'Why is a circle a circle?' We need not, therefore, take much notice of the advocates of unreason. They show by their advocacy that they are not too clear on what they are talking about.

How is it that 'Should I follow reason?' is a tautological question like 'Is a circle a circle?' Questions of the form 'Shall I do this?' or 'Should I do this?' or 'Ought I to do this?' are . . . requests to someone (possibly oneself) to deliberate on one's behalf. That is to say, they are requests to survey the facts and weigh the reasons for and against this course of action. These questions could therefore be paraphrased as follows. 'I wish to do what is supported by the best reasons. Tell me whether this is so supported.' As already mentioned, 'following reason' means 'doing what is supported by the best reasons.' Hence the question 'Shall (should, ought) I follow reason?' must be paraphrased as 'I wish to do what is supported by the best reasons. Tell me whether doing what is supported by the best reasons is doing what is supported by the best reasons.' It is, therefore, not worth asking.

The question '*Why* should I follow reason?' simply does not make sense. Asking it shows complete lack of understanding of the meaning of 'why questions.' 'Why should I do this?' is a request to be given the reason for saying that I should do this. It is normally asked when someone has already said, 'You should do this' and answered by giving the reason. But since 'Should I follow reason?' means 'Tell me whether doing what is supported by the best reasons is doing what is supported by the best reasons,' there is simply no possibility of adding 'Why?' For the question now comes to this, 'Tell me the reason why doing what is supported by the best reasons is doing what is supported by the best reasons.' It is exactly like asking, 'Why is a circle a circle?'

However, it must be admitted that there is another possible interpretation to our question according to which it makes sense and can even be answered. 'Why should I follow reason?' may not be a request for a reason in support of a tautological remark, but a request for a reason why one should enter on the theoretical task of deliberation. . . . Following reason involves the completion of two tasks, the theoretical and the practical. The point of the theoretical is to give guidance in the practical task. We perform the theoretical only because we wish to complete the practical task in accordance with the outcome of the theoretical. On our first interpretation, 'Should I follow reason?' meant 'Is the practical task completed when it is completed in accordance with the outcome of the theoretical task?' And the answer to this is obviously 'Yes,' for that is what we mean by 'completion of the practical task.' On our second interpretation, 'Should I follow reason?' is not a question about the practical but about the theoretical task. It is not a question about whether, given that one is prepared to perform both these tasks, they are properly completed in the way indicated. It is a question about whether one should enter on the whole performance at all, whether the "game" is worth playing. And this is a meaningful question. It might be better to "follow inspiration" than to "follow reason," in this sense: better to close one's eyes and wait for an answer to flash across the mind.

But while, so interpreted, 'Should I follow reason?' makes sense, it seems to me obvious that the answer to it is 'Yes, because it pays.' Deliberation is the only reliable method. Even if there were other reliable methods, we could only tell whether they were reliable by checking them against this method. Suppose some charismatic leader counsels, 'Don't follow reason, follow me. My leadership is better than that of reason'; we would still have to check his claim against the ordinary methods of reason. We would have to ascertain whether in following his advice we were doing the best thing. And this we can do only by examining whether he has advised us to do what is supported by the best reasons. His claim to be better than reason can in turn only be supported by the fact that he tells us precisely the same as reason does.

Is there any sense, then, in his claim that his guidance is preferable to that of reason? There may be, for working out what is supported by the best reasons takes a long time. Frequently, the best thing to do is to do something quickly now rather than the most appropriate thing later. A leader may have the ability to "see," to "intuit," what is the best thing to do more quickly than it is possible to work this out by the laborious methods of deliberation. In evaluating the qualities of leadership of such a person, we are evaluating *his ability to perform correctly the practical task of following reason* without having to go through the lengthy operations of the theoretical. Reason is required to tell us whether anyone has qualities of leadership better than ordinary, in the same way that pencil and paper multiplications are required to tell us whether a mathematical prodigy is genuine or a fraud. . . .

CHAPTER 2

RELATIVISM

This chapter confronts the fact that people and cultures differ widely on what they consider to be ethical behavior and act accordingly. Upon arriving at college, one of the first things you notice is that your roommate has some very strange customs and ideas. You have a similar feeling about many other students in your dormitory, and some of them feel the same about you. Individual opinions about right and wrong vary sharply. So does the behavior of individuals—at least within certain cultural constraints. What implications does this individual diversity of opinion and action have for ethical decision-making?

Although there is wide variety in individual beliefs about ethics and in the corresponding individual behavior, there are cultural restraints—cultural standards. In our culture, we disagree about abortion. Some favor it; others do not. We don't have a group speaking up for infanticide, however. Yet, as several readings in this chapter show, infanticide has been accepted in some cultures. The things our culture most abhors have been accepted or perhaps even required by some other culture at some period in history.

Anthropologists, psychologists, sociologists, and other social scientists study the different behavior patterns of individuals and cultures. They catalog the different beliefs that individuals and cultures have about right and wrong. Some of the more startling differences on matters of ethics among different cultures are briefly described in the article by Wellman. That people and cultures disagree as to what counts as right and wrong, good and bad, and behave accordingly can be accepted as a fact. What implications does this fact have for ethical decision-making?

Some have argued that the diversity of "moral" behavior shows that the theory of moral relativism is true. How do relativists establish their position? Many relativists have pointed to the *fact* that different individuals and cultures hold different views about what constitutes moral behavior as *evidence* for the truth of their position. Philosophers are virtually unanimous in the opinion that this is an invalid argument.

First, many philosophers claim that the "facts" aren't really what they seem. Several writers refer to the fact that in some cultures after a certain age parents are put to death. In our culture such behavior would be murder. We take care of our parents. Does this difference in behavior prove that the two cultures disagree about matters of ethics? No it does not. Suppose the other culture believes that people exist in the afterlife in the same condition that they leave their life. It would be very cruel to have one's parents exist eternally in an unhealthy state. By killing them when they are relatively active and vigorous you ensure their happiness for all eternity. The underlying ethical principle of this culture is that children have duties to their parents, including the duty to be concerned with their parents' happiness as they approach old age. This ethical principle is identical with our own. What looked like a difference in ethics between our culture and another turned out, upon close examination, to be a difference on matters of fact.

Here is a second way that the "facts" really aren't what they seem. Cultures differ in physical setting, in economic development, in the state of their science and technology, in their literacy rate, and in many other ways. Even if there were universal moral principles, they would have to be applied in these different cultural contexts. Given the different situations in which cultures exist, it would come as no surprise to find universal principles applied in different ways. Hence, the differences in so-called ethical behavior among cultures would be surface differences only. The cultures would agree on the fundamental universal moral principles. In later chapters of this book some very general principles of ethics will be discussed. One such principle appeals to the public good. It says that social institutions and individual behavior should be so ordered that they lead to the greatest good for the greatest number. Many different forms of social organization and individual behavior are consistent with this principle.

Both of the arguments outlined above are developed in the selection by John Hospers. The point of these two arguments is that surface diversities among cultures on so-called ethical behavior may not reflect genuine disagreement about ethics. Unless the relativist can establish basic differences about matters of ethics, the case for relativism cannot be made.

This discussion is important for anyone concerned with making an ethical decision. Ethical judgments are bound up in some complicated way with the facts. The existence of simple, safe birth-control methods has implications for sexual morality. The existence of sophisticated mechanical techniques for prolonging human life has implications for medical ethics. Since our ethical judgments depend in part upon what the facts are, the first step in resolving disputes about ethics should be to determine whether or not the disputants are disagreeing over the facts. If the disagreement is factual, it will need to be resolved before tackling any ethical disagreement. If the factual disagreement is resolved, the ethical disagreement often dissolves.

Some philosophers have made the strong claim that ultimately all the disagreement between cultures is either disagreement about the facts or nothing more than the attempt to apply universal moral principles to specific situations. These philosophers claim that the apparent diversity in behavior among cultures is only apparent, and that ultimately cultures do agree on certain fundamental ethical standards. A discussion of this claim would take us beyond philosophy to anthropology, history, theology, and a host of other disciplines. The discussion thus far should have established the early contention that you can't claim that cultural relativism is true because in fact cultures do have different moral standards.

Another common strategy for criticizing relativism is to show that the consequences of taking the perspective of ethical relativism lead to some rather bizarre results. One of the bizarre results is that if relativism is true, then agreement on morals is, in principle, impossible. Of course "agreement" here means agreement on the basis of reasons. There can be agreement by force. That's equivalent to "Worship my God or I'll cut off your head." Why there can be no rational agreement is obvious on an examination of the definition of relativism. Cultural relativism is the view that what is right or wrong is determined by culture. So if one culture says that abortion is right and another says it is wrong, that has to be the end of the matter. Abortion *is* morally permissible in one culture and morally wrong in the other.

But suppose a person from one culture moves to another and tries to persuade the other culture to change its view. Suppose someone moves from a culture where slavery is immoral to one where slavery is morally permitted. Normally if a person were to try to convince the culture where slavery was permitted that slavery was morally wrong, we would refer to such a person as a moral reformer. But if cultural relativism were true, there would be no place for the concept of a moral reformer. Slavery is right in those cultures that say it is right and wrong in those cultures that say it is wrong. If the reformer fails to persuade a slaveholding country to change its mind, the reformer's antislavery position was never right. If the reformer is successful in persuading a country to change its mind, the reformer's antislavery views were wrong until the country did in fact change its view. Then the reformer's antislavery view was right. Now that's a bizarre result.

Underlying these two objections is the broader objection that relativism is inconsistent with our use of moral language. When Russia and the United States argue about the moral rights that human beings have, they seem to be genuinely disagreeing about a matter of ethics. How unfortunate it would be if that dispute had to be resolved by nonrational means, since rational agreement is in principle impossible. People do marshal arguments in behalf of ethical views. If relativism is true, such arguments are doomed to failure or are a mere subterfuge to create agreement. Similarly we do have a place in our language for the concept of a moral reformer. Is this use of language really deviant, as it would have to be if relativism were true?

Finally, there is an argument which tries to show that if relativism is true, then it sometimes really is immoral to hold true beliefs. The argument works like this:

1 In Iran, holding a position of cultural relativism is considered wrong.

2 In the United States, holding a position of cultural relativism is morally permissible (not wrong).

By the definition of cultural relativism both (1) and (2) can be true. (As a matter of fact they probably are.) If relativism is true, then holding a position of cultural relativism really is wrong in Iran, and we have the bizarre result that in Iran holding a true moral theory is morally wrong.

By the arguments developed so far we see that you can't move from the facts of diversity in so-called ethical behavior and disagreement in ethics to moral relativism. The facts really don't establish ethical relativism, and the facts about our use of moral language are inconsistent with a relativist theory.

Actually the facts about the diversity of moral behavior are often used to support another position which is often confused with relativism. The common name for this position is "moral skepticism." Moral skepticism holds that there is no way to rationally establish a culture's moral views or to show that the moral views of one culture are rationally superior to the moral views of another culture.

What creates so much confusion is that some moral skeptics then go on to take a moral position—namely, that we should tolerate the divergent moral views of other countries. This is ultimately the position taken by Westermarck. However, many philosophers have found this plea for tolerance by moral skeptics to be deficient. Basically the criticisms, found in the selections by Taylor and Wellman, are of two types. First, a moral skeptic cannot consistently defend the judgment that tolerance is morally right. Second, the fact of cultural diversity about matters of ethics does not establish the truth of moral skepticism.

Recall that a moral skeptic argues that ethical judgments cannot be adequately justified. However, surely the judgment that people ought to be tolerant is an ethical judgment. Hence moral skeptics who argue for tolerance really cannot justify their opinion, and if they can, they are no longer consistent moral skeptics. They would be arguing that no ethical judgment can be justified but that "You ought to be tolerant" can be justified.

Many of the arguments against relativism apply equally well against the type of moral skepticism being considered here. Apparent disagreement in beliefs about right and wrong does not establish ultimate disagreement of ethical belief. The disagreement, as we have seen, may be about the facts rather than about the ethical judgments per se. But suppose the disagreement is about the moral judgment per se rather than about the facts on which the moral judgment is based. What does the mere fact of disagreement prove? There is disagreement about all kinds of things, but that disagreement does not commit anyone to the view that one of the parties in the disagreement can't be wrong. Perhaps the real issue is that the moral skeptic does not believe that disagreements in ethics can be resolved by using the scientific method, and perhaps the moral skeptic is right in that. What would the inapplicability of the scientific method prove? To establish this point the moral skeptic would have to show that all adequate justification is scientific in nature. That is a tall order.

Of course, nothing I have said here proves that moral skepticism is false. Arguments similar to those used against relativism would show that moral skepticism is inconsistent with our use of moral language. Such arguments are powerful, but they are not conclusive. Later chapters will provide positive arguments to show how ethical judgments can be justified.

The Variability of Moral Judgments

Edward Westermarck

. . . The variability of moral valuation depends in a very large measure upon intellectual factors of another kind, namely, different ideas relating to the objective nature of similar modes of conduct and their consequences. Such differences of ideas may arise from different situations and external conditions of life, which consequently influence moral opinion. We find, for instance, among many peoples the custom of killing or abandoning parents worn out with age or disease. It prevails among a large number of savage tribes and occurred formerly among many Asiatic and European nations, including the Vedic people and peoples of Teutonic extraction; there is an old English tradition of "the Holy Mawle, which they fancy hung behind the church door, which when the father was seaventie, the sonne might fetch to knock his father in the head, as effete and of no more use." This custom is particularly common among nomadic hunting tribes, owing to the hardships of life and the inability of decrepit persons to keep up in the march. In times when the food-supply is insufficient to support all the members of a community it also seems more reasonable that the old and useless should have to perish than the young and vigorous. And among peoples who have reached a certain degree of wealth and comfort, the practice of killing the old folks, though no longer justified by necessity, may still go on, partly through survival of a custom inherited from harder times, and partly from the humane intent of putting an end to lingering misery. What appears to most of us as an atrocious practice may really be an act of kindness, and is commonly approved of, or even insisted upon, by the old people themselves. . . .

The variability of moral judgments largely originates in different measures of knowledge, based on experience of the consequences of conduct, and in different beliefs. In almost every branch of conduct we notice the influence which the belief in supernatural forces or beings or in a future state has exercised upon the moral ideas of mankind, and the great diversity of this influence. Religion or superstition has on the one hand stigmatized murder and suicide, on the other hand it has commended human sacrifice and certain cases of voluntary self-destruction. It has inculcated humanity and charity, but has also led to cruel persecutions of persons embracing another creed. It has emphasized the duty of truth-speaking, and has itself been a cause of pious fraud. It has prompted cleanly habits and filthiness. It has enjoined labour and abstinence from labour, sobriety and drunkenness, marriage and celibacy, chastity and temple prostitution. It has introduced a great variety of new duties and virtues, quite different from those which are recognized by the moral consciousness when left to itself, but nevertheless in many cases considered more important than any other duties or virtues. . . .

In so far as differences of moral opinion depend on knowledge or ignorance of facts, on specific religious or superstitious beliefs, on different degrees of reflection, or on different conditions of life or other external circumstances, they do not clash with that universality which is implied in the notion of the objective validity of moral judgments. We shall now examine whether the same is the case with other differences that, at least apparently, are not due to purely cognitive causes.

When we study the moral rules laid down by the customs of savage peoples we find that they in a very large measure resemble the rules of civilized nations. In every savage community homicide is prohibited by custom, and so is theft. Savages also regard charity as a duty and praise generosity as a virtue, indeed their customs relating to mutual aid are often much more exacting than our own; and many of them are conspicuous for their avoidance of telling lies. But in spite of the great similarity of moral commandments, there is at the same time a difference between the regard for life, property, truth, and the general well-being of a neighbour which displays itself in savage rules of morality and that which is found among ourselves: it has, broadly speaking, only reference to members of the same community or tribe. Primitive peoples carefully distinguish between an act of homicide committed within their own community and one where the victim is a stranger: while the former is in ordinary circumstances disapproved of, the latter is in most cases allowed and often considered worthy of praise. And the same holds true of theft and lying and the infliction of other injuries. Apart from the privileges granted to guests, which are always of very short duration, a stranger is in early society devoid of all rights. And the same is the case not only among savages but among nations of archaic culture as well.

When we pass from the lower races to peoples more advanced in civilization we find that the social unit has grown larger, that the nation has taken the place of the tribe, and that the circle within which the infliction of injuries is prohibited has been extended accordingly. But the old distinction between injuries committed against compatriots and harm done to foreigners remains. In Greece in early times the "contemptible stranger" had no legal rights, and was protected only if he was the guest of a citizen; and even later on, at Athens, while the intentional killing of a citizen was punished with death and confiscation of the murderer's property, the intentional killing of a non-citizen was punished only with exile. . . . In the thirteenth century there were still several places in France in which a stranger who remained there for a year and a day became the serf of the lord of the manor. In England, till upwards of two centuries after the Conquest, foreign merchants were considered only as sojourners who had come to a fair or market, and were obliged to employ their landlords as brokers to buy and sell the commodities; and one stranger was often arrested for the debt or punished for the misdemeanour of another. . . .

It would be in vain to deny that the old distinction between a tribesman or fellow-countryman and a foreigner is dead among ourselves. . . . But both law and public opinion certainly show a very great advance in humanity with regard to the treatment of foreigners. And if we pass to the rules laid down by moralists and professedly accepted by a large portion of civilized humanity, the change from the savage attitude has been enormous. The doctrine of universal love is not peculiar to Christianity. The Chinese moralists inculcated benevolence to all men, without making any reference to national distinctions. Mih-tsze, who lived in the interval between Confucius and Mencius, even taught that we ought to love all men equally; . . . Buddhism enjoins the duty of universal love: . . . In Greece and Rome philosophers arose who opposed national narrowness and prejudice. Thus the Cynics attached slight value to the citizenship of any special state, declaring themselves to be citizens of the world. But it was the Stoic philosophy that first gave to the idea of a world-citizenship a definite positive meaning and raised it to historical importance.

It is obvious that the expansion of the moral rules has been a consequence of the expansion of the social unit and of increased intercourse between different societies, and if, as I maintain, the range of the moral emotions varies with the range of the altruistic sentiment, there is every reason to assume that an immediate cause of the greater comprehensiveness of the moral rules has been a corresponding widening of that sentiment. Among gregarious animals it is apt to be felt towards any member of their species that is not an object of their fear or anger. In mankind it has been narrowed by social isolation, by differences in race, language, habits, and customs, by enmity and suspicion. But peaceful intercourse leads to conditions favourable to its expansion, as well as to friendly behaviour for prudential reasons in the relations between those who come into contact with each other. People of different nationalities feel that in spite of all dissimilarities there is much that they have in common; and frequent intercourse makes the differences less marked or obliterates many of them altogether. . . .

It will perhaps be argued that the impartiality which is a characteristic of all moral judgments required a universalization of the moral rules, and that this could only be accomplished by a process of reasoning, which gradually extended them to wider and wider circles of men and finally to the whole human race. But let us remember what the impartiality of moral judgments really implies. . . . When a person pronounces an act right or wrong, it implies that *ceteris paribus* it is so whether he, or some friend or enemy of his, does it to another; *or* another does it to him, or to some friend or enemy of his. This impartiality has nothing to do with the question whether the agent and he to whom the act is done belong to the same or different families, tribes, nations, or other social groups. If it is considered wrong of a person to cheat another belonging to his own group but not wrong to cheat a foreigner, the impartiality of the moral emotion of disapproval, which underlies the concept of wrongness, merely leads to a general rule that applies to all similar cases independently of the nationality of him who holds the view. If I maintain that a foreigner, or a member of another class in my own society, has a duty towards me but that I have not the same duty towards him, my opinion can be justified only on condition that there is some difference in the circumstances affecting the morality of the case. People are certainly only too prone to assume that there are such differences. When they attribute different rights to different individuals, or classes of individuals, they are often in reality influenced by the relationship in which they stand to them; and reflection may be needed to decide whether the assumed impartiality of their moral judgment is real or illusory. Indeed, some degree of reasoning, however small, may always be needed in order to know whether a retributive emotion is felt impartially. . . . But it seems to me to be a sheer illusion to maintain that reason requires of us an impartiality in our conduct which makes no difference between one man and another. . . . I cannot find it unreasonable to endeavour to promote the welfare of my own family or country in preference to that of other families or countries. But my moral emotions tell me that I must allow anybody else to show a similar preference for *his* family or country.

I think that the question, why moral rules should differ because the persons to whom they refer are members of different social groups, would hardly arise unless there were a correspondingly broad altruistic sentiment behind it. Whatever part reflection may have played in the expansion of the moral rules—prudence has also, no doubt had something to do with the matter—it seems to me obvious that the dominant cause has been the widening of the altruistic sentiment. Beyond its limits the equalization of duties in our moral consciousness cannot go, whatever theorists may have to say on the subject; and the varying strength of this sentiment with regard to its objects will always prevent the rules from being anything like uniform and always make their equalization extremely incomplete. . . .

The variations of the altruistic sentiment in range and strength are also responsible for other differences of moral opinion. Even among ourselves there is no unanimity as to the dictates of duty in cases where a person's own interests collide with those of his fellow-men. . . . In some men, the altruistic sentiment is stronger than in others and, consequently, more apt to influence their consciences with regard to their own conduct and their judgments on other people's conduct. And while everybody will no doubt agree that some amount of self-sacrifice is a duty in certain circumstances, the amount and the circumstances can hardly be fixed in general rules, and on the whole, in cases of conflicting interests the judgment must to a large extent remain a matter of private opinion. . . .

To ethical writers who believe in the objective validity of moral judgments moral evolution implies a progressive discovery of values as a matter of reflection or thought, which follows in the wake of experience. They are fond of arguing that the changes of moral opinion are on a par with the discoveries made in mathematics, physics, and other sciences, which have been disputed quite as fiercely as any differences of moral valuation. . . . But while the objectivists cannot be accused of exaggerating the changes in our theoretical knowledge as compared with those in moral opinion, they have failed to see that the causes of these changes are in a large measure fundamentally different. The theoretical differences can be removed by sufficient observation and reflection, owing to the general uniformity of our sense-perceptions and intellect. It has been said that "the moral convictions of thoughtful and well-educated people are the data of ethics just as sense-perceptions are the data of a natural science. Just as some of the latter have to be rejected as illusory, so have some of the former; but as the latter are rejected only when they are in conflict with other more accurate sense-perceptions, the former are rejected only when they are in conflict with other convictions which stand better the test of reflection." But, surely, there is an enormous difference between the possibility of harmonizing conflicting sense-perceptions and that of harmonizing conflicting moral convictions. When the sense-perceptions vary in the presence of the same object, as when the object looks different under different objective conditions or if the beholding eye is normal or colour-blind, the variations can be accounted for by reference to the external conditions or the structure of the organ, and they in no way affect our conceptions of things as they really are. So also a hallucination is easily distinguished from a perception when we learn by experience that its object does not exist, whereas the perception has an existing object. On the other hand we all know that there often is a conflict between the moral convictions of "thoughtful and well-educated people," nay, even between the moral "intuitions" of philosophers, which proves irreconcilable. This is just what may be expected if moral opinions are based on emotions. The moral emotions depend upon cognitions, but the same cognitions may give rise to emotions that differ, in quality or intensity, in different persons or in the same person on different occasions, and then there is nothing that could make the emotions uniform. Certain cognitions inspire fear into nearly every breast, but there are brave men and cowards in the world, independently of the accuracy with which they realize impending danger. Some cases of suffering can hardly fail to call forth compassion in the most pitiless heart; but men's disposition to feel pity varies greatly, both in regard to the beings for whom it is felt and as to the intensity of the emotion. The same holds true of the moral emotions. To a large extent, as we have seen, their differences depend upon the presence of different cognitions, but very frequently the emotions also differ though the cognitions are the same. The variations of the former kind do not interfere with the belief in the universality of moral judgments, but when the variations of the moral emotions may be traced to different persons' tendencies to feel differently in similar circumstances on account of the particular nature of their altruistic sentiments, the supposed universality of moral judgments is a delusion.

It will perhaps be argued that, with sufficient insight into facts, there would be no diversity of moral opinion if only the moral consciousness of all men were "sufficiently developed"; . . . But what is meant by a sufficiently developed moral consciousness? Practically, I suppose, nothing else than agreement with the speaker's own moral convictions. The expression is faulty and deceptive, because, if intended to mean anything more, it presupposes a universality of moral judgments which they do not possess, and at the same time may appear to prove what it presupposes. We may speak of an intellect sufficiently developed to grasp a certain truth, because truth is one; but it is not proved to be one by the fact that it is recognized as such by a "sufficiently" developed intellect. The universality of truth lies in the recognition of judgments as true by all who have a *full* knowledge of the facts concerned, and the appeal to a *sufficient* knowledge rightly *assumes* that truth is universal.

That moral judgments could not possibly possess that universality which is characteristic of truth becomes particularly obvious when we consider that their predicates vary not only in quality but in quantity. There are no degrees of truth and falsehood; but there are degrees of goodness and badness, virtues and merits may be greater or smaller, a duty may be more or less stringent, and if there are no degrees of rightness, the reason for it is that right simply means conformity to the rule of duty. . . .

The quantitative differences of moral estimates are plainly due to the emotional origin of all moral concepts. Emotions vary in intensity almost indefinitely, and the moral emotions form no exception to this rule. Indeed, it may be fairly doubted whether the same mode of conduct ever arouses exactly the same degree of approval or disapproval in any two individuals. Many of these differences are of course too slight to manifest themselves in the moral judgment; but very frequently the intensity of the emotion is indicated by some special word, or by the tone in which the judgment is pronounced. It should be noticed, however, that the quantity of the estimate expressed in a moral predicate is not identical with the intensity of the moral emotion which a certain course of conduct arouses on a particular occasion. We are liable to feel more indignant if an injury is committed before our eyes than if we read of it in a newspaper, and yet we admit that the degree of badness is in both cases the same. The comparative quantity of moral estimates is determined by the intensity of the emotions which their objects tend to evoke in exactly similar circumstances.

The Ethical Implications of Cultural Relativity
Carl Wellman

It is often thought that the discoveries of anthropology have revolutionary implications for ethics. Readers of Sumner, Benedict, and Herskovits are apt to come away with the impression that the only moral obligation is to conform to one's society, that polygamy is as good as monogamy, or that no ethical judgment can be rationally justified. While these anthropologists might complain that they are being misinterpreted, they would not deny that their real intent is to challenge the traditional view of morals. Even the anthropologist whose scientific training has made him skeptical of sweeping generalities and wary of philosophical entanglements is inclined to believe that the scientific study of cultures has undermined the belief in ethical absolutes of any kind.

Just what has been discovered that forces us to revise our ethics? Science has shown that certain things that were once thought to be absolute are actually relative to culture. Something is relative to culture when it varies with and is causally determined by culture. Clearly, nothing can be both relative to culture and absolute, for to be absolute is to be fixed and invariable, independent of man and the same for all men.

Exactly which things are relative and in what degree is a question still being debated by cultural anthropologists. Important as this question is, I do not propose to discuss it. It is the empirical scientist who must tell us which things vary from culture to culture and to what extent each is causally determined by its culture. It is not for me to question the findings of the anthropologists in this area. Instead, let me turn to the philosophical problem of the implications of cultural relativity. Assuming for the moment that cultural relativity is a fact, what follows for ethics? . . .

I

It has long been recognized that mores are relative to culture. Mores are those customs which are enforced by social pressure. They are established patterns of action to which

By permission. *The Journal of Philosophy*, Vol. 60, no. 7, March 28, 1963. Copyright © 1963 by Journal of Philosophy, Inc.

the individual is expected to conform and from which he deviates only at the risk of disapproval and punishment. It seems clear that mores vary from society to society and that the mores of any given society depend upon its culture. What does this imply for ethics?

The conclusion most frequently drawn is that what is right in one society may be wrong in another. For example, although it would be wrong for one of us to kill his aged parents, this very act is right for an Eskimo. This is because our mores are different from those of Eskimo society, and it is the mores that make an act right or wrong.

Let us grant, for the sake of discussion, that different societies do have different mores. Why should we grant that the mores make an act right or wrong? It has been claimed that this is true by definition. 'Right' simply means according to the mores, and 'wrong' means in violation of the mores. There is something to be said for this analysis of our concepts of right and wrong. It seems to explain both the imperativeness and the impersonality of obligation. The "ought" seems to tell one what to do and yet to be more than the command of any individual; perhaps its bindingness lies in the demands of society. Attractive as this interpretation appears at first glance, I cannot accept it. . . . This particular analysis is objectionable in that it makes it self-contra-dictory to say that any customary way of acting is wrong. No doubt social reformers are often confused, but they are not always inconsistent.

If the view that the mores make an act right or wrong is not true by definition, it amounts to the moral principle that one ought always to conform to the mores of his society. None of the ways in which this principle is usually supported is adequate. *(a)* Any society unconsciously develops those mores which are conducive to survival and well-being under its special circumstances. Each individual ought to obey the mores of his society because this is the best way to promote the good life for the members of that society. I admit that there is a tendency for any society to develop those mores which fit its special circumstances, but I doubt that this is more than a tendency. There is room for reform in most societies, and this is particularly true when conditions are changing for one reason or another. *(b)* One ought to obey the mores of his society because disobedience would tend to destroy those mores. Without mores any society would lapse into a state of anarchy that would be intolerable for its members. It seems to me that this argument deserves to be taken seriously, but it does not prove that one ought always to obey the mores of his society. What it does show is that one ought generally to obey the mores of his society and that whenever he considers disobedience he should give due weight to the effects of his example upon social stability. *(c)* One ought to obey the mores of his society because disobedience tends to undermine their existence. It is important to preserve the mores, not simply to avoid anarchy, but because it is their mores which give shape and meaning to the life of any people. I grant that the individual does tend to think of his life in terms of the mores of his group and that anything which disrupts those mores tends to rob his life of significance. But once again, all this shows is that one should conform to the mores of his society on the whole. Although there is some obligation to conformity, this is not the only nor the most important obligation on the member of any society.

Therefore, it does not seem to me that one can properly say that the mores make an act right or wrong. One cannot define the meaning of these ethical words in terms of the mores, nor can one maintain the ethical principle that one ought always to obey the mores of his society. If the mores do not make acts right or wrong, the fact that different societies have different mores does not imply that the same kind of act can be right in one society and wrong in another. . . .

II

Both linguistic and psychological studies have suggested that people living in different societies conceptualize their experience in different ways. Probably moral concepts vary from society to society depending upon the cultural backgrounds from which they arise. The ancient Greek thought of virtue quite differently from the modern American; the Christian conception of obligation is probably absent from the mind of the African who has escaped the influence of any missionary. What are we to conclude from the fact that moral concepts are relative to culture?

The obvious implication appears to be that people of different cultural backgrounds are almost sure to disagree on any ethical question. Obvious as it may seem, this is not implied at all. In fact, people using different concepts could never disagree, for disagreement presupposes that both parties are thinking in the same terms. For one thing, on what question are they supposed to be disagreeing? If each person is using his own set of concepts, each person formulates his own question in his own terms. And if the two persons do not have any common set of ethical concepts, there is no way for formulating a single question that will be intelligible to both of them. Again, in what sense do their respective answers disagree? When an American says that Poland is undemocratic and a Russian insists that it is a fine example of democracy, it appears that they are disagreeing. No doubt they do disagree in many ways, but not in their utterances. Their statements are quite compatible, for they are using the words 'democracy' in different senses. Similarly, people of different cultures would only seem to disagree, if they attached different concepts to their ethical words.

The proper conclusion to draw is that any comparison between the ethical views of the members of different cultures can be only partial. As long as each view is stated only in its own terms there can be no comparison between them; comparison becomes possible only when they are stated in the same set of concepts. But if the sets of concepts are not identical, any translation of one view into the language of the other or of both into some neutral language will be approximate at best. Even where something approaching adequate translation is possible, some of the meaning will be lost or something will be added that was not in the original concept. For this reason, any claim that the ethical views of people in different societies are either identical or contradictory is likely to tell only part of the story. To some extent, at least, the ethics of different cultures are incommensurate.

III

The aspect of cultural relativity most often emphasized is that pertaining to moral judgments. Objects that the members of one society think to be good are considered bad by another group; acts considered wrong in one society are thought of as right in another. Moreover, these differences in judgments of value and obligation seem to reflect cultural differences between the respective societies. There is a great deal of evidence to suggest that ethical judgments are relative to culture.

To many anthropologists and philosophers it is a corollary of this fact that one of a set of contrary ethical judgments is no more valid than another, or, put positively, that all ethical judgments are equally valid. Unfortunately, there is a crucial ambiguity [here]. . . . Ethical judgments might have equal validity either because all are valid or because none are: similarly one ethical judgment might be no more valid than another either because both are equally valid or because both are equally lacking in validity. Since these two interpretations are quite different, let us consider them separately.

On the first interpretation, the conclusion to be drawn from the fact that ethical judgments are relative to culture is that every moral judgment is valid for the society in which it is made. Instead of denying the objective validity of ethical judgments, this view affirms it, but in a qualified form which will allow for the variations in ethical belief.

There seem to be three main ways of defending this position. *(a)* Ethical judgments have objective validity because it is possible to justify them rationally. However, this validity is limited to a given society because the premises used in such justification are those which are agreed upon in that society. Since there are no universally accepted premises, no universal validity is possible. I would wish to deny that justification is real if it is limited in this way. If all our reasoning really does rest on certain premises which can be rejected by others without error, then we must give up the claim to objective validity. When I claim validity for ethical judgments, I intend to claim more than that it is possible to support them with logical arguments; I also claim that it is incorrect to deny the premises of such arguments. *(b)* Any ethical judgment is an expression of a total pattern of culture. Hence it is possible to justify any single judgment in terms of its coherence with the total cultural configuration of the judger. But one cannot justify the culture as a whole, for it is not part of a more inclusive pattern. Therefore, ethical judgments have objective validity, but only in terms of a given cultural pattern. I would make the same objection to this view as to the preceding one. Since it allows justification to rest upon an arbitrary foundation, it is inadequate to support any significant claim to objective validity. *(c)* Any ethical judgment has objective validity because it is an expression of a moral code. The validity of a moral code rests on the fact that without conformity to a common code social cohesion breaks down, leading to disastrous results. Since any given moral code provides cohesion for one and only one society, each ethical judgment has validity for a single society. There are at least two difficulties with this defence of objectivity. Surely one could deny some ethical judgments without destroying the entire moral code they reflect; not every judgment could be shown to be essential to social stability. Moreover, the argument seems to rest on the ethical judgment that one ought not to contribute to the breakdown of social stability. How is this judgment to be shown to be valid? One must either appeal to some other basis of validity or argue in a circle. None of these arguments to show that every moral judgment is valid for the society in which it is made is adequate.

On the second interpretation, the conclusion to be drawn from the fact that moral judgments are relative to culture is that moral judgments have no objective validity. This amounts to saying that the distinction between true and false, correct and incorrect, does not apply to such judgments. This conclusion obviously does not follow simply from the fact that people disagree about ethical questions. We do not deny the objective validity of scientific judgments either on the grounds that different scientists propose alternative theories or on the grounds that the members of some societies hold fast to many unscientific beliefs.

Why, then, does the fact that moral judgments are relative to culture imply that they have no objective validity? *(a)* Individuals make different ethical judgments because they judge in terms of different frames of reference, and they adopt these frames of reference uncritically from their cultures. Since ethical judgments are the product of enculturation rather than reasoning, they cannot claim rational justification. I do not find this argument convincing, for it seems to confuse the origin of a judgment with its justification. The causes of a judgment are one thing; the reasons for or against it are another. It remains to be shown that any information about what causes us to judge as we do has any bearing on the question of whether or not our judgments are correct. *(b)* It is impossible to settle ethical questions by using the scientific method. Therefore, there is no objective way to show that one ethical judgment is any more correct than another, and, in the absence of any method of establishing the claim to objective validity, it makes no sense to continue to make the claim. I will concede that, if there is no rational method of establishing ethical judgments, then we might as well give up the claim to objective validity. And if the scientific method is restricted to the testing of hypotheses by checking the predictions they imply against the results of observation and experiment, it does seem to be inapplicable to ethical questions. What I will not concede is the tacit assumption that the scientific method is the only method of establishing the truth. Observation and experimentation do not figure prominently in the method used by mathematicians. I even wonder whether the person who concludes that ethical judgments have no objective validity can establish *this* conclusion by using the scientific method. The fact that ethical judgments cannot be established scientifically does not by itself prove that they cannot be established by any method of reasoning. . . .

CONCLUSION

It is fashionable either to ignore the facts of cultural relativity or to draw startling conclusions from them. . . . The various arguments by which these conclusions are usually derived from the facts of cultural relativity are, in my opinion, either invalid or inconclusive. On the other hand, there are some important ethical conclusions which can and should be drawn from these same facts. Among the genuine implications of cultural relativity I would include these: Our own institutions are far from inevitable. Generically similar objects or situations may have different values in different societies. Generically similar acts may be right or good in one society and wrong or bad in another. Any comparison between the ethical views of the members of different societies can be only partial.

No doubt the reader will wish to challenge my acceptance or rejection of this or that particular conclusion. Quite apart from such specific ethical questions, however, there are certain over-all logical conclusions which seem to me inevitable. (1) What conclusions one can legitimately draw from the facts of cultural relativity will depend upon *which* facts one starts from. It is worth distinguishing between the relativity of mores, social institutions, human nature, acts, goals, value experiences, moral emotions, moral concepts, moral judgments, and moral reasoning; for each of these has different implications for ethics. (2) By themselves the facts of cultural relativity do not imply anything for ethics. Any argument that is both interesting and valid requires additional premises. Thus it is only in conjunction with certain statements that go beyond anthropology that the findings of anthropology have any bearing at all on ethics. (3) What conclusions one should draw will obviously depend upon which of these additional premises one accepts. Therefore, one's ethical and epistemological theory will determine the significance one will attach to cultural relativity. (4) Before we can criticize or even understand the arguments by which ethical conclusions are derived from the facts of such relativity, we must make these additional premises explicit and see what can be said for or against them. My main purpose in this paper has been to make a start in this complicated yet crucial task.

Relativism

John Hospers

Relativism, when analyzed, breaks down into several different views.

1. *Sociological relativism* is simply the view that different groups of people—different tribes, different cultures, different civilizations—have different moral standards for evaluating acts as right or wrong. For example, in our society we believe that it is better to be caught for stealing than to escape capture; but the Spartan youth who allowed the fox to gnaw at his vital organs rather than be caught for stealing . . . reflected a popular belief that being caught was bad but stealing was not. The Dobu tribesmen of New Guinea believe that growing your own vegetables is honorable but stealing your neighbor's vegetables is still more honorable. The ancient Romans, unlike the Christians, had more respect for honor than for pity. They could be forgiving if they could gain some advantage from being so; otherwise they had virtually no feeling for victims, such as prisoners of war. Courage was prized; mercy and humility were not. Some desert tribes, such as those discussed in our previous example of T. E. Lawrence, think it a sacred obligation, when one of their number has been killed or captured by an opposing tribe, to capture and kill (by slow torture) a member of that tribe, even if he is not the same man who committed the offense—a perfectly innocent man will do just as well. The Eskimos think it right to kill their parents after

the parents have reached a certain age—indeed, the parents expect this—rather than take them along on their hazardous journeys. . . .

No one is likely to deny relativism in this sense. It would ill become the moral philosopher to say, "You sociologists and anthropologists are all wrong in the alleged facts which you report. It is all a tissue of lies!" Those who are best qualified to know what the Dobu tribesmen believe are those who have lived among the Dobu and seen for themselves.

Even so, the term "sociological relativism" is ambiguous. If the term merely means that there are moral beliefs held by one group which are not held by another, this is obviously true—an empirical fact. But if the term means that different groups have different *basic* moral principles, the statement is not obviously true and may even be false. Different groups *may* be using the same basic moral principles but applying them in different ways to different situations. Imagine two tribes, each believing that they should do what is most conducive to the survival of as many people as possible within the tribe. One of the tribes lives in the desert, and the other where there is plenty of water. In the first tribe wasting even a small amount of water is considered a grave moral offense, perhaps even a capital offense; in the second tribe there are no rules at all about wasting water. This is an example of sociological relativism in the first sense; the one believes that wasting water is wrong and the other does not. But it is not an example of sociological relativism in the second sense, for both moral rules equally illustrate one basic moral principle, that what is right is what promotes survival. On this assumption they do not differ at all; what differs is the application of this one principle to different circumstances.

2. Sociological relativism is not an ethical doctrine at all; it tries to describe what people's moral beliefs *are;* it says nothing about whether any of them are preferable to others. *Ethical relativism,* however, goes further; it has a definite view about right and wrong, and thus it enters the domain of ethics. According to ethical relativism, if there are two tribes or societies, and in one of them it is believed that acts of a certain kind are wrong while in the other it is believed that acts of that same kind are right, *both beliefs* are true: in the first society acts of that kind *are* wrong and in the other society they *are* right. Polygamy is right in polygamous societies but not in monogamous societies. Thus there is no overall standard of right and wrong—what is right and what is wrong depends on the society of which you are a member.

Here at once we have an ambiguity. Let us suppose, for the moment, that slavery is right in one society and wrong in another—not just that it is thought to be so, which would be sociological relativism, but that it really is so, as ethical relativism says. But a person who holds this belief need not be a relativist at all. He may believe in some one over-all standard of right, such as the maximum happiness of the people concerned. . . . And if so, since he has one standard of rightness, he is no relativist. A certain practice might make for the happiness of one society but not of another, and in that event it would be right in the one society but not in the other; only the application of the moral principle differs from one society to another, not the principle itself. Probably most people who call themselves ethical relativists are not so at all, for they believe in one moral standard which applies in different ways to different societies because of the various conditions in which they live. One might as well talk about gravitational relativism because a stone falls and a balloon rises; yet both events are equally instances of one law of universal gravitation.

But suppose that the person believes that there *is* no one over-all standard and that what is right and what is wrong varies from one society to another without reference to any one overall moral principle. A person might believe that what is right for one group may be wrong for another and what is right for one individual may be wrong for another, though *not* because there is one over-all moral principle of which these are different applications. The relativist will be hard put to it to give any reason *why* he believes this to be so, but he may state the position without any attempt to give reasons. In that event he can truly be called a relativist. But now he must face certain problems:

a. If we ask him *why* a practice that is right in one society is wrong in another, he will have no reason to present. There seems to be no general principle from which his position follows. This weakness, to put it mildly, will leave many people dissatisfied.

b. "What is right in one group is wrong in another," he says. But what exactly is a group? and which group is one to select? Every person is a member of many different groups—his nation, his state, his city, his club, his school, church, fraternity, or athletic association. Suppose that most of the people in his club think that a certain kind of act is wrong and that most of the people in his nation think it is right; what then?

c. How many of the group—whatever group it turns out to be—must think it is wrong before it really is wrong? The usual answer is, "The majority." Presumably this means anything over 50 per cent. If 51 per cent of his countrymen think adultery is wrong, then it is wrong for the people in that country; but if only 49 per cent of them think it wrong, then it isn't. This conclusion is strange, to say the least. Can't a majority be mistaken? A minority view may sometimes spread and become a majority view later; in that event, was the act wrong before and right now? It is very easy to say, "Head hunting is right in a headhunting society, and if most of the people in the United States became headhunters, then headhunting would be right for us," and the same with such practices as polygamy, witchburning, conviction without a trial, cannibalism. But is there any reason why what most people believe should be true?

d. If what the majority of a society or group approves is *ipso facto* right in that society, how can there be any such thing as moral improvement? If someone in a headhunting society were convinced that headhunting was cruel, barbarous, and wrong and proceeded to share these sentiments with his chieftain, the relativistic chieftain would reply, "But the majority in our tribe considers it right, so it *is* right." In a society in which most people cheated the government on their income tax, it would be right to do so, though it would no longer be right once the percentage of cheaters dropped below 50. If ethical relativism is correct, it is clearly impossible for the moral beliefs of a society to be mistaken because the certainty of the majority that its beliefs were right would prove that those beliefs *were* right for that society at that time. The minority view would therefore be mistaken, no matter what it was. Needless to say, most people who state that "in morals everything is relative" and who proceed to call themselves ethical relativists are unaware of these implications of their theory.

Normative Ethical Relativism

Paul W. Taylor

The statement, "What is right in one society may be wrong in another," is a popular way of explaining what is meant by the "relativity of morals." It is usually contrasted with "ethical universalism," taken as the view that "right and wrong do not vary from society to society." These statements are ambiguous, however, and it is important for us to be mindful of their ambiguity. For they may be understood either as factual claims or as normative claims, and it makes a great deal of difference which way they are understood. . . .

When it is said that what is right in one society may be wrong in another, this may be understood to mean that what is *believed* to be right in one society is *believed* to be wrong in another. And when it is said that moral right and wrong vary from society to society, this may be understood to mean that different moral norms are adopted by different societies, so that an act which fulfills the norms of one society may violate the norms of another. If this is what is meant, then we are here being told merely of the cultural variability of specific standards and rules. . . .

But the statement, "What is right in one society may be wrong in another," may be interpreted in quite a different way. It may be taken as a normative claim rather than as a factual assertion. Instead of asserting the unsurprising fact that what is believed to be right in one society is believed to be wrong in another, it expresses the far more radical and seemingly paradoxical claim that what *actually is* right in one society may *actually be* wrong in another. According to this view, moral norms are to be considered valid only within the society which has adopted them as part of its way of life. Such norms are not to be considered valid outside that society. The conclusion is then drawn that it is not legitimate to judge people in other societies by applying the norms of one's own society to their conduct. This is the view we shall designate "normative ethical relativism." In order to be perfectly clear about what it claims, we shall examine two ways in which it can be stated, one focusing our attention upon moral judgments, the other on moral norms.

With regard to moral judgments, normative ethical relativism holds that two *apparently* contradictory statements can both be true. The argument runs as follows. Consider the two statements:

(1) It is wrong for unmarried women to have their faces unveiled in front of strangers.

(2) It is not wrong for . . . (as above).

Here it seems as if there is a flat contradiction between two moral judgments, so that if one is true the other must be false. But the normative ethical relativist holds that they are both true, because the statements as given in (1) and (2) are incomplete. They should read as follows:

(3) It is wrong for unmarried women *who are members of society S* to have their faces unveiled in front of strangers.

(4) It is not wrong for unmarried women *outside of society S* to have their faces unveiled in front of strangers.

Statements (3) and (4) are not contradictories. To assert one is not to deny the other. The normative ethical relativist simply translates all moral judgments of the form "Doing act X is right" into statements of the form "Doing X is right when the agent is a member of society S." The latter statement can then be seen to be consistent with statements of the form "Doing X is wrong when the agent is not a member of society S."

The normative ethical relativist's view of moral norms accounts for the foregoing theory of moral judgments. A moral norm, we have seen, is either a standard used in a judgment of good and bad character or a rule used in a judgment of right and wrong conduct. Thus a person is judged to be good insofar as he fulfills the standard, and an action is judged to be right or wrong according to whether it conforms to or violates the rule. Now when a normative ethical relativist says that moral norms vary from society to society, he does not intend merely to assert the fact that different societies have adopted different norms. He is going beyond descriptive relativism and is making a normative claim. He is denying any universal validity to moral norms. He is saying that a moral standard or rule is correctly applicable only to the members of the particular society which has adopted the standard or rule as part of its actual moral code. He therefore thinks it is illegitimate to judge the character or conduct of those outside the society by such a standard or rule. Anyone who uses the norms of one society as the basis for judging the character or conduct of persons in another society is consequently in error.

It is not that a normative ethical relativist necessarily believes in *tolerance* of other people's norms. Nor does his position imply that he grants others the *right* to live by their own norms, for he would hold a relativist view even about tolerance itself. A society whose code included a rule of tolerance would be right in tolerating others, while one that denied tolerance would be right (relative to its own norm of intolerance) in prohibiting others from living by different norms. The normative ethical relativist would simply say that *we* should not judge the tolerant society to be any better than the intolerant one, for this would be applying our own norm of tolerance to other societies. Tolerance, like any other norm, is culture-bound. Anyone who claims that every society has a *right* to live by its own norms, provided that it respects a similar right in other societies, is an ethical universalist, since he holds at least one norm valid for all societies, namely, the right to practice a way of life without interference from others. And he deems this universal norm a valid one, whether or not every society does in fact accept it.

If the normative ethical relativist is challenged to prove his position, he may do either of two things. On the one hand, he may try to argue that his position follows from, or is based on, the very same facts that are cited by the descriptive relativist as evidence for *his* position. Or, on the other hand, he may turn for support to metaethical considerations. Putting aside the second move for the moment, let us look more closely at the first.

The most frequent argument given in defense of normative ethical relativism is that, if the facts pointed out by the descriptive relativist are indeed true, then we must accept normative ethical relativism as the only position consistent with those facts. For it seems that if each person's moral judgments are formed within the framework of the norms of his own culture and historical epoch, and if such norms vary among cultures and epochs, it would follow necessarily that it is unwarranted for anyone to apply his own norms to conduct in other societies and times. To do so would be ethnocentrism, which is . . . a kind of blind, narrow-minded dogmatism. To escape the irrationality of being ethnocentric, we need but realize that the only norms one may legitimately apply to any given group are the ones accepted by that group. Since different peoples accept different norms, there are no universal norms applicable to everyone throughout the world. Now, to say that there are no universal norms applicable worldwide is to commit oneself to normative ethical relativism. Thus, the argument concludes, normative ethical relativism follows from the facts of descriptive relativism.

Is this a valid argument? Suppose one accepts the facts pointed out by the descriptive relativist. Must he then also accept normative ethical relativism? Let us examine some of the objections that have been raised to this argument. In the first place, it is claimed that the facts of cultural variability do not, *by themselves,* entail normative ethical relativism. The reason is that it is perfectly possible for someone to accept those facts and deny normative ethical relativism without contradicting himself. No matter how great may be the differences in the moral beliefs of different cultures and in the moral norms they accept, it is still possible to hold that some of these beliefs are true and others false, or that some of the norms are more correct, justified, or enlightened than others. The fact that societies differ about what is right and wrong does not mean that one society may not have better reasons for holding its views than does another. After all, just because two people (or two groups of people) disagree about whether a disease is caused by bacteria or by evil spirits does not lead to the conclusion that there is no correct or enlightened view about the cause of the disease. So it does not follow from the fact that two societies differ about whether genocide is right that there is no correct or enlightened view about this moral matter.

A similar argument can be used with regard to the second set of facts asserted by the descriptive relativist. No contradiction is involved in affirming that all moral beliefs come from the social environment and denying normative ethical relativism. The fact that a belief is learned from one's society does not mean that it is neither true nor false, or that if it is true, its truth is "relative" to the society in which it was learned. All of our beliefs, empirical ones no less than moral ones, are learned from our society. We are not born with any innate beliefs about chemistry or physics; we learn these only in our schools. Yet this does not make us skeptical about the universal validity of these sciences. So the fact that our moral beliefs come from our society and are learned in our homes and schools has no bearing on their universal validity. The origin or cause of a person's *acquiring* a belief does not determine whether the *content* of the belief is true or false, or even whether there are good grounds for his accepting that content to be true or false.

If it is claimed that our moral beliefs are based on attitudes or feelings culturally conditioned in us from childhood, the same point can still be made. Suppose, for example, that a person who believes slavery is wrong feels disapproval, dislike, or even abhorrence towards the institution of slavery. His negative attitude, which has undoubtedly been influenced by the value system of his culture, may be contrasted with a positive stance (approval, liking, admiring) of someone brought up in an environment where slave owning was accepted. Here are positive and negative attitudes toward slavery, each being causally conditioned by the given cultural environment. It does not follow from this that the two are equally justified, or that neither can be justified. The question of whether a certain attitude toward slavery is justified or unjustified depends on whether good reasons can be given *for* anyone taking the one attitude and *against* anyone taking the other. This question requires the exercise of our reasoning powers. . . . The mere fact that the attitudes which underlie moral beliefs are all learned from the social environment leaves open the question of what attitudes an intelligent, rational, and well-informed person would take toward a given action or social practice.

The same kind of argument also holds with respect to the third fact of descriptive relativism: ethnocentrism. People who are ethnocentric *believe* that the one true moral code is that of their own society. But this leaves open the question, Is their belief true or false? Two people of different cultures, both ethnocentric but with opposite moral beliefs, may each think his particular moral norms are valid for everyone; however, this has no bearing on whether either one—or neither one—is correct. We must inquire independently into the possibility of establishing the universal validity of a set of moral norms, regardless of who might or might not believe them to be universally true.

It should be noted that these various objections to the first argument for normative ethical relativism, even if sound, are not sufficient to show that normative ethical relativism is false. They only provide reasons for rejecting one argument in support of that position. To show that the position is false, it would be necessary to give a sound argument in defense of ethical universalism. The sorts of arguments set forth by philosophers to establish universalism will be disclosed in later chapters. It is only if one or more of these arguments proves acceptable that normative ethical relativism is refuted.

CHAPTER 3

MORAL RESPONSIBILITY

In any discipline, students appreciate a catchy phrase that accurately summarizes a fairly fundamental point. Philosophy is a subject that doesn't have many catchy phrases. But it does have a few. One of the best-known is from ethics, "ought implies can." The point of the expression is that if I say you ought to do something, then I presume that you have the capability to do it (i.e., that you are free to do it). Another way of explaining the expression is by saying that human freedom is a presupposition of ethical practice. Unless human beings are free, ethical behavior is impossible. The logical sequence works like this: To be a moral being, I must be an agent who can be held responsible for any of my actions which are subject to praise or blame. To be responsible for those actions, I must have been free in some sense or other either to do or not to do those acts. In the absence of freedom in this sense, it would be bizarre to hold me morally responsible for them.

In our first selection, Samuel Butler describes a world (Erewhon) where people are held morally responsible for being ill. The citizens of Erewhon are brought to trial and punished when they are found guilty of being sick. What we consider criminal conduct, stealing for example, is treated in Erewhon the way we treat the sick. A person who steals is treated. Social practice in Erewhon is indeed bizarre. What makes it bizarre is that we believe people are not responsible for getting cancer or catching the flu but that they usually are responsible for stealing. That's why we put sick people in hospitals and thieves in jail. What distinguishes our culture from that of Erewhon is a difference about the facts concerning responsibility. It's not just that Erewhon has different customs from us. It is that we and the citizens of Erewhon disagree about the nature of the world.

The view that human beings are free to do or not do acts for which they are traditionally held morally responsible is not universally shared. A number of social scientists deny that human beings are free in that sense, and hence they could comfortably accept one-half of the social practices of Erewhon; we—like the citizens of Erewhon—should treat criminals rather than punish them. Criminal behavior does resemble being ill, after all. One of the most articulate exponents of this point of view is the behavioral psychologist B. F. Skinner. In the selection reproduced here, Skinner admits that "treating" crime and other uses of psychological conditioning would undermine the traditional views on human freedom and dignity. But let's not mourn excessively; their usefulness—at least according to Skinner—has passed. Traditionally, Skinner argues, freedom has been understood primarily in terms of *feeling* free. But, he maintains, "feeling free" doesn't show that a person is free. Skinner provides many instances of people who feel free but really aren't free—the happy slave. Skinner maintains that all positive reinforcement (the habitual use of rewards to affect behavior) denies freedom to a certain extent, since it affects behavior. Childrearing and teaching which make heavy use of reward provide examples. For the sake of argument, let's grant Skinner's contention that psychological conditioning denies freedom to a certain extent.

By focusing on positive reinforcement in childrearing and training, Skinner is able to make his moral point. Most positive reinforcement is not wrong—even if it does deny freedom. All behavior responds to reinforcement techniques. What makes a reinforcement technique right or wrong is the use to which it is put. If reinforcement produces a happier, more productive individual, as with typical childrearing, then the reinforcement technique is good. If reinforcement harms the individual, even if the reinforced behavior serves the interests of others, then the reinforcement technique is bad.

Behind this distinction between "good" and "bad" reinforcement techniques is Skinner's conviction that behavioral psychology is a benign scientific advance. The view of human nature depicted in the freedom and dignity literature is a superstitious view. The view of the person depicted by behavioral psychology is the scientific view, and our understanding of human beings is enhanced by the scientific view. All human beings really lose in accepting the scientific view is their vanity.

But is that all we have to lose? If Skinner's views prevailed, our legal (and moral) institutions would have to be completely redesigned. Rehabilitation and treatment would be emphasized at the expense of due process and finding of fault. The standards of fault and due process have no real role to play in settings where behavior is controlled by operant conditioning. If societal practice changed extensively toward the behavioral model, a radical and revolutionary change would have to take place in the practice of law and morals.

A few behaviorists, like Skinner, recognize the radical implications of their views. The fact that legal and moral institutions would look very different in a world where psychological conditioning, rather than establishing fault and intent, was the norm would not count as an objection. Behaviorists like Skinner would concede this point—joyfully. The real issue is not whether the world would be different but whether we would be justified in having institutional arrangements which emphasize operant conditioning at the expense of establishing fault and intent. To answer that question, two very distinct questions need to be addressed. First, are the traditional legal and moral institutions morally superior to the alternatives proposed by Skinner? Second are the "facts" of human nature upon which Skinner's view depends backed by sufficient empirical evidence and scrupulous conceptual rigor?

Many argue that Skinner's alternative view fails both these tests. As for the moral test, Skinner has no way of providing an objective test for what is right and wrong. The type of person we are, including our beliefs about matters of ethics, is a result of environmental forces, including the forces of other human conditioners. Hence my views about what is right and wrong depend on the views of others—specifically on the views of those that condition behavior. But what about the ethical views of the conditioners? Either those views were in turn conditioned, and we have the start of an infinite regress, or the ethical views of the conditioners were not established by conditioning. The behaviorist who opts for the latter alternative must admit that not all behavior and beliefs are conditioned. But that contradicts the behaviorist's central postulate. Ultimately, under Skinner's analysis what is good is what those in charge of conditioning say is good. But what reason do we have to think that the conditioners are right? I think the reader can see why Skinner's behavioral-psychological assumptions are considered, by some, to be ethically dangerous. What is right or wrong is determined by a cultural-scientific elite. For society to be governed (conditioned) in that way is frightening—whether the citizens accept conditioning happily or not. The behavioral psychologist fails the ethical test because there is no room in the theory for the discipline of ethics, specifically for the assessment of the arguments in behalf of or opposed to an ethical position.

What about the charge that Skinner's view of human nature lacks conceptual rigor? Skinner contends that positive reinforcement denies freedom to a certain extent, since it affects behavior. But does it? A debate on this question leads us to the traditional free will problem.

In this introduction the most we can accomplish is to separate the genuine issues, where there is real controversy, from the spurious issues, which can be definitively settled. Most philosophers agree that an action which can neither be explained nor caused cannot be evaluated from the moral point of view. Suppose that a mother was asked why she had sacrificed her own interests so that she could send her daughter to college. Her response was, "I didn't have any reason, I just did. I really can't explain it further." Compare that response with this one: "Since I stand in a unique relationship to my daughter, I have special obligations to her—obligations which override my own interests." While the second response provides moral reasons, the first response really isn't an answer to the question at all. Behavior subject to the first account isn't moral behavior at all; it's mysterious behavior. Hence, to claim that ought implies can or to say that persons are morally responsible does not commit us to the view that moral actions are done without a reason. They are done for a reason—e.g., supporting the interests of others. Consider the following three events:

1 A plant gradually grows toward the sun.
2 A fifth-grader correctly computes that $3 \times 3 = 9$.
3 A mother saves a large percentage of her income to pay for her daughter's college education.

In each case there is an explanation for the event. The question why the event happened can be answered with a great deal of certainty. However, which events, if any, occurred voluntarily? For which events, if any, was the agent responsible?

Most of us would agree that the plant's turning to the sun was caused, and involuntary. Given the laws of nature and the composition of the plant, the plant couldn't do anything else but grow toward the sun. It would be a misuse of language to say that the plant was responsible for growing toward the sun. The philosophical question is whether or not *all* events can be explained in just the way we explain the plant's growing toward the sun.

Many philosophers answer that question with a resounding no. Aristotle, for example, defines a free action as a voluntary act of choice. For Aristotle a voluntary act is an act which is done without external compulsion and without ignorance. What makes a voluntary act an act of choice is the element of rational deliberation, and we can only rationally deliberate about things which are in our power. A mother's saving for her daughter's education is a free act.

In a selection included in this chapter, Sartre distinguishes human *actions* from all other events by the fact that human actions are intentional. Note that not all human behavior can be classified as actions. Burps, twitches, and sneezes are not actions; they are not intentional behavior.

Sartre accepts the fact that human beings exist within a situation. Persons live in an environment, have limited powers, have a history, and interact with others. What human beings can do within the total situation is to postulate some ideal (goal) which represents a state of affairs other than that which currently exists and then work to bring their situation in line with the postulated ideal. On the mundane level I can postulate the ideal of "going to the Coke machine to purchase a Coke which will quench my thirst" and then undertake the appropriate behavior. On a more elevated plane I can postulate the ideal of "bringing about a more democratic and peace-loving society" and then undertake the appropriate behavior to bring that about. This postulating of ideals which move us beyond our given situations is the ground of human action and constitutes Sartre's concept of freedom. That a mother is poor is a given. That a mother can postulate the ideal of educating her daughter and undertake the appropriate behavior (saving) is a free action. The mother didn't have to respond to her circumstances in the way she did. None of us do. For this reason, there is a legitimate reason for saying we are responsible for our situation. We are responsible for what we do in a given context and how we attempt to transform it. This is what Sartre means when he declares that man "is responsible for the world and for himself as a way of being."

After these explanations the student may wonder what all the fuss is about. Human behavior can be explained, but some human behavior has special characteristics which enable us to say that it is free and that persons are responsible for such behavior. Such behavior can be morally evaluated and is suitable for praise or blame.

C. A. Campbell, as well as most other philosophers, believes that the free will problem cannot be dissolved so quickly and simply. So much depends on the meaning of the word *cause*. Determinism is the view that all events in the world are caused wholly and only by antecedent (past) events. Under this definition, it looks as if all events must be as they are and could not be otherwise. It looks as if following a mathematical rule, such as computing that $3 \times 3 = 9$, is just like the plant's growing toward the sun. Ditto for the mother's act of saving. If that is what is meant by saying that all events are caused, then clearly our intentions result wholly and only from past causes, all behavior is nonvoluntary, and hence we cannot be held morally responsible for it. Moreover, most social scientists prefer this materialistic, mechanistic notion of causality because it makes all human behavior reducible to laws of the type that govern the disciplines of physics and chemistry.

However, the fact that a definition of causality is convenient for the "scientific" study of behavior is not a sufficient reason for adopting it. The right question to ask is whether the scientific view is plausible in terms of helping us understand human behavior. It seems to me that it is not. The implications of the scientific definition of causality give us a very bizarre world. A wider definition of cause which includes all lawlike behavior might well be better. We could then have different kinds of causes— physical and chemical ones for the plant's growing toward the sun, rule-guided ones for mathematics, games, etc., and intentional ones for moral and prudential behavior. Such an account of cause would in principle enable us to explain (but not predict) all human behavior and would still allow a place for genuine responsibility. In any case the remainder of this book rests on the assumption that we do have what Campbell calls "contracausal" or creative, freedom.

Erewhon

Samuel Butler

This is what I gathered. That in that country if a man falls into ill health, or catches any disorder, or fails bodily in any way before he is seventy years old, he is tried before a jury of his countrymen, and if convicted is held up to public scorn and sentenced more or less severely as the case may be. There are subdivisions of illnesses into crimes and misdemeanours as with offences amongst ourselves — a man being punished very heavily for serious illness, while failure of eyes or hearing in one over sixty-five, who has had good health hitherto, is dealt with by fine only, or imprisonment in default of payment. But if a man forges a cheque, or sets his house on fire, or robs with violence from the person, or does any other such things as are criminal in our own country, he is either taken to a hospital and most carefully tended at the public expense, or if he is in good circumstances, he lets it be known to all his friends that he is suffering from a severe fit of immorality, just as we do when we are ill, and they come and visit him with great solicitude, and inquire with interest how it all came about, what symptoms first showed themselves, and so forth, — questions which he will answer with perfect unreserve; for bad conduct, though considered no less deplorable than illness with ourselves, and as unquestionably indicating something seriously wrong with the individual who misbehaves, is nevertheless held to be the result of either pre-natal or post-natal misfortune.

The strange part of the story, however, is that though they ascribe moral defects to the effect of misfortune either in character or surroundings, they will not listen to the plea of misfortune in cases that in England meet with sympathy and commiseration only. Ill luck of any kind, or even ill treatment at the hands of others, is considered an offence against society, inasmuch as it makes people uncomfortable to hear of it. Loss of fortune, therefore, or loss of some dear friend on whom another was much dependent is punished hardly less severely than physical delinquency. . . .

The fact, therefore, that the Erewhonians attach none of that guilt to crime which they do to physical ailments, does not prevent the more selfish among them from neglecting a friend who has robbed a bank, for instance, till he has fully recovered; but it does prevent them from even thinking of treating criminals with that contemptuous tone which would seem to say, 'I, if I were you, should be a better man than you are,' a tone which is held quite reasonable in regard to physical ailment. Hence, though they conceal ill health by every cunning and hypocrisy and artifice which they can devise, they are quite open about the most flagrant mental diseases, should they happen to exist, which to do the people justice is not often. Indeed, there are some who are, so to speak, spiritual valetudinarians, and who make themselves exceedingly ridiculous by their nervous supposition that they are wicked, while they are very tolerable people all the time. This however is exceptional; and on the whole they use much the same reserve or unreserve about the state of their moral welfare as we do about our health.

From Samuel Butler, *Erewhon*. Published by Jonathan Cape Ltd., London.

Hence all the ordinary greetings among ourselves, such as, How do you do? and the like, are considered signs of gross illbreeding; nor do the politer classes tolerate even such a common complimentary remark as telling a man that he is looking well. They salute each other with, 'I hope you are good this morning;' or 'I hope you have recovered from the snappishness from which you were suffering when I last saw you;' and if the person saluted has not been good, or is still snappish, he says so at once and is condoled with accordingly. Indeed, the straighteners have gone so far as to give names from the hypothetical language (as taught at the Colleges of Unreason), to all known forms of mental indisposition, and to classify them according to a system of their own, which, though I could not understand it, seemed to work well in practice; for they are always able to tell a man what is the matter with him as soon as they have heard his story, and their familiarity with the long names assures him that they thoroughly understand his case.

The reader will have no difficulty in believing that the laws regarding ill health were frequently evaded by the help of recognised fictions, which every one understood, but which it would be considered gross ill-breeding to even seem to understand. Thus, a day or two after my arrival at the Nosnibors', one of the many ladies who called on me made excuses for her husband's only sending his card, on the ground that when going through the public market-place that morning he had stolen a pair of socks. I had already been warned that I should never show surprise, so I merely expressed my sympathy, and said that though I had only been in the capital so short a time, I had already had a very narrow escape from stealing a clothes brush, and that though I had resisted temptation so far, I was sadly afraid that if I saw any object of special interest that was neither too hot nor too heavy, I should have to put myself in the straightener's hands.

Mrs. Nosnibor, who had been keeping an ear on all that I had been saying, praised me when the lady had gone. Nothing she said, could have been more polite according to Erewhonian etiquette. She then explained that to have stolen a pair of socks, or 'to have the socks' (in more colloquial language), was a recognised way of saying that the person in question was slightly indisposed.

In spite of all this they have a keen sense of the enjoyment consequent upon what they call being 'well.' They admire mental health and love it in other people, and take all the pains they can (consistently with their other duties) to secure it for themselves. They have an extreme dislike to marrying into what they consider unhealthy families. They send for the straightener at once whenever they have been guilty of anything seriously flagitious—often even if they think that they are on the point of committing it; and though his remedies are sometimes exceedingly painful, involving close confinement for weeks, and in some cases the most cruel physical tortures, I never heard of a reasonable Erewhonian refusing to do what his straightener told him, any more than of a reasonable Englishman refusing to undergo even the most frightful operation, if his doctors told him it was necessary. . . .

In Erewhon as in other countries there are some courts of justice that deal with special subjects. Misfortune generally, as I have above explained, is considered more or less criminal, but it admits of classification, and a court is assigned to each of the main heads under which it can be supposed to fall. Not very long after I had reached the capital I strolled into the Personal Bereavement Court, and was both much interested and pained by listening to the trial of a man who was accused of having just lost a wife to whom he had been tenderly attached, and who had left him with three little children, of whom the eldest was only three years old.

The defence which the prisoner's counsel endeavoured to establish was, that the prisoner had never really loved his wife; but it broke down completely, for the public prosecutor called witness after witness who deposed to the fact that the couple had been devoted to one another, and the prisoner repeatedly wept as incidents were put in evidence that reminded him of the irreparable nature of the loss he had sustained. The jury returned a verdict of guilty after very little deliberation, but recommended the prisoner to mercy on the ground that he had but recently insured his wife's life for a considerable sum, and might be deemed lucky inasmuch as he had received the money without demur from the insurance company, though he had only paid two premiums.

I have just said that the jury found the prisoner guilty. When the judge passed sentence, I was struck with the way in which the prisoner's counsel was rebuked for having referred to a work in which the guilt of such misfortunes as the prisoner's was extenuated to a degree that roused the indignation of the court.

'We shall have,' said the judge, 'these crude and subversionary books from time to time until it is recognised as an axiom of morality that luck is the only fit object of human veneration. How far a man has any right to be more lucky and hence more venerable than his neighbours, is a point that always has been, and always will be, settled proximately by a kind of higgling and haggling of the market, and ultimately by brute force; but however this may be, it stands to reason that no man should be allowed to be unlucky to more than a very moderate extent.'

Then, turning to the prisoner, the judge continued: — 'You have suffered a great loss. Nature attaches a severe penalty to such offences, and human law must emphasise the decrees of nature. But for the recommendation of the jury I should have given you six months' hard labour. I will, however, commute your sentence to one of three months, with the option of a fine of twenty-five per cent of the money you have received from the insurance company.'

The prisoner thanked the judge, and said that as he had no one to look after his children if he was sent to prison, he would embrace the option mercifully permitted him by his lordship, and pay the sum he had named. He was then removed from the dock.

The next case was that of a youth barely arrived at man's estate, who was charged with having been swindled out of large property during his minority by his guardian, who was also one of his nearest relations. His father had been long dead, and it was for this reason that this offence came on for trial in the Personal Bereavement Court. The lad, who was undefended, pleaded that he was young, inexperienced, greatly in awe of his guardian, and without independent professional advice. 'Young man,' said the judge sternly, 'do not talk nonsense. People have no right to be young, inexperienced, greatly in awe of their guardians, and without independent professional advice. If by such indiscretions they outrage the moral sense of their friends, they must expect to suffer accordingly.' He then ordered the prisoner to apologise to his guardian, and to receive twelve strokes with a cat-of-nine-tails. . . .

Beyond Freedom and Dignity

B. F. Skinner

I

Almost all living things act to free themselves from harmful contacts. A kind of freedom is achieved by the relatively simple forms of behavior called reflexes. A person sneezes and frees his respiratory passages from irritating substances. He vomits and frees his stomach from indigestible or poisonous food. He pulls back his hand and frees it from a sharp or hot object. More elaborate forms of behavior have similar effects. When confined, people struggle ("in rage") and break free. When in danger they flee from or attack its source. Behavior of this kind presumably evolved because of its survival value; it is as much a part of what we call the human genetic endowment as breathing, sweating, or digesting food. And through conditioning similar behavior may be acquired with respect to novel objects which could have played no role in evolution. These are no doubt minor instances of the struggle to be free, but they are significant. We do not attribute them to any love of freedom; they are simply forms of behavior which have proved useful in reducing various threats to the individual and hence to the species in the course of evolution.

A much more important role is played by behavior which weakens harmful stimuli in another way. It is not acquired in the form of conditioned reflexes, but as the product of a different process called operant conditioning. When a bit of behavior is followed by a certain kind of consequence, it is more likely to occur again, and a consequence having this effect is called a reinforcer. Food, for example, is a reinforcer to a hungry organism; anything the organism does that is followed by the receipt of food is more likely to be done again whenever the organism is hungry. Some stimuli are called negative reinforcers; any response which reduces the intensity of such a stimulus—or ends it—is more likely to be emitted when the stimulus recurs. Thus, if a person escapes from a hot sun when he moves under cover, he is more likely to move under cover when the sun is again hot. The reduction in temperature reinforces the behavior it is "contingent upon"—that is, the behavior it follows. Operant conditioning also occurs when a person simply avoids a hot sun—when, roughly speaking, he escapes from the *threat* of a hot sun.

Negative reinforcers are called aversive in the sense that they are the things organisms "turn away from." The term suggests a spatial separation—moving or running away from something—but the essential relation is temporal. In a standard apparatus used to study the process in the laboratory, an arbitrary response simply weakens an aversive stimulus or brings it to an end. A great deal of physical technology is the result of this kind of struggle for freedom. Over the centuries, in erratic ways, men have constructed a world in which they are relatively free of many kinds of threatening or harmful stimuli—extremes of temperature, sources of infection, hard labor, danger, and even those minor aversive stimuli called discomfort.

Escape and avoidance play a much more important role in the struggle for freedom when the aversive conditions are generated by other people. Other people can be aversive without, so to speak, trying: they can be rude, dangerous, contagious, or annoying, and one escapes from them or avoids them accordingly. They may also be "intentionally" aversive—that is, they may treat other people aversively because of what follows. Thus, a slave driver induces a slave to work by whipping him when he stops; by resuming work the slave escapes from the whipping (and incidentally reinforces the slave driver's behavior in using the whip). A parent nags a child until the child performs a task; by performing the task the child escapes nagging (and reinforces the parent's behavior). The blackmailer threatens exposure unless the victim pays; by paying, the victim escapes from the threat (and reinforces the practice). A teacher threatens corporal punishment or failure until his students pay attention; by paying attention the students escape from the threat of punishment (and reinforce the teacher for threatening it). In one form or another intentional aversive control is the pattern of most social coordination—in ethics, religion, government, economics, education, psychotherapy, and family life.

A person escapes from or avoids aversive treatment by behaving in ways which reinforce those who treated him aversively until he did so, but he may escape in other ways. For example, he may simply move out of range. A person may escape from slavery, emigrate or defect from a government, desert from an army, become an apostate from a religion, play truant, leave home, or drop out of a culture as a hobo, hermit, or hippie. Such behavior is as much a product of the aversive conditions as the behavior the conditions were designed to evoke. The latter can be guaranteed only by sharpening the contingencies or by using stronger aversive stimuli.

Another anomalous mode of escape is to attack those who arrange aversive conditions and weaken or destroy their power. We may attack those who crowd us or annoy us, as we attack the weeds in our garden, but again the struggle for freedom is mainly directed toward intentional controllers—toward those who treat others aversively in order to induce them to behave in particular ways. Thus, a child may stand up to his parents, a citizen may overthrow a government, a communicant may reform a religion, a student may attack a teacher or vandalize a school, and a dropout may work to destroy a culture. . . .

The literature of freedom has encouraged escape from or attack upon all controllers. It has done so by making any indication of control aversive. Those who manipulate human behavior are said to be evil men, necessarily bent on exploitation. Control is clearly the opposite of freedom, and if freedom is good, control must be bad. What is overlooked is control which does not have aversive consequences at any time. Many social practices essential to the welfare of the species involve the control of one person by another, and no one can suppress them who has any concern for human achievements. . . .

The problem is to free men, not from control, but from certain kinds of control, and it can be solved only if our analysis takes all consequences into account. How people feel about control, before or after the literature of freedom has worked on their feelings, does not lead to useful distinctions.

Were it not for the unwarranted generalization that all control is wrong, we should deal with the social environment as simply as we deal with the nonsocial. Although technology has freed men from certain aversive features of the environment, it has not freed them from the environment. We accept the fact that we depend upon the world around us, and we simply change the nature of the dependency. In the same way, to make the social environment as free as possible of aversive stimuli we do not need to destroy that environment or escape from it; we need to redesign it.

II

It is in the nature of an experimental analysis of human behavior that it should strip away the functions previously assigned to autonomous man and transfer them one by one to the controlling environment. The analysis leaves less and less for autonomous man to do. But what about man himself? Is there not something about a person which is more than a living body? Unless something called a self survives, how can we speak of self-knowledge or self-control? To whom is the injunction "Know thyself" addressed? . . .

A self is a repertoire of behavior appropriate to a given set of contingencies. A substantial part of the conditions to which a person is exposed may play a dominant role, and under other conditions a person may report, "I'm not myself today," or "I couldn't have done what you said I did, because that's not like me." The identity conferred upon a self arises from the contingencies responsible for the behavior. Two or more repertoires generated by different sets of contingencies compose two or more selves. A person possesses one repertoire appropriate to his life with his friends and another appropriate to his life with his family, and a friend may find him a very different person if he sees him with his family or his family if they see him with his friends. The problem of identity arises when situations are intermingled, as when a person finds himself with both his family and his friends at the same time. . .

The picture which emerges from a scientific analysis is not of a body with a person inside, but of a body which is a person in the sense that it displays a complex repertoire of behavior. The picture is, of course, unfamiliar. The man thus portrayed is a stranger, and from the traditional point of view he may not seem to be a man at all. . . .

What is being abolished is autonomous man—the inner man, the homunculus, the possessing demon, the man defended by the literatures of freedom and dignity. His abolition has long been overdue. Autonomous man is a device used to explain what we cannot explain in any other way. He has been constructed from our ignorance, and as our understanding increases, the very stuff of which he is composed vanishes. Science does not dehumanize man, it de-homunculizes him, and it must do so if it is to prevent the abolition of the human species. To man *qua* man we readily say good riddance. Only by dispossessing him can we turn to the real causes of human behavior. Only then can we turn from the inferred to the observed, from the miraculous to the natural, from the inaccessible to the manipulable. . . .

Science has probably never demanded a more sweeping change in a traditional way of thinking about a subject, nor has there ever been a more important subject. In the traditional picture a person perceives the world around him, selects features to be perceived, discriminates among them, judges them good or bad, changes them to make them better (or, if he is careless, worse), and may be held responsible for his action and justly rewarded or punished for its consequences. In the scientific picture a person is a member of a species shaped by evolutionary contingencies of survival, displaying behavioral processes which bring him under the control of the environment in which he lives, and largely under the control of a social environment which he and millions of others like him have constructed and maintained during the evolution of a culture. The direction of the controlling relation is reversed: a person does not act upon the world, the world acts upon him.

It is difficult to accept such a change simply on intellectual grounds and nearly impossible to accept its implications. The reaction of the traditionalist is usually described in terms of feelings. One of these, to which the Freudians have appealed in explaining the resistance to psychoanalysis, is wounded vanity. Freud himself expounded, as Ernest Jones has said, "the three heavy blows which narcissism or self-love of mankind had suffered at the hands of science. The first was cosmological and was dealt by Copernicus; the second was biological and was dealt by Darwin; the third was psychological and was dealt by Freud." (The blow was suffered by the belief that something at the center of man knows all that goes on within him and that an instrument called will power exercises command and control over the rest of one's personality.) But what are the signs or symptoms of wounded vanity, and how shall we explain them? What people *do* about such a scientific picture of man is call it wrong, demeaning, and dangerous, argue against it, and attack those who propose or defend it. They do so not out of wounded vanity but because the scientific formulation has destroyed accustomed reinforcers. If a person can no longer take credit or be admired for what he does, then he seems to suffer a loss of dignity or worth, and behavior previously reinforced by credit or admiration will undergo extinction. Extinction often leads to aggressive attack. . . .

The traditional conception of man is flattering; it confers reinforcing privileges. It is therefore easily defended and can be changed only with difficulty. It was designed to build up the individual as an instrument of countercontrol, and it did so effectively but in such a way as to limit progress. We have seen how the literatures of freedom and dignity, with their concern for autonomous man, have perpetuated the use of punishment and condoned the use of only weak nonpunitive techniques, and it is not difficult to demonstrate a connection between the unlimited right of the individual to pursue happiness and the catastrophes threatened by unchecked breeding, the unrestrained affluence which exhausts resources and pollutes the environment, and the imminence of nuclear war.

Physical and biological technologies have alleviated pestilence and famine and many painful, dangerous, and exhausting features of daily life, and behavioral technology can begin to alleviate other kinds of ills. In the analysis of human behavior it is just possible that we are slightly beyond Newton's position in the analysis of light, for we are beginning to make technological applications. There are wonderful possibilities— and all the more wonderful because traditional approaches have been so ineffective.

It is hard to imagine a world in which people live together without quarreling, maintain themselves by producing the food, shelter, and clothing they need, enjoy themselves and contribute to the enjoyment of others in art, music, literature, and games, consume only a reasonable part of the resources of the world and add as little as possible to its pollution, bear no more children than can be raised decently, continue to explore the world around them and discover better ways of dealing with it, and come to know themselves accurately and, therefore, manage themselves effectively. Yet all this is possible, and even the slightest sign of progress should bring a kind of change which in traditional terms would be said to assuage wounded vanity, offset a sense of hopelessness or nostalgia, correct the impression that "we neither can nor need to do anything for ourselves," and promote a "sense of freedom and dignity" by building "a sense of confidence and worth." In other words, it should abundantly reinforce those who have been induced by their culture to work for its survival.

An experimental analysis shifts the determination of behavior from autonomous man to the environment—an environment responsible both for the evolution of the species and for the repertoire acquired by each member. Early versions of environmentalism were inadequate because they could not explain how the environment worked, and much seemed to be left for autonomous man to do. But environmental contingencies now take over functions once attributed to autonomous man, and certain questions arise. Is man then "abolished"? Certainly not as a species or as an individual achiever. It is the autonomous inner man who is abolished, and that is a step forward. But does man not then become merely a victim or passive observer of what is happening to him? He is indeed controlled by his environment, but we must remember that it is an environment largely of his own making. The evolution of a culture is a gigantic exercise in self-control. It is often said that a scientific view of man leads to wounded vanity, a sense of hopelessness, and nostalgia. But no theory changes what it is a theory about; man remains what he has always been. And a new theory may change what can be done with its subject matter. A scientific view of man offers exciting possibilities. We have not yet seen what man can make of man.

Freedom: An Existential Explanation

Jean-Paul Sartre

I

It is strange that philosophers have been able to argue endlessly about determinism and free-will, to cite examples in favor of one or the other thesis without ever attempting first to make explicit the structures contained in the very idea of *action*. The concept of an act contains, in fact, numerous subordinate notions which we shall have to organize and arrange in a hierarchy: to act is to modify the *shape* of the world; it is to arrange means in view of an end; it is to produce an organized instrumental complex such that by a series of concatenations and connections the modification effected on one of the links causes modifications throughout the whole series and finally produces an anticipated result. But this is not what is important for us here. We should observe first that an action is on principle *intentional*. The careless smoker who has through negligence caused the explosion of a powder magazine has not *acted*. On the other hand the worker who is charged with dynamiting a quarry and who obeys the given orders has acted when he has produced the expected explosion; he knew what he was doing or, if you prefer, he intentionally realized a conscious project. . . .

Since freedom is identical with my existence, it is the foundation of ends which I shall attempt to attain either by the will or by passionate efforts. Therefore it can not be limited to voluntary acts. Volitions, on the contrary, like passions are certain subjective attitudes by which we attempt to attain the ends posited by original freedom. By original freedom, of course, we should not understand a freedom which would be prior to the voluntary or passionate act but rather a foundation which is strictly contemporary with the will or the passion and which these *manifest*, each in its own way. . . .

If these ends are already posited, then what remains to be decided at each moment is the way in which I shall conduct myself with respect to them; in other words, the attitude which I shall assume. Shall I act by volition or by passion? Who can decide except me? In fact, if we admit that circumstances decide for me (for example, I can act by volition when faced with a minor danger but if the peril increases, I shall fall into passion), we thereby suppress all freedom. It would indeed be absurd to declare that the will is autonomous when it appears but that external circumstances strictly determine the moment of its appearance. . . .

This does not mean that I am free to get up or to sit down, to enter or to go out, to flee or to face danger—if one means by freedom here a pure capricious, unlawful, gratuitous, and incomprehensible contingency. To be sure, each one of my acts, even the most trivial, is entirely free in the sense which we have just defined; but this does not mean that my act can be anything whatsoever or even that it is *unforeseeable*. Someone, nevertheless, may object and ask how if my act can be understood *neither* in terms of the state of the world *nor* in terms of the ensemble of my past taken as an irremediable thing, it could possibly be anything but gratuitous. Let us look more closely.

Common opinion does not hold that to be free means only to choose oneself. A choice is said to be free if it is such that it could have been other than what it is. I start out on a hike with friends. At the end of several hours of walking my fatigue increases and finally becomes very painful. At first I resist and then suddenly I let myself go, I give up, I throw my knapsack down on the side of the road and let myself fall down beside it. Someone will reproach me for my act and will mean thereby that I was free—that is, not only was my act not determined by any thing or person, but also I could have succeeded in resisting my fatigue. . . .

II

The decisive argument which is employed by common sense against freedom consists in reminding us of our impotence. Far from being able to modify our situation at our whim, we seem to be unable to change ourselves. I am not "free" either to escape the lot of my class, of my nation, of my family, or even to build up my own power or my fortune or to conquer my most insignificant appetites or habits. I am born a worker, a Frenchman, an hereditary syphilitic, or a tubercular. The history of a life, whatever it may be, is the history of a failure. The coefficient of adversity of things is such that years of patience are necessary to obtain the feeblest result. Again it is necessary "to obey nature in order to command it"; that is, to insert my action into the network of determinism. Much more than he appears "to make himself," man seems "to be made" by climate and the earth, race and class, language, the history of the collectivity of which he is a part, heredity, the individual circumstances of his childhood, acquired habits, the great and small events of his life.

This argument has never greatly troubled the partisans of human freedom. . . . Many of the facts set forth by the determinists do not actually deserve to enter into our considerations. In particular the coefficient of adversity in things can not be an argument against our freedom, for it is *by* us—i.e., by the preliminary positing of an end—that this coefficient of adversity arises. A particular crag, which manifests a profound resistance if I wish to displace it, will be on the contrary a valuable aid if I want to climb upon it in order to look over the countryside. In itself—if one can even imagine what the crag can be in itself—it is neutral; that is, it waits to be illuminated by an end in order to manifest itself as adverse or helpful. Again it can manifest itself in one or the other way only within an instrumental-complex which is already estab- lished. Without picks and piolets, paths already worn, and a technique of climbing, the crag would be neither easy nor difficult to climb; the question would not be posited, it would not support any relation of any kind with the technique of mountain climbing. Thus although brute things . . . can from the start limit our freedom of action, it is our freedom itself which must first constitute the framework, the technique, and the ends in relation to which they will manifest themselves as limits. Even if the crag is revealed as "too difficult to climb," and if we must give up the ascent, let us note that the crag is revealed as such only because it was originally grasped as "climbable"; it is therefore our freedom which constitutes the limits which it will subsequently encounter. . . .

The essential consequence of our earlier remarks is that man being condemned to be free carries the weight of the whole world on his shoulders; he is responsible for the world and for himself as a way of being. We are taking the word "responsibility" in its ordinary sense as "consciousness (of) being the incontestable author of an event or of an object." . . .

He must assume the situation with the proud consciousness of being the author of it, for the very worst disadvantages or the worst threats which can endanger my person have meaning only in and through my project; and it is on the ground of the engagement which I am that they appear. It is therefore senseless to think of complaining since nothing foreign has decided what we feel, what we live, or what we are.

Furthermore this absolute responsibility is not resignation; it is simply the logical requirement of the consequences of our freedom. What happens to me happens through me, and I can neither affect myself with it nor revolt against it nor resign myself to it. Moreover everything which happens to me is *mine*. By this we must understand first of all that I am always equal to what happens to me *qua* man, for what happens to a man through other men and through himself can be only human. The most terrible situations of war, the worst tortures do not create a non-human state of things; there is no non-human situation. It is only through fear, flight, and recourse to magical types of conduct that I shall decide on the non-human, but this decision is human, and I shall carry the entire responsibility for it. But in addition the situation is *mine* because it is the image of my free choice of myself, and everything which it presents to me is *mine* in that this represents me and symbolizes me. Is it not I who decide the coefficient of adversity in things and even their unpredictability by deciding myself?

Thus there are no *accidents* in a life; a community event which suddenly bursts forth and involves me in it does not come from the outside. If I am mobilized in a war, this war is *my* war; it is in my image and I deserve it. I deserve it first because I could always get out of it by suicide or by desertion; these ultimate possibles are those which must always be present for us when there is a question of envisaging a situation. For lack of getting out of it, I have *chosen* it. This can be due to inertia, to cowardice in the face of public opinion, or because I prefer certain other values to the value of the refusal to join in the war (the good opinion of my relatives, the honor of my family, etc.). Anyway you look at it, it is a matter of a choice. This choice will be repeated later on again and again without a break until the end of the war. . . .

But in addition the war is *mine* because by the sole fact that it arises in a situation which I cause to be and that I can discover it there only by engaging myself for or against it, I can no longer distinguish at present the choice which I make of myself from the choice which I make of the war. To live this war is to choose myself through it and to choose it through my choice of myself. There can be no question of considering it as "four years of vacation" or as a "reprieve," as a "recess," the essential part of my responsibilities being elsewhere in my married, family, or professional life. In this war which I have chosen I choose myself from day to day, and I make it mine by making myself. If it is going to be four empty years, then it is I who bear the responsibility for this. . . .

Yet this responsibility is of a very particular type. Someone will say, "I did not ask to be born." This is a naive way of throwing greater emphasis on our facticity. I am responsible for everything, in fact, except for my very responsibility, for I am not the foundation of my being. Therefore everything takes place as if I were compelled to be responsible. I am *abandoned* in the world, not in the sense that I might remain abandoned and passive in a hostile universe like a board floating on the water, but rather in the sense that I find myself suddenly alone and without help, engaged in a world for which I bear the whole responsibility without being able, whatever I do, to tear myself away from this responsibility for an instant. For I am responsible for my very desire of fleeing responsibilities. To make myself passive in the world, to refuse to act upon things and upon Others is still to choose myself, and suicide is one mode among others of being-in-the-world. . . . That is why I can not ask, "*Why* was I born?" or curse the day of my birth or declare that I did not ask to be born, for these various attitudes toward my birth—i.e., toward the *fact* that I realize a presence in the world— are absolutely nothing else but ways of assuming this birth in full responsibility and of making it *mine*. . . . The one who realizes in anguish his condition as *being* thrown into a responsibility which extends to his very abandonment has no longer either remorse or regret or excuse; he is no longer anything but a freedom which perfectly reveals itself and whose being resides in this very revelation. But . . . most of the time we flee anguish in bad faith.

Is "Freewill" A Pseudo-Problem?

C. A. Campbell

I

So far as the *meaning,* as distinct from the *conditions,* of moral responsibility is concerned, the common view is very simple. If we ask ourselves whether a certain person is morally responsible for a given act. . . , what we are considering, it would be said, is whether or not that person is a fit subject upon whom to pass moral judgment; whether he can fittingly be deemed morally good or bad, morally praiseworthy or blameworthy. This does not take us any great way: but . . . so far as it goes it does not seem to me seriously disputable. The really interesting and controversial question is about the *conditions* of moral responsibility, and in particular the question whether freedom of a contra-causal kind is among these conditions.

The answer of the common man to the latter question is that it most certainly *is* among the conditions. Why does he feel so sure about this? Not . . . because the common man supposes that causal law exercises 'compulsion' in the sense that pre-

By permission. C. A. Campbell, "Is 'Freewill' a Pseudo-Problem?" in *Mind,* vol. LX, no. 239, July 1951. Edited by Professor Gilbert Ryle. Edinburgh: T. Nelson & Sons, Ltd., Parkside Works.

scriptive laws do, but simply because he does not see how a person can be deemed morally praiseworthy or blameworthy in respect of an act which he could not help performing. From the stand-point of moral praise and blame, he would say—though not necessarily from other stand-points—it is a matter of indifference whether it is by reason of some external constraint or by reason of his own given nature that the man could not help doing what he did. It is quite enough to make moral praise and blame futile that in either case there were no genuine alternatives, no open possibilities, before the man when he acted. He could not have acted otherwise than he did. And the common man might not unreasonably go on to stress the fact that we all, even if we are linguistic philosophers, do in our actual practice of moral judgment appear to accept the common view. He might insist upon the point . . . that we do all, in passing moral censure, 'make allowances' for influences in a man's hereditary nature or environmental circumstances which we regard as having made it more than ordinarily difficult for him to act otherwise than he did: the implication being that if we supposed that the man's heredity and environment made it not merely very *difficult* but actually *impossible* for him to act otherwise than he did, we could not properly assign moral blame to him at all.

Let us put the argument implicit in the common view a little more sharply. The moral 'ought' implies 'can'. If we say that A morally ought to have done X, we imply that in our opinion, he could have done X. But we assign moral blame to a man only for failing to do what we think he morally ought to have done. Hence if we morally blame A for not having done X, we imply that he could have done X even though in fact he did not. In other words, we imply that A could have acted otherwise than he did. And that means that we imply, as a necessary condition of a man's being morally blameworthy, that he enjoyed a freedom of a kind not compatible with unbroken causal continuity.

II

Now what is it that is supposed to be wrong with this simple piece of argument? . . . The argument looks as though it were doing little more than reading off necessary implications of the fundamental categories of our moral thinking. One's inclination is to ask 'If one is to think morally at all, how else than this *can* we think?'.

In point of fact, there is pretty general agreement among the contemporary critics as to what is wrong with the argument. Their answer in general terms is as follows. No doubt A's moral responsibility does imply that he could have acted otherwise. But this expression 'could have acted otherwise' stands in dire need of analysis. When we analyse it, we find that it is not, as is so often supposed, simple and unambiguous, and we find that in *some* at least of its possible meanings it implies *no* breach of causal continuity between character and conduct. Having got this clear, we can further discern that only in one of these *latter* meanings is there any compulsion upon our moral thinking to assert that if A is morally blameworthy for an act, A 'could have acted otherwise than he did'. It follows that, contrary to common belief, our moral thinking does *not* require us to posit a contra-causal freedom as a condition of moral responsibility. . . .

What then *does* one mean in this class of cases by 'A could have acted otherwise'? I submit that the expression is taken in its simple, categorical meaning, without any suppressed 'if' clause to qualify it. Or perhaps, in order to keep before us the important truth that it is only as expressions of *will* or *choice* that acts are of moral import, it might be better to say that a condition of A's moral responsibility is that he could have *chosen* otherwise. . . . There is a very real question, at least for any person who approaches the question of moral responsibility at a tolerably advanced level of reflexion, about whether A could have *chosen* otherwise. Such a person will doubtless be acquainted with the claims advanced in some quarters that causal law operates universally: or/and with the theories of some philosophies that the universe is throughout the expression of a single supreme principle; or/and with the doctrines of some theologians that the world is created, sustained and governed by an Omniscient and Omnipotent Being. Very understandably such world-views awaken in him doubts about the validity of his first, easy, instinctive assumption that there are genuinely open possibilities before a man at the moment of moral choice. It thus becomes for him a real question whether a man could have chosen otherwise than he actually did, and, in consequence, whether man's moral responsibility is really defensible. For how can a man be morally responsible, he asks himself, if his choices, like all other events in the universe, could not have been otherwise than they in fact were? It is precisely against the background of world-views such as these that for reflective people the problem of moral responsibility normally arises. . . .

The unreflective or unsophisticated person, the ordinary 'man in the street', who does not know or much care what scientists and theologians and philosophers have said about the world, sees well enough that A is morally responsible only if he could have acted otherwise, but in his intellectual innocence he will, very probably, envisage nothing capable of preventing A from having acted otherwise except some material impediment. Accordingly, for the unreflective person, 'A could have acted otherwise, as a condition of moral responsibility', *is* apt to mean no more than 'A could have acted otherwise *if* he had so chosen'.

It would appear, then, that the view now favoured by many philosophers, that the freedom required for moral responsibility is merely freedom from external constraint, is a view which they share only with the less reflective type of layman. Yet it should be plain that on a matter of this sort the view of the unreflective person is of little value by comparison with the view of the reflective person. There are some contexts, no doubt, in which lack of sophistication is an asset. But this is not one of them. The question at issue here is as to the kind of impediments which might have prevented a man from acting otherwise than he in fact did: and on this question knowledge and reflexion are surely prerequisites of any answer that is worth listening to. It is simply on account of the limitations of his mental vision that the unreflective man interprets the expression 'could have acted otherwise', in its context as a condition of moral responsibility, solely in terms of external constraint. He has failed (as yet) to reach the intellectual level at which one takes into account the implications for moral choices of the world-views of science, religion, and philosophy. If on a matter of this complexity the philosopher finds that his analysis accords with the utterances of the uneducated he has, I suggest, better cause for uneasiness than for self-congratulation. . . .

III

A contra-causal freedom, it is argued, such as is implied in the 'categorical' interpretation of the proposition 'A could have chosen otherwise than he did', posits a breach of causal continuity between a man's character and his conduct. Now apart from the general presumption in favour of the universality of causal law, there are special reasons for disallowing the breach that is here alleged. It is the common assumption of social intercourse that our acquaintances will act 'in character'; that their choices will exhibit the 'natural' response of their characters to the given situation. And this assumption seems to be amply substantiated, over a wide range of conduct, by the actual success which attends predictions made on this basis. Where there should be, on the contra-causal hypothesis, chaotic variability, there is found in fact a large measure of intelligible continuity. Moreover, what is the alternative to admitting that a person's choices flow from his character? Surely just that the so-called 'choice' is not *that person's* choice at all: that, relatively to the person concerned, it is a mere 'accident'. Now we cannot really believe this. But if it *were* the case, it would certainly not help to establish *moral* freedom, the freedom required for *moral* responsibility. For clearly a man cannot be morally responsible for an act which does not express his own choice but is, on the contrary, attributable simply to chance. . . .

To begin with the less troublesome of the two main objections indicated—the objection that the break in causal continuity which free will involves is inconsistent with the predictability of conduct on the basis of the agent's known character. All that is necessary to meet this objection, I suggest, is the frank recognition, which is perfectly open to the Libertarian, that there is a wide area of human conduct, determinable on clear general principles, within which free will does not effectively operate. The most important of these general principles . . . has often enough been stated by Libertarians. Free will does not operate in these practical situations in which no conflict arises in the agent's mind between what he conceives to be his 'duty' and what he feels to be his 'strongest desire'. It does not operate here because there just is no occasion for it to operate. There is no reason whatever why the agent should here even contemplate choosing any course other than that prescribed by his strongest desire. In all such situations, therefore, he naturally wills in accordance with strongest desire. But his 'strongest desire' is simply the specific *ad hoc* expression of that system of conative and emotive dispositions which we call his 'character'. In all such situations, therefore, whatever may be the case elsewhere, his will is in effect determined by his character as so far formed. Now when we bear in mind that there are an almost immeasurably greater number of situations in a man's life that conform to *this* pattern than there are situations in which an agent is aware of a conflict between strongest desire and duty, it is apparent that a Libertarianism which accepts the limitation of free will to the *latter* type of situation is not open to the stock objection on the score of 'predictability'.

For there still remains a vast area of human behaviour in which prediction on the basis of known character may be expected to succeed: an area which will accommodate without difficulty, I think, all these empirical facts about successful prediction which the critic is apt to suppose fatal to Free Will.

So far as I can see, such a delimitation of the field of effective free will denies to the Libertarian absolutely nothing which matters to him. For it is precisely that small sector of the field of choices which our principle of delimitation still leaves open to free will—the sector in which strongest desire clashes with duty—that is crucial for moral responsibility. It is, I believe, with respect to such situations, and in the last resort to such situations alone, that the agent himself recognises that moral praise and blame are appropriate. They are appropriate, according as he does or does not 'rise to duty' in the face of opposing desires; always granted, that is, that he is free to choose between these courses as genuinely open possibilities. If the reality of freedom be conceded *here,* everything is conceded that the Libertarian has any real interest in securing.

But, of course, the most vital question is, can the reality of freedom be conceded even here? In particular, can the standard objection be met which we stated, that if the person's choice does not, in these situations as elsewhere, flow from his *character,* then it is not *that person's* choice at all.

This is, perhaps, of all the objections to a contra-causal freedom, the one which is generally felt to be the most conclusive. For the assumption upon which it is based, *viz.* that no intelligible meaning can attach to the claim that an act which is not an expression of the self's *character* may nevertheless be the *self's* act, is apt to be regarded as self-evident. The Libertarian is accordingly charged with being in effect an *In*determinist, whose 'free will', in so far as it does not flow from the agent's character, can only be a matter of 'chance'. Has the Libertarian—who invariably repudiates this charge and claims to be a *Self*-determinist—any way of showing that, contrary to the assumption of his critics, we *can* meaningfully talk of an act as the self's act even though, in an important sense, it is not an expression of the self's 'character'?

I think that he has. I want to suggest that what prevents the critics from finding a meaning in this way of talking is that they are looking for it in the wrong way; or better, perhaps, with the wrong orientation. They are looking for it from the stand-point of the *external observer;* the stand-point proper to, because alone possible for, apprehension of the physical world. Now from the external stand-point we may observe processes of change. But one thing which, by common consent, *cannot* be observed from without is *creative activity.* Yet—and here lies the crux of the whole matter—it is precisely creative activity which we are trying to understand when we are trying to understand what is traditionally designated by 'free will'. For if there should be an act which is genuinely the self's act and is nevertheless not an expression of its character, such an act, in which the self 'transcends' its character as so far formed, would seem to be essentially of the nature of creative activity. It follows that to look for a meaning in 'free will' from the external stand-point is absurd. It is to look for it in a way that ensures that it will not be found. Granted that a creative activity of any kind is at least *possible* (and I know of no ground for its *a priori* rejection), there is one way, and one way only, in which we can hope to apprehend it, and that is from the *inner* stand-point of direct participation.

It seems to me therefore, that if the Libertarian's claim to find a meaning in a 'free' will which is genuinely the self's will, though not an expression of the self's character, is to be subjected to any test that is worth applying, that test must be undertaken from the inner stand-point. We ought to place ourselves imaginatively at the stand-point of the agent engaged in the typical moral situation in which free will is claimed, and ask ourselves whether from *this* stand-point the claim in question does or does not have meaning for us. That the appeal must be to introspection is no doubt unfortunate. But he would be a very doctrinaire critic of introspection who declined to make use of it when in the nature of the case no other means of apprehension is available. Everyone must make the introspective experiment for himself: but I may perhaps venture to report, though at this late stage with extreme brevity, what I at least seem to find when I make the experiment myself.

In the situation of moral conflict, then, I (as agent) have before my mind a course of action X, which I believe to be my duty; and also a course of action Y, incompatible with X, which I feel to be that which I most strongly desire. Y is, as it is sometimes expressed, 'in the line of least resistance' for me—the course which I am aware I should take if I let my purely desiring nature operate without hindrance. It is the course towards which I am aware that my *character,* as so far formed, naturally inclines me. Now, as actually engaged in this situation, I find that I cannot help believing that I *can* rise to duty and choose X; the 'rising to duty' being effected by what is commonly called 'effort of will'. And I further find, if I ask myself just what it is I am believing when I believe that I 'can' rise to duty, that I cannot help believing that it lies with me here and now, quite absolutely, which of two genuinely open possibilities I adopt; whether, that is, I make the effort of will and choose X, or, on the other hand, let my desiring nature, my character as so far formed, 'have its way', and choose Y, the course 'in the line of least resistance'. These beliefs may, of course, be illusory, but that is not at present in point. For the present argument all that matters is whether beliefs of this sort are in fact discoverable in the moral agent in the situation of 'moral temptation'. For my own part, I cannot doubt the introspective evidence that they are.

Now here is the vital point. No matter which course, X or Y, I choose in this situation, I cannot doubt, *qua* practical being engaged in it, that my choice is *not* just the expression of my formed character, and yet *is* a choice made by my *self*. For suppose I make the effort and choose X (my 'duty'). Since my very purpose in making the 'effort' is to enable me to act against the existing 'set' of desire, which is the expression of my character as so far formed, I cannot possibly regard the act itself as the expression of my *character*. On the other hand, introspection makes it equally clear that I am certain that it is *I* who choose; that the act is not an 'accident', but is genuinely *my* act. Or suppose that I choose Y (the end of 'strongest desire'). The course chosen here is, it is true, in conformity with my 'character'. But since I find myself unable to doubt that I *could* have made the effort and chosen X, I cannot possibly regard the choice of Y as *just* the expression of my character. Yet here again

I find that I cannot doubt that the choice is *my* choice, a choice for which *I* am justly to be blamed.

What this amounts to is that I *can* and *do* attach meaning, *qua* moral agent, to an act which is not the self's character and yet is genuinely the self's act. And having no good reason to suppose that other persons have a fundamentally different mental constitution, it seems to me probable that anyone else who undertakes a similar experiment will be obliged to submit a similar report. I conclude, therefore, that the argument against 'free will' on the score of its 'meaninglessness' must be held to fail. 'Free Will' does have meaning; though, because it is of the nature of a creative activity, its meaning is discoverable only in an intuition of the practical consciousness of the participating agent. To the agent making a moral choice in the situation where duty clashes with desire, his 'self' is known to him as a creatively active self, a self which declines to be identified with his 'character' as so formed. Not, of course, that the self's character—let it be added to obviate misunderstanding—either is, or is supposed by the agent to be, devoid of bearing upon his choices, even in the 'sector' in which free will is held to operate. On the contrary, such a bearing is manifest in the empirically verifiable fact that we find it 'harder' (as we say) to make the effort of will required to 'rise to duty' in proportion to the extent that the 'dutiful' course conflicts with the course to which our character as so far formed inclines us. It is only in the polemics of the critics that a 'free' will is supposed to be incompatible with recognising the bearing of 'character' upon choice. . . .

TWO

THE SCOPE OF MORALITY

CHAPTER **4**

LAW, RELIGION, AND ETHICS

Suppose you were to take a survey of people on the street. The question to be asked: "How do you know what is right and wrong?" There would, of course, be a wide variety of answers. However, many people would answer something like this: "My religion"; "My spiritual upbringing"; "The Bible." Many others would answer something like this: "The law"; "If it's illegal it's immoral; if it's not illegal, it must be O.K."

These answers reflect the view that the ethical is bound up with the legal and the religious. No one would deny that there is considerable overlap among the three. Many of the things that are morally prohibited are legally forbidden as well. And many moral principles are deeply embedded in religious tradition. However, most philosophers would insist on the autonomy and authority of ethics. This means, first, that moral principles are neither identical with nor can be reduced to the principles of any religion or to legal rules; second, that the ultimate justification for ethical decisions can be found neither in religion nor in the law. The ultimate justification for moral principles, most philosophers would argue, is in human reason or human understanding, or in human experience. Hence, they would maintain that although religion, law, and ethics have much in common, there are fundamental distinctions among them. The task of this chapter is to make clear how the law, religion, and ethics are fundamentally different yet at the same time share considerable content.

The first two selections, by Plato and Kierkegaard, raise the issue of ultimate authority. Many theologians wish to defend the view that the ultimate authority (the ultimate court of appeal) is God. But suppose we ask, "Is something wrong because God forbids it, or does God forbid it because it is wrong?" If you say that God forbids it because it is wrong, then it appears as if there is some ultimate standard apart from

God which indicates what is right and wrong. On the other hand, if something is wrong because God forbids it, then morality depends on God. In an important sense God is beyond or above morality. Kierkegaard takes the option that God is above or beyond morality. Something is right or wrong because God commands or forbids it. But suppose God commands something that human morality forbids—for example, sacrificing your only son. This is precisely the sacrifice that God asked of Abraham. Kierkegaard does not shrink from the conclusion that if God commands it, our duty is to follow God's command. But how do we distinguish a genuine command of God's from the promptings of a sick mind? So long as what God commands is approved by morality there is no difficulty; God would not command something contrary to moral reflection. But if God's commandment makes something right, such an appeal is closed off. There is no way to distinguish the command of God from the promptings of a sick mind.

Although the Kierkegaard selection raises the issue of ultimate authority in a rather vivid manner, placing ultimate authority on matters of morality in God, it raises other issues as well. There are many different conceptions of God (many different religions) and equally many different conceptions of what God commands. If you are not a member of any religion, how could you decide what you ought to do? Or suppose a country has citizens from many different religions. If religion is the ultimate authority, how could disputes about morality be rationally resolved? In point of fact they are often "resolved" by violence.

Although technically Plato's *Euthyphro* ends indecisively, it seems fairly clear that Plato rejects the notion that something is pious because the gods love it. Rather the theological term *piety* must be explained in reference to a moral term, *justice*. Moreover, we cannot understand pious behavior in terms of providing service to the gods—of meeting their needs, so to speak. To give the discussion a further twist, isn't there something strange about gods depending on humans for the fulfillment of their needs? Indeed wouldn't piety in part be motivated by the recognition that God has no needs? God is complete or whole. To be complete or whole is in part to be good or just. It is the goodness of God compared with the lack of goodness in humankind that inspires piety. The pious is explained in terms of the good. These considerations and the difficulties in conflict resolution and in distinguishing the commands of God from the promptings of a sick mind have led many philosophers to reject the option that something is right or wrong because God commands or forbids it. Such philosophers tend to embrace the option that God commands or forbids it because it is right or wrong. However, even if we accept the view that the justification of ethical principles is independent of any religious doctrine, there is considerable overlap between religion and ethics. Religion provides an account of the human being which inspires and enriches ethical theory. Most religions insist that their doctrines represent the epitome of morality.

Just as ethics is distinguishable from and independent of religion, so most philosophers agree that ethics is distinguishable from and independent of the law. Since so many immoral acts are also illegal, and since there is a moral obligation to obey the law, characterizing the differences between the two is not an easy task.

Some philosophers have tried to enumerate characteristics possessed by morality but not possessed by the law. For example H. L. A. Hart believes that such characteristics as importance, immunity from deliberate change, the voluntary character of moral offenses, and the form of moral pressure are sufficient to separate the moral from the legal. Other thinkers look to the problems that law and morality are supposed to address. These thinkers believe that there are many types of undesirable conduct that can't be handled by the law. For example Christopher Stone points out that the law is reactive; usually the law responds to an evil. Morality typically prohibits behavior before the behavior is established. Morality provides a mode of criticism and hence a sanction against undesirable conduct before there is a law against it. Morality can assist individuals when there is no consensus in the body politic and hence no law. Our society permits calves to be cruelly treated before they are slaughtered for veal. There is no law against this, but we can refuse to buy veal on moral grounds and try to convince others to join us.

Still other philosophers have drawn a distinction between moral duties and moral ideals. Moral duties, such as "Don't lie," "Don't steal," and "Don't kill," are necessary for the existence of a society. Being constrained by such moral duties is a necessary condition for society. Hence, moral duties are absolute demands, and behavior by everyone in accordance with moral duties is expected. Moral ideals, on the other hand, are goals. We try to live up to them, but a certain amount of slippage is expected. Since the moral duties apply to everyone, and conforming to them is necessary to the survival of society, failure to conform is made illegal. Breaches of moral duty often fall into the classification of illegal acts. Breaches of moral ideals should not be classified as illegal. The distinction between moral duties and moral ideals is so important that Chapter 5 is entirely devoted to a discussion of it.

One aspect of that discussion is important to the issues discussed in this chapter. One of the great debates in contemporary society is over what kinds of behavior should be made illegal. Some people hold that the distinction between moral duties and moral ideals coincides with the distinction between public morality and private morality. Conduct that impinges on other people falls in the domain of public morality. Behavior which is essentially a choice of lifestyle falls in the domain of private morality. The law may regulate matters of public morality but not matters of private morality—or so the supporters of this distinction maintain. On their view laws against rape are appropriate, but laws against forms of sexual behavior among consenting adults (e.g., against homosexuality) are inappropriate.

The final two selections in this chapter present competing positions on the distinction between public and private morality. Lord Devlin argues that departures from private morality can threaten the existence of society just as much as departures from public morality. In principle there is no moral matter that cannot become a matter of law. What determines whether conduct should be made illegal is the effect of that conduct on the fabric of society. If conduct endangers the fabric of society it should be prohibited, whether it falls in what is traditionally called "private morality" or not. Often this argument for the enforcement of private morality is buttressed by what the predominant religion of the society counts as sinful. There is often great pressure to pass laws against sinful behavior regardless of whether the sinful behavior takes place in private or not.

H. L. A. Hart concedes Devlin's point that acceptance of some moral principles is necessary for the preservation of society, but maintains that these principles govern public morality rather than private morality. If Devlin is concerned with the preservation of morality, Hart is concerned with the dangers of dogmatism and moral stagnation. He is also concerned with the negative impact of the use of coercion rather than argument, advice, and exhortation to defend the moral status quo.

What conclusions can be drawn from this discussion? First, there are good explanations for the fact that ethics, religion, and the law overlap. All three have as their objective the regulation of human conduct in accordance with a conception of the good. Ethics and religion—and perhaps even the law—inspire us to more noble thoughts and actions. Yet the law, religion, and ethics are also separate and distinct. One cannot be reduced to the other. Most philosophers contend that ethics is an independent, autonomous discipline. This chapter provides some of the arguments for that contention, and future chapters will so treat the discipline of ethics. Nonetheless, future chapters will also draw on religion and the law, since they can enrich our discussion of ethics even as they have enriched ethics itself.

Euthyphro

Plato

Socr. Tell me, then, what is piety and what is impiety?

Euth. Well, then, I say that piety means prosecuting the unjust individual who has committed murder or sacrilege, or any other such crime, as I am doing now, whether he is your father or your mother or whoever he is; and I say that impiety means not prosecuting him. And observe, Socrates, I will give you a clear proof, which I have already given to others, that it is so, and that doing right means not letting off unpunished the sacrilegious man, whosoever he may be. Men hold Zeus to be the best and the most just of the gods; and they admit that Zeus bound his own father, Cronos, for wrongfully devouring his children; and that Cronos, in his turn, castrated his father for similar reasons. And yet these same men are incensed with me because I proceed against my father for doing wrong. So, you see, they say one thing in the case of the gods and quite another in mine. . . .

Socr. Very likely. But many other actions are pious, are they not, Euthyphro?

Euth. Certainly.

Socr. Remember, then, I did not ask you to tell me one or two of all the many pious actions that there are; I want to know what is characteristic of piety which makes all pious actions pious. You said, I think, that there is one characteristic which makes all pious actions pious, and another characteristic which makes all impious actions impious. Do you not remember?

Euth. I do.

Socr. Well, then, explain to me what is this characteristic, that I may have it to turn to, and to use as a standard whereby to judge your actions and those of other men, and be able to say that whatever action resembles it is pious, and whatever does not, is not pious.

Euth. Yes, I will tell you that if you wish, Socrates.

Socr. Certainly I do.

Euth. Well, then, what is pleasing to the gods is pious, and what is not pleasing to them is impious.

Socr. Fine, Euthyphro. Now you have given me the answer that I wanted. Whether what you say is true, I do not know yet. But, of course, you will go on to prove that it is true.

Euth. Certainly.

Socr. Come, then, let us examine our statement. The things and the men that are pleasing to the gods are pious, and the things and the men that are displeasing to the gods are impious. But piety and impiety are not the same; they are as opposite as possible—was not that what we said?

Euth. Certainly.

By permission. Plato, *Euthyphro, Apology, Crito,* translated by F. J. Church, The Bobbs-Merrill Company, Inc., Indianapolis, Indiana, 1948, 1956.

Socr. And it seems the appropriate statement?

Euth. Yes, Socrates, certainly.

Socr. Have we not also said, Euthyphro, that there are quarrels and disagreements and hatreds among the gods?

Euth. We have. . . .

Socr. Then, my good Euthyphro, you say that some of the gods think one thing just, the others another; and that what some of them hold to be honorable or good, others hold to be dishonorable or evil. For there would not have been quarrels among them if they had not disagreed on these points, would there?

Euth. You are right.

Socr. And each of them loves what he thinks honorable, and good, and just; and hates the opposite, does he not?

Euth. Certainly.

Socr. But you say that the same action is held by some of them to be just, and by others to be unjust; and that then they dispute about it, and so quarrel and fight among themselves. Is it not so?

Euth. Yes.

Socr. Then the same thing is hated by the gods and loved by them; and the same thing will be displeasing and pleasing to them.

Euth. Apparently.

Socr. Then, according to your account, the same thing will be pious and impious.

Euth. So it seems.

Socr. Then, my good friend, you have not answered my question. I did not ask you to tell me what action is both pious and impious; but it seems that whatever is pleasing to the gods is also displeasing to them. And so, Euthyphro, I should not be surprised if what you are doing now in punishing your father is an action well pleasing to Zeus, but hateful to Cronos and Uranus, and acceptable to Hephaestus, but hateful to Hera; and if any of the other gods disagree about it, pleasing to some of them and displeasing to others.

Euth. But on this point, Socrates, I think that there is no difference of opinion among the gods: they all hold that if one man kills another unjustly, he must be punished. . . .

Socr. Suppose that Euthyphro were to prove to me as clearly as possible that all the gods think such a death unjust, how has he brought me any nearer to understanding what piety and impiety are? This particular act, perhaps, may be displeasing to the gods, but then we have just seen that piety and impiety cannot be defined in that way; for we have seen that what is displeasing to the gods is also pleasing to them. So I will let you off on this point, Euthyphro; and all the gods shall agree in thinking your father's action wrong and in hating it, if you like. But shall we correct our definition and say that whatever all the gods hate is impious, and whatever they all love is pious; while whatever some of them love, and others hate, is either both or neither? Do you wish us now to define piety and impiety in this manner?

Euth. Why not, Socrates?

Socr. There is no reason why I should not, Euthyphro. It is for you to consider whether that definition will help you to teach me what you promised.

Euth. Well, I should say that piety is what all the gods love, and that impiety is what they all hate.

Socr. Are we to examine this definition, Euthyphro, and see if it is a good one? Or are we to be content to accept the bare statements of other men or of ourselves without asking any questions? Or must we examine the statements?

Euth. We must examine them. But for my part I think that the definition is right this time.

Socr. We shall know that better in a little while, my good friend. Now consider this question. Do the gods love piety because it is pious, or is it pious because they love it?

Euth. I do not understand you, Socrates.

Socr. I will try to explain myself: we speak of a thing being carried and carrying, and being led and leading, and being seen and seeing; and you understand that all such expressions mean different things, and what the difference is.

Euth. Yes, I think I understand.

Socr. And we talk of a thing being loved, of a thing loving, and the two are different?

Euth. Of course.

Socr. Now tell me, is a thing which is being carried in a state of being carried because it is carried, or for some other reason?

Euth. No, because it is carried.

Socr. And a thing is in a state of being led because it is led, and of being seen because it is seen?

Euth. Certainly.

Socr. Then a thing is not seen because it is in a state of being seen: it is in a state of being seen because it is seen; and a thing is not led because it is in a state of being led: it is in a state of being led because it is led; and a thing is not carried because it is in a state of being carried: it is in a state of being carried because it is carried. Is my meaning clear now, Euthyphro? I mean this: if anything becomes or is affected, it does not become because it is in a state of becoming: it is in a state of becoming because it becomes; and it is not affected because it is in a state of being affected: it is in a state of being affected because it is affected. Do you not agree?

Euth. I do.

Socr. Is not that which is being loved in a state either of becoming or of being affected in some way by something?

Euth. Certainly.

Socr. Then the same is true here as in the former cases. A thing is not loved by those who love it because it is in a state of being loved; it is in a state of being loved because they love it.

Euth. Necessarily.

Socr. Well, then, Euthyphro, what do we say about piety? Is it not loved by all the gods, according to your definition?

Euth. Yes.

Socr. Because it is pious, or for some other reason?

Euth. No, because it is pious.

Socr. Then it is loved by the gods because it is pious; it is not pious because it is loved by them?

Euth. It seems so.

Socr. But, then, what is pleasing to the gods is pleasing to them, and is in a state of being loved by them, because they love it?

Euth. Of course.

Socr. Then piety is not what is pleasing to the gods, and what is pleasing to the gods is not pious, as you say, Euthyphro. They are different things.

Euth. And why, Socrates?

Socr. Because we are agreed that the gods love piety because it is pious, and that is not pious because they love it. Is not this so?

Euth. Yes.

Socr. And that what is pleasing to the gods because they love it, is pleasing to them by reason of this same love, and that they do not love it because it is pleasing to them.

Euth. True.

Socr. Then, my dear Euthyphro, piety and what is pleasing to the gods are different things. If the gods had loved piety because it is pious, they would also have loved what is pleasing to them because it is pleasing to them; but if what is pleasing to them had been pleasing to them because they loved it, then piety, too, would have been piety because they loved it. But now you see that they are opposite things, and wholly different from each other. For the one is of a sort to be loved because it is loved, while the other is loved because it is of a sort to be loved. My question, Euthyphro, was, What is piety? But it turns out that you have not explained to me the essential character of piety; you have been content to mention an effect which belongs to it— namely, that all the gods love it. You have not yet told me what its essential character is. Do not, if you please, keep from me what piety is; begin again and tell me that. Never mind whether the gods love it, or whether it has other effects: we shall not differ on that point. Do your best to make clear to me what is piety and what is impiety.

Euth. But, Socrates, I really don't know how to explain to you what is in my mind. Whatever statement we put forward always somehow moves round in a circle, and will not stay where we put it. . . .

Socr. I will do my best to help you to explain to me what piety is, for I think that you are lazy. Don't give in yet. Tell me, do you not think that all piety must be just?

Euth. I do.

Socr. Well, then, is all justice pious, too? Or, while all piety is just, is a part only of justice pious, and the rest of it something else?

Euth. I do not follow you, Socrates. . . .

Socr. . . . I think that where there is reverence there also is fear. Does any man feel reverence and a sense of shame about anything, without at the same time dreading and fearing the reputation of wickedness?

Euth. No, certainly not.

Socr. Then, though there is fear wherever there is reverence, it is not correct to say that where there is fear there also is reverence. Reverence does not always accompany fear; for fear, I take it, is wider than reverence. It is a part of fear, just as the odd is a part of number, so that where you have the odd you must also have number, though where you have number you do not necessarily have the odd. Now I think you follow me?

Euth. I do.

Socr. Well, then, this is what I meant by the question which I asked you. Is there always piety where there is justice? Or, though there is always justice where there is piety, yet there is not always piety where there is justice, because piety is only a part of justice? Shall we say this, or do you differ?

Euth. No, I agree. I think that you are right.

Socr. Now observe the next point. If piety is a part of justice, we must find out, I suppose, what part of justice it is? Now, if you had asked me just now, for instance, what part of number is the odd, and what number is an odd number, I should have said that whatever number is not even is an odd number. Is it not so?

Euth. Yes.

Socr. Then see if you can explain to me what part of justice is piety, that I may tell Meletus that now that I have been adequately instructed by you as to what actions are righteous and pious, and what are not, he must give up prosecuting me unjustly for impiety.

Euth. Well, then, Socrates, I should say that righteousness and piety are that part of justice which has to do with the careful attention which ought to be paid to the gods; and that what has to do with the careful attention which ought to be paid to men is the remaining part of justice.

Socr. And I think that your answer is a good one, Euthyphro. But there is one little point about which I still want to hear more. I do not yet understand what the careful attention is to which you refer. I suppose you do not mean that the attention which we pay to the gods is like the attention which we pay to other things. We say, for instance, do we not, that not everyone knows how to take care of horses, but only the trainer of horses?

Euth. Certainly.

Socr. For I suppose that the skill that is concerned with horses is the art of taking care of horses.

Euth. Yes.

Socr. And not everyone understands the care of dogs, but only the huntsman.

Euth. True.

Socr. For I suppose that the huntsman's skill is the art of taking care of dogs.

Euth. Yes.

Socr. And the herdsman's skill is the art of taking care of cattle.

Euth. Certainly.

Socr. And you say that piety and righteousness are taking care of the gods, Euthyphro?

Euth. I do.

Socr. Well, then, has not all care the same object? Is it not for the good and benefit of that on which it is bestowed? For instance, you see that horses are benefited and improved when they are cared for by the art which is concerned with them. Is it not so?

Euth. Yes, I think so.

Socr. And dogs are benefited and improved by the huntsman's art, and cattle by the herdsman's, are they not? And the same is always true. Or do you think care is ever meant to harm that which is cared for?

Euth. No, indeed; certainly not.

Socr. But to benefit it?

Euth. Of course.

Socr. Then is piety, which is our care for the gods, intended to benefit the gods, or to improve them? Should you allow that you make any of the gods better when you do a pious action?

Euth. No indeed; certainly not.

Socr. No, I am quite sure that that is not your meaning, Euthyphro. It was for that reason that I asked you what you meant by the careful attention which ought to be paid to the gods. I thought that you did not mean that.

Euth. You were right, Socrates. I do not mean that.

Socr. Good. Then what sort of attention to the gods will piety be?

Euth. The sort of attention, Socrates, slaves pay to their masters.

Socr. I understand; then it is a kind of service to the gods?

Euth. Certainly.

Socr. Can you tell me what result the art which serves a doctor serves to produce? Is it not health?

Euth. Yes.

Socr. And what result does the art which serves a shipwright serve to produce?

Euth. A ship, of course, Socrates.

Socr. The result of the art which serves a builder is a house, is it not?

Euth. Yes.

Socr. Then tell me, my good friend: What result will the art which serves the gods serve to produce? You must know, seeing that you say that you know more about divine things than any other man. . . .

Euth. There are many notable results, Socrates.

Socr. So are those, my friend, which a general produces. Yet it is easy to see that the crowning result of them all is victory in war, is it not?

Euth. Of course.

Socr. And, I take it, the farmer produces many notable results; yet the principal result of them all is that he makes the earth produce food.

Euth. Certainly.

Socr. Well, then, what is the principal result of the many notable results which the gods produce?

Euth. I told you just now, Socrates, that accurate knowledge of all these matters is not easily obtained. However, broadly I say this: if any man knows that his words and actions in prayer and sacrifice are acceptable to the gods, that is what is pious; and it preserves the state, as it does private families. But the opposite of what is acceptable to the gods is sacrilegious, and this it is that undermines and destroys everything.

Socr. Certainly, Euthyphro, if you had wished, you could have answered my main question in far fewer words. But you are evidently not anxious to teach me. Just now, when you were on the very point of telling me what I want to know, you stopped short. If you had gone on then, I should have learned from you clearly enough by this time what piety is. But now I am asking you questions, and must follow wherever you lead me; so tell me, what is it that you mean by piety and impiety? Do you not mean a science of prayer and sacrifice?

Euth. I do.

Socr. To sacrifice is to give to the gods, and to pray is to ask of them, is it not?

Euth. It is, Socrates.

Socr. Then you say that piety is the science of asking of the gods and giving to them?

Euth. You understand my meaning exactly, Socrates.

Socr. Yes, for I am eager to share your wisdom, Euthyphro, and so I am all attention; nothing that you say will fall to the ground. But tell me, what is this service of the gods? You say it is to ask of them, and to give to them?

Euth. I do.

Socr. Then, to ask rightly will be to ask of them what we stand in need of from them, will it not?

Euth. Naturally.

Socr. And to give rightly will be to give back to them what they stand in need of from us? It would not be very skillful to make a present to a man of something that he has no need of.

Euth. True, Socrates.

Socr. Then piety, Euthyphro, will be the art of carrying on business between gods and men?

Euth. Yes, if you like to call it so.

Socr. But I like nothing except what is true. But tell me, how are the gods benefited by the gifts which they receive from us? What they give is plain enough. Every good thing that we have is their gift. But how are they benefited by what we give them? Have we the advantage over them in these business transactions to such an extent that we receive from them all the good things we possess, and give them nothing in return?

Euth. But do you suppose, Socrates, that the gods are benefited by the gifts which they receive from us?

Socr. But what *are* these gifts, Euthyphro, that we give the gods?

Euth. What do you think but honor and praise, and, as I have said, what is acceptable to them.

Socr. Then piety, Euthyphro, is acceptable to the gods, but it is not profitable to them nor loved by them?

Euth. I think that nothing is more loved by them.

Socr. Then I see that piety means that which is loved by the gods.

Euth. Most certainly.

Socr. After that, shall you be surprised to find that your statements move about instead of staying where you put them? . . . Do you not see that our statement has come round to where it was before? Surely you remember that we have already seen that piety and what is pleasing to the gods are quite different things. Do you not remember?

Euth. I do.

Socr. And now do you not see that you say that what the gods love is pious? But does not what the gods love come to the same thing as what is pleasing to the gods?

Euth. Certainly.

Socr. Then either our former conclusion was wrong or, if it was right, we are wrong now.

Euth. So it seems.

Is There Such a Thing as a Teleological Suspension of the Ethical?

Søren Kierkegaard

The ethical as such is the universal, and as the universal it applies to everyone, which may be expressed from another point of view by saying that it applies every instant. . . . Conceived immediately as physical and psychical, the particular individual is the individual who has his *telos* in the universal, and his ethical task is to express himself constantly in it, to abolish his particularity in order to become the universal. As soon as the individual would assert himself in his particularity over against the universal he sins, and only by recognizing this can he again reconcile himself with the universal. Whenever the individual after he has entered the universal feels an impulse to assert himself as the particular, he is in temptation, and he can labor himself out of this only by penitently abandoning himself as the particular in the universal. If this be the highest thing that can be said of man and of his existence, then the ethical has the same character as man's eternal blessedness, . . .

Faith is precisely this paradox, that the individual as the particular is higher than the universal, is justified over against it, is not subordinate but superior—yet in such a way, be it observed, that it is the particular individual who, after he has been subordinated as the particular to the universal, now through the universal becomes the individual who as the particular is superior to the universal, for the fact that the individual as the particular stands in an absolute relation to the absolute. This position cannot be mediated, for all mediation comes about precisely by virtue of the universal; it is and remains to all eternity a paradox, inaccessible to thought. . . .

That for the particular individual this paradox may easily be mistaken for a temptation is indeed true, but one ought not for this reason to conceal it. That the whole constitution of many persons may be such that this paradox repels them is indeed true, but one ought not for this reason to make faith something different in order to be able to possess it, but ought rather to admit that one does not possess it, whereas those who possess faith should take care to set up certain criteria so that one might distinguish the paradox from a temptation. . . .

Now the story of Abraham contains such a teleological suspension of the ethical. . . . He acts by virtue of the absurd, for it is precisely absurd that he as the particular is higher than the universal. This paradox cannot be mediated; for as soon as he begins to do this he has to admit that he was in temptation, and if such was the case, he never gets to the point of sacrificing Isaac, or, if he has sacrificed Isaac, he must turn back repentantly to the universal. By virtue of the absurd he gets Isaac again. Abraham is therefore at no instant a tragic hero but something quite different, either a murderer or a believer. The middle term which saves the tragic hero, Abraham has not. Hence it is that I can understand the tragic hero but cannot understand Abraham, though in a certain crazy sense I admire him more than all other men.

Abraham's relation to Isaac, ethically speaking, is quite simply expressed by saying that a father shall love his son more dearly than himself. Yet within its own compass the ethical has various gradations. Let us see whether in this story there is to be found any higher expression for the ethical such as would ethically explain his conduct, ethically justify him in suspending the ethical obligation toward his son, without in this search going beyond the teleology of the ethical. . . .

When a son is forgetful of his duty, when the state entrusts the father with the sword of justice, when the laws require punishment at the hand of the father, then will the father heroically forget that the guilty one is his son, he will magnanimously conceal his pain, but there will not be a single one among the people, not even the son, who will not admire the father, and whenever the law of Rome is interpreted, it will be remembered that many interpreted it more learnedly, but none so gloriously as Brutus. . . .

The difference between the tragic hero and Abraham is clearly evident. The tragic hero still remains within the ethical. He lets one expression of the ethical find its *telos* in a higher expression of the ethical; the ethical relation between father and son, or daughter and father, he reduces to a sentiment which has its dialectic in its relation to the idea of morality. Here there can be no question of a teleological suspension of the ethical itself.

With Abraham the situation was different. By his act he overstepped the ethical entirely and possessed a higher *telos* outside of it, in relation to which he suspended the former. For I should very much like to know how one would bring Abraham's act into relation with the universal, and whether it is possible to discover any connection whatever between what Abraham did and the universal . . . except the fact that he transgressed it. It was not for the sake of saving a people, not to maintain the idea of the state, that Abraham did this, and not in order to reconcile angry deities. If there could be a question of the deity being angry, he was angry only with Abraham, and Abraham's whole action stands in no relation to the universal, is a purely private undertaking. Therefore, whereas the tragic hero is great by reason of his moral virtue, Abraham is great by reason of a purely personal virtue. In Abraham's life there is no higher expression for the ethical than this, that the father shall love his son. Of the ethical in the sense of morality there can be no question in this instance. In so far as the universal was present, it was indeed cryptically present in Isaac, hidden as it were in Isaac's loins, and must therefore cry out with Isaac's mouth, "Do it not! Thou art bringing everything to naught."

Why then did Abraham do it? For God's sake, and (in complete identity with this) for his own sake. He did it for God's sake because God required this proof of his faith; for his own sake he did it in order that he might furnish the proof. The unity of these two points of view is perfectly expressed by the word which has always been used to characterize this situation: it is a trial, a temptation. A temptation—but what does that mean? What ordinarily tempts a man is that which would keep him from doing his duty, but in this case the temptation is itself the ethical . . . which would keep him from doing God's will. But what then is duty? Duty is precisely the expression for God's will. . . .

Therefore, though Abraham arouses my admiration, he at the same time appalls me. He who denies himself and sacrifices himself for duty gives up the finite in order to grasp the infinite, and that man is secure enough. The tragic hero gives up the certain for the still more certain, and the eye of the beholder rests upon him confidently. But he who gives up the universal in order to grasp something still higher which is not the universal—what is he doing? Is it possible that this can be anything else but a temptation? And if it be possible . . . but the individual was mistaken—what can save him? He suffers all the pain of the tragic hero, he brings to naught his joy in the world, he renounces everything . . . and perhaps at the same instant debars himself from the sublime joy which to him was so precious that he would purchase it at any price. Him the beholder cannot understand nor let his eye rest confidently upon him. Perhaps it is not possible to do what the believer proposes, since it is indeed unthinkable. Or if it could be done, but if the individual had misunderstood the deity—what can save him? . . .

The Enforcement of Morals

Lord Patrick Devlin

. . . In jurisprudence, as I have said, everything is thrown open to discussion and, in the belief that they cover the whole field, I have framed three interrogatories addressed to myself to answer:

1 Has society the right to pass judgement at all on matters of morals? Ought there, in other words, to be a public morality, or are morals always a matter for private judgement?

2 If society has the right to pass judgement, has it also the right to use the weapon of the law to enforce it?

3 If so, ought it to use that weapon in all cases or only in some; and if only in some, on what principles should it distinguish?

I shall begin with the first interrogatory and consider what is meant by the right of society to pass a moral judgement, that is, a judgement about what is good and what is evil. . . . What makes a society of any sort is community of ideas, not only political ideas but also ideas about the way its members should behave and govern their lives; these latter ideas are its morals. Every society has a moral structure as well as a political one: or rather, since that might suggest two independent systems, I should say that the structure of every society is made up both of politics and morals. Take, for example, the institution of marriage. Whether a man should be allowed to take more than one wife is something about which every society has to make up its mind one way or the other. In England we believe in the Christian idea of marriage and therefore adopt monogamy as a moral principle. Consequently the Christian institution of marriage has become the basis of family life and so part of the structure of our society. It is there not because it is Christian. It has got there because it is Christian, but it remains there because it is built into the house in which we live and could not be removed without bringing it down. The great majority of those who live in this country accept it because it is the Christian idea of marriage and for them the only true one. But a non-Christian is bound by it, not because it is part of Christianity but because, rightly or wrongly, it has been adopted by the society in which he lives. It would be useless for him to stage a debate designed to prove that polygamy was theologically more correct and socially preferable; if he wants to live in the house, he must accept it as built in the way in which it is.

We see this more clearly if we think of ideas or institutions that are purely political. Society cannot tolerate rebellion; it will not allow argument about the rightness of the cause. Historians a century later may say that the rebels were right and the Government was wrong and a percipient and conscientious subject of the State may think so at the time. But it is not a matter which can be left to individual judgement.

The institution of marriage is a good example for my purpose because it bridges the division, if there is one, between politics and morals. Marriage is part of the structure of our society and it is also the basis of a moral code which condemns fornication and adultery. The institution of marriage would be gravely threatened if individual judgements were permitted about the morality of adultery; on these points there must be a public morality. But public morality is not to be confined to those moral principles which support institutions such as marriage. People do not think of monogamy as something which has to be supported because our society has chosen to organize itself upon it; they think of it as something that is good in itself and offering a good way of life and that it is for that reason that our society has adopted it. I return to the statement that I have already made, that society means a community of ideas; without shared ideas on politics, morals, and ethics no society can exist. Each one of us has ideas about what is good and what is evil; they cannot be kept private from the society in which we live. If men and women try to create a society in which there is no fundamental agreement about good and evil they will fail; if, having based it on common agreement, the agreement goes, the society will disintegrate. For society is not something that is kept together physically; it is held by the invisible bonds of common thought. If the bonds were too far relaxed the members would drift apart. A common morality is part of the bondage. The bondage is part of the price of society; and mankind, which needs society, must pay its price. . . .

You may think that I have taken far too long in contending that there is such a thing as public morality, a proposition which most people would readily accept, and may have left myself too little time to discuss the next question which to many minds may cause greater difficulty: to what extent should society use the law to enforce its moral judgements? But I believe that the answer to the first question determines the way in which the second should be approached and may indeed very nearly dictate the answer to the second question. If society has no right to make judgements on morals, the law must find some special justification for entering the field of morality: if homosexuality and prostitution are not in themselves wrong, then the onus is very clearly on the lawgiver who wants to frame a law against certain aspects of them to justify the exceptional treatment. But if society has the right to make a judgement and has it on the basis that a recognized morality is as necessary to society as, say, a recognized government, then society may use the law to preserve morality in the same way as it uses it to safeguard anything else that is essential to its existence. If therefore the first proposition is securely established with all its implications, society has a prima facie right to legislate against immorality as such. . . .

I think, . . . that it is not possible to set theoretical limits to the power of the State to legislate against immorality. It is not possible to settle in advance exceptions to the general rule or to define inflexibly areas of morality into which the law is in no circumstances to be allowed to enter. Society is entitled by means of its laws to protect itself from dangers, whether from within or without. Here again I think that the political parallel is legitimate. The law of treason is directed against aiding the king's enemies and against sedition from within. The justification for this is that established government is necessary for the existence of society and therefore its safety against violent over-throw must be secured. But an established morality is as necessary as good government to the welfare of society. Societies disintegrate from within more frequently than they are broken up by external pressures. There is disintegration when no common morality is observed and history shows that the loosening of moral bonds is often the first stage of disintegration, so that society is justified in taking the same steps to preserve its moral code as it does to preserve its government and other essential institutions. The suppression of vice is as much the law's business as the suppression of subversive activities; it is no more possible to define a sphere of private morality than it is to define one of private subversive activity. It is wrong to talk of private morality or of the law not being concerned with immorality as such or to try to set rigid bounds to the part which the law may play in the suppression of vice. There are no theoretical limits to the power of the State to legislate against treason and sedition, and likewise I think there can be no theoretical limits to legislation against immorality. You may argue that if a man's sins affect only himself it cannot be the concern of society. If he chooses to get drunk every night in the privacy of his own home, is any one except himself the worse for it? But suppose a quarter or a half of the population got drunk every night, what sort of society would it be? You cannot set a theoretical limit to the number of people who can get drunk before society is entitled to legislate against drunkenness. The same may be said of gambling. . . .

In what circumstances the State should exercise its power is the third of the interrogatories I have framed. But before I get to it I must raise a point which might have been brought up in any one of the three. How are the moral judgements of society to be ascertained? By leaving it until now, I can ask it in the more limited form that is now sufficient for my purpose. How is the law-maker to ascertain the moral judgements of society? It is surely not enough that they should be reached by the opinion of the majority; it would be too much to require the individual assent of every citizen. English law has evolved and regularly uses a standard which does not depend on the counting of heads. It is that of the reasonable man. He is not to be confused with the rational man. He is not expected to reason about anything and his judgement may be largely a matter of feeling. It is the viewpoint of the man in the street—or to use an archaism familiar to all lawyers—the man in the Clapham omnibus. He might also be called the right-minded man. For my purpose I should like to call him the man in the jury box, for the moral judgement of society must be something about which any twelve men or women drawn at random might after discussion be expected to be unanimous. This was the standard the judges applied in the days before Parliament was as active as it is now and when they laid down rules of public policy. They did not think of themselves as making law but simply as stating principles which every right-minded person would accept as valid. It is what Pollock called 'practical morality', which is based not on theological or philosophical foundations but 'in the mass of continuous experience half-consciously or unconsciously accumulated and embodied in the morality of common sense.' He called it also 'a certain way of thinking on questions of morality which we expect to find in a reasonable civilized man or a reasonable Englishman, taken at random.'[1]

Immorality then, for the purpose of the law, is what every right-minded person is presumed to consider to be immoral. Any immorality is capable of affecting society injuriously and in effect to a greater or lesser extent it usually does; this is what gives the law its *locus standi*. It cannot be shut out. But—and this brings me to the third question—the individual has a *locus standi* too; he cannot be expected to surrender to the judgement of society the whole conduct of his life. It is the old and familiar question of striking a balance between the rights and interests of society and those of the individual. This is something which the law is constantly doing in matters large and small. To take a very down-to-earth example, let me consider the right of the individual whose house adjoins the highway to have access to it; that means in these days the right to have vehicles stationary in the highway, sometimes for a considerable time if there is a lot of loading or unloading. There are many cases in which the courts have had to balance the private right of access against the public right to use the highway without obstruction. It cannot be done by carving up the highway into public and private areas. It is done by recognizing that each have rights over the whole; that if each were to exercise their rights to the full, they would come into conflict; and

---

[1]*Essays in Jurisprudence and Ethics* (1882), Macmillan, pp. 278 and 353.

therefore that the rights of each must be curtailed so as to ensure as far as possible that the essential needs of each are safeguarded.

I do not think that one can talk sensibly of a public and private morality any more than one can of a public or private highway. Morality is a sphere in which there is a public interest and a private interest, often in conflict, and the problem is to reconcile the two. This does not mean that it is impossible to put forward any general statements about how in our society the balance ought to be struck. Such statements cannot of their nature be rigid or precise; they would not be designed to circumscribe the operation of the law-making power but to guide those who have to apply it. While every decision which a court of law makes when it balances the public against the private interest is an *ad hoc* decision, the cases contain statements of principle to which the court should have regard when it reaches its decision. In the same way it is possible to make general statements of principle which it may be thought the legislature should bear in mind when it is considering the enactment of laws enforcing morals.

I believe that most people would agree upon the chief of these elastic principles. There must be toleration of the maximum individual freedom that is consistent with the integrity of society. . . . The principle appears to me to be peculiarly appropriate to all questions of morals. Nothing should be punished by the law that does not lie beyond the limits of tolerance. It is not nearly enough to say that a majority dislike a practice; there must be a real feeling of reprobation. . . . We should ask ourselves in the first instance whether, looking at it calmly and dispassionately, we regard it as a vice so abominable that its mere presence is an offense. If that is the genuine feeling of the society in which we live, I do not see how society can be denied the right to eradicate it. Our feeling may not be so intense as that. We may feel about it that, if confined, it is tolerable, but that if spread it might be gravely injurious; it is in this way that most societies look upon fornication, seeing it as a natural weakness which must be kept within bounds but which cannot be rooted out. It becomes then a question of balance, the danger to society in one scale and the extent of the restriction in the other. . . .

The limits of tolerance shift. This is supplementary to what I have been saying but of sufficient importance in itself to deserve statement as a separate principle which law-makers have to bear in mind. . . . It may be that over-all tolerance is always increasing. The pressure of the human mind, always seeking greater freedom of thought, is outwards against the bonds of society forcing their gradual relaxation. It may be that history is a tale of contraction and expansion and that all developed societies are on their way to dissolution. I must not speak of things I do not know; and anyway as a practical matter no society is willing to make provision for its own decay. I return therefore to the simple and observable fact that in matters of morals the limits of tolerance shift. Laws, especially those which are based on morals, are less easily moved. It follows as another good working principle that in any new matter of morals the law should be slow to act. By the next generation the swell of indignation may have abated and the law be left without the strong backing which it needs. But it is then difficult to alter the law without giving the impression that moral judgement is being weakened. . . .

A third elastic principle must be advanced more tentatively. It is that as far as possible privacy should be respected. This is not an idea that has ever been made explicit in the criminal law. Acts or words done or said in public or in private are all brought within its scope without distinction in principle. But there goes with this a strong reluctance on the part of judges and legislators to sanction invasions of privacy in the detection of crime. The police have no more right to trespass than the ordinary citizen has; there is no general right of search; to this extent an Englishman's home is still his castle. The Government is extremely careful in the exercise even of those powers which it claims to be undisputed. Telephone tapping and interference with the mails afford a good illustration of this. . . .

This indicates a general sentiment that the right to privacy is something to be put in the balance against the enforcement of the law. Ought the same sort of consideration to play any part in the formation of the law? Clearly only in a very limited number of cases. When the help of the law is invoked by an injured citizen, privacy must be irrelevant; the individual cannot ask that his right to privacy should be measured against injury criminally done to another. But when all who are involved in the deed are consenting parties and the injury is done to morals, the public interest in the moral order can be balanced against the claims of privacy. . . .

The Preservation of Morality

H. L. A. Hart

. . . Is the fact that certain conduct is by common standards immoral sufficient to justify making that conduct punishable by law? Is it morally permissible to enforce morality as such? Ought immorality as such to be a crime? . . .

I shall consider this dispute mainly in relation to the special topic of sexual morality where it seems *prima facie* plausible that there are actions immoral by accepted standards and yet not harmful to others. . . .

Lord Devlin bases his affirmative answer to the question on the quite general principle that it is permissible for any society to take the steps needed to preserve its own existence as an organized society, and he thinks that immorality—even private sexual immorality—may, like treason, be something which jeopardizes a society's existence. Of course many of us may doubt this general principle, and not merely the suggested analogy with treason. We might wish to argue that whether or not a society is justified in taking steps to preserve itself must depend both on what sort of society it is and what the steps to be taken are. If a society were mainly devoted to the cruel persecution of a racial or religious minority, or if the steps to be taken included hideous tortures, it is arguable that what Lord Devlin terms the "disintegration" of such a society would be morally better than its continued existence, and steps ought not to be taken to preserve it. Nonetheless Lord Devlin's principle that a society may take the steps required to preserve its organized existence is not itself tendered as an item of English popular morality, deriving its cogency from its status as part of our institutions. He puts it forward as a principle, rationally acceptable, to be used in the evaluation or criticism of social institutions generally. And it is surely clear that anyone who holds the question whether a society has the "right" to enforce morality, or whether it is morally permissible for any society to enforce its morality by law, to be discussable at all, must be prepared to deploy some such general principles of critical morality. In asking the question, we are assuming the legitimacy of a standpoint which permits criticism of the institutions of any society, in the light of general principles and knowledge of the facts. . . .

This last consideration brings us to what is really the central issue. . . . Let us suppose, contrary to much evidence, . . . that there really is a moral code in sexual matters supported by an overwhelming majority and that they are deeply disturbed when it is infringed even by adults in private; that the punishment of offenders really does sustain the sense that the conduct is immoral and without their punishment the prevalent morality would change in a permissive direction. The central question is: Can anything or nothing be said to support the claim that the prevention of this change and the maintenance of the moral *status quo* in a society's morality are values sufficient to offset the cost in human misery which legal enforcement entails? Is it simply a blank assertion, or does it rest on any critical principles connecting what is said to be of value here with other things of value?

Here certain discriminations are needed. There are three propositions concerning the value of preserving social morality which are in perennial danger of confusion. The first of these propositions is the truth that since all social moralities, whatever else they may contain, make provision in some degree for such universal values as individual freedom, safety of life, and protection from deliberately inflicted harm, there will always be much in social morality which is worth preserving even at the cost in terms of these same values which legal enforcement involves. It is perhaps misleading to say with Lord Devlin that social morality, so far as it secures these things, is of value because they are required for the preservation of society; on the contrary, the preservation of any particular society is of value because among other things it secures for human beings some measure of these universal values. It is indeed arguable that a human society in which these values are not recognised at all in its morality is neither an empirical nor a logical possibility, and that even if it were, such a society could be of no practical value for human beings. In conceding this much, however, we must beware of following Lord Devlin in thinking of social morality as a seamless web and of all its provisions as necessary for the existence of the society whose morality it is. We should . . . be alive to the truth that though these essential universal values must be secured, society can not only survive individual divergences in other fields from its prevalent morality, but profit from them.

Secondly, there is the truth, less familiar and less easy to state in precise terms, that the spirit or attitude of mind which characterises the practice of a social morality is something of very great value and indeed quite vital for men to foster and preserve in any society. For in the practice of any social morality there are necessarily involved what may be called *formal* values as distinct from the *material* values of its particular rules or content. In moral relationships with others the individual sees questions of conduct from an impersonal point of view and applies general rules impartially to himself and to others; he is made aware of and takes account of the wants, expectations, and reactions of others; he exerts self-discipline and control in adapting his conduct to a system of reciprocal claims. These are universal virtues and indeed constitute the specifically moral attitude to conduct. It is true that these virtues are learnt in conforming to the morality of some particular society, but their value is not derived from the fact that they are there accounted virtues. We have only to conduct the Hobbesian experiment of imagining these virtues totally absent to see that they are vital for the conduct of any cooperative form of human life and any successful personal life. No principles of critical morality which paid the least attention to the most elementary facts of human nature and the conditions in which human life has to be led could propose to dispense with them. Hence if by the preservation of morality is meant the preservation of the moral attitude to conduct and its formal values, it is certainly true that it is a value. But, though true, this is really irrelevant to the issue before us; for the preservation of morality in this sense is not identical with and does not require the preservation from change of a society's moral code as it is at any given moment of that society's existence; and *a fortiori* it does not require the legal enforcement of its rules. The moral attitude to conduct has often survived the criticism, the infringement, and the ultimate relaxation of specific moral institutions. The use of legal punishment to freeze into immobility the morality dominant at a particular time in a society's existence may possibly succeed, but even where it does it contributes nothing to the survival of the animating spirit and formal values of social morality and may do much to harm them.

From the preservation of morality in this sense which is so clearly a value we must, then, distinguish mere moral conservatism. This latter amounts to the proposition that the preservation from change of any existent rule of a social morality, whatever its content, is a value and justifies its legal enforcement. This proposition would be at least intelligible if we could ascribe to all social morality the status which theological systems or the doctrine of the Law of Nature ascribes to some fundamental principles. Then, at least, some general principle would have been adduced to support the claim that preservation of any rule of social morality was a value justifying its legal enforcement; something would have been said to indicate the source of this asserted value. The application of these general principles to the case in hand would then be something to be discussed and argued, and moral conservatism would then be a form of critical morality to be used in the criticism of social institutions. It would not then be—as it is when dissociated from all such general principles—a brute dogma, asserting that the preservation of any social morality necessarily outweighs its cost in human misery and deprivation of freedom. In this dogmatic form it in effect withdraws positive morality from the scope of any moral criticism. . . .

To use coercion to maintain the moral *status quo* at any point in a society's history would be artificially to arrest the process which gives social institutions their value.

CHAPTER **5**

MORAL DUTIES AND MORAL IDEALS

Suppose a student prefers to keep late hours and prefers partying to studying. Is that student being immoral? In answering the question, would it make a difference whether the student's education was funded by the student's parents, the student's own resources, or the taxpayers in general? Are the citizens of the United States immoral because they purchase video-cassette recorders, cosmetics, fast foods, and home computers while millions of people are starving? Is it wrong for a student not to report another student who violates the honor code? Is it wrong not to "blow the whistle" on a dangerous product manufactured by your employer if whistle-blowing is likely to result in the loss of your job? Is the captain of a ship obligated to go down with it? A general question arises from the consideration of these examples: What are the nature and scope of our ethical obligations?

Let's begin with something close to a philosophical consensus. Nearly all philosophers—and nonphilosophers for that matter—agree that it is wrong to cause avoidable harm to others. One of the most recent examples of this viewpoint is Charles Fried's book *Right and Wrong*. Fried considers the duty not to cause avoidable harm as a given in our western tradition. The duty is assumed rather than argued for. Rather than develop arguments in defense of a duty not to cause avoidable harm, Fried sees the task of ethics as spelling out what duties (categorical norms) follow from the basic moral duty and showing how so-called exceptions to these duties do not detract from their absolute binding power.

Perhaps one of the most difficult tasks for Fried and others who make the duty not to cause avoidable harm to other persons an essential duty of ethics is to define what is to count as a harm. The difficulty arises because in ordinary language *harm* is used loosely to refer to any injury whatsoever. People are obviously harmed when their property is stolen, or when their person is attacked. But in addition, if someone libels or slanders them, they can sue for harm to their reputation. People may also claim to be harmed when they are offended by something—the existence of X-rated movie theaters, for example. Still another wrinkle occurs when you count harm caused by inaction—you are harmed because I didn't help you; or by action which indirectly lessens your opportunities—I buy the last ticket to the World Series, so that there is none available for you.

Philosophers who appeal to the duty not to cause avoidable harm cannot use *harm* as it is used in ordinary language. (In ordinary language almost any negative influence directly or indirectly caused by another person or event would count as a harm.) If you adopt a use of *harm* that broad, almost every action you take will cause avoidable harm to someone. Hence almost any act you do would have ethical import. The scope of ethics would have to be expanded to cover almost every decision we make.

A number of strategies for solving this problem have been adopted. Sometimes an ethical theorist will simply stipulate a limited application of *harm*. For example, "social injury [harm] is defined as particularly including activities which violate, or frustrate the enforcement of, rules of domestic or international law intended to protect individuals against deprivation of health, safety, or basic freedoms."[1] Fried stipulates that "harm" is to be limited to physical harm. To distinguish directly caused harm from indirectly caused harm which results from inaction or from a lessening of opportunities, Fried appeals to more theoretical considerations between harms and benefits. What is significant about direct harm is that the agent chooses the victim. Not helping someone is not benefiting them. In those cases, Fried argues, "If a stranger can say to me, 'You might have benefited me,' I can always reply, 'No more than countless other persons.' In harm this problem does not exist." Ditto with the last World Series ticket. The person who purchased the last ticket did not pick out a specific victim but simply bought the last ticket, and many people were disappointed.

Fried also makes use of the distinction between intentionally caused harm and the unforeseen and unanticipated harmful side-effects of actions. Harms which result from unforeseen and unanticipated side-effects do not fall under the duty not to cause avoidable harm. Hence, for Fried there is a moral prohibition against causing avoidable physical harm so long as we understand that we are not talking about unintended harm. Moreover, the duty refers to directly caused harm; the duty does not include the harm which is equivalent to not benefiting someone.

Fried is a good example of a philosopher who tries to limit the scope of our moral obligations. For Fried, only a limited number of our decisions raise genuinely ethical obligations. Many decisions that we make are morally neutral. But perhaps the attempt to limit the scope of morality to one basic moral duty is to go to the extreme—even if that basic moral duty covers many of the decisions we actually make. Another theory which attempts to limit the scope of our moral obligations rests on the question: What moral obligations must be accepted by members of a society if there is to be a society at all? Moral prohibitions against killing, physical attack, and theft are paradigm

[1]John G. Simon, Charles W. Powers, and Jon P. Gunnemann, "The Responsibilities of Corporations and Their Owners," in Tom L. Beauchamp and Norman E. Bowie (eds.), *Ethical Theory and Business,* 2d ed., Prentice-Hall, Englewood Cliffs, N.J., 1983, p. 89.

examples. If these moral prohibitions didn't exist and weren't generally respected, Hobbes's war of all against all would surely exist. These prohibitions are absolute moral duties, since they are necessary for the functioning of society. Not causing avoidable physical harm is an excellent example of one such absolute duty. The set of these absolute duties and prohibitions can be called the "moral minimum." To be a moral person one must at least respect these duties and prohibitions.

But many philosophers argue that there is more to morality than the moral minimum. There are ideals of human excellence—standards of what a person ought to be, and the duty or obligation to achieve this ideal of human excellence is a duty one has to oneself. The notion of a moral ideal is developed in the selection by R. M. Hare. Consider people who spend inordinate amounts of time watching soap operas or playing video games. Presumably these people have not violated any absolute duties or prohibitions, but they lead morally undesirable lives, don't they? The notion of an ideal of human excellence is also captured by ordinary language. Sometimes we say that someone lives like a pig. A fraternity comes to be known as "Animal House." The use of nonhuman terms to describe human behavior is a way of showing moral condemnation of that behavior—even if the behavior causes no real harm.

What is the relation of moral ideals and the moral minimum? The obligations that constitute the moral minimum are absolute. Most philosophers would agree that obligations to oneself to fulfill ideals of human excellence are less stringent than the obligations which constitute the moral minimum. Some would argue that duties to oneself aren't genuine obligations at all. It would be nice if people didn't behave like pigs, but so long as they don't harm others, they can behave like pigs if they want to. These philosophers would say that behaving like a pig is morally permissible even if behaving like a pig can correctly be described as bad. On this view, some decisions which are bad are morally permissible. Other philosophers, like Daniel Callahan, take sharp exception to this view. They believe that the duties to oneself to achieve human ideals are genuine moral obligations.

But some people decide to pursue human ideals even when pursuing these ideals causes some harm to others. People who are opposed to all forms of gambling would prohibit lotteries and church bingo even though the proceeds from these forms of gambling would be used to help the needy. Are decisions which promote moral ideals while causing harm ever morally acceptable? Using the distinction between social morality and individual ideals, P. F. Strawson considers that issue. Chapter 4 raised the issue of whether everything that was immoral should also be illegal. The distinction between social morality and individual ideals provides a theoretical way of answering that question in the negative. Social morality should be legally enforced. It's the morality that provides the glue for keeping society together. Moral ideals, on the other hand, should not be legally enforced. Society can tolerate a wide diversity of individual lifestyles, and these lifestyles should in fact be tolerated. Strawson, like many philosophers, argues that a society which tolerates a diversity of individual ideals is a morally better society.

However, even if philosophers like Strawson are basically correct in their assessment that a diversity of individual ideals within a society is good, there are limits to toleration. Some persons adopt ideals which are racist, sexist, or elitist in ways that harm others.

Ideals which violate the moral minimum must be constrained to the point where persons aren't harmed. Racists may preach their doctrine but shouldn't be allowed to practice it. It is a principle of morality that individual ideals must be consistent with the moral minimum of the society.

At this point our conception of morality includes a moral minimum which establishes very stringent duties and obligations which are required and which must be generally followed if we are to have a society at all. Any other moral obligations must be consistent with the requirements of the moral minimum. Some of these other obligations include obligations to strive to meet ideals of human excellence. We ought to adopt lifestyles which promote the best in human nature. However, whereas divergence and disagreement about the moral minimum is destabilizing and dangerous, divergence and disagreement about human excellence is not so destabilizing and dangerous. Indeed many ethical theorists consider divergences in lifestyles to be a positive good.

Does this mean that the scope of ethics can be captured by the stringent obligations of the moral minimum and the less stringent obligations to achieve moral ideals? No, it does not. We can start with an example from Peter Singer.[2] Suppose on the way to my lecture I see a baby about to drown in a shallow pond. By simply getting the bottom of my pants wet and being a few minutes late to class, I can save the baby's life. Don't I have a duty to save the baby? And isn't my duty in this case absolute, even though I didn't cause the baby's predicament? Most of us would say that we do have a very stringent duty to save the baby's life. In fact the principle "You have a moral duty to benefit others when you can do so with little inconvenience to yourself" seems every bit as stringent as the principle "You have a moral duty not to cause avoidable physical harm."

But once you allow one obligation to benefit others to be a stringent moral obligation equal in weight to the obligations which constitute the moral minimum, you need some basis for drawing the line. Otherwise ethics would become very demanding indeed. Suppose all obligations to benefit others were as stringent as the obligations which constitute the moral minimum. For any decision that we made, we would have to ask whether there was an alternative decision that would better enable us to benefit others. But then matters like deciding when to brush your teeth, have lunch with a friend, or go to a movie become ethical decisions. Isn't that carrying ethics a bit far?

Most philosophers agree that making ethical decisions should not be especially onerous in most circumstances. Normally doing the right thing shouldn't require a lot of work. Generally we should be free to pursue our own interests, and deliberations over what actions to pursue would not raise any particularly moral considerations. That's the advantage to a minimalist ethics. Keeping the obligations necessary for society to exist or keeping the obligation to avoid causing harm, where harm is defined as Fried does, does not usually require us to do anything. It simply requires that we refrain from doing certain things, like killing, lying, and stealing.

On the other hand, the drowning-baby example indicates that we can't limit the scope of ethics to the obligations constituted by the moral minimum. In addition there are other objections to a minimalist ethics. In a penetrating critique included in this

---

[2]Peter Singer, "Rich and Poor," in Beauchamp and Bowie, op. cit., p. 622.

chapter, Daniel Callahan urges us to broaden our horizons. Callahan's overriding objection to minimalist ethics is that other important ethical issues are either distorted or ignored. Among Callahan's charges are the fact that limiting the scope of ethics to minimalist ethics has (1) made the attempt to discover objective human ideals subversive, (2) limited moral criticism to issues involving direct public harm, and (3) created a false dichotomy between our public and private lives.

Another way of raising Callahan's concern is to take some paradigm case of an individual ideal and show how a choice concerning that ideal has a direct impact on whether or not the world will be a better place. On a minimalist morality, most questions of that type are relatively unimportant. Persons of Callahan's persuasion would argue that such a point of view is seriously mistaken. Norman Care presents career choice as one such paradigm.[3] Most students look at career choice as either a simple problem of maximizing one's income or as a more complex problem of adding depth and meaning to one's individual life. Seldom do students ask whether selection of this career or that will contribute to a better world. But philosophers like Callahan would argue that such decisions are basically ethical, since the choice of our individual ideals has an impact for good or evil on others.

Still another way of raising Callahan's concern is to consider people who act to benefit others at great costs to themselves. A soldier who jumps on a grenade to save the lives of fellow soldiers and a whistle-blower who is fired for trying to protect the public are excellent examples. We refer to such people as saints or heroes.[4] Even if no one has a stringent duty to be a hero or a saint, ethical theory must have a conceptual framework broad enough to provide an analysis of what counts as ethically heroic behavior. Limiting the scope of ethics to the moral minimum will not provide that framework.

We can conclude that people can be held responsible for their decisions for or against morality when following our moral obligations is within the reach of most individuals. Following the absolute duties and prohibitions that make society possible provides a moral minimum and is within the reach of most individuals. But the concept of a moral minimum is too austere to capture the full dimensions of the scope of moral life. In some circumstances we have an absolute duty to help others. We also have decisions to make concerning individual ideals, and these decisions must be made with the recognition that our choice of individual ideals affects others for better or worse. Finally one choice—the decision to help others at extraordinary cost to ourselves—moves us to the realm of the ethically heroic. Adding these dimensions to the moral minimum places morality at the center of our lives, but these added dimensions do not mean that all our actions have great moral import. Whether I buy my gas at Shell or Exxon is morally neutral. Whether I become a doctor or a financier does have moral import. Whether or not I refrain from harming others is morally crucial.

---

[3]Norman Care, "Career Choice," in *Ethics,* Chicago: University of Chicago Press, 1983.

[4]This term was made popular by J. O. Urmson's article "Saints and Heroes," A. I. Melden (ed.), *Essays in Moral Philosophy,* University of Washington Press, Seattle, 1958.

Right and Wrong

Charles Fried

RIGHT AND WRONG AS ABSOLUTE

. . .Ordinary moral understanding, as well as many major traditions of Western moral theory, recognize that there are some things which a moral man will not do, no matter what. The harming of innocent people, lying, enslavement, and degradation—these are all things decent people shrink from, though great good might seem to come in particular cases from resorting to them. . . .

It is part of the idea that lying or murder are wrong, not just bad, that these are things you must not do—no matter what. They are not mere negatives that enter into a calculus to be outweighed by the good you might do or the greater harm you might avoid. Thus the norms which express deontological judgments—for example, Do not commit murder—may be said to be absolute. They do not say: "Avoid lying, other things being equal" but "Do not lie, period." This absoluteness is an expression of how deontological norms or judgments differ from those of consequentialism. But absoluteness is only a suggestive first approximation of a much more complex characteristic. This characteristic can only be fully appreciated as a number of such norms are considered in detail and contrasted with their consequentialist versions. In every case the norm has boundaries and what lies outside those boundaries is not forbidden at all. Thus lying is wrong, while withholding a truth which another needs may be perfectly permissible—but that is because withholding truth is not lying. Murder is wrong but killing in self-defense is not. The absoluteness of the norm is preserved in these cases, but only by virtue of a process which defines its boundaries. That process is different from the process by which good and bad are weighed in consequentialism, and so the distinctiveness of judgments of right and wrong is preserved.

Even within such boundaries we can imagine extreme cases where killing an innocent person may save a whole nation. In such cases it seems fanatical to maintain the absoluteness of the judgment, to do right even if the heavens will in fact fall. And so the catastrophic may cause the absoluteness of right and wrong to yield, but even then it would be a non sequitur to argue (as consequentialists are fond of doing) that this proves that judgments of right and wrong are always a matter of degree, depending on the relative goods to be attained and harms to be avoided. I believe, on the contrary, that the concept of the catastrophic is a distinct concept just because it identifies the extreme situations in which the usual categories of judgment (including the category of right and wrong) no longer apply. . . .

When we say that one must not grievously harm an innocent person, that one must not lie, these are categorical prohibitions in the sense that (within limits) no amount of good can justify them. But they are not absolute in the sense that we may never be justified in doing acts which have these very results—the death of an innocent person, the propagation of false beliefs—as a consequence. They are absolute in the sense that they point out certain *acts* we must not perform. They are not absolute in the consequentialist's sense; they do not state that a certain state of the world is of such supreme importance that the value of everything else must be judged by its tendency to produce that state. . . . We must indeed be concerned with producing good in the world, but without violating the absolute norms of right and wrong.

It is a crucial thesis of this work, then, that there are categorical norms, and that judgments of right and wrong take the form of categorical norms. Given the centrality of this concept, I offer this specification. First, a *norm* is a judgment addressed to an agent, directing choice. Thus a norm differs from value judgments in general in that value judgments do not necessarily direct choice, although choices may be made by reference to them. If I say that the August moon is particularly beautiful or that Hadrian was a wise emperor, consistency requires that I take the opportunity to gaze upon the moon in August when nothing stands in the way or emulate Hadrian should I find myself in his situation, but it is obviously not the point of these judgments to prescribe such conduct. To say, however, that lying is wrong is just to direct all potential auditors to avoid lies. Second, a norm is *categorical* when its application is not contingent upon the agent's adopting some other independent end, which the norm will lead him to attain; it is not like the norm "If you wish to live to be ninety, don't smoke." . . . But third, my conception contains a further element, which is captured (though with more rigor than I ultimately intend) by the term absoluteness. A categorical norm does more than direct that a particular value be given weight in making choices. It is not like the directive that the suffering of animals be taken into account in one's choices, and that if the cost is not too great that their suffering be minimized. Rather, a categorical norm displaces other judgments in its domain, so that other values and ends may not be urged as reasons for violating the norm. It is preemptive. This latter characteristic of categorical norms is the most distinctive and the most troublesome. In fact, I have already indicated that in a sense it is an approximation of a more complex notion. A categorical norm may be overwhelmed by extreme circumstances. So also it may be underwhelmed, as it were, by the triviality of the instance of its application. But so long as the consequences fall within a very broad range, the categorical norm holds, no matter what those consequences. To propound a categorical norm, to argue that an action is wrong, is to invite inquiry into the kinds of action intended to be covered, but not an inquiry into the costs of compliance. . . .

In this [section] I examine one crucial categorical norm: that it is wrong to do physical harm to an innocent person. Now, physical harm is not the only or necessarily the worst kind of injury. A man's liberty to speak his mind or travel freely may be more important to him than security against some sorts of harm, as may be his property or his reputation. Certain violations of these other interests may also be wrong, just as wrong as doing physical harm. I shall not offer accounts of all such wrongs. I suppose that arguments analogous to those I give regarding harm and lying are available in other cases. I claim only that the norm forbidding physical harm has priority, at least in the exposition of a theory of right and wrong.

By physical harm I mean an impingement upon the body which either causes pain or impairs functioning. Thus a sharp, painful blow which, however, neither cuts nor bruises would constitute harm. So also would a laceration of the skin, since any break in the skin impairs the functioning of that tissue. On the other hand, to cut hair or a fingernail or to paint the skin with some nontoxic substance might constitute an offense to dignity but would not stand as a physical harm. This definition covers a wide range of consequences. It covers everything from killing to pinching and thus raises an important theoretical question. Can it be that pinching has the same moral quality as killing? I shall offer very little in the way of enlightenment regarding the morality of pinching, although if one takes physical harms further along the line of seriousness—maiming, blinding, or even temporary infliction of severe pain—I have no difficulty concluding that, in all of these cases, the formal nature of the moral judgment, the categorical prohibition, is the same. These are harms we must not intend to inflict, and consideration of consequences as such cannot outweigh that judgment. As we shall see, there are excuses and justifications for killing, and so there must be also for maiming and the infliction of pain. . . .

Consider these two cases:

1 Plunging a dagger into someone's heart.

2 Revaluing your currency with the foreseeable result that your country's wheat crop will be more expensive and less readily available for famine relief and the further foreseeable result that some persons weakened by hunger in distant lands will die.

It is our intuitive response that without some very special and narrowly drawn justification, the conduct in case 1 is wrong, while the moral quality of the conduct in case 2 depends on a wide variety of considerations: the purpose of the revaluation, the likely response of other countries, the history behind the move, the background of international practice, and so on. In short, it seems natural to bring the first of these cases within the ambit of the categorical norm "Do no harm." The conduct in the second case, however, must inevitably be subjected to some form of consequentialist analysis. . . . If we could not distinguish between cases 1 and 2, if we could not say that directly harming was wrong in some special way, if we had to weigh and balance all the consequences to see if stabbing an innocent person to death was wrong, then our whole position as free moral agents, our status as persons, would be grievously undermined. . . .

. . . It is the individual person who is the ultimate entity of value, so that even a person's happiness is only important because it is that person's happiness. Happiness is not a kind of undifferentiated abstract plasma waiting to be attached to a particular person but the aim and outcome of individual *choice*, the success of the self in realizing its own values through its choices and efficacy. Accordingly, the maintenance of the integrity of the individual as the locus of valuation and choice is more important than the abstractions of happiness, pleasure, or excellence. These latter are, after all, rather the *objects* of individual valuation. And if the primacy of the individual is to be maintained, if it is individuality, personality, which is the point of departure of ethical judgments, then the "irrelevantly" particular must be allowed significance.

The integrity of the person as the center of moral choice and judgment requires that we find room for the inescapably particular in personality. . . . The absolute norm

"Do no harm" expresses this centrality of the person on both ends of the relation: it gives special prominence to the physical person as the object (victim) of the relation, and it makes the person as agent both more responsible for what he does directly or intentionally and less responsible for what merely comes about as a side effect of his purposes. . . .

Direct Harm

It is a natural point of departure for any containment and highlighting of personal responsibility to give special prominence to that which we accomplish by touching, that which is accomplished by our physical bodies. Our ethical constructs attach a peculiar importance to that which is done directly, immediately, because it is through such actions that we first learn about our capacities and our efficacy. As we touch and produce results in the world by touching, we learn that we are able to produce results and that we as individuals are different from the results we produce. It is by touching that the notions of acting and efficacy develop in us. It is by touching that we learn that we are different from the world, that we become acquainted with our identity, and that we become acquainted with our capacity for causal efficacy. . . .

Physical harm inflicted directly, personally as it were . . . provides a paradigm for the kind of relation between persons which is the subject of the categorical prohibition. And, though the discussion has been concerned so far explicitly only with one side, the agent's side, of the relation encompassed by the norm "Do no harm," the argument is symmetric. The same factors, which identify the importance of the particular embodied person for the purpose of anchoring the causal chain of responsibility in the immediate and direct *production* of results, operate as well to bind the person of the victim with peculiar closeness to what he *suffers* in his physical person.

The Analogy to Benefit

. . . The distinction between benefit and harm arises in this way: If everyone who passed us by in a crowded street had a claim to our special *and positive* concern, a claim to be specially benefited, then little would be left over for those undoubted and strong cases—affection, kinship—in which a special claim to benefit seems justified. Nor would the problem be significantly less severe if we limited the strangers' claims to those strangers who asked for our help. The intrusion on our ability to limit and control the numbers and identities of those who have a privileged call on our help could be as bad in the latter case as in the former. . . . But these problems are not with us in respect to harm. *It is not the victim who chooses the agent, but the agent who chooses the victim.* The agent retains control of his circle of concern; it cannot engulf. In direct harm, the agent focuses on the victim, knowing that his actions will impinge directly on him. It is the agent who makes the victim an issue and who must therefore take account of his particularity.

Thus some choice, some special circumstance, must single out the face in the crowd to whom the agent will stand bound by the special bond—for if he stood specially bound by everyone he met, in the end there would be no special bond to anyone. In the case of benefit, something has to reach out to particularize the beneficiary of the relation other than the general fact—applicable across too indefinite a range—of a susceptibility to benefit. If a stranger can say to me, "You might have benefited me," I can always reply, "No more than countless other persons." In harm this problem does not exist. The conscious, volitional infliction of harm directly by my person upon the person of the victim *ipso facto* sufficiently particularizes the victim. I cannot in general and always say, "If I had not harmed you, I would have harmed someone else," for usually it is open to me to harm no one at all.

Now, I do insist that the direct impingement be conscious, a volitional gesture. If I harm you directly but inadvertently—through carelessness or even against my will, as when pushed—this may or may not create a relation such that I am to be blamed, must apologize or try to make it up to you, but I have not made a conscious decision to inflict harm on your person by my person. It is that decision which is the subject of the absolute norm "Do no harm.". . .

FROM DIRECTNESS TO INTENTION

. . . Direct harm deals with both too easy and too limited a range of cases. The complexities encountered in cases of more remote harming scarcely arise where the harm is direct. The effects we produce directly are generally the first steps in a planned chain of causality radiating out from our persons. The problems about unwanted reverberations, the "mere" side effects, begin further out, after the causal sequence has left the range of our immediate person. It is to those more classically troubling cases that I now turn.

The more remote cases are, of course, crucial. Man's technical progress from the spear to the radio-actuated Mars lander epitomizes the history of his attempt to extend his efficacy in precisely targeted projects beyond the range of his own body. So, just as the concept of directness gathers its moral force from its connection with the primitive fact of personal efficacy, the concept of intention corresponds to the equally human phenomenon of planned and contrived *distant* efficacy. Direct efficacy may be the first experience of efficacy, but as intelligence is essentially human, so the mastery of increasingly complex causal processes is of the essence of intelligent agency. The *person* may be invested at first in direct efficacy, but his *intelligence* is invested in his remote projects and his person invests his intelligence. Thus planned results are the natural extension of direct results, and intention of directness.

If you would grasp the fundamentality of intelligent purposive action, consider the difference between two states of affairs, both removed from the physical and temporal proximity of the person and both equally beneficial to his ultimate goals and situation. One comes about without any intervention on his part, though he well knows that processes lead to the result. The other he brings about: he considers what he wants, he takes stock of the resources at his command and of the laws by which events unfold, he charts the course and then acts, setting the whole thing in motion. In both cases there is the result and there is the desire, but in the second there is purposive action, plan, intention. The two cases are basically different courses of events. Initiating one is the intimate, personal fact of immediate action, direct efficacy. But that is not all. Intelligence, foresight, the channel dug for events by our minds in imagination, carries that first intimate thrust forward and invests the final results with the same personal attachment as was present at the outset.

This is not an argument, it is a picture, a picture of what it is to be a human being in the world of events. And it is according to this picture that we can see why means are different from concomitants. For means are part of our plans and thus are invested with our persons in a way that concomitants are not. The means we choose are the steps along a way we have mapped out in advance. Concomitants just happen; they belong to the domain of naturally occurring processes in which we might intervene if we choose. And of course we are sometimes responsible for what just happens, but really no more responsible for what happens as a concomitant of our plans than we are for what just happens because we choose not to act at all or to concern ourselves with other things. Directness is the kernel of personal investment from which we set out. From it, the world of events takes two courses: (1) the course of events in which we are, through plan and purpose, equally as invested as in the outset and (2) those sequences of events which radiate out from the starting point in the infinite concentric circles of mere causality. If we were responsible in the fullest measure for the second, then disintegrating universality would be upon us. If we were *not* responsible for the first, then the power of our reach would to that crucial extent be truncated. The special responsibility we bear for our projects is an appropriate recognition of our special involvement in those projects.

Thus the considerations explaining the absolute characters of the norm "Do no harm" in the case of *direct* harm must be generalized to the case of *intentional* harm. Direct harm describes a wrongful relation between two particular persons, just because it so intimately involves their particularity. Intended harm is wrong for closely analogous reasons. The harm, of course, on the victim's side of the relation is the same, but my account of the significance of intention shows why the agent's personal investment in his fellow's harm is just as great as if he produced it directly. It was the agent's very plan to bring about that harm; he formed a project in his mind and included the victim's harm in that project. Thus the intended injury is a result of personal agency, while in the case of a side effect or accident the injury is the product of natural causality (even if some human actions appear in the causal chain). Another person, who after all has the same capacity for reflection and the same concern to maintain his integrity, his person, as I do, has chosen to make my body, my person, a means to some end of his own.

None of this should be understood to excuse the evil of moral callousness, of disregard of the harm which our projects produce as a side effect, or of the harm which we might by some affirmative effect have avoided. I agree that our increased capacity to produce (or avoid) distant harm extends the range of our moral responsibility for all of those results. Starving populations in distant lands are our concern. Nothing I say here should be taken to deny this. I argue for a complex, not for a myopic sense of responsibility. The absolute norm forbids direct or intentional harm, but it does not excuse all other harms. The norm does not, however, forbid those harms absolutely.

(As I have argued, it could not coherently do so.) There are duties of concern and beneficence toward all human beings, but they are not absolute. They allow for weighing and calculation—inevitably—as the absolute norm does not. Often these are impersonal duties to abstract persons and so they can be fulfilled in abstract ways—through governments, institutions, and the like. As we see next, very little can override the absolute norm "Do no harm," but the duty to care for abstract humanity may be overcome in many ways. Finally, there can be no doubt that my argument for an absolute prohibition of direct or intentional harm must operate to some extent at the expense of the interest of all those others who do not come into this specially stringent circle of concern. For there must be instances where only by doing intentional harm could I ward off greater harm from perhaps many others. And still I must do no harm.

COMPLETING THE STRUCTURE: DEFENSE

There is an obvious objection to the proposal that "Do no harm" is an absolute norm: the categorical judgment cannot plausibly be asserted in the face of our tolerance of direct, intentional injuries inflicted in sports, medical treatment, punishment, and combat. Harm is inflicted directly, though not as a means or an end, when we push through a crowd on some urgent errand. It is inflicted in protecting property and warding off dangers. Any theory which would always condemn such actions is obviously extreme and unacceptable.

Consent, authorization, defense of legitimate interest must be accommodated somehow in our moral deliberations. Now we might assign some weight to the negative term, here the physical injury, and recognize these justifications as positive terms to be weighed and balanced off against the negative term. But this is precisely what I have said must not be done. If consent and self-defense were to enter the arguments simply as counterweights, then they would enter the argument in exactly the same way that good purposes enter the argument when the harm is produced unintentionally or when the harm is just something we have failed to avoid. And that would destroy the distinctiveness of the thesis regarding the categorical norm. Thus consent, duress, self-defense do not just constitute excuses and justifications (which is the traditional and familiar point about them) but they must exist in a peculiarly close theoretical relationship with the very wrong they serve to qualify. Whatever theoretical explanation can be offered for giving the norm categorical status must itself provide the basis for the particular qualifications of that norm. These generalities are well illustrated by the example of defense as a justification for intentional harm. The system of justification, it will be seen, not only makes more plausible but fills out the substantive concept of harm as a paradigm of a forbidden relation.

Defense of the Person

Physical harm is permissible if it is intended as a means of defense against a proportional physical harm. Thus the absolute norm is qualified even further than by its limitation to intentional or direct harm, for here is a case of permissible *intentional* harm. . . .

The defender does indeed intend to kill; the death of the aggressor is the means to the defense, even though (as is often the case with intentional harm) the defender may prefer to have some less drastic means available to him. . . . What is wrong about intentionally harming is the relation it asserts between agent and victim. The agent is using his victim's *person* as a means to an end, and this is what constitutes the offense against respect, the offense against the person of the victim. The agent's principle of action, though it need not deny the human bond in general, would exclude the victim from it. And here is the special offense. But in the case of self-defense, the defender asserts no moral priority over his attacker, for the defender's intention is sufficiently justified by an assertion that his (the defender's) person, while of no greater moral significance than the attacker's, is of no *less* consequence either. The reciprocity of interests and the similarity between the actor-defender and the victim-aggressor are crucial. Self-defense describes a form of relation whose structure we may affirm.

All this is straightforward and familiar. The inquiry into self-defense is intended primarily to illustrate a method and to give content to some very general ideas. Now let us take the argument for self-defense further by considering intentional harm to protect against values other than physical integrity or to defend against an aggressor who is acting on a mistaken or insane belief that his conduct is justified, or indeed an aggressor who is not acting intentionally at all.

Defense of Other Values

I own some valuable object which another tries to take from me. What may I do to protect my interests? American law provides in general that I may use whatever force short of deadly force is reasonably necessary to protect my property against immediate loss. Or I am walking on the sidewalk and a bully insists I walk in the street to humiliate me. May I insist on my right if I know this may provoke perhaps a deadly attack, and may I then use deadly force in my defense? The answers to these questions will depend to a great extent on the general social context. It is not surprising that in some times and places even deadly force has been authorized to protect property. On the other hand, a person threatened with deadly force anywhere but in his home is usually required to retreat if he safely can before using deadly force, but no common-law jurisdiction deprives a man of the right to defend himself—if need be with deadly force—on the ground that he might have avoided the occasion of the attack in the first place by acceding to a threat or yielding some right. Now I am not primarily concerned with law but with morals, and the law is significant as it illuminates these moral questions. . . .

Consider a schematized version of the encounter: The defender warns that he will inflict bodily injury if necessary to protect his property; and only after this warning is defied does the defender inflict injury. I assume further that the aggression is against a substantial value and that the aggression is wrong and known to be wrong. The defender's action differs from wrongful infliction of harm not because there is a substantive value (the property) to be balanced against the injury he inflicts, for that fact is usually present and I have argued that it is insufficient, but because the "aggressor-victim" himself intends a violation of the agent's rights. It is the threatened violation of the defender's rights which is crucial. Since I have made no point of the concept of rights so far . . . suffice it to say now that we are assuming that the invasion of the actor's property interest would be a wrong toward him in the same sense (though not necessarily to the same degree) as would the earlier paradigm case of intentional physical harm. And thus an agent who inflicts injury on a robber does not affirm a principle asserting moral superiority to the robber any more than he does when he defends his person. Nor does he assert that the robber's person is available to him for his ends—only that his (the defender's) rights are not available for the robber's ends.

Though this may seem obvious, how would we answer the doubter who insists that in this case too one intentionally uses the injury of another to further (protect) some end of one's own? The robber would use the actor here by violating his rights, would subject his victim to this unjust use. The defender, by resisting, intends to inflict injury to be sure, but all this may also be correctly characterized by saying that he intends to protect his rights. Thus, far from asserting a moral superiority to the robber, far from implying a degrading relation to him, the actor intends to prevent just such a degrading relation from coming about. This intention of the defender to prevent wrong may not do the whole job, but at least the shoe is on the other foot: the actor's intention is capable of a statement which seems consistent with the arguments used to account for the norm "do no harm." . . .

But we do on occasion feel justified in preventing someone from choosing to suffer death or maiming for some trivial end—even if the attainment of that end injures no one. Should we not hesitate as well to allow this extension of the notion of consent to justify grave harm inflicted by a victim defending against a trivial transgression? . . . We assume from the outset that whatever harm is inflicted is necessary to defend the imperiled value. But if society by police and courts can assure that the threatened property will eventually be restored, then recourse to force is no longer necessary. And of course the extent to which a society is willing and able to give such assurances will vary.

Ideals

R. M. Hare

Consider the question, discussed on the wireless recently, of whether it is wrong for a pretty girl to earn good money by undressing herself at a 'strip club' for the pleasure of an audience of middle-aged business-men. If this is not a moral question in an accepted sense of the word, it is hard to say what would be. The enlightened may not think it an important one; but there is no doubt that many people think it very important. Yet those who call such exhibitions immoral do not do so because of their effect on other people's interests; for, since everybody gets what he or she wants, nobody's interests are harmed. They are likely, rather, to use such words as 'degrading'. This gives us a clue to the sort of moral question with which we are dealing. It is a question not of interests but of *ideals*. Such conduct offends against an ideal of human excellence held by many people; that is why they condemn it. Even if their condemnation is put in the terminology of 'interests', this is only because, like Plato, they think that to make somebody a worse man is to do him the greatest possible harm. But this Platonic way of speaking should not conceal from us the difference between two distinct grounds on which we can commend or condemn actions, one of which is connected with the interests of other people, and the other with ideals of human excellence. One reason why it is wrong to confine the term 'moral question' by a terminological fiat to questions concerning the effect of our actions upon other people's interests, is that such a restriction would truncate moral philosophy by preventing it saying anything about ideals.

It is not difficult to find other examples. Suppose that somebody is trying to decide whether to make his career that of a stockbroker or an army officer. It may be that he thinks that, by and large, it will not make a predictable difference to other people's interests which he chooses. If he becomes a stockbroker, he will make money for some people, deprive other people indirectly of the same amount of money, and promote the existence of an active market in stocks and shares, which, it is said, is of service to the industrial and commercial well-being of the community. If he becomes a soldier, he will kill a lot of people, protect a lot of others, and perhaps, if his government's policy is a wise one, contribute in some small measure to the stability of international relations. In both cases there is direct gain to the man's clients or countrymen, and the direct and indirect gains and losses to other people make up, with this, a rough balance, so far as prediction is possible at all. But these somewhat imponderable factors may not be what weigh most with him when he is trying to decide which life it would be best to choose. He may be moved more by the thought (perhaps an unjust one) that stockbroking is a sedentary and sordid occupation, and the military life an active one, requiring courage and self-sacrifice. If on these grounds he chooses to enter an army career, are we to say that he has been swayed by *moral* considerations?

This . . . may be merely a terminological question. But if we say that the grounds are not moral, we shall be at a loss for a word to describe the kind of ideals which led him to this choice of career. And this might make us think that we do need the word 'moral' in this application. . . . Once we get away from the terminological problem, the facts begin to look clearer; there are at least two kinds of grounds on which a man might say that the best thing to do would be so and so; one of these is concerned with interests, and the other with ideals. These sorts of grounds must be kept distinct from each other, even if later they turn out to be related in some way; but 'moral' may, all the same, be the word used in our common speech for both of them.

In order to avoid confusion, let us call one of these kinds of ground 'utilitarian' and the other 'idealist'. A utilitarian might argue that there is a logical (and not merely an historical) connexion between the two, because moral ideals are always framed, and have to be framed, to encourage the development of qualities which will conduce to the furthering of people's interests, or those of society in general. But this is too sweeping a claim. Just as, at Cruft's, dogs called retrievers are given prizes for qualities which are unrelated to their performance as gun-dogs, so many people have ideals of human excellence whose utilitarian basis is vestigial. It would be a hazardous claim, at any rate in modern society, that the moral quality of so-called 'physical' courage is on the whole conducive to human well-being; yet we both admire this quality and encourage the young to cultivate it. This may be only because at one time it was vital to the preservation of society that the majority, at any rate, of its male citizens should possess this virtue; and perhaps, if this is no longer the case in the present state of military science, we may come to abandon this ideal, or to give it less weight. But this is irrelevant to the present argument. It may indeed be that there is a strong tendency for our ideals to be framed in accordance with the utilitarian needs of society in past generations; but nevertheless the ideals are logically independent of the needs, and can survive their disappearance. We must not commit a mistake similar to that which would be committed by an anthropologist who said that the Hindus wash five times a day for purely hygienic reasons; they wash as a religious duty, and though the custom may have grown originally out of vague ideas of hygiene, it would survive the proof that more disease is spread than prevented by it.

Moral ideals have a very close resemblance, in some ways, to aesthetic ideals; they are logically more like them than either are like those grounds for moral judgements which I have called utilitarian. Consider yet another example of a choice between moral ideals in which golden-rule arguments are out of place. The leader of a Himalayan expedition has the choice of either leading the final assault on the mountain himself, or staying behind at the last camp and giving another member of his party the opportunity. Here it is obvious that different ideals will conflict; yet it is easy to suppose that no argument concerned with the interests of the parties will settle the question—for the interests may be very precisely balanced. The questions that arise are likely to be concerned, not with the interests of the parties, but with ideals of what a man should *be*. Is it better to be the sort of man who, in face of great obstacles and dangers, gets to the top of the *n*th highest mountain in the world; or the sort of man who uses his position of authority to give a friend this opportunity instead of claiming it for himself? These questions are very like aesthetic ones. It is as if a man were regarding his own life and character as a work of art, and asking how it should best be completed.

It may be asked whether, if golden-rule arguments are out of place here, there are any other arguments which can be brought to bear on such questions. Now this might depend on what we are prepared to count as an argument; but nevertheless it is not a merely terminological question. There certainly are arguments that would be cogent in such a case, if the parties already accepted some ideal of human excellence; facts could then be adduced to show that such and such a line of conduct would or would not be in accord with the ideal. . . . There are also arguments which attempt to show the inconsistency of two moral opinions, both of which a man claims to hold. Such arguments may make use of the requirement of universalizability; if we find a man making judgements about himself which are quite different from those which he makes about others in similar situations, we can compel him logically either to abandon one set of judgements or the other, or to show differences between the situations. Further, we can seek to show inconsistencies, not between two sets of moral judgements, but between moral judgements and other prescriptions to which he assents. If, for example, as a result of accepting certain singular prescriptions (the expression of his desires), he habitually acts in a way that conflicts with his professed ideals, there comes a point at which his advocacy of his ideals altogether loses force.

Nevertheless, it is impossible, and moral philosophers ought not to try, to find methods of argument which will settle, determinately, disputes between upholders of different ideals in all cases. Suppose, for example, that one man has the ideals of an ascetic and another those of a *bon vivant*. Is it at all likely that moral arguments between them will be such as to compel one of them to adopt the other's point of view—assuming that neither is, by pursuing his own ideal, affecting one way or another the interests of other parties? The moral philosopher who thinks that he is failing his public if he does not provide a logic for settling such questions, would do well to ask almost any member of the public whether he *expects* them ever to be settled. . . .

The conclusion, then, of our discussion of ideals seems to be this. Where interests are not concerned, conflicts between ideals are not susceptible to very much in the way of argument; on the other hand, conflicts between interests, if ideals are not involved, admit of reconciliation by means of the forms of argument which the logic of the moral words generates. The large question remains of what happens when interests conflict with ideals. . . .

Social Morality and Individual Ideal

P. F. Strawson

Men make for themselves pictures of ideal forms of life. Such pictures are various and may be in sharp opposition to each other; and one and the same individual may be captivated by different and sharply conflicting pictures at different times. At one time it may seem to him that he should live—even that *a man* should live—in such-and-such a way; at another that the only truly satisfactory form of life is something totally different, incompatible with the first. In this way, his outlook may vary radically, not only at different periods of his life, but from day to day, even from one hour to the next. It is a function of so many variables: age, experiences, present environment, current reading, current physical state are some of them. As for the ways of life that may thus present themselves at different times as each uniquely satisfactory, there can be no doubt about their variety and opposition. The ideas of self-obliterating devotion to duty or to the service of others; of personal honour and magnanimity; of asceticism,

"Social Morality and Individual Ideal," in *Philosophy* by P. F. Strawson, vol. 36, no. 136, 1961. Reprinted by permission of Cambridge University Press.

contemplation, retreat; of action, dominance and power; of the cultivation of "an exquisite sense of the luxurious"; of simple human solidarity and co-operative endeavour; of a refined complexity of social existence; of a constantly maintained and renewed affinity with natural things—any of these ideas, and a great many others too, may form the core and substance of a personal ideal. At some times such a picture may present itself as merely appealing or attractive; at others it may offer itself in a stronger light, as, perhaps, an image of the only sane or non-ignoble human reaction to the situation in which we find ourselves. "The nobleness of life is to do thus" or, sometimes, "The sanity of life is to do thus": such may be the devices with which these images present themselves. . . .

I think there can be no doubt that what I have been talking about falls within the region of the ethical. I have been talking about evaluations such as *can* govern choices and decisions which are of the greatest importance to men. Whether it falls within the region of the moral, however, is something that may be doubted. Perhaps the region of the moral falls within it. Or perhaps there are no such simple inclusion-relations between them. The question is one I shall come back to later. I should like first to say something more about this region of the ethical. It could also be characterized as a region in which there are truths which are incompatible with each other. There exist, that is to say, many profound general statements which are capable of capturing the ethical imagination in the same way as it may be captured by those ideal images of which I spoke. They often take the form of general descriptive statements about man and the world. They can be incorporated into a metaphysical system, or dramatized in a religious or historical myth. . . . I will not give examples, but I will mention names. One cannot read Pascal or Flaubert, Nietzsche or Goethe, Shakespeare or Tolstoy, without encountering these profound truths. It is certainly possible, in a coolly analytical frame of mind, to mock at the whole notion of the profound truth; but we are guilty of mildly bad faith if we do. For in most of us the ethical imagination succumbs again and again to *these* pictures of man, and it is precisely as truths that we wish to characterize them while they hold us captive. But these truths have the same kind of relation to each other as those ideal images of which I have already spoken. For pictures of the one kind reflect and are reflected by pictures of the other. They capture our imagination in the same way. Hence it is as wholly futile to think that we could, without destroying their character, systematize these truths into one coherent body of truth as it is to suppose that we could, without destroying their character, form a coherent composite image from these images. . . .

Now what are the relations between the region of the ethical and the sphere of morality? One widely accepted account of the latter is in terms of the idea of rules or principles governing human behaviour which apply universally within a community or class. The class may be variously thought of as a definite social group or the human species as a whole or even the entire class of rational beings. It is not obvious how these contrasting conceptions, of diversity of ideal and of community of rule, are related to each other; and in fact, I think, the relationship is complicated. One way of trying to harmonize the ideas would be as follows. This way is extremely crude and inadequate, but it may serve as a starting point. It is obvious that many, if not all, of the ideal images of which I spoke demand for their realization the existence of some form of social organization. The demand is in varying degrees logical or empirical. Some ideals only make sense in a complex social context, and even in a particular kind of complex social context. For others, some complexity of social organization seems, rather, a practically necessary condition of the ideal's being realized in any very full or satisfactory way. Now it is a condition of the existence of any form of social organization, of any human community, that certain expectations of behaviour on the part of its members should be pretty regularly fulfilled: that some duties, one might say, should be performed, some obligations acknowledged, some rules observed. We might begin by locating the sphere of morality here. It is the sphere of the observance of rules, such that the existence of some such set of rules is a condition of the existence of a society. This is a minimal interpretation of morality. It represents it as what might literally be called a kind of public convenience: of the first importance as a condition of everything that matters, but only as a condition of everything that matters, not as something that matters in itself.

I am disposed to see considerable merit in this minimal conception of morality. By this I mean not that it is really, or nearly, an adequate conception—only that it is a useful analytical idea . . .

Let me set out some of its merits. First we must be clearer about what this minimal interpretation is. The fundamental idea is that of a socially sanctioned demand made on an individual in virtue merely of his membership of the society in question, or in virtue of a particular position which he occupies within it or a particular relation in which he stands to other members of it. I spoke of rules in this connection; and the rules I meant would simply be the generalized statements of demands of this type. The formula I employ for the fundamental idea is deliberately flexible, the notions of a society and of social sanctioning deliberately vague. This flexibility is necessary to do justice to the complexities of social organization and social relationships. For instance, we can regard ourselves as members of many different social groups or communities, some of which fall within others; or again, when I speak of the social sanctioning of a demand which is made on an individual member of a group in virtue of his position in the group, we may think of the social sanction of that demand sometimes as arising only within the limited group in question, sometimes as arising also within a wider group which includes that limited group. A position in a society may or may not also be, so to speak, a position in society. Thus a position in a family generally gives rise to certain demands upon the holder of that position which are recognized both within the family and within some wider group or groups within which the family falls. The same may be true of membership of a profession or even of a professional association. On the other hand, some of the demands of certain class or caste moralities receive little or no extraneous reinforcement from the wider social groupings to which the members of the limited class also belong. Or again what one might call the internal morality of an intimate personal relationship may be as private as the relationship itself. One of the merits I should claim for this approach to morality is precisely that it so easily makes room for many concepts which we habitually employ, but which tend to be neglected in moral philosophy. Thus we talk of medical ethics, of the code of honour of a military caste, of bourgeois morality and of working-class morality. Such ideas fit more easily into an account of morality which sees it as essentially, or at any rate fundamentally, a function of social groupings than they do into the more apparently individualistic approaches which are generally current.

Another merit which I shall claim for the present approach is that it makes it relatively easy to understand such notions as those of conscientiousness, duty and obligation in a concrete and realistic way. These notions have been treated almost entirely abstractly in moral philosophy in the recent past, with the result that they have come to some of our contemporaries[1] to seem to be meaningless survivals of discarded ideas about the government of the universe. But as most ordinarily employed I do not think they are that at all. There is nothing in the least mysterious or metaphysical in the fact that duties and obligations go with offices, positions and relationships to others. The demands to be made on somebody in virtue of his occupation of a certain position may indeed be, and often are, quite explicitly listed in considerable detail. And when we call someone conscientious or say that he has a strong sense of his obligations or of duty, we do not ordinarily mean that he is haunted by the ghost of the idea of supernatural ordinances; we mean rather such things as this, that he can be counted on for sustained effort to do what is required of him in definite capacities, to fulfil the demand made on him as student or teacher or parent or soldier or whatever he may be. A certain professor once said: "For me to be moral is to behave like a professor". . . .

But now it is time to return to the question of the relation between social moralities and those ideal pictures of forms of life which I spoke of at the outset. . . . The possibilities of collision, absorption and interplay are many. The way I have just expressed the matter perhaps makes most obvious the possibility of collision; and this possibility is worth stressing. It is worth stressing that what one acknowledges or half-acknowledges as obligation may conflict not only, crudely, with interest and, weakly, with inclination but also with ideal aspiration, with the vision that captures the ethical imagination. On the other hand, it may be that a picture of the ideal life is precisely one in which the interests of morality are dominant, are given an ideal, overriding value. To one dominated temporarily or permanently by such a picture the "consciousness of duty faithfully performed" will appear as the supremely satisfactory state, and being moral not merely as something that matters but as the thing that supremely matters. Or again the ideal picture may be, not that in which the interests of morality in general are dominant, but rather one in which the dominating idea operates powerfully to reinforce some, but not perhaps others, of a system of moral demands. So it is with that ideal picture in which obedience to the command to love one another appears as the supreme value.

This is still to draw too simple a picture. Let us remember the diversity of communities to which we may be said to belong, and the diversity of systems of moral demand which belong to them. To a certain extent, though to an extent which we must not exaggerate, the systems of moral relationships into which we enter are a matter of choice—or at least a matter in which there are alternative possibilities; and different systems of moral demand are variously well or ill adapted to different ideal

[1]Cf. G. E. M. Anscombe, "Modern Moral Philosophy," *Philosophy,* January 1958.

pictures of life. The ideal picture, moreover, may call for membership not merely of communities in which certain interests are safeguarded by a system of moral demands, but for membership of a community or of a system of relationships in which the system of demands reflects in a positive way the nature of the ideal. For one crude instance of this, we may think again of the morality of a military caste in connection with the ideal of personal honour. In general, in a society as complex as ours, it is obvious that there are different moral environments, different sub-communities within the community, different systems of moral relationships, interlocking indeed and over- lapping with one another, but offering some possibilities of choice, some possibilities of adjustment of moral demand and individual aspiration. But here again, at least in our time and place, it is the limits of the direct relevance of each to the other that must finally be stressed. Inside a single political human society one may indeed find different, and perhaps widely different, moral environments, social groupings in which different systems of moral demand are recognized. But if the one grouping is to form part of the wider society, its members must be subject too to a wider system of reciprocal demand, a wider common morality; and the relative significance of the wider common morality will grow in proportion as the sub-groups of the society are closely interlocked, in proportion as each individual is a member of a plurality of subgroups and in proportion as the society is not rigidly stratified, but allows of relatively free access to, and withdrawal from, its subgroups. In a political society which thus combines a wide variety of social groupings with complex interlocking and freedom of movement between them the dissociation of idiosyncratic ideal and common moral demand will doubtless tend to be at its maximum. On the other hand an ideal picture of man *may* tend, in fact or in fancy, to demand the status of a comprehensive common morality. Thus Coleridgean or Tolstoyan dreamers may play with the thought of self-enclosed ideal communities in which the system of moral demands shall answer exactly, or as exactly as possible, to an ideal picture of life held in common by all their members. Such fancies are bound to strike many as weak and futile; for the price of preserving the purity of such communities is that of severance from the world at large. More seriously, there may be some attempt to make the whole moral climate of an existing national state reflect some ideal image of human solidarity or religious devotion or military honour. In view of the natural diversity of human ideals—to mention only that—such a state (or its members) will evidently be subject to at least some stresses from which a liberal society is free.

To conclude. I have spoken of those ideal images of life of which one individual may sympathize with many, and desire to see many realized in some degree. I have spoken also of those systems—though the word is too strong—of recognized reciprocal claim that we have on one another as members of human communities, or as terms of human relationships, many of which could scarcely exist or have the character they have but for the existence of such systems of reciprocal claim. I have said something, though too little, of the complex and various relations which may hold between these two things, viz. our conflicting visions of the ends of life and the systems of moral demand which make social living possible. Finally I have glanced at the relations of both to the political societies in which we necessarily live. The field of phenomena over which I have thus loosely ranged is, I think, very much more complex and many- sided than I have been able to suggest; but I have been concerned to suggest something of its complexity. Some implications for moral philosophy I have hinted at in passing, mainly by way of an attempt to correct some typical exaggerations of contemporary theory. But the main practical implications for moral and political philosophy are, I think, that more attention should be concentrated on types of social structure and social relation, and on those complex interrelationships which I have mentioned as well as others which I have not. For instance, it is hard not to believe that understanding of our secular morality would be enhanced by considering the historical role that religion has played in relation to morality. Or again, I doubt if the nature of morality can be properly understood without some consideration of its relationship to law. It is not merely that the spheres of morality and law are largely overlapping, or that their demands often coincide. It is also that in the way law functions to give cohesiveness to the most important of all social groupings we may find a coarse model of the way in which systems of moral demand function to give cohesiveness to social groupings in general. Similarly, in the complexity of our attitudes towards existing law we may find a model of the complexity of our attitude towards the systems of moral demand which impinge upon us in our social relations at large—or upon others, in theirs.

Finally, I do not think there is any very definite invitation to moral or political commitment implicit in what I have said. But perhaps one question can be raised, and in part answered. What will be the attitude of one who experiences sympathy with a variety of conflicting ideals of life? It seems that he will be most at home in a liberal society, in a society in which there are variant moral environments but in which no ideal endeavours to engross, and determine the character of, the common morality. He will not argue in favour of such a society that it gives the best chance for the truth about life to prevail, for he will not consistently believe that there is such a thing as the truth about life. Nor will he argue in its favour that it has the best chance of producing a harmonious kingdom of ends, for he will not think of ends as necessarily capable of being harmonized. He will simply welcome the ethical diversity which the society makes possible, and in proportion as he values that diversity he will note that he is the natural, though perhaps the sympathetic, enemy of all those whose single intense vision of the ends of life drives them to try to make the requirements of the ideal co-extensive with those of common social morality.

Minimalist Ethics

Daniel Callahan

The attraction of morality in times of affluence is that not much of it seems needed. More choices are available and thus fewer harsh dilemmas arise. If they arise, money can be used to buy out of or evade the consequences of choice. The wages of sin are offset by the cheapness of therapy, drugs, liquor, economy flights, and a career change.

If all else fails, public confessions can profitably be produced as a miniseries. Vice is rewarded because everything is rewarded, even virtue.

Matters are otherwise in hard times. Options are fewer, choices nastier. Where forgiveness and therapeutic labels could once be afforded, blaming and denunciation become more congenial. If life is going poorly, someone obviously must be at fault, if not the government, then my neighbor, wife, or child. The warm, expansive self, indulgent of the foibles of others, gives way to the harsh, competitive self; enemies abound, foreign and domestic. It is not so much that the "least well-off" cease to count (though they do), but that all imagine they are now in that category. Nastiness becomes the standard of civility, exposé the goal of journalism, a lawsuit the way friends, families, and colleagues reconcile their differences. . . .

What, then, is the problem to be diagnosed? Here is the question I want to ask, and attempt to address: As we move into what will most likely be chronically hard economic times, how can our society muster the moral resources necessary to endure as a viable human culture? Three assumptions underlie that question. The first is that economic strength and military power have no necessary ethical connection with the internal human and moral viability of a culture; they can only help assure its mere existence. The second is that the era of sustained economic growth is over, and with it the perennially optimistic psychology of affluence. The prospects are for at best a steady-state economy, one where the next generation can only hope that it will do as well as the previous generation; only that, and no more, and probably less.

My third assumption is that the kind of morality that was able to flourish during times of affluence will, if carried over unchanged into hard times, lead to moral chaos and maybe worse. What has been that morality? It has been one that stressed the transcendence of the individual over the community, the need to tolerate all moral viewpoints, the autonomy of the self as the highest human good, and the voluntary, informed consent contract as the model of human relationships. . . .

Now all of that autonomy is doubtless fine, and lofty, and lovely. But to live that kind of life, you need to have money at hand, good health, and a clinic full of psychological counselors at the ready. It is a good-time philosophy for comfortable people living in the most powerful, rich nation on earth. Will it work in hard times? Some doubt is in order.

Hard times require self-sacrifice and altruism—but there is nothing in an ethic of moral autonomy to sustain or nourish those values. Hard times necessitate a sense of community and the common good—but the putative virtues of autonomy are primarily directed toward the cultivation of independent selfhood. Hard times demand restraint in the blaming of others for misfortune—but one outcome of moral autonomy as an ideal is to make more people blameworthy for the harms they supposedly do others. Hard times need a broad sense of duty toward others, especially those out of sight— but an ethic of autonomy stresses responsibility only for one's freely chosen, consenting-adult relationships. . . .

I want to define one set of moral values that emerged during our recent decades of affluence, and try to show how peculiarly ill suited they are, and even dangerous, for the hard times ahead. For lack of a more graceful term, I will call those values a "minimalist ethic." I have already hinted at some of the features of that ethic, but will now try to be more specific. That ethic can be stated in a simple proposition: *one may morally act in any way one chooses so far as one does not do harm to others.* . . .

I call this a "minimalist ethic" because, put crudely, it seems to be saying that the sole test of the morality of an action, or of a whole way of life, is whether it avoids harm to others. If that minimal standard can be met, then there is no further basis for judging personal or communal moral goods and goals, for praising or blaming others, or for educating others about higher moral obligations to self or community. In the language of our day: the only judgment we are permitted on the way others make use of their moral autonomy is to assess whether they are doing harm to others. If we can discern no such harm, then we must suspend any further judgment. Should we fail to suspend that judgment, we are then guilty of a positive violation of their right to privacy and self-determination.

The pervasiveness of this ethic has had a number of consequences:

1 A minimalist ethic has tended to confuse useful principles for government regulation and civil liberties with the broader requirements of the moral life, both individual and communal.

2 It has misled many in our society into thinking that a sharp distinction can be drawn between the public and the private sphere, and that different standards of morality apply to each.

3 It has given us a thin and shriveled notion of personal and public morality. We are obliged under the most generous reading of a minimalist ethic only to honor our voluntarily undertaken family obligations, to keep our promises, and to respect contracts freely entered into with other freely consenting adults. Beyond those minimal standards, we are free to do as we like, guided by nothing other than our private standards of good and evil. Altruism, beneficence, and self-sacrifice beyond that tight circle are in no sense moral obligations and, in any case, cannot be universally required. My neighbor can and will remain a moral stranger unless and until, as an exercise of my autonomy, I choose to enter into a contract with him; and I am bound to no more toward him than the letter of that contract. Although I ought to treat my neighbor with justice, that is because I may otherwise do harm to him, or owe it to him as a way of discharging the debt of former injustices, or because it seems a rational idea to develop a social contract with others as a way of enhancing my own possibilities for greater liberty and the gaining of some primary goods.

4 A minimalist ethic has deprived us of meaningful language to talk about our life together outside of our contractual relationships. The only language that does seem common is that of "the public interest," a concept that for most translates into the aggregate total of individual desires and demands. The language of "rights" is common enough (though not of putatively archaic "natural" or "God-given" rights). But it is to be understood that the political and moral purpose of both negative and positive rights is to protect and advance individual autonomy. It is not the kind of language that can comfortably be used any longer to talk about communal life, shared values, and the common good.

5 A minimalist ethic has made the ancient enterprise of trying to determine the inherent or intrinsic good of human beings a suspect, probably subversive activity. It assumes no one can answer such lofty and vague questions, that attempts to try probably

pose a threat to liberty, and that, in any event, any purported answers should be left resolutely private.

6 Unless I can show in a demonstrable way that the behavior of others poses some direct public harm, I am not allowed to question that behavior, much less to pass a public negative judgment on it. The culture of a minimalist ethic is one of rigid and rigorous toleration. Who am I to judge what is good for others? One is—maybe—entitled to personal moral opinions about the self-regarding conduct of others. But a public expression of those opinions would contribute to an atmosphere of moral suppression in the civil order, and of an anti-autonomous moral repression in the private psychological order. One question is taken to be the definitive response to anyone who should be so un-civil as to talk about ethics *tout simpliciter:* "But whose ethics?"

In some quarters, a minimalist ethic has gone a step further, to a de-listing of many behavioral choices as moral problems at all. Thus abortion becomes a "religious" rather than a moral issue, and it is well-known that all religious issues are private, arational, and idiosyncratic; questions of sex, and most recently homosexuality, become matters of "alternative lifestyles" or "sexual preference"; and the use of pleasure-enhancing drugs becomes an amusing choice between two valued-soaked (and thus subjective) norms, "psychotropic hedonism" or "pharmacological calvinism."[1]

7 Under the terms of a "minimalist ethic" only a few moral problems are worth bothering with at all. The issue of liberty versus justice is one of them, and that of autonomy versus paternalism is another. The former is important because distributive justice is required to finally enthrone a community of fully autonomous individuals. The latter is vital because it is well recognized that paternalism, even the beneficently motivated and kindly sort, poses the most direct threat to individual liberty. A lack of informed consent, decisions taken by experts, and a failure to observe due process will be high on the list of evils of a minimalist ethic. Anything less than a full egalitarianism—equal decisions made by equally autonomous moral agents—is seen as an eschatological failure.

I have drawn here an exaggerated picture of a minimalist ethic. It fits the views of no one person precisely and, to be sure, cannot be taken to represent any single, coherent, well-developed ethical theory. Not all those who favor a perfect egalitarianism would equally favor (or favor at all) a moral de-listing of matters of sex and drugs. There is no necessary incompatibility between favoring a civil-libertarian political ethic and holding a view of the community that affirms the value of close community ties, of seeking transcendent values, and of recognizing duties over and above those of self-realization. Permutations of and exceptions to this general portrait are then easy enough to find. Nonetheless, I believe it sufficiently accurate as a composite portrait of a mainstream set of values in American culture to take seriously, and to reject. A society heavily composed of those who aspire to, or unwittingly accept, a minimalist ethic cannot be a valid human community. In times of stress, it could turn into a very nasty community.

I suggest . . . that a minimalist ethic sounds very much like a close relative of John

---

[1]Gerald L. Klerman, "Psychotropic Hedonism vs. Pharmacological Calvinism," *Hastings Center Report,* September 1972, pp. 1–3.

Stuart Mill's position in "On Liberty" (1859), but also that it represents a pressing of that position beyond the limits he intended. . . . Recall Mill's famous principle and point of departure in "On Liberty":

> the sole end for which mankind are warranted, individually or collectively, in interfering with the liberty of action of any of their number, is self-protection. That the only purpose for which power can be rightfully exercised over any member of a civilized community, against his will, is to prevent harm to others.[2]

Mill goes on to reiterate and embellish that principle in a variety of ways, stressing not only that society ought to be solely concerned with individual conduct that "concerns others," but also that "over himself, over his own body and mind, the individual is sovereign."[3]

Nor is it sufficient that the individual be protected "against the tyranny of the magistrate." Protection is also needed

> against the tyranny of the prevailing opinion and feeling; against the tendency of society to impose, by other means than civil penalties, its own ideas and practices or rules of conduct on those who dissent from them.[4] . . .

With an even more contemporary flavor, Mill wrote that:

> the principle requires liberty of tastes and pursuits; of framing the plan of our life to suite our own character; of doing as we like, subject to such consequences as may follow: without impediment from our fellow creatures, as long as what we do does not harm them, even though they should think our conduct foolish, perverse, or wrong.[5] . . .

Mill is by no means unaware of the possibility that the kind of liberty he seeks can lead to some undesirable outcomes:

> I fully admit that the mischief which a person does to himself may seriously affect, both through their sympathies and their interests, those nearly connected with him and, in a minor degree, society at large.[6] . . .

In another place, he writes that "mankind are greater gainers by suffering each other to live as seems good to themselves, than by compelling each to live as seems good to the rest."[7]

That is too confident a utilitarian conclusion. . . . Whatever its other failings, Mill lived in a time and a culture that could take many if not most western moral values for granted. He did not have to specify or defend the standards by which his countrymen should judge the self-regarding behavior of others, or the moral principles to be inculcated in children, or the norms on which the moral exhortations he countenanced were based.

---

[2]John Stuart Mill, "On Liberty," in *John Stuart Mill: Selected Writings,* ed. Mary Warnock (New York: Meridian Books, 1962), p. 135.

[3]Ibid.

[4]Ibid., p. 130.

[5]Ibid., p. 138.

[6]Ibid., p. 212.

[7]Ibid., p. 138.

Increasingly, no such background—tacitly held and almost superfluous to state—can be assumed. Precisely because that is so, and because a minimalist ethic has been one outcome of the train of thought that Mill helped set in motion, we are now forced to reexamine the relationship between public and private morality. Can they, in the first place, be sharply distinguished as Mill thought possible?

The evidence provided by the emergence of a minimalist ethic is hardly encouraging. It would have us not only obsessively make such a distinction; it would also have us go a step further and eschew moral judgment on the private lives of others as well. In response, I want to argue three points. The first is that the distinction between the private and the public is a cultural artifact only, varying with time and place. The second is that only a thoroughly dulled (or self-interested) imagination could even pretend to think that there can be private acts with no public consequences. The third point is that the effort to sharply distinguish the two spheres can do harm to our general moral life. . . .

Our more recent historical experience indicates that the distinction between the public and the private is at the least a cultural artifact and quite possibly a matter of the sheerest ideology. I earlier pointed to a "de-listing" phenomenon in our society—the attempt to remove whole spheres of behavior from moral scrutiny and judgment. That point needs a complementary one: a number of activities once thought to be private only in their moral significance are now judged to be of public importance. The common moral wisdom at present tells us, for example—in a way it did not tell Mill's generation—that we have among other things: no right to pollute the water and the air; to knowingly procreate defective children or even to have too many healthy children; to utter private slurs against females, ethnic, or racial groups, or to ignore the private domestic life of public officials. Family planning was, in the days of Margaret Sanger, an entirely public and proscribed matter. Then, with the triumph of the family-planning movement, it became an issue of wholly private morality. And then, with the perception of a world population explosion, it became once again a public matter. The frequenting of prostitutes was once legal in many places, and thought to be a concern of private morality only. Not many feminists, aware of the degradation of women that has been a part of prostitution, are likely to be impressed with a private-morality-consenting-adult rationale any longer. They are hardly keen on pornography either, and for the same kind of reason.

If it is so hard in the end to separate the private and the public, why does the idea continue to persist? One reason is that, on occasion, it can serve to buttress our personal predilections or ideologies. I know that I cannot make a good moral case to myself about why I continue to smoke in the face of all that distressing health evidence. Yet I do not have to try quite so hard when I can persuade myself that the issue is between myself and myself and is no one else's affair. (That others ordinarily believe it necessary to cite potential harm to others as the essence of their moral point against me only confirms the power of a minimalist ethic.) Think also how much more arduous it would be morally for the "prochoice" group in the abortion debate to have to admit that abortion decisions are fully public in their direct implications, and then to be forced to make the case for the public benefits of abortion. It is an argument that, perhaps, could be made in some cases—but it is much, much easier to relegate the whole issue to the private realm, where the standards of moral rigor are more accommodating.

There are other, less self-serving reasons for the persistence of the distinction. We need some language and concepts for finding a limit to the right of the government, or the populace, to intervene in our lives. That was Mill's concern and it is as legitimate now as it was in his day. In groping around for a solution, our legal system stumbled on a "right to privacy." That concept represents a latter-day reading of the Constitution, and has resisted efforts to give it a clear meaning. Even so, it has its heuristic uses and no better formulation to get at some kinds of civil-liberties issues has been proposed. Yet to say that it is useful does not entail that we need to go so far as to reify, as if it represented reality, a sharp distinction between private and public life. A loose, shifting, casual distinction, taken with a nice grain of salt, may be equally serviceable.

The problem we now face is twofold. Do those of us who want to protect civil liberties have the nerve at the same time to recognize and openly admit the possibility that our society is paying an increasingly high moral cost for isolating the "private" sphere from moral judgment? . . .

If that was done, we would be driven to grapple with the need to set some kind of limits to those liberties that, in balance, produce an intolerable level of moral nihilism and relativism as a cultural outcome. It is not, and ought not to be, just the Moral Majority that worries about violence and more-tolerant-than-thou sex on television; or about children neglected by parental quests for greater psychological fulfillment; or about casual stealing, cheating, lying, and consenting-adult infidelity; or about rising assault and murder rates. Whatever the gain to liberty of the private standards and dispositions that tacitly support those developments, they all point to the emergence of an intolerable society, destructive as much to private as to public life. A legitimate respect for civil liberties does not require a forgoing of standards by which to judge private behavior any more than respect for freedom of speech requires a suspension of judgment on the contents of free speech.

Mill's problem was to find a "limit" to "the legitimate interference of collective opinion with individual independence."[8] Although our task may not exactly be the opposite, the weight of inquiry may now have to shift. What ought to be the limits of liberty, and how can we identify those points at which "collective opinion" ought to hold sway against claims of private moral autonomy? To even ask that question implies that we must be prepared once again to judge the private lives of others, the way they use their liberty, and that the standards of judgment ought to be more demanding than those required by a minimalist ethic. . . .

[8]Ibid., p. 130.

CHAPTER 6

MORAL RULES

Most people are introduced to ethics through moral rules. Parents find that rule-making is a very effective way to get children to do what they want them to do when they are not physically present. (One hopes there is some rough correlation between what parents want their children to do and what morality requires.) The parental emphasis on rules is reinforced by religion. One of the first tasks of young Christians and Jews is to learn the Ten Commandments. Moreover, moral rules are not things that are discarded when children become adults. Moral rules are just as central in adult ethical decision-making. Note the emphasis on professional rules of conduct. Recently, business codes of ethics have been widely adopted. Private clubs and lodges all have elaborate rules for conduct—many of which can be characterized as moral. And, of course, many of the moral rules one learned as a child, such as "Don't lie," "Don't steal," "Don't cheat," continue to govern adult behavior. When asked to justify why they did or did not do something, adults, no less than children, appeal to the moral rules.

Philosophers, on this issue, are not out of step with the general population. Nearly all ethicists either develop an ethical theory in terms of rules or spend a large amount of time and space giving an account of how the traditional concern for moral rules can be accommodated into their system.

However, neither everyone in the general public nor all serious thinkers about ethics are unanimous in their praise of moral rules. The basic charge is that an overemphasis on rules stultifies and deadens morality. Moral decision-making gets done in a bureaucratic manner; as a result, the uniqueness of the individual situation is lost. Emphasizing the rules often makes the ethical decision-maker less sensitive to the needs of persons. Also, rules become etched in stone and are followed blindly even after the circumstances which produced the rules have changed radically. Rules also tend to become self-justifying, and, hence, the purpose of the rule is forgotten. Think of the rules governing college students. These rules were created to solve particular problems or to respond to centrally held values. Rules forbidding students on scholarship to have cars were created on the basis of the beliefs that cars were a luxury and interfered with study. So long as these beliefs were widely held, it was easy for a dean to justify the rule when a scholarship student asked, "Why do you have a rule forbidding scholarship students to have cars?" With the passage of time and changing beliefs and values, the justification is either forgotten or becomes fuzzy. In many circumstances, a car is a necessity rather than a luxury, and, hence, *failure* to have a car, rather than having one, would interfere with study. If a rule against scholarship students' having cars existed today, the question "How do we justify this rule?" would likely be answered by, "Because it's the rule." That kind of answer won't do.

Sometimes the whole set of ethical rules becomes sufficiently divorced from changed circumstances that a wholesale rebellion against the rules takes place. Such a rebellion actually did take place in the 1960s. Students today—even in a more traditional period—have no idea how different the life of a college student is today than it was in 1962. In the 1950s and early 1960s rigid course requirements, class attendance policies, and even compulsory chapel were commonplace. Dormitories were sexually segregated; often eating facilities were as well. Members of the opposite sex did not meet you in your room. Rules against alcohol and cigarette smoking existed—although even then they were not rigorously enforced. Pornography was definitely under the table. Movies and plays did not contain nudity.

The Broadway play *Hair,* the birth-control pill, the free-speech movement at Berkeley, and both the civil rights struggle and the anti-Vietnam protests helped bring about a moral revolution. The old rules collapsed in a few years—evidence that they had outlived their usefulness. Intellectual thinking influenced and was influenced by changes in the popular culture. A theory of ethics arose which claimed that rules were no longer needed and that following rules in ethical decision-making was positively harmful. This theory, formulated primarily by Christian ethicists, acquired the name "situation ethics." The New Testament of love was an ethics that broke through the bond of rules—the Old Testament ethics of law.

This debate between those who make rules central in ethical decision-making and those who wish to deemphasize rules is not new. Plato and Aristotle had much the same debate. In matters of morality, Plato put his faith in the ultimate authority of the philosopher-king rather than in rules (law). Only the philosopher-king had the wisdom and experience necessary to make moral judgments. The analogue of the philosopher-king is King Solomon. Aristotle, on the other hand, put his faith in the ultimate authority of the law. The law was more stable than human personalities, both in terms of surviving individual persons and in being less subject to temporary personal idiosyncrasies. Of course, the Platonists could correctly point out that law had to be interpreted and applied, so that human personalities were required after all.

This chapter considers the role that moral rules play in ethical decision-making. Most of the selection will argue for the necessity of rules, but Stephen Toulmin's article warns about ethical decision-making which emphasizes rules.

In the opening selection, R. M. Hare argues for the necessity of rules. His argument is extremely clever, but also easy to understand. Rules are required for any kind of teaching. Hare uses learning to drive as his case in point. What is true of teaching someone to drive is also true of teaching someone to make ethical decisions. Moral rules are central to ethics because that is the only way ethics can be taught.

On the side of deemphasizing rules, Stephen Toulmin calls on his experiences as a member of the National Commission for the Protection of Human Subjects of Biomedical and Behavioral Research. Toulmin was struck by the fact that so long as the members of the commission worked on a case-by-case basis, they could agree on detailed recommendations, but they argued endlessly about the adequacy of the underlying principles. This insight reminded Toulmin of the history of the role of law in ethics and of an ethic for governing relationships among strangers. Even among strangers, considerations of law were sometimes counterbalanced by considerations of equity. Toulmin argues that the chief task for ethics today should be to find ways for "reviving the friendly society." The ethics of rules is ill-equipped for this task.

However, the purpose of this chapter is not limited to the debate between those who emphasize rules and those who deemphasize them. Probably the best-known moral philosopher is Immanuel Kant (1724–1804). The selection by Kant provides a classical example of a philosopher who builds his entire ethical theory on a rule base. He accepted most of the popular morality of his day, but wanted to place it on a secure foundation. Kant was no relativist. He wanted a test for any act which *everyone* would accept as valid for determining whether or not doing the act would be moral. But what could provide the basis for such a test? It couldn't be human wants, desires, and inclinations because they are notoriously individual; any agreement would be impossible. The only other candidate is human reason. Human reason, unlike human desires, is universal. All human beings follow the same rules to solve mathematical problems or to launch a rocket ship. Ethics had to be placed on a similar foundation, and, hence, it had to be based on reason. The chief law of reason is the principle of noncontradiction. A contradiction occurs when you assert and deny the same judgment. If on one occasion, you say $2 + 2 = 4$, and on another, similar occasion, you say $2 + 2 \neq 4$, you are contradicting yourself. Kant thought he could base his ultimate moral rule on this principle of noncontradiction. Suppose you were considering whether it was morally permissible to tell a lie. The principle of noncontradiction would require that you make the same judgment in *all* similar cases. Suppose you say it is permissible to tell a lie; then you must agree to say it is permissible for all others to lie in similar situations. But what would happen if it was permissible for everyone to lie? The use of language would be undermined. We would never know whether people were telling the truth or not, and, hence, the communication function of language would break down. Hence, it is impossible to argue that it is permissible to lie, since a universalized practice of lying would undermine language, which you need in order to lie in the first place. Hence it is morally wrong to lie.

This example provides the basis for Kant's fundamental moral principle, which he calls the "categorical imperative": "Act only according to that maxim by which you can at the same time will that it should become a universal law." The maxim "it is permissible to lie" cannot, for the reason shown, become a universal law. Therefore, you ought not to lie. Three other applications of the categorical imperative are provided in the selections included in this chapter. Another important version of the categorical imperative, "Treat persons as ends, never as means merely" is discussed in Chapter 7.

Although most philosophers agree that Kant has something very important to say about moral philosophy, his work on ethics suffers from two distinct problems. First, he uses a technical terminology which makes him difficult to understand. Second, his account of morality is certainly incomplete. The categorical imperative might provide a necessary test for determining whether an action is moral, but there is more to it than that. In addition, there are objections to the categorical imperative itself.

Most of the technical terminology has been edited out of the selections included in this chapter. Something must be said, however, about the term *categorical imperative*. An imperative is a requirement of reason. Kant speaks of hypothetical and categorical imperatives. A hypothetical imperative is a requirement of reason with respect to goals you have. Thus, if you want an A in this course, you must study. Since reason recognizes that you must study to get an A, then the requirement to study is a hypothetical imperative. It is hypothetical because it holds only if you want to get an A. A categorical imperative is a requirement of reason that holds no matter what your goals or purposes. It holds with no "ifs," "ands," or "buts," and it holds for all persons. If an imperative is to serve as the foundation for ethics, it must be categorical.

As for the difficulties with the categorical imperative, one of the more vexing is how to handle exceptions. Lying is wrong, and one reason may be that if lying were universalized, lying would be self-defeating. But some lies are not wrong. Lying to save a life is not wrong, and if that stipulation were built into the maxim, it would pass the test of the categorical imperative. Kant provided little help in telling us how narrowly or widely the maxims governing actions are to be construed. If they are construed too widely, then the categorical imperative seems too inflexible. Some lies are not immoral, even if the practice of lying cannot be universalized. On the other hand, if you narrow the maxims, by building in hundreds of exceptions, then you allow so many cases of lying that the categorical imperative is undermined.

Kant also expects one fundamental moral rule to do too much work. Consider any moral discussion involving tradeoffs. I have a duty of loyalty to my employer and a duty of loyalty to my children. Often both demand more of me than I can give. How do I make that decision? The categorical imperative doesn't have anything to say in these types of cases. After all, any of a number of tradeoffs would pass the test of the categorical imperative.

One further issue for discussion is created by a dilemma which many of us will face in our lives. We will be in a position where we have the responsibility to make a decision based on the rules but doubt that the rules are adequate either for cases of this type or for this particular case. Should we bury our scruples and make the decision our position or role dictates, or should we violate our responsibility? John Rawls's distinction between justifying a practice and justifying a particular action falling under the practice is of some help here. With respect to justifying a practice—our system of criminal law, for example—the justification is to be based on consequences. Does this particular practice lead to the public good? Of course a positive answer to that question at this particular time does not require a positive answer in the future. Practices are modified or even replaced because they no longer lead to good consequences.

However, if one has a position of responsibility within a practice—is a judge, for example—then one should follow the rules of that practice. Judges should use the current rules of law to determine sentencing. A judge who finds the current rules inadequate certainly ought to question them. However, a judge shouldn't question the rules while functioning as a judge at the time of sentencing. The scholarly journal or the annual convention is the place for such questioning.

The rules of an institution or practice are different from most practical rules, including many rules of morality. Many rules we follow are what Rawls calls "summary rules." Perhaps a more apt term would be "rules of thumb." Generally, drivers should stay to the right. A good rule to follow when the barometer is falling and clouds are lowering in the southwest is "take an umbrella to work." When people ask about the boss, follow the rule, "you must be loyal to the boss." These rules are good rules of thumb; they work in most situations. However, when there is *good* reason to think that following the rule will lead to undesirable consequences, little further thought should be given to violating the rule. A rule of thumb is simply the kind of rule that can be easily overthrown.

But not all rules are rules of thumb. Practices and human institutions are created by people according to rules. These rules make the practices what they are; these rules are constitutive of the practice (e.g., the rules for making a contract or getting married). If you causally tamper with these rules, you change the practice. Of course the rules of a practice can be changed, but there are formal procedures for doing so. You can't just abandon a rule constituting a practice whenever doing so would create better consequences. Rules constituting practices aren't like rules of thumb. And since these rules have their special status, there is a theoretical basis for Rawls's conclusion that participants within a practice should follow the rules of that practice even if following the rules in this case would lead to bad consequences. Were the rules in question mere summary rules, there should be no hesitancy in abandoning them. However, much more is at stake with rules that constitute a practice.

In a way, this discussion of Rawls brings us full circle. Moral rules are absolutely fundamental in the moral life. They are necessary for teaching ethics; some rules actually constitute the practices of our community and, hence, achieve a special status. Perhaps morality itself is constituted by a rule or set of rules. Yet, moral rules do have their dangers and their limitations.

The Necessity of Rules for Teaching Morals

R. M. Hare

. . . Without principles, most kinds of teaching are impossible, for what is taught is in most cases a principle. In particular, when we learn *to do* something, what we learn is always a principle. Even to learn or be taught a fact (like the names of the five rivers of the Punjab) is to learn how to answer a question; it is to learn the principle 'When asked "What are the names of the five rivers of the Punjab?" answer "The Jhelum, the Chenab, &c.".'. . . To learn to do anything is never to learn to do an individual act; it is always to learn to do acts of a certain kind in a certain kind of situation; and this is to learn a principle. Thus, in learning to drive, I learn, not to change gear *now,* but to change gear when my engine makes a certain kind of noise. If this were not so, instruction would be of no use at all; for if all an instructor could do were to tell us to change gear *now,* he would have to sit beside us for the rest of our lives in order to tell us just when, on each occasion, to change gear.

Thus without principles we could not learn anything whatever from our elders. This would mean that every generation would have to start from scratch and teach itself. But even if each generation were able to teach itself, it could not do so without principles; for self-teaching, like all other teaching, is the teaching of principles. . . . Let us suppose that [a] clairvoyant made all his choices on some principle, but always forgot, as soon as he had made the choice, what the principle had been. He would have, accordingly, each time he made a decision, to go over all the effects of the alternative actions. This would be so time-consuming that he would not have the leisure to make many decisions in the course of his life. He would spend his whole time deciding matters like whether to step off with the right or the left foot, and would never reach what we should call the more important decisions. But if he could remember the principles on which he acted, he would be in a much better position; he could *learn* how to act in certain kinds of circumstance; he could learn to single out quickly the relevant aspects of a situation, including the effects of the various possible actions, and so choose quickly, and in many cases habitually. Thus his powers of considered decision would be set free for more momentous decisions. When the cabinet-maker has learnt how to make a dovetail without thinking much about it, he will have time to think about such things as the proportions and aesthetic appearance of the finished product. And it is the same with our conduct in the moral sphere; when the performance of the lesser duties has become a matter of habit, we have time to think about the greater.

There is a limit in practice to the amount that can be taught to someone by someone else. Beyond this point, self-teaching is necessary. The limit is set by the variety of conditions which may be met with in doing whatever is being taught; and this variety

The Language of Morals by R. M. Hare (1952), pp. 60–65, 74–78. Reprinted by permission of Oxford University Press.

is greater in some cases than in others. A sergeant can teach a recruit almost all there is to be known about fixing bayonets on parade, because one occasion of fixing bayonets on parade is much like another; but a driving instructor cannot do more than begin to teach his pupil the art of driving, because the conditions to be met with in driving are so various. In most cases, teaching cannot consist in getting the learner to perform faultlessly a fixed drill. One of the things that has to be included in any but the most elementary kinds of instruction is the opportunity for the learner to make decisions for himself, and in so doing to examine, and even modify to suit particular types of case, the principles which are being taught. The principles that are taught us initially are of a provisional kind. . . . Our training, after the initial stages, consists in taking these principles, and making them less provisional; we do this by using them continually in our own decisions, and sometimes making exceptions to them; some of the exceptions are made because our instructor points out to us that certain cases are instances of classes of exceptions to the principle; and some of the exceptions we decide on for ourselves. This presents no more difficulty than our clairvoyant had in deciding between two sets of effects. If we learn from experiment that to follow a certain principle would have certain effects, whereas to modify it in a certain way would have certain other effects, we adopt whichever form of the principle leads to the effects which we choose to pursue.

We may illustrate this process of modifying principles from the example already used, that of learning to drive. I am told, for instance, always to draw into the side of the road when I stop the car; but later I am told that this does not apply when I stop before turning into a side-road to the offside—for then I must stop near the middle of the road until it is possible for me to turn. Still later I learn that in this manoeuvre it is not necessary to stop at all if it is an uncontrolled junction and I can see that there is no traffic which I should obstruct by turning. When I have picked up all these modifications to the rule, and the similar modifications to all the other rules, and practice them habitually as so modified, then I am said to be a good driver, because my car is always in the right place on the road, travelling at the right speed, and so on. The good driver is, among other things, one whose actions are so exactly governed by principles which have become a habit with him, that he normally does not have to *think* just what to do. But road conditions are exceedingly various, and therefore it is unwise to let all one's driving become a matter of habit. One can never be certain that one's principles of driving are perfect—indeed, one can be very sure that they are not; and therefore the good driver not only drives well from habit, but constantly attends to his driving habits, to see whether they might not be improved; he never stops learning. . . .

Drivers often know just what to do in a certain situation without being able to enunciate in words the principle on which they act. This is a very common state of affairs with all kinds of principles. Trappers know just where to set their traps, but often cannot explain just why they have put a trap in a particular place. We all know how to use words to convey our meaning; but if a logician presses us for the exact definition of a word we have used, or the exact rules for its use, we are often at a loss. This does not mean that the setting of traps or the use of words or the driving of cars does not proceed according to principles. One may know how, without being able to say how—though if a skill is to be taught, it is easier if we *can* say how.

We must not think that, if we can decide between one course and another without further thought (it seems self-evident to us, which we should do), this necessarily implies that we have some mysterious intuitive faculty which tells us what to do. A driver does not know when to change gear by intuition; he knows it because he has learnt and not forgotten; what he knows is a principle, though he cannot formulate the principle in words. The same is true of moral decisions which are sometimes called 'intuitive'. We have moral 'intuitions' because we have learnt how to behave, and have different ones according to how we have learnt to behave.

It would be a mistake to say that all that had to be done to a man to make him into a good driver was to tell him, or otherwise inculcate into him, a lot of general principles. This would be to leave out the factor of decision. Very soon after he begins to learn, he will be faced with situations to deal with which the provisional principles so far taught him require modification; and he will then have to decide what to do. He will very soon discover which decisions were right and which wrong, partly because his instructor tells him, and partly because having seen the effects of the decisions he determines in future not to bring about such effects. On no account must we commit the mistake of supposing that decisions and principles occupy two separate spheres and do not meet at any point. All decisions except those, if any, that are completely arbitrary are to some extent decisions of principle. We are always setting precedents for ourselves. It is not a case of the principle settling everything down to a certain point, and decision dealing with everything below that point. Rather, decision and principles interact throughout the whole field. Suppose that we have a principle to act in a certain way in certain circumstances. Suppose then that we find ourselves in circumstances which fall under the principle, but which have certain other peculiar features, not met before, which make us ask 'Is the principle really intended to cover cases like this, or is it incompletely specified—is there here a case belonging to a class which should be treated as exceptional?' Our answer to this question will be a decision, but a decision of principle, as is shown by the use of the value-word 'should'. If we decide that this should be an exception, we thereby modify the principle by laying down an exception to it.

Suppose, for example, that in learning to drive I have been taught always to signal before I slow down or stop, but have not yet been taught what to do when stopping in an emergency; if a child leaps in front of my car, I do not signal, but keep both hands on the steering-wheel; and thereafter I accept the former principle with this exception, that in cases of emergency it is better to steer than to signal. I have, even on the spur of the moment, made a decision of principle. To understand what happens in cases like this is to understand a great deal about the making of value-judgements.

The question 'How shall I bring up my children?'. . . is one to the logic of which, since ancient times, few philosophers have given much attention. A child's moral upbringing has an effect upon him which will remain largely untouched by anything that happens to him thereafter. If he has had a stable upbringing, whether on good principles or on bad ones, it will be extremely difficult for him to abandon those principles in later life—difficult but not impossible. They will have for him the force of an objective moral law; and his behaviour will seem to give much evidence in support of intuitionist ethical theories, provided that it is not compared with the behaviour of those who stick just as firmly to quite different principles. But nevertheless, unless our education has been so thorough as to transform us into automata, we can come to doubt or even reject these principles; that is what makes human beings, whose moral systems change, different from ants, whose moral system does not. Therefore, even if for me the question 'What shall I do in such and such a situation?' is almost invariably answered without ambiguity by the moral intuition which my upbringing has given me, I may, if I ask myself 'How shall I bring up my children?' pause before giving an answer. It is here that the most fundamental moral decisions of all arise; and it is here, if only moral philosophers would pay attention to them, that the most characteristic uses of moral words are to be found. Shall I bring up my children *exactly* as I was brought up, so that they have the same intuitions about morals as I have? Or have circumstances altered, so that the moral character of the father will not provide a suitable equipment for the children? Perhaps I shall try to bring them up like their father, and shall fail; perhaps their new environment will be too strong for me, and they will come to repudiate my principles. Or I may have become so bewildered by the strange new world that, although I still act from force of habit on the principles that I have learnt, I simply do not know what principles to impart to my children, if, indeed, one in my condition can impart any settled principles at all. On all these questions, I have to make up my mind; only the most hide-bound father will try to bring up his children, without thinking, in exactly the way that he himself was brought up; and even he will usually fail disastrously.

Many of the dark places of ethics become clearer when we consider this dilemma in which parents are liable to find themselves. We have already noticed that, although principles have in the end to rest upon decisions of principle, decisions as such cannot be taught; only principles can be taught. It is the powerlessness of the parent to make for his son those many decisions of principle which the son during his future career will make, that gives moral language its characteristic shape. The only instrument which the parent possesses is moral education—the teaching of principles by example and precept, backed up by chastisement and other more up-to-date psychological methods. Shall he use these means, and to what extent? Certain generations of parents have had no doubts about this question. They have used them to the full; and the result has been to turn their children into good intuitionists, able to cling to the rails, but bad at steering round corners. At other times parents—and who shall blame them?— suffer from lack of confidence; they are not sure enough what they themselves think, to be ready to impart to their children a stable way of life. The children of such a generation are likely to grow up opportunists, well able to make individual decisions, but without the settled body of principles which is the most priceless heritage that any generation can leave to its successors. For though principles are in the end built upon decisions of principle, the building is the work of many generations, and the man who has to start from the beginning is to be pitied; he will not be likely, unless he is a genius, to achieve many conclusions of importance, any more than the average boy, turned loose without instruction upon a desert island, or even in a laboratory, would be likely to make any of the major scientific discoveries.

The dilemma between these two extreme courses in education is plainly a false one. Why it is a false one is apparent, if we recall what was said earlier about the dynamic relation between decisions and principles. It is very like learning to drive. It would be foolish, in teaching someone to drive, to try to inculcate into him such fixed and comprehensive principles that he would never have to make an independent decision. It would be equally foolish to go to the other extreme and leave it to him to find his own way of driving. What we do, if we are sensible, is to give him a solid basis of principles, but at the same time ample opportunity of making the decisions upon which these principles are based, and by which they are modified, improved, adapted to changed circumstances, or even abandoned if they become entirely unsuited to a new environment. To teach only the principles, without giving the opportunity of subjecting them to the learner's own decisions of principle, is like teaching exclusively from the textbooks without entering the laboratory. On the other hand, to abandon one's child or one's driving-pupil to his own self-expression is like putting a boy into a laboratory and saying 'Get on with it'. The boy may enjoy himself or kill himself, but will probably not learn much science.

The moral words, of which we may take 'ought' as an example, reflect in their logical behaviour this double nature of moral instruction—as well they may, for it is in moral instruction that they are most typically used. The sentences in which they appear are normally the expression of decisions of principle—and it is easy to let the decisions get separated, in our discussion of the subject, from the principles. This is the source of the controversy between the 'objectivists', as intuitionists sometimes call themselves, and the 'subjectivists', as they often call their opponents. The former lay stress on the fixed principles that are handed down by the father, the latter on the new decisions which have to be made by the son. The objectivist says 'Of course you know what you ought to do; look at what your conscience tells you, and if in doubt go by the consciences of the vast majority of men'. He is able to say this, because our consciences are the product of the principles which our early training has indelibly planted in us, and in one society these principles do not differ much from one person to another. The subjectivist, on the other hand, says 'But surely, when it comes to the point—when I have listened to what other people say, and given due weight to my own intuitions, the legacy of my upbringing—I have in the end to decide for myself what I ought to do. To deny this is to be a conventionalist; for both common moral notions and my own intuitions are the legacy of tradition, and—apart from the fact that there are so many different traditions in the world—traditions cannot be started without someone doing what I now feel called upon to do, decide. If I refuse to make my own decisions, I am, in merely copying my fathers, showing myself a lesser man than they; for whereas they must have initiated, I shall be merely accepting.' This plea of the subjectivist is quite justified. It is the plea of the adolescent who wants to be adult. To become morally adult is to reconcile these two apparently conflicting positions by learning to make decisions of principle; it is to learn to use 'ought'-sentences in the realization that they can only be verified by reference to a standard or set of principles which we have by our own decision accepted and made our own. This is what our present generation is so painfully trying to do.

The Tyranny of Principles

Stephen Toulmin

. . . These days, public debates about ethical issues oscillate between, on the one hand, a narrow dogmatism that confines itself to unqualified general assertions dressed up as "matters of principle" and, on the other, a shallow relativism that evades all firm stands by suggesting that we choose our "value systems" as freely as we choose our clothes. Both approaches suffer from the same excess of generality. The rise of anthropology and the other human sciences in the early twentieth century encouraged a healthy sense of social and cultural differences; but this was uncritically taken as implying an end to all objectivity in practical ethics. The subsequent reassertion of ethical objectivity has led, in turn, to an insistence on the absoluteness of moral principles that is not balanced by a feeling for the complex problems of discrimination that arise when such principles are applied to particular real-life cases. So, the relativists have tended to overinterpret the need for discrimination in ethics, discretion in public administration, and equity in law, as a license for general personal subjectivity. The absolutists have responded by denying all real scope for personal judgment in ethics, insisting instead on strict construction in the law, on unfeeling consistency in public administration, and—above all—on the "inerrancy" of moral principles.

I propose to concentrate my attention on this last phenomenon—the revival of a tyrannical absolutism in recent discussions about social and personal ethics. I find it reflected in attitudes toward politics, public affairs, and the administration of justice, as much as toward questions of "ethics" in a narrower and more personal sense. My main purpose will be to ask: What is it about our present situation that inclines us to move in that direction? By way of reply, I shall argue that, in all large industrialized societies and cultures—regardless of their economic and political systems—ethics, law, and public administration have recently undergone similar historical transformations, so that all three fields are exposed to the same kinds of pressures, face common difficulties, and share in the same resulting public distrust. And I shall try to show what we can learn about those shared problems, and about the responses that they call for, by studying the common origins of our basic ethical, legal, and political ideas. All my central examples will be concerned with the same general topic: the nature, scope, and force of "rules" and "principles" in ethics and in law. Three personal experiences helped to bring these problems into focus for me.

Reprinted by permission of The Hastings Center and Stephen Toulmin. © Institute of Society, Ethics and The Life Sciences, 360 Broadway, Hastings-on-Hudson, NY 10706.

THREE PERSONAL EXPERIENCES

Human Subjects Research

For several years in the mid-1970s, I worked as a staff member with the National Commission for the Protection of Human Subjects of Biomedical and Behavioral Research, which was established by the U.S. Congress, with the task of reporting and making recommendations about the ethics of using human subjects in medical and psychological research. Eleven commissioners—five of them scientists, the remaining six lawyers, theologians, and other nonscientists—were instructed to make recommendations about publicly financed human experimentation: in particular, to determine under what conditions subjects belonging to certain vulnerable groups (such as young children and prisoners) could participate in such research without moral objection.

Before the Commission began work, many onlookers assumed that its discussions would degenerate into a Babel of rival opinions. One worldly commentator remarked in the *New England Journal of Medicine,* "Now (I suppose) we shall see matters of eternal principle decided by a six to five vote."[1] But things did not work out that way. In practice, the commissioners were never split along the line between scientists and nonscientists. In almost every case they came close to agreement even about quite detailed recommendations—at least for so long as their discussions proceeded taxonomically, taking one difficult class of cases at a time and comparing it in detail with other clearer and easier classes of cases.

Even when the Commission's recommendations were not unanimous, the discussions in no way resembled Babel: the commissioners were never in any doubt what it was that they were *not quite unanimous about.* Babel set in only afterwards. When the eleven individual commissioners asked themselves what "principles" underlay and supposedly justified their adhesion to the consensus, each of them answered in his or her own way: the Catholics appealed to Catholic principles, the humanists to humanist principles, and so on. They could agree; they could agree what they were agreeing about; but, apparently, they could not agree why they agreed about it.

This experience prompted me to wonder what this final "appeal to principles" really achieved. Certainly it did not add any weight or certitude to the commissioners' specific ethical recommendations, for example, about the kind of consent procedures required in biomedical research using five-year-old children. They were, quite evidently, surer about these shared, particular judgments than they were about the discordant general principles on which, in theory, their practical judgments were based. If anything, the appeal to principles undermined the recommendations by suggesting to onlookers that there was more disharmony than ever showed up in the commissioners' actual discussions. So, by the end of my tenure with the Commission I had begun to suspect that the point of "appealing to principles" was something quite else: not to give particular ethical judgments a more solid foundation, but rather to square the collective ethical conclusions of the Commission as a whole with each individual commissioner's other *non*ethical commitments. So (it seemed to me) the principles of Catholic ethics tell us more about Catholicism than they do about ethics, the principles of Jewish or humanist ethics more about Judaism or humanism than about ethics. Such principles serve less as foundations, adding intellectual strength or force to particular moral opinions, than they do as corridors or curtain walls linking the moral perceptions of all reflective human beings, with other, more general positions—theological, philosophical, ideological, or *Weltanschaulich.*

Abortion

The years of the National Commission's work were also years during which the morality of abortion became a matter of public controversy. In fact, the U.S. Congress established the Commission in the backwash of the Supreme Court's ruling on the legality of abortion, following a public dispute about research on the human fetus. And before long the public debate about abortion acquired some of the same puzzling features as the proceedings of the Commission itself. On the one hand, there were those who could discuss the morality of abortion temperately and with discrimination, acknowledging that here, as in other agonizing human situations, conflicting considerations are involved and that a just, if sometimes painful, balance has to be struck between different rights and claims, interests and responsibilities. That temperate approach underlay traditional common law doctrines about abortion before the first statutory restrictions were enacted in the years around 1825. It was also the approach adopted by the U.S. Supreme Court in the classic case, *Roe* v. *Wade;* and, most important, it was the approach clearly spelled out by Thomas Aquinas, whose position was close to that of the common law and the Supreme Court. (He acknowledged that the balance of moral considerations necessarily tilts in different directions at different stages in a woman's pregnancy, with crucial changes beginning around the time of "quickening."[2]) On the other hand, much of the public rhetoric increasingly came to turn on "matters of principle." As a result, the abortion debate became less temperate, less discriminating, and above all less resolvable. Too often, in subsequent years, the issue has boiled down to pure head-butting: an embryo's unqualified "right to life" being pitted against a woman's equally unqualified "right to choose." Those who have insisted on dealing with the issue at the level of high theory thus guarantee that the only possible practical outcome is deadlock.

Social Welfare Benefits

My perplexities about the force and value of "rules" and "principles" were further sharpened as the result of a television news magazine program about a handicapped young woman who had difficulties with the local Social Security office. Her Social Security payments were not sufficient to cover her rent and food, so she started an answering service, which she operated through the telephone at her bedside. The income from this service—though itself less than a living wage—made all the difference to her. When the local Social Security office heard about this extra income, however, they reduced her benefits accordingly; in addition, they ordered her to repay some of the money she had been receiving. (Apparently, they regarded her as a case of "welfare fraud.") The television reporter added two final statements. Since the report had been filmed, he told us, the young woman, in despair, had taken her own life. To this he added his personal comment that "there should be a *rule* to prevent this kind of thing from happening."

Notice that the reporter did not say, "The local office should be given discretion to waive, or at least bend, the existing rules in hard cases." What he said was,"There should be an *additional* rule to prevent such inequities in the future." Justice, he evidently believed, can be ensured only by establishing an adequate system of rules, and injustice can be prevented only by adding more rules.

Hence, the questions that arise from these experiences: What force and function do rules or principles truly possess, either in law or in ethics? What social and historical circumstances make it most natural and appropriate to discuss legal and ethical issues in the language of "rules" and "principles"? Why are our own contemporary legal and ethical discussions so preoccupied with rules and principles? And to what extent would we do better to look for justice and morality in other directions?

RULES IN ROMAN LAW

Far from playing an indispensable part in either law or ethics, "rules" have only a limited and conditional role. The current vogue for rules and principles is the outcome of certain powerful factors in recent social history; but these factors have always been balanced against counterweights. Justice has always required both law and equity, while morality has always demanded both fairness and discrimination. When this essential duality is ignored, reliance on unchallengeable principles can generate, or become the instrument of, its own subtle kind of tyranny.

My reading soon led me back to Peter Stein's *Regulae Juris,* which traces the development of the concept of a "rule" in Roman law from its beginnings to the modern era.[3] His account of the earliest phases of Roman law was for me the most striking part. For the first three hundred years of Roman history, the legal system made no explicit use of the concept of rules. The College of Pontiffs acted as the city's judges, and individual pontiffs gave their adjudications on the cases submitted to them. But they were not required to cite any general rules as justifications for their decisions. Indeed, they were not required to give reasons at all. Their task was not to argue, but rather to pontificate.

How was this possible? How can any system of law operate in the absence of rules, reasons, and all the associated apparatus of binding force and precedent? Indeed, in such a situation can we say a true system of law exists at all? Those questions require us to consider the historical and anthropological circumstances of early Rome. Initially Rome was a small and relatively homogeneous community, whose members shared a correspondingly homogeneous tradition of ideas about justice and fairness, property and propriety. . . . In any such community the functions of adjudication tend to be more arbitral than regulatory. Like labor arbitrators today, the judges will not be as sharply bound by precedent as contemporary high court judges. So the disputes that the pontiffs adjudicated were typically ones about which the traditional consensus was ambiguous; the balance of rights and obligations between the parties required the judgment call of a trusted and disinterested arbitrator. In these marginal cases all that the arbitrator may be able to say is, "Having taken all the circumstances into account, I find that on this particular occasion it would, all in all, be more reasonable to tilt the scale to A rather than to B." This ruling will rest, not on the application of general legal rules, but rather on the exercise of judicial discrimination in assessing the balance of particulars. Initially, "pontificating" did not mean laying down the law in a dogmatic manner. Rather, it meant resolving marginal disputes by an equitable arbitration, and the pontiffs had the trust of their fellow citizens in doing so.

This state of affairs did not last. Long before the first Imperial codification, Roman law began to develop the full apparatus of "rules" with which we ourselves are familiar. Stein suggests that five sets of factors contributed to this new reliance on *regulae*.[4] First, as the city grew, the case load increased beyond what the pontiffs themselves could manage. Junior judges, who did not possess the same implicit trust as the pontiffs, were brought in to resolve disputes; so the consistency of their rulings had to be "regularized." Second, with the rise of lawyering as a profession, law schools were set up and *regulae* were articulated for the purpose of teaching the law. Discretion, which had rested earlier on the personal characters of the pontiffs themselves and which is not so easy to teach, began to be displaced by formal rules and more teachable argumentative skills. Third, Rome acquired an empire, and foreign peoples came under the city's authority. Their systems of customary law had to be put into harmony with the Roman system, and this could be done only by establishing a concordance between the "rules" of different systems. Fourth, the empire itself developed a bureaucracy, which could not operate except on the basis of rules. Finally, the intellectual discussion of law was pursued in the context of Greek philosophy. Although Cicero, for example, was a practicing attorney, he was also a philosophical scholar with a professional interest in the Stoic doctrine of the *logos,* or "universal reason."

What followed the resulting proliferation of rules and laws is common knowledge. First, a functional differentiation grew up between two kinds of issues. On the one hand, there were issues that could be decided by applying *general* rules or laws, on the basis of the maxim that like cases should be treated alike. On the other hand, there were issues that called for discretion, with an eye to the *particular* features of each case, in accordance with the maxim that significantly different cases should be treated differently. This functional differentiation became the ancestor of our own distinction between legal and equitable jurisdiction. Second, the Emperor Constantine decided as a matter of imperial policy to bring equitable jurisdiction under his personal control by reserving the equitable function to his own personal court and chancellor. Out in the public arena, judges were given the menial task of applying general rules with only the minimum of discretion. Once legal proceedings were exhausted, the aggrieved citizen could appeal to the Emperor as *parens patriae* ("father of the fatherland") for the benevolent exercise of clemency or equity. Politically, this division of labor certainly did the Emperor no harm; but it also sowed the first seeds of public suspicion that the Law is one thing, Justice another.

Carried over into the modern English-speaking world, the resulting division between courts of law and courts of equity is familiar to readers of Charles Dickens. And although during the twentieth century most Anglo-American jurisdictions have merged legal and equitable functions in the same courts, it is still widely the case that equitable remedies can be sought only in cases where legal remedies are unavailable or un-workable—so that in this respect the dead hand of Constantine still rules us from the grave.

THE ETHICS OF STRANGERS

Life in late-twentieth-century industrial societies clearly has more in common with life in Imperial Rome than it has with the Rome of Horatius at the Bridge or with Mrs. Gaskell's *Cranford*. Our cities are vast, our populations are mixed and frag-mented, our public administration is bureaucratic, our jurisdictions (both domestic and foreign) are many and varied. As a result, the moral consensus and civic trust on which the pontificate of early Rome depended for its general respect and efficacy often appear to be no more than a beguiling dream. The way we live now, people have come to value uniformity above responsiveness, to focus on law at the expense of equity, and to confuse "the rule of law" with a law of rules. Yet the balance between law and equity still needs to be struck, even if new ways need to be found that answer our new needs. From this point on, I shall work my way toward the question: how, in our actual situation, can that balance best be redressed?

In law, in ethics, and in public administration alike, there is nowadays a similar preoccupation with general principles and a similar distrust of individual discretion. In the administration of social services, the demand for equality of treatment makes us unwilling to permit administrators to "temper the wind to the shorn lamb"—that strikes us as unfair, and therefore unjust. (The equation of justice with fairness is thus a two-edged sword.) In the professions, a widespread fear that professionals are taking unfair advantage of their fiduciary positions has contributed to the recent wave of malpractice suits. In the courts, judges are given less and less room to exercise discretion, and many lawyers view juries as no more trustworthy than judges; the more they are both kept in line by clear rules, or so it seems, the better. As for public discussions of ethics, the recognition of genuine moral complexities, conflicts, and tragedies, that can be dealt with only on a case-by-case basis, is simply unfashionable. Victory in public argument goes, rather, to the person with the more imposing principle. Above all, many people involved in the current debate seem to have forgotten what the term "equity" actually means. They assume that it is just a literary synonym for "equality." So, a demand for the uniform application of public policies leads to a submerging of the discretionary by the rigorous, the equitable by the equal. Faced with judicial injustices, we react like the television reporter, declaring, "There ought to be a law against it," even where it would be more appropriate to say, "In this particular case, the law is making an ass of itself." The same applies to the operation of our bureaucracies, and to the emphasis on principles in moral judgments.

In all three fields, we need to be reminded that equity requires not the imposition of uniformity or equality on all relevant cases, but rather reasonableness or respon-siveness (*epieikeia*) in applying general rules to individual cases. Equity means doing justice with discretion around, in the interstices of, and in areas of conflict between our laws, rules, principles, and other general formulas. It means being responsive to the limits of all such formulas, to the special circumstances in which one can properly make exceptions, and to the trade-offs required where different formulas conflict. The degree to which such marginal judgments can be regularized or routinized remains limited today, just as it was in early Rome. Faced with the task of balancing the equities of different parties, a judge today may well be guided by previous precedents; but these precedents only illuminate broad maxims, they do not invoke formal rules. Likewise, professional practice may be described in cut-and-dried terms as a matter of "routine and accepted" procedures only in the artificial context of a malpractice suit. In the actual exercise of his profession, a surgeon, say, may sometimes simply have to use his or her own best judgment in deciding how to proceed conscientiously. Finally, in ethics, moral wisdom is exercised not by those who stick by a single principle come what may, absolutely and without exception, but rather by those who understand that, in the long run, no principle—however absolute—can avoid running up against another equally absolute principle; and by those who have the experience and discrimination needed to balance conflicting considerations in the most humane way.

By looking at the effects of changing social conditions and modes of life on our ethical perceptions, I believe we can best hit on the clues that will permit us to unravel this whole tangle of problems. A century ago in *Anna Karenina* Leo Tolstoy expressed a view which, though in my opinion exaggerated, is none the less illuminating. During his lifetime Tolstoy lived to see the abolition of serfdom, the introduction of railways, the movement of population away from the country to the cities, and the consequent emergence of modern city life; and he continued to have deep reservations about the possibility of living a truly moral life in a modern city. As he saw matters, genuinely "moral" relations can exist only between people who live, work, and associate together: inside a family, between intimates and associates, within a neighborhood. The natural limit to any person's moral universe, for Tolstoy, is the distance he or she can walk, or at most ride. By taking the train, a moral agent leaves the sphere of truly moral actions for a world of strangers, toward whom he or she has few real obligations and with whom dealings can be only casual or commercial. Whenever the moral pressures and demands become too strong to bear, Tolstoy has Anna go down to the railway station and take a train somewhere, anywhere. The final irony of Tolstoy's own painful life was that he finally broke away from his home and family, only to die in the local stationmaster's office. Matters of state policy and the like, in Tolstoy's eyes, lay quite outside the realm of ethics. Through the figure of Constantin Levin, he made clear his skepticism about all attempts either to turn ethics into a matter of theory or to make political reform an instrument of virtue.

What Tolstoy rightly emphasized is the sharp difference that exists between our moral relations with our families, intimates, and immediate neighbors or associates, and our moral relations with complete strangers. In dealing with our children, friends, and immediate colleagues, we both expect to—and are expected to—make allowances for their individual personalities and tastes, and we do our best to time our actions according to our perception of their current moods and plans. In dealing with the bus driver, the sales clerk in a department store, the hotel barber, and other such casual contacts, there may be no basis for making these allowances, and so no chance of doing so. In these transient encounters, our moral obligations are limited and chiefly negative—for example, to avoid acting offensively or violently. So, in the ethics of strangers, respect for rules is all, and the opportunities for discretion are few. In the ethics of intimacy, discretion is all, and the relevance of strict rules is minimal. For Tolstoy, of course, only the ethics of intimacy was properly called "ethics" at all— that is why I described his view as exaggerated. But in this respect the ethics of John Rawls is equally exaggerated, though in the opposite direction. In our relations with casual acquaintances and unidentified fellow citizens, absolute impartiality may be a prime moral demand; but among intimates a certain discreet partiality is, surely, only equitable, and certainly not unethical. So a system of ethics that rests its principles on "the veil of ignorance" may well be "fair," but it will also be—essentially—an ethics for relations between strangers.[5]

THE STRESSES OF LAWSUITS

Seeing how Tolstoy felt about his own time, what would he have thought about the life we lead today? The effects of the railways, in blurring the boundary between the moral world of the immediate community and the neutral world beyond, have been only multiplied by the private car, which breaks that boundary down almost completely. Living in a high-rise apartment building, taking the car from its underground garage to the supermarket and back, the modern city dweller may sometimes wonder whether he has any neighbors at all. For many of us, the sphere of intimacy has shrunk to the nuclear family, and this has placed an immense strain on family relations. Living in a world of comparative strangers, we find ourselves short on civic trust and increasingly estranged from our professional advisors. We are less inclined to give judges and bureaucrats room to use their discretion, and more determined to obtain equal (if not always equitable) treatment. In a world of complete strangers, indeed, equality would be about the only virtue left.

Do not misunderstand my position. I am not taking a nostalgia trip back to the Good Old Days. The world of neighborliness and forced intimacy, of both geographical and social immobility, had its vices as well as its virtues. Jane Austen's caricature of Lady Catherine de Burgh in *Pride and Prejudice* reminds us that purchasing equity by submitting to gross condescension can make its price too dear.

> God bless the Squire and his relations,
> and keep us in our proper stations.

Any biography of Tolstoy reminds us that his world, too, had a darker side. Those who are seduced by his admiration for the moral wisdom of the newly emancipated peasantry will find an antidote in Frederick Douglass's memoirs of slave life on the Maryland shore. Nor am I deploring apartment buildings and private cars. People usually have reasons for living as they do, and attacking modernity in the name of the morality of an earlier time is an act of desperation, like building the Berlin Wall. No, my question is only: If we accept the modern world as it is—apartment buildings, private cars, and all—how can we strike the central balance between the ethics of intimates and the ethics of strangers, between uniformity of treatment and administrative discretion, and between equity and law, in ways that answer our contemporary needs?

To begin with the law: current public stereotypes focus on the shortcomings of the adversary process, but what first needs to be explained is just where the adversary system has gone astray, and in what fields of law we should be most concerned to replace it. That should not be hard to do. Given that we handle our moral relations with intimates and associates differently from our moral relations with strangers, is not some similar differentiation appropriate between our legal relations with strangers, on the one hand, and with intimates, associates, and close family members on the other?

Even in the United States, the homeland of the adversary system, at least two types of disputes—labor-management conflicts and the renegotiation of commercial contracts—are dealt with by using arbitration or conciliation rather than confrontation. That is no accident. In a criminal prosecution or a routine civil damage suit arising out of a car collision, the parties are normally complete strangers before the proceedings and have no stake in one another's future, so no harm is done if they walk out of the court vowing never to set eyes on each other again. By contrast, the parties to a labor grievance will normally wish to continue working together after the adjudication, while the disputants in a commercial arbitration may well retain or resume business dealings with one another despite the present disagreement. In cases of these kinds, the psychological stresses of the adversary system can be quite destructive: by the time an enthusiastic litigating attorney has done his bit, further labor relations or commercial dealings may be psychologically impossible. So in appraising different kinds of court proceedings, we need to consider how particular types of judicial episodes fit into the larger life histories of the individuals who are parties to them, and what impact the form of proceedings can have on those life histories.

A lawsuit that pits the full power of the state against a criminal defendant is one thing: in that context, Monroe Freedman may be right to underline the merits of the adversary mode, and the positive obligations of zealous defense advocacy.[6] A civil suit that pits colleagues, next-door neighbors, or family members against each other is another thing: in that context resort to adversary proceedings may only make a bad situation worse. So, reasonably enough, the main locus of dissatisfaction with the adversary system is those areas of human life in which the psychological outcomes are most damaging: family law, for example. By the time that the father, mother, and children involved in a custody dispute have all been zealously represented in court, the bad feelings from which the suit originally sprang may well have become irremediable. It is just such areas as family law that other nations (such as West Germany) have chosen to handle by arbitration rather than litigation, in chambers rather than in open court, so providing much more room for discretion.

I am suggesting, then, that a system of law consisting wholly of rules would treat all parties coming before it in the ways appropriate to strangers. By contrast, in legal issues that arise between parties who wish to continue as close associates on an intimate or familiar level, the demands of equality and rule conformity lose their central place. There, above all, the differences between the desires, personalities, hopes, capacities, and ambitions of the parties most need to be taken into account; and only an adjudicator with authority to interpret existing rules, precedents, and maxims in the light of, and in response to, those differences will be in a position to respect the equities of all the parties involved.

REVIVING THE FRIENDLY SOCIETY

In public administration, especially in the field of social services, the crucial historical changes were more recent, yet they appear much harder to reverse. Two centuries ago most of what we now call the social services—then known, collectively, as "charity"—were still dispensed through the churches. Local ministers of religion were generally trusted to perform this duty equitably and conscientiously; and in deciding to give more to (say) Mrs. Smith than Mrs. Jones, they were not strictly answerable to any supervisor, still less bound by a book of rules. . . . Even a hundred years ago many such charitable functions were still carried on by private organizations, like those in Britain which were charmingly known as "friendly societies." But by this time things were beginning to change. A friendly clergyman is one thing, but a friendly *society* is more of an anomaly: in due course irregularities in the administration of those organizations—like those in some trade union pension funds today—provoked government supervision, and a Registrar of Friendly Societies was appointed to keep an eye on them.

From that point on, the delivery of social services has become ever more routinized, centralized, and subject to bureaucratic routine. It should not take horror stories, like that of the handicapped young woman's answering service, to make us think again about the whole project of delivering human services through a bureaucracy: one only has to read Max Weber. The imperatives of bureaucratic administration require determinate procedures and full accountability; while a helping hand, whether known by the name of "charity" or "social services," can be truly equitable only if it is exercised with discretion, on the basis of substantive and informed judgments about need rather than formal rules of entitlement.

What might be done, then, to counter the rigors of bureaucracy in this field? Or should late-twentieth-century societies look for other ways of lending a collective hand to those in need? In an exemplary apologia for bureaucracy, Herbert Kaufman of the Brookings Institution has put his finger on many of the key points.[7] If we find public administration today complex, unresponsive, and procedure-bound, he argues that this is almost entirely our own fault. These defects are direct consequences of the demands that we ourselves have placed on our public servants in a situation increasingly marked by diversity, democracy, and distrust. Since we are unwilling to grant discretion to civil servants for fear that it will be abused, we leave ourselves with no measure for judging administrators' performance other than *equality*. As Kaufman remarks, "If people in one region discover that they are treated differently from people in other regions under the same program, they are apt to be resentful and uncooperative."[8]

Hence there arises a "general concern for uniform application of policy," which can be guaranteed only by making the rulebook even more inflexible. Yet is our purchase it at any price? If we were certain that our own insistence on absolute fairness made the social services dehumanizing and dehumanized, might we not consider opting for other, more *equitable* procedures even though their outcomes might be less *equal?*

Alternatively, perhaps we should reconsider the wholesale nationalization of charity that began in the early twentieth century. Plenty of uncorrupt private pension funds still operate alongside governmental retirement and old-age pension schemes, and a few communally based systems of welfare and charity remain trusted just because their accountability is to a particular community. Among the Ismailis, for instance, the world-wide branch of Islam of which the Aga Khan is the head, tithing is still the rule, and no promising high school graduate misses the chance of going to college merely because he comes from a poor family. Despite governmental programs, that is no longer true of the United States. So perhaps we have let ourselves become too skeptical too soon about the friendliness of "friendly societies," and we should take more seriously the possibility of reviving social instruments with local roots, which do not need to insist on rigidly rule-governed procedures. That is of course a large "perhaps." The social changes that led to the nationalization of charity are powerful and longstanding, and thus far they have shown little sign of weakening. Given a choice, people may prefer to continue putting up with bureaucratic forms and procedures that they can grumble at with impunity if in this way they can avoid putting themselves at the mercy of social or communal relationships that they may find onerous.

FRAIL HOPES AND SLENDER FOUNDATIONS

In the field of ethics, all these difficulties are magnified. There I have one firm intellectual conviction, and one somewhat frailer hope on the social level.

In a 1932 poem Robert Frost wrote:

Don't join too many gangs. Join few if any.
Join the United States, and join the family.
But not much in between, unless a college.[9]

Frost, in his curmudgeonly way, captures that hostility toward communal ties and restraints which, since Tolstoy's day, has continued to undermine our "intermediate institutions" or "mediating structures." Toward the nuclear family and the nation, people do indeed still feel some natural loyalty; "but not much in between, unless a college." During the last thirty years, even the nation-state has lost much of its mystique, leaving the family exposed to stresses that it can hardly support. It is my frail social hope that we may find some new ways of shaping other intermediate institutions toward which we can develop a fuller loyalty and commitment: associations larger than the nuclear family, but not so large that they defeat in advance the initial presumption that our fellow members are trustworthy. For it is only in that context, I suspect, that the ethics of discretion and intimacy can regain the ground it has lost to the ethics of rules and strangers.

Where might we look for the beginnings of such associations? Traditionally their loci were determined by religious and ethnic ties, and these are still sometimes used constructively to extend the range of people's moral sympathies beyond the immediate household. But we scarcely need to look as far as Ulster or Lebanon to see the other side of that particular coin. Membership in schools and colleges has some of the same power, as Frost grudgingly admits, though it is a power that tends to operate exclusively rather than generously. The great ethical hope of the Marxists was that "working-class solidarity" would, in effect, create a vast and cohesive extended family within which the dispossessed would find release from psychological as well as from political and economic oppression. But by now, alas, the evidence of history seems to show that awareness of shared injuries sets different groups against one another quite as often as it unites them. For some of us, the bonds of professional association are as powerful as any. The physicians of Tarrytown or the attorneys of Hyde Park probably have a close understanding of, feeling for, and even trust in one another; and despite all other reservations about my fellow academics, I do still have a certain implicit trust in their professional responsibility and integrity. So each year, without any serious anxiety, I vote for colleagues whom I have never even met to serve on the boards that manage my pension funds. If it were proved that those elected representatives had been milking the premiums and salting them away in a Swiss bank, that revelation would shake up my moral universe more radically than any dishonesty among public figures on the national level.

True, these are frail hopes and provide only slender foundations to build on. Yet, in the realm of ethics, frail hopes and slender foundations may be what we should learn to live with as much better than nothing. And that brings me to the intellectual point about which I am much more confident. If the cult of absolute principles is so attractive today, that is a sign that we still find it impossible to break with the "quest for certainty" that John Dewey tried so hard to discredit.[10] Not that we needed Dewey to point out the shortcomings of absolutism. Aristotle himself had insisted that there are no "essences" in the realm of ethics, and so no basis for any rigorous "theory" of ethics. Practical reasoning in ethics, as elsewhere, is a matter of judgment, of weighing different considerations against one another, never a matter of formal theoretical deduction from strict or self-evident axioms. It is a task less for the clever arguer than for the *anthropos megalopsychos,* the "large-spirited human being."

It was not for nothing, then, that the members of the National Commission for the Protection of Human Subjects were able to agree about the ethical issues for just so long as they discussed those issues taxonomically. In doing so they were reviving the older, Aristotelian procedures of the casuists and rabbinical scholars, who understood all along that in ethics, as in law, the best we can achieve in practice is for good-hearted, clear-headed people to triangulate their way across the complex terrain of moral life and problems. So, starting from the paradigmatic cases that we do understand—what in the simplest situations harm is, and fairness, and cruelty, and generosity—we must simply work our way, one step at a time, to the more complex and perplexing cases in which extremely delicate balances may have to be struck. For example, we must decide on just what conditions, if any, it would be acceptable to inject a sample group of five-year-old children with an experimental vaccine from which countless other children should benefit even though the risks fall on those few individuals alone. Ethical argumentation thus makes most effective progress if we think of the "common morality" in the same way as we think about the common law: if, for instance, we develop our perception of moral issues by the same kind of progressive triangulation that has extended common law doctrines of tort into the areas, first of negligence and later of strict liability.

Meanwhile, we must remain on guard against the moral enthusiasts. In their determination to nail their principles to the mast, they succeed only in blinding themselves to the equities embodied in real-life situations and problems. Their willingness to legislate morality threatens to transform the most painful and intimate moral quandaries into adversarial confrontations between strangers. To take one example, by reintroducing uncompromising legal restraints to enjoin all procedures of abortion whatever, they are pitting a woman against her own newly implanted zygote in some ghastly parody of a landlord-tenant dispute. This harsh inflexibility sets the present day moral enthusiasts in sharp contrast to Aristotle's *anthropoi megalopsychoi,* and recalls Tolstoy's portrait of Alexei Karenin's associate, the Countess Ivanovna, who in theory was a supporter of all fashionable good causes but in practice was ready to act harshly and unforgivingly.

When Pascal attacked the Jesuit casuists for being too ready to make allowances in favor of penitents who were rich or highborn, he no doubt had a point. But when he used this point as a reason for completely rejecting the case method in ethics, he set the bad example that is so often followed today: assuming that we must withdraw discretion entirely when it is abused and impose rigid rules in its place, instead of inquiring how we could adjust matters so that necessary discretion would continue to be exercised in an equitable and discriminating manner. I vote without hesitation against Pascal and for the Jesuits and the Talmudic scholars. We do not need to go as far as Tolstoy and claim that an ethics modeled on law rather than on equity is no ethics at all. But we do need to recognize that a morality based entirely on general rules and principles is tyrannical and disproportioned, and that only those who make equitable allowances for subtle individual differences have a proper feeling for the deeper demands of ethics. In practice the casuists may occasionally have been lax; but they grasped the essential, Aristotelian point about applied ethics: it cannot get along on a diet of general principles alone. It requires a detailed taxonomy of particular, detailed types of cases and situations. So, even in practice, the faults of the casuists—such as they were—were faults on the right side.

NOTES

1 So, at any rate, current legend reports. On the other hand, having worked through the files of the *Journal* for 1974–75 without finding any article or editorial on the subject, I am inclined to suspect that this may have been a casual remark by the late Dr. Franz Ingelfinger, the distinguished editor of the periodical.

2 Thomas Aquinas, *Commentarium Libro Tertio Sententiarum,* D.3, Q.5, A.2, Solutio.

3 Peter Stein, *Regulae Juris* (Edinburgh: Edinburgh University Press, 1966), pp. 4–10.

4 Stein, pp. 26ff, 80–82, 124–27.

5 John Rawls, *Theory of Justice,* (Cambridge, Mass: Harvard University Press, 1971).

6 Monroe Freedman, *Lawyers' Ethics in an Adversary System* (Indianapolis: Bobbs Merrill, 1975). In this connection, current Chinese attempts to turn criminal proceedings into a

species of chummy conciliation between the defendant and his fellow citizens can too easily serve to conceal tyranny behind a mask of paternalistic goodwill.

7 Herbert Kaufman, *Red Tape: Its Origins, Uses and Abuses* (Washington, D.C.: Brookings Institution 1977).

8 *Ibid.*, p. 77.

9 Robert Frost, "Build Soil—a Political Pastoral." in *Complete Poems of Robert Frost* (New York: Holt, Rinehart & Winston, 1949), pp. 421–32, at p. 430.

10 John Dewey. *The Quest for Certainty* (New York: Putnam, 1929).

The Fundamental Principle of Ethics

Immanuel Kant

Everything in nature works according to laws. Only a rational being has the capacity of acting according to the conception of laws, i.e., according to principles. This capacity is will. . . . The conception of an objective principle, so far as it constrains a will, is a command (of reason), and the formula of this command is called an *imperative*.

All imperatives are expressed by an "ought" and thereby indicate the relation of an objective law of reason to a will which is not in its subjective constitution necessarily determined by this law. This relation is that of constraint. Imperatives say that it would be good to do or to refrain from doing something, but they say it to a will which does not always do something simply because it is presented as a good thing to do. Practical good is what determines the will by means of the conception of reason and hence not by subjective causes but, rather, objectively, i.e., on grounds which are valid for every rational being as such. . . .

All imperatives command either hypothetically or categorically. The former present the practical necessity of a possible action as a means to achieving something else which one desires (or which one may possibly desire). The categorical imperative would be one which presented an action as of itself objectively necessary, without regard to any other end.

Since every practical law presents a possible action as good and thus as necessary for a subject practically determinable by reason, all imperatives are formulas of the determination of action which is necessary by the principle of a will which is in any way good. If the action is good only as a means to something else, the imperative is hypothetical; but if it is thought of as good in itself, and hence as necessary in a will which of itself conforms to reason as the principle of this will, the imperative is categorical. . . . It concerns not the material of the action and its intended result but the form and the principle from which it results. What is essentially good in it consists

Immanuel Kant, *Foundations of the Metaphysics of Morals and What Is Enlightenment.* © 1959 The Liberal Arts Press, Inc. A Division of the Bobbs-Merrill Company, Inc.

in the intention, the result being what it may. This imperative may be called the imperative of morality. . . . For instance, when it is said, "Thou shalt not make a false promise," we assume that the necessity of this avoidance is not a mere counsel for the sake of escaping some other evil, so that it would read, "Thou shalt not make a false promise so that, if it comes to light, thou ruinest thy credit"; we assume rather that an action of this kind must be regarded as of itself bad and that the imperative of the prohibition is categorical. . . .

There is . . . only one categorical imperative. It is: Act only according to that maxim by which you can at the same time will that it should become a universal law.

Now if all imperatives of duty can be derived from this one imperative as a principle, we can at least show what we understand by the concept of duty and what it means, even though it remain undecided whether that which is called duty is an empty concept or not.

The universality of law according to which effects are produced constitutes what is properly called nature in the most general sense (as to form), i.e., the existence of things so far as it is determined by universal laws. [By analogy], then, the universal imperative of duty can be expressed as follows: Act as though the maxim of your action were by your will to become a universal law of nature.

We shall now enumerate some duties, adopting the usual division of them into duties to ourselves and to others and into perfect and imperfect duties.

1 A man who is reduced to despair by a series of evils feels a weariness with life but is still in possession of his reason sufficiently to ask whether it would not be contrary to his duty to himself to take his own life. Now he asks whether the maxim of his action could become a universal law of nature. His maxim, however, is: For love of myself, I make it my principle to shorten my life when by a longer duration it threatens more evil than satisfaction. But it is questionable whether this principle of self-love could become a universal law of nature. One immediately sees a contradiction in a system of nature whose law would be to destroy life by the feeling whose special office is to impel the improvement of life. In this case it would not exist as nature; hence that maxim cannot obtain as a law of nature, and thus it wholly contradicts the supreme principle of all duty.

2 Another man finds himself forced by need to borrow money. He well knows that he will not be able to repay it, but he also sees that nothing will be loaned him if he does not firmly promise to repay it at a certain time. He desires to make such a promise, but he has enough conscience to ask himself whether it is not improper and opposed to duty to relieve his distress in such a way. Now, assuming he does decide to do so, the maxim of his action would be as follows: When I believe myself to be in need of money, I will borrow money and promise to repay it, although I know I shall never do so. Now this principle of self-love or of his own benefit may very well be compatible with his whole future welfare, but the question is whether it is right. He changes the pretension of self-love into a universal law and then puts the question: How would it be if my maxim became a universal law? He immediately sees that it could never hold as a universal law of nature and be consistent with itself; rather it must necessarily contradict itself. For the universality of a law which says that anyone who believes

himself to be in need could promise what he pleased with the intention of not fulfilling it would make the promise itself and the end to be accomplished by it impossible; no one would believe what was promised to him but would only laugh at any such assertion as vain pretense.

3 A third finds in himself a talent which could, by means of some cultivation, make him in many respects a useful man. But he finds himself in comfortable circumstances and prefers indulgence in pleasure to troubling himself with broadening and improving his fortunate natural gifts. Now, however, let him ask whether his maxim of neglecting his gifts, besides agreeing with his propensity to idle amusement, agrees also with what is called duty. He sees that a system of nature could indeed exist in accordance with such a law, even though man (like the inhabitants of the South Sea Islands) should let his talents rust and resolve to devote his life merely to idleness, indulgence, and propagation—in a word, to pleasure. But he cannot possibly will that this should become a universal law of nature or that it should be implanted in us by a natural instinct. For, as a rational being, he necessarily wills that all his faculties should be developed, inasmuch as they are given to him for all sorts of possible purposes.

4 A fourth man, for whom things are going well, sees that others (whom he could help) have to struggle with great hardships, and he asks, "What concern of mine is it? Let each one be as happy as heaven wills, or as he can make himself; I will not take anything from him or even envy him; but to his welfare or to his assistance in time of need I have no desire to contribute." If such a way of thinking were a universal law of nature, certainly the human race could exist, and without doubt even better than in a state where everyone talks of sympathy and good will, or even exerts himself occasionally to practice them while, on the other hand, he cheats when he can and betrays or otherwise violates the rights of man. Now although it is possible that a universal law of nature according to that maxim could exist, it is nevertheless impossible to will that such a principle should hold everywhere as a law of nature. For a will which resolved this would conflict with itself, since instances can often arise in which he would need the love and sympathy of others, and in which he would have robbed himself, by such a law of nature springing from his own will, of all hope of the aid he desires.

The foregoing are a few of the many actual duties, or at least of duties we hold to be actual, whose derivation from the one stated principle is clear. We must be able to will that a maxim of our action become a universal law; this is the canon of the moral estimation of our action generally. Some actions are of such a nature that their maxim cannot even be *thought* as a universal law of nature without contradiction, far from it being possible that one could will that it should be such. In others this internal impossibility is not found, though it is still impossible to *will* that their maxim should be raised to the universality of a law of nature, because such a will would contradict itself. . . .

When we observe ourselves in any transgression of a duty, we find that we do not actually will that our maxim should become a universal law. That is impossible for us; rather, the contrary of this maxim should remain as a law generally, and we only take the liberty of making an exception to it for ourselves or for the sake of our inclination, and for this one occasion. Consequently, if we weighed everything from one and the same standpoint, namely, reason, we would come upon a contradiction in our own will, viz., that a certain principle is objectively necessary as a universal law and yet subjectively does not hold universally but rather admits exceptions. . . .

Two Concepts of Rules

John Rawls

In this paper I want to show the importance of the distinction between justifying a practice and justifying a particular action falling under it, and I want to explain the logical basis of this distinction and how it is possible to miss its significance. . . .

To explain how the significance of the distinction may be overlooked, I am going to discuss two conceptions of rules. One of these conceptions conceals the importance of distinguishing between the justification of a rule or practice and the justification of a particular action falling under it. The other conception makes it clear why this distinction must be made and what is its logical basis.

I

The subject of punishment, in the sense of attaching legal penalties to the violation of legal rules, has always been a troubling moral question. The trouble about it has not been that people disagree as to whether or not punishment is justifiable. Most people have held that, freed from certain abuses, it is an acceptable institution. Only a few have rejected punishment entirely, which is rather surprising when one considers all that can be said against it. The difficulty is with the justification of punishment: various arguments for it have been given by moral philosophers, but so far none of them has won any sort of general acceptance; no justification is without those who detest it. . . .

For our purposes we may say that there are two justifications of punishment. What we may call the retributive view is that punishment is justified on the grounds that wrongdoing merits punishment. It is morally fitting that a person who does wrong should suffer in proportion to his wrongdoing. That a criminal should be punished follows from his guilt, and the severity of the appropriate punishment depends on the depravity of his act. The state of affairs where a wrongdoer suffers punishment is morally better than the state of affairs where he does not; and it is better irrespective of any of the consequences of punishing him.

What we may call the utilitarian view holds that on the principle that bygones are bygones and that only future consequences are material to present decisions, punishment is justifiable only by reference to the probable consequences of maintaining it

John Rawls, "Two Concepts of Rules," *Philosophical Review*, vol. 64, no. 1, January 1955, pp. 3–32.

as one of the devices of the social order. Wrongs committed in the past are, as such, not relevant considerations for deciding what to do. If punishment can be shown to promote effectively the interest of society it is justifiable, otherwise it is not.

I have stated these two competing views very roughly to make one feel the conflict between them: one feels the force of *both* arguments and one wonders how they can be reconciled. From my introductory remarks it is obvious that the resolution which I am going to propose is that in this case one must distinguish between justifying a practice as a system of rules to be applied and enforced, and justifying a particular action which falls under these rules; utilitarian arguments are appropriate with regard to questions about practices, while retributive arguments fit the application of particular rules to particular cases.

We might try to get clear about this distinction by imagining how a father might answer the question of his son. Suppose the son asks, "Why was *J* put in jail yesterday?" The father answers, "Because he robbed the bank at *B*. He was duly tried and found guilty. That's why he was put in jail yesterday." But suppose the son had asked a different question, namely, "Why do people put other people in jail?" Then the father might answer, "To protect good people from bad people" or "To stop people from doing things that would make it uneasy for all of us; for otherwise we wouldn't be able to go to bed at night and sleep in peace." There are two very different questions here. One question emphasizes the proper name: it asks why *J* was punished rather than someone else, or it asks what he was punished for. The other question asks why we have the institution of punishment: why do people punish one another rather than, say, always forgiving one another?

Thus the father says in effect that a particular man is punished, rather than some other man, because he is guilty, and he is guilty because he broke the law (past tense). In his case the law looks back, the judge looks back, the jury looks back, and a penalty is visited upon him for something he did. That a man is to be punished, and what his punishment is to be, is settled by its being shown that he broke the law and that the law assigns that penalty for the violation of it.

On the other hand we have the institution of punishment itself, and recommend and accept various changes in it, because it is thought by the (ideal) legislator and by those to whom the law applies that, as a part of a system of law impartially applied from case to case arising under it, it will have the consequence, in the long run, of furthering the interests of society.

One can say, then, that the judge and the legislator stand in different positions and look in different directions: one to the past, the other to the future. The justification of what the judge does, *qua* judge, sounds like the retributive view; the justification of what the (ideal) legislator does, *qua* legislator, sounds like the utilitarian view. Thus both views have a point (this is as it should be since intelligent and sensitive persons have been on both sides of the argument); and one's initial confusion disappears once one sees that these views apply to persons holding different offices with different duties, and situated differently with respect to the system of rules that make up the criminal law. . . .

The answer, then, to the confusion engendered by the two views of punishment is quite simple: one distinguishes two offices, that of the judge and that of the legislator, and one distinguishes their different stations with respect to the system of rules which make up the law; and then one notes that the different sorts of considerations which would usually be offered as reasons for what is done under the cover of these offices can be paired off with the competing justifications of punishment. One reconciles the two views by the time-honored device of making them apply to different situations. . . .

II

I shall now consider the question of promises. The objection to utilitarianism in connection with promises seems to be this: it is believed that on the utilitarian view when a person makes a promise the only ground upon which he should keep it, if he should keep it, is that by keeping it he will realize the most good on the whole. So that if one asks the question "Why should I keep *my* promise?" the utilitarian answer is understood to be that doing so in *this* case will have the best consequences. And the answer is said, quite rightly, to conflict with the way in which the obligation to keep promises is regarded.

Now of course critics of utilitarianism are not unaware that one defense sometimes attributed to utilitarians is the consideration involving the practice of promise-keeping.[1] In this connection they are supposed to argue something like this: it must be admitted that we feel strictly about keeping promises, more strictly than it might seem our view can account for. But when we consider the matter carefully it is always necessary to take into account the effect which our action will have on the practice of making promises. The promisor must weigh, not only the effects of breaking his promise on the particular case, but also the effect which his breaking his promise will have on the practice itself. Since the practice is of great utilitarian value, and since breaking one's promise always seriously damages it, one will seldom be justified in breaking one's promise. If we view our individual promises in the wider context of the practice of promising itself we can account for the strictness of the obligation to keep promises. There is always one very strong utilitarian consideration in favor of keeping them, and this will insure that when the question arises as to whether or not to keep a promise it will usually turn out that one should, even where the facts of the particular case taken by itself would seem to justify one's breaking it. In this way the strictness with which we view the obligation to keep promises is accounted for.

Ross has criticized this defense as follows:[2] however great the value of the practice of promising, on utilitarian grounds, there must be some value which is greater, and one can imagine it to be obtainable by breaking a promise. Therefore there might be a case where the promisor could argue that breaking his promise was justified as leading to a better state of affairs on the whole. And the promisor could argue in this way no matter how slight the advantage won by breaking the promise. If one were to challenge the promisor his defense would be that what he did was best on the whole in view of all the utilitarian considerations, which in this case *include* the importance of the practice. Ross feels that such a defense would be unacceptable. I think he is right insofar as he is protesting against the appeal to consequences in general and without further explanation. Yet it is extremely difficult to weigh the force of Ross's argument. The kind of case imagined seems unrealistic and one feels that it needs to be described. One is inclined to think that it would either turn out that such a case came under an exception defined by the practice itself, in which case there would not be an appeal to consequences in general on the particular case, or it would happen that the circumstances were so peculiar that the conditions which the practice presupposes no longer obtained. But certainly Ross is right in thinking that it strikes us as wrong for a person to defend breaking a promise by a general appeal to consequences. For a general utilitarian defense is not open to the promisor: it is not one of the defenses allowed by the practice of making promises.

Ross gives two further counterarguments.[3] First, he holds that it overestimates the damage done to the practice of promising by a failure to keep a promise. One who breaks a promise harms his own name certainly, but it isn't clear that a broken promise always damages the practice itself sufficiently to account for the strictness of the obligation. Second, and more important, I think, he raises the question of what one is to say of a promise which isn't known to have been made except to the promisor and the promisee, as in the case of a promise a son makes to his dying father concerning the handling of the estate. In this sort of case the consideration relating to the practice doesn't weigh on the promisor at all, and yet one feels that this sort of promise is as binding as other promises. The question of the effect which breaking it has on the practice seems irrelevant. The only consequence seems to be that one can break the promise without running any risk of being censured; but the obligation itself seems not the least weakened. Hence it is doubtful whether the effect on the practice ever weighs in the particular case; certainly it cannot account for the strictness of the obligation where it fails to obtain. It seems to follow that a utilitarian account of the obligation to keep promises cannot be successfully carried out.

From what I have said in connection with punishment, one can foresee what I am going to say about these arguments and counterarguments. They fail to make the distinction between the justification of a practice and the justification of a particular action falling under it, and therefore they fall into the mistake of taking it for granted that the promisor . . . is entitled without restriction to bring utilitarian considerations to bear in deciding whether to keep *his* promise. But if one considers what the practice of promising is one will see, I think, that it is such as not to allow this sort of general discretion to the promisor. Indeed, the point of the practice is to abdicate one's title to act in accordance with utilitarian and prudential considerations in order that the future may be tied down and plans coordinated in advance. There are obvious utilitarian advantages in having a practice which denies to the promisor, as a defense, any general appeal to the utilitarian principle in accordance with which the practice itself may be justified. There is nothing contradictory, or surprising, in this: utilitarian (or aesthetic) reasons might properly be given in arguing that the game of chess, or baseball, is satisfactory just as it is, or in arguing that it should be changed in various respects, but a player in a game cannot properly appeal to such considerations as reasons for his making one move rather than another. It is a mistake to think that if the practice is justified on utilitarian grounds then the promisor must have complete liberty to use utilitarian arguments to decide whether or not to keep his promise. The practice forbids this general defense; and it is a purpose of the practice to do this. Therefore what the above arguments presuppose—the idea that if the utilitarian view is accepted then the promisor is bound if, and only if, the application of the utilitarian principle to his own case shows that keeping it is best on the whole—is false. The promisor is bound because he promised: weighing the case on its merits is not open to him.

III

So far I have tried to show the importance of the distinction between the justification of a practice and the justification of a particular action falling under it by indicating how this distinction might be used to defend utilitarianism against two long-standing objections. One might be tempted to close the discussion at this point by saying that utilitarian considerations should be understood as applying to practices in the first instance and not to particular actions falling under them except insofar as the practices admit of it. One might say that in this modified form it is a better account of our considered moral opinions and let it go at that. But to stop here would be to neglect the interesting question as to how one can fail to appreciate the significance of this rather obvious distinction and can take it for granted that utilitarianism has the consequence that particular cases may always be decided on general utilitarian grounds. I want to argue that this mistake may be connected with misconceiving the logical status of the rules of practices; and to show this I am going to examine two conceptions of rules, two ways of placing them within the utilitarian theory.

The conception which conceals from us the significance of the distinction I am going to call the summary view. It regards rules in the following way: one supposes that each person decides what he shall do in particular cases by applying the utilitarian principle; one supposes further that different people will decide the same particular case in the same way and that there will be recurrences of cases similar to those previously decided. Thus it will happen that in cases of certain kinds the same decision will be made either by the same person at different times or by different persons at the same time. If a case occurs frequently enough one supposes that a rule is formulated to cover that sort of case. I have called this conception the summary view because rules are pictured as summaries of past decisions arrived at by the *direct* application of the utilitarian principle to particular cases. Rules are regarded as reports that cases of a certain sort have been found on *other* grounds to be properly decided in a certain way (although, of course, they do not *say* this).

There are several things to notice about this way of placing rules within the utilitarian theory.

1 The point of having rules derives from the fact that similar cases tend to recur and that one can decide cases more quickly if one records past decisions in the form of rules. If similar cases didn't recur, one would be required to apply the utilitarian principle directly, case by case, and rules reporting past decisions would be of no use.

2 The decisions made on particular cases are logically prior to rules. Since rules gain their point from the need to apply the utilitarian principle to many similar cases, it follows that a particular case (or several cases similar to it) may exist whether or not there is a rule covering that case. We are pictured as recognizing particular cases prior to there being a rule which covers them, for it is only if we meet with a number

of cases of a certain sort that we formulate a rule. Thus we are able to describe a particular case as a particular case of the requisite sort whether there is a rule regarding *that* sort of case or not. . . .

To illustrate this consider a rule, or maxim, which could arise in this way: suppose that a person is trying to decide whether to tell someone who is fatally ill what his illness is when he has been asked to do so. Suppose the person to reflect and then decide, on utilitarian grounds, that he should not answer truthfully; and suppose that on the basis of this and other like occasions he formulates a rule to the effect that when asked by someone fatally ill what his illness is, one should not tell him. The point to notice is that someone's being fatally ill and asking what his illness is, and someone's telling him, are things that can be described as such whether or not there is this rule. The performance of the action to which the rule refers doesn't require the stage-setting of a practice of which this rule is a part. This is what is meant by saying that on the summary view particular cases are logically prior to rules.

3 Each person is in principle always entitled to reconsider the correctness of a rule and to question whether or not it is proper to follow it in a particular case. As rules are guides and aids, one may ask whether in past decisions there might not have been a mistake in applying the utilitarian principle to get the rule in question, and wonder whether or not it is best in this case. The reason for rules is that people are not able to apply the utilitarian principle effortlessly and flawlessly; there is need to save time and to post a guide. On this view a society of rational utilitarians would be a society without rules in which each person applied the utilitarian principle directly and smoothly, and without error, case by case. On the other hand, ours is a society in which rules are formulated to serve as aids in reaching these ideally rational decisions on particular cases, guides which have been built up and tested by the experience of generations. If one applies this view to rules, one is interpreting them as maxims, as "rules of thumb"; and it is doubtful that anything to which the summary conception did apply would be called a *rule*. Arguing as if one regarded rules in this way is a mistake one makes while doing philosophy.

4 The concept of a *general* rule takes the following form. One is pictured as estimating on what percentage of the cases likely to arise a given rule may be relied upon to express the correct decision, that is, the decision that would be arrived at if one were to correctly apply the utilitarian principle case by case. If one estimates that by and large the rule will give the correct decision, or if one estimates that the likelihood of making a mistake by applying the utilitarian principle directly on one's own is greater than the likelihood of making a mistake by following the rule, and if these considerations held of persons generally, then one would be justified in urging its adoption as a general rule. In this way *general* rules might be accounted for on the summary view. It will still make sense, however, to speak of applying the utilitarian principle case by case, for it was by trying to foresee the results of doing this that one got the initial estimates upon which acceptance of the rule depends. That one is taking a rule in accordance with the summary conception will show itself in the naturalness with which one speaks of the rule as a guide, or as a maxim, or as a generalization from experience, and as something to be laid aside in extraordinary cases where there

is no assurance that the generalization will hold and the case must therefore be treated on its merits. Thus there goes with this conception the notion of a particular exception which renders a rule suspect on a particular occasion.

The other conception of rules I will call the practice conception. On this view rules are pictured as defining a practice. Practices are set up for various reasons, but one of them is that in many areas of conduct each person's deciding what to do on utilitarian grounds case by case leads to confusion, and that the attempt to coordinate behavior by trying to foresee how others will act is bound to fail. As an alternative one realizes that what is required is the establishment of a practice, the specification of a new form of activity; and from this one sees that a practice necessarily involves the abdication of full liberty to act on utilitarian and prudential grounds. It is the mark of a practice that being taught how to engage in it involves being instructed in the rules which define it, and that appeal is made to those rules to correct the behavior of those engaged in it. Those engaged in a practice recognize the rules as defining it. The rules cannot be taken as simply describing how those engaged in the practice in fact behave: it is not simply that they act as if they were obeying the rules. Thus it is essential to the notion of a practice that the rules are publicly known and understood as definitive; and it is essential also that the rules of a practice can be taught and can be acted upon to yield a coherent practice. On this conception, then, rules are not generalizations from the decisions of individuals applying the utilitarian principle directly and independently to recurrent particular cases. On the contrary, rules define a practice and are themselves the subject of the utilitarian principle.

To show the important differences between this way of fitting rules into the utilitarian theory and the previous way, I shall consider the differences between the two conceptions on the points previously discussed.

1 In contrast with the summary view, the rules of practices are logically prior to particular cases. This is so because there cannot be a particular case of an action falling under a rule of a practice unless there is the practice. This can be made clearer as follows: in a practice there are rules setting up offices, specifying certain forms of action appropriate to various offices, establishing penalties for the breach of rules, and so on. We may think of the rules of a practice as defining offices, moves, and offenses. Now what is meant by saying that the practice is logically prior to particular cases is this: given any rule which specifies a form of action (a move), a particular action which would be taken as falling under this rule given that there is the practice would not be *described as* that sort of action unless there was the practice. In the case of actions specified by practices it is logically impossible to perform them outside the stage-setting provided by those practices, for unless there is the practice, and unless the requisite proprieties are fulfilled, whatever one does, whatever movements one makes, will fail to count as a form of action which the practice specifies. What one does will be described in some *other* way.

One may illustrate this point from the game of baseball. Many of the actions one performs in a game of baseball one can do by oneself or with others whether there is the game or not. For example, one can throw a ball, run, or swing a peculiarly shaped piece of wood. But one cannot steal base, or strike out, or draw a walk, or make an error, or balk; although one can do certain things which appear to resemble these actions such as sliding into a bag, missing a grounder and so on. Striking out, stealing a base, balking, etc., are all actions which can only happen in a game. No matter what a person did, what he did would not be described as stealing a base or striking out or drawing a walk unless he could also be described as playing baseball, and for him to be doing this presupposes the rule-like practice which constitutes the game. The practice is logically prior to particular cases: unless there is the practice the terms referring to actions specified by it lack a sense.

2 The practice view leads to an entirely different conception of the authority which each person has to decide on the propriety of following a rule in particular cases. To engage in a practice, to perform those actions specified by a practice, means to follow the appropriate rules. If one wants to do an action which a certain practice specifies then there is no way to do it except to follow the rules which define it. Therefore, it doesn't make sense for a person to raise the question whether or not a rule of a practice correctly applies to *his* case where the action he contemplates is a form of action defined by a practice. If someone were to raise such a question, he would simply show that he didn't understand the situation in which he was acting. If one wants to perform an action specified by a practice, the only legitimate question concerns the nature of the practice itself ("How do I go about making a will?").

This point is illustrated by the behavior expected of a player in games. If one wants to play a game, one doesn't treat the rules of the game as guides as to what is best in particular cases. In a game of baseball if a batter were to ask "Can I have four strikes?" it would be assumed that he was asking what the rule was; and if, when told what the rule was, he were to say that he meant that on this occasion he thought it would be best on the whole for him to have four strikes rather than three, this would be most kindly taken as a joke. One might contend that baseball would be a better game if four strikes were allowed instead of three; but one cannot picture the rules as guides to what is best on the whole in particular cases, and question their applicability to particular cases as particular cases.

3 and 4 To complete the four points of comparison with the summary conception, it is clear from what has been said that rules of practices are not guides to help one decide particular cases correctly as judged by some higher ethical principle. And neither the quasi-statistical notion of generality, nor the notion of a particular exception, can apply to the rules of practices. A more or less general rule of a practice must be a rule which according to the structure of the practice applies to more or fewer of the kinds of cases arising under it; or it must be a rule which is more or less basic to the understanding of the practice. Again, a particular case cannot be an exception to a rule of a practice. An exception is rather a qualification or a further specification of the rule.

It follows from what we have said about the practice conception of rules that if a person is engaged in a practice, and if he is asked why *he* does what *he* does, or if he is asked to defend what he does, then his explanation, or defense, lies in referring the questioner to the practice. He cannot say of *his* action, if it is an action specified by a practice, that he does it rather than some other because he thinks it is best on the whole. When a man engaged in a practice is queried about his action he must assume that the questioner either doesn't know that he is engaged in it ("Why are you in a hurry to pay him?" "I promised to pay him today") or doesn't know what the practice is. One doesn't so much justify one's particular action as explain, or show, that it is in accordance with the practice. The reason for this is that it is only against the stage-setting of the practice that one's particular action is described as it is. Only by reference to the practice can one *say* what one is doing. To explain or to defend one's own action, as a particular action, one fits it into the practice which defines it. If this is not accepted it's a sign that a different question is being raised as to whether one is justified in accepting the practice, or in tolerating it. When the challenge is to the practice, citing the rules (saying what the practice is) is naturally to no avail. But when the challenge is to the particular action defined by the practice, there is nothing one can do but refer to the rules. Concerning particular actions there is only a question for one who isn't clear as to what the practice is, or who doesn't know that it is being engaged in. This is to be contrasted with the case of a maxim which may be taken as pointing to the correct decision on the case as decided on *other* grounds, and so giving a challenge on the case a sense by having it question whether these other grounds really support the decision on this case.

If one compares the two conceptions of rules I have discussed, one can see how the summary conception misses the significance of the distinction between justifying a practice and justifying actions falling under it. On this view rules are regarded as guides whose purpose it is to indicate the ideally rational decision on the given particular case which the flawless application of the utilitarian principle would yield. One has, in principle, full option to use the guides or to discard them as the situation warrants without one's moral office being altered in any way: whether one discards the rules or not, one always holds the office of a rational person seeking case by case to realize the best on the whole. But on the practice conception, if one holds an office defined by a practice then questions regarding one's actions in this office are settled by reference to the rules which define the practice. If one seeks to question these rules, then one's office undergoes a fundamental change: one then assumes the office of one empowered to change and criticize the rules, or the office of a reformer, and so on. The summary conception does away with the distinction of offices and the various forms of argument appropriate to each. On that conception there is one office and so no offices at all. It therefore obscures the fact that the utilitarian principle must, in the case of actions and offices defined by a practice, apply to the practice, so that general utilitarian arguments are not available to those who act in offices so defined.[4]

Some qualifications are necessary in what I have said. First, I may have talked of the summary and the practice conceptions of rules as if only one of them could be true of rules, and if true of any rules, then necessarily true of *all* rules. I do not, of course, mean this. (It is the critics of utilitarianism who make this mistake insofar as their arguments against utilitarianism presuppose a summary conception of the rules of practices.) Some rules will fit one conception, some rules the other; and so there are rules of practices (rules in the strict sense), and maxims and "rules of thumb."

Secondly, there are further distinctions that can be made in classifying rules, distinctions which should be made if one were considering other questions. The distinctions which I have drawn are those most relevant for the rather special matter I have discussed, and are not intended to be exhaustive.

Finally, there will be many border-line cases about which it will be difficult, if not impossible, to decide which conception of rules is applicable. One expects border-line cases with any concept, and they are especially likely in connection with such involved concepts as those of a practice, institution, game, rule, and so on. . . . What I have done is to emphasize and sharpen two conceptions for the limited purpose of this paper.

NOTES

1 Ross, *The Right and the Good,* pp. 37–39, and *Foundations of Ethics* (Oxford, 1939), pp. 92–94. I know of no utilitarian who has used this argument except W. A. Pickard-Cambridge in "Two Problems about Duty," *Mind,* n.s., XLI (April, 1932), 153–157, although the argument goes with G. E. Moore's version of utilitarianism in *Principia Ethica* (Cambridge, 1903). To my knowledge it does not appear in the classical utilitarians; and if one interprets their view correctly this is no accident.

2 Ross, *The Right and the Good,* pp. 38–39.

3 Ross, *ibid.,* p. 39. The case of the nonpublic promise is discussed again in *Foundations of Ethics,* pp. 95–96, 104–105. It occurs also in J. D. Mabbott, "Punishment," *Mind,* n.s., vol. XLVIII (April, 1939), pp. 155–157, and in A. I. Melden, "Two Comments on Utilitarianism," *Philosophical Review,* LX (October, 1951), 519–523. . . .

4 How do these remarks apply to the case of the promise known only to father and son? Well, at first sight the son certainly holds the office of promisor, and so he isn't allowed by the practice to weigh the particular case on general utilitarian grounds. Suppose instead that he wishes to consider himself in the office of one empowered to criticize and change the practice, leaving aside the question as to his right to move from his previously assumed office to another. Then he may consider utilitarian arguments as applied to the practice; but once he does this he will see that there are such arguments for not allowing a general utilitarian defense in the practice for this sort of case. For to do so would make it impossible to ask for and to give a kind of promise which one often wants to be able to ask for and to give. Therefore he will not want to change the practice, and so as a promisor he has no option but to keep his promise.

PART **THREE**

FUNDAMENTAL ETHICAL PRINCIPLES AND CONCEPTS

CHAPTER 7

RESPECT FOR PERSONS

All of us have at least occasionally said or heard someone saying, "Don't treat me like a doormat" or "I am not simply a sex object, I am a person" or "I am somebody." We often criticize bureaucrats because they don't treat us as individuals. Behind these popular expressions is a fundamental moral principle—the principle of respect for persons. Moreover, this principle is as fundamental in theoretical discussions of ethics as it is in popular discussions. This chapter provides an analysis of the fundamental ethical principle of respect for persons. Although an appeal to the principle of respect for persons usually receives a sympathetic response, it does need some defense. After all, what's so important about us? Isn't this appeal to our special nature just the kind of appeal that ethical skeptics and behaviorists like Skinner reject? An early thinker noted that humans painted the gods to resemble humans and that if animals could paint they would paint their gods to look like animals. Contemporary science fiction writers have created a number of interesting episodes around the following plot: Human beings rule the world and treat all other living creatures as means to their own ends. This behavior is justified on the basis that human beings are superior. Then aliens from another solar system arrive on earth. They are clearly superior to us and the tables are turned. Instead of being cooks, the human beings are cooked, and the aliens justify their treatment of us in exactly the same way that we justify our treatment of animals. Surely these science fiction writers have a point. Recognition that we are special, if we are, ought to carry with it a good dose of humility; we must recognize that there may be other forms of life in the universe which are superior to us. However, the science fiction writers do not undercut the point that we are superior to other animals; they undercut using that superiority as a basis for treating other animals the way we do.

What is needed is some argument on behalf of the fundamental principle, "Respect persons." The justification of the principle has two parts. On the one hand, an argument is needed to show that the principle should include humans but should not include reference to any other living thing. On the other hand, an argument is needed to show that the principle should not rule anyone out on arbitrary grounds, e.g., that it not be used to exclude blue-eyed people as nonpersons.

Let's consider arguments for including only human beings. One of the most developed arguments is Aristotle's. Think of Aristotle as the great classifier. Alexander the Great, a pupil of Aristotle's, sent Aristotle the equivalent of the contents of a huge garage sale—everything from different species of animals to different constitutions. How should the garage sale be organized? Isn't it rational to begin by putting like with like? But almost any two objects have some characteristics they share and some characteristics which differentiate them. How is the selection to be made? Aristotle looked for unique characteristics—what do these individuals have which no other individuals have? Human beings have the capacity to reason. This differentiates them from all other things. Aristotle believed that since human beings had the same capacities as other living things as well as this additional capacity to reason, human beings were superior. This belief usually operates as an unanalyzed assumption, but it is an assumption that is deeply embedded in our language and practice. As previously indicated, one of the great put-downs is to charge that someone is no more than an animal. "He's just a male-chauvinist pig!"

Another account which addresses both questions is provided in the selection by Immanuel Kant. Kant's initial formulation of the categorical imperative was discussed in Chapter 6. Kant formulated another version of the categorical imperative which serves as one way of stating the principle of respect for persons. Kant's statement is "Treat persons as ends and never as merely a means." In defense of his principle Kant draws on the distinction between conditional value and unconditional value and then asks the question, "How does anything come to be valued?" How does a painting by Picasso or the Grand Canyon get its value? The painting, the Grand Canyon, and everything else come to be valued because human beings bestow value on them. All these things have conditional values. All things that have value have value with respect to us. Since we human beings are rational and autonomous, Kant argues, human beings have unconditional value. Our value does not depend on anyone else.

But what gives human beings this special place? Why are human beings the only objects which have unconditional value? Is it just an accident of nature based on the fact that human beings have more power? That wouldn't be Kant's view. Rather Kant appeals to reason. It is in our capacity as rational creatures that we bestow value on other creatures and that human beings have unconditional value. Indeed Kant views human beings as a kind of ideal rational community (a realm of ends) whose members are both subject and sovereign at the same time. They are sovereign because they formulate the rules that apply to all, and they are subject because they should obey the rules made by themselves and others. However, since in the ideal rational community all rule-making is rational, the rules are universal, and hence we can be both subject and sovereign with respect to them. Construe Kant's fundamental principles as analogous to fundamental principles in mathematics. The same fundamental moral rules hold for all rational moral beings just as the same mathematical principles hold for all mathematicians. It is just this capacity to legislate universal moral rules on the basis of reason which gives human beings their dignity. Human beings are special because they are capable of being moral agents.

It is this analysis of human reason that enables us to show how Kant's version of the respect-for-persons principle, "Treat persons as ends and never as merely a means," avoids arbitrarily excluding anyone from the realm of persons. The ability to use moral reason, like the ability to use mathematical reason, does not depend on any other feature associated with being human—with height, weight, race, or sex. No subgroup of human beings can be excluded, because all types of human beings share the capacity for moral thought.

Of course, Kant needs a theory of potential capacity and diminished capacity to make room for infants and the brain-damaged. Moreover, Kant ignored the people that today are classified as social psychopaths. On his definition they wouldn't be persons because they are incapable of subjecting themselves to the moral law—they have no sense of right and wrong. And even here Kant may not be totally wrong; such creatures are considered human beings in a very diminished sense—if they are considered human beings at all. A son who murders his mother, cuts her up, and puts her in the garbage can and feels no guilt or shame isn't considered human by a lot of people. A moral sensitivity and a capacity for reason are considered essential human characteristics and are not the sole property of any sex, race, or class. That is Kant's point.

Another defense of the Kantian principle is provided in a recent book by Alan Donagan. His strategy was to survey the western tradition, including its Jewish and Christian theological components, in search of a common underlying principle. He believes that such a common underlying principle is found in a variation of Kant's, viz., "It is impermissible not to respect every human being, oneself or any other, as a rational creature." Donagan believes that this variation has much in common with the scriptural commandment, "Thou shalt love thy neighbor as thyself." The common tradition constitutes the principle's ground. Rather than provide additional defenses of the common principle, Donagan provides a detailed analysis of how specific duties can be derived from it. For example, Donagan derives such familiar moral obligations as "Don't kill," "Don't commit suicide," "Don't do anything to impair your health," and "Adopt some coherent plan of life which will develop your capabilities."

Yet another twist on the argument in defense of Kant's principle is based on a theory of a person's moral development. If one is to fully develop as a person—that is, move from dependency to autonomous, rational adulthood—then a human being can't be servile. To be servile is to be dependent, and self-respect is a necessary condition for avoiding the attitude of servility. This basic argument is accepted and developed in the selection by Thomas E. Hill, Jr. He shows that there are two types of servility, and that in both cases what is needed to correct servility is a kind of self-respect. Hill then goes on to show why an attitude of servility is not only a defect but a particularly moral defect. In other words, the attitude of servility can be criticized on moral grounds.

Suppose Hill's argument is pretty much on the mark. The sad fact is that many minorities and most women throughout the world have either been kept in servility or have acquiesced in it. It is a moral imperative that such servility be ended. But immoral or unjust situations cannot be corrected overnight. It is almost always easier to be just at the outset than it is to correct injustice once it has occurred. Efforts in the United States to correct years of injustice against blacks serve as the obvious example. Many of the victims are dead and can't be compensated. In a stagnant economy something (for example, either cash through increased taxes or actual jobs) must be taken from the majority and given to the blacks. Often the members of the majority who are penalized were only slight and indirect beneficiaries of discrimination, yet they pay a high price. Resentment inevitably results. "White backlash" is an oft-discussed phenomenon. The situation in the United States concerning the attempt to correct for racial discrimination serves as a paradigm for the general question: Given the difficulties of correction, how long should the victims of an unjust policy wait until the situation is corrected? Virginia Held tries to answer that question in terms of the rate of progress which would be consistent with the victim's self-respect.

If one had to identify one principle which has stood as the bedrock of nonconsequentialist ethics, it would be Immanuel Kant's "Treat persons as ends, never as merely a means" principle or some other version of the respect-for-persons principle. Indeed the respect-for-persons principle is so strongly entrenched that even consequentialists find it necessary to argue that consequentialist ethical theory can accommodate it. (For a distinction between nonconsequentialists and consequentialists, see the General Introduction.) Moreover, strong arguments can be marshaled on behalf of the principle. Since it is strongly entrenched in our moral consciousness, defended by strong arguments, and directly or indirectly accepted by all moral theories, the principle of respect for persons is a candidate for the status of ultimate and fundamental moral principle. This means that so long as it is properly understood, the basic idea behind both the Kantian principle of respect for persons and the variations on it is morally sound. Any adequate moral theory must give the principle or some acceptable version of it a significant role. No adequate moral theory can contain principles, rules, or concepts which are substantially inconsistent with it. Many, but not all, philosophers believe that with respect to this principle, relativism is mistaken. We have an ethical absolute.

Persons as Ends

Immanuel Kant

. . . Now, I say, man and, in general, every rational being exists as an end in himself and not merely as a means to be arbitrarily used by this or that will. In all his actions, whether they are directed to himself or to other rational beings, he must always be regarded at the same time as an end. All objects of inclinations have only a conditional worth, for if the inclinations and the needs founded on them did not exist, their object would be without worth. The inclinations themselves as the sources of needs, however, are so lacking in absolute worth that the universal wish of every rational being must be indeed to free himself completely from them. Therefore, the worth of any objects to be obtained by our actions is at all times conditional. Beings whose existence does not depend on our will but on nature, if they are not rational beings, have only a relative worth as means and are therefore called "things"; on the other hand, rational beings are designated "persons" because their nature indicates that they are ends in themselves, i.e., things which may not be used merely as means. Such a being is thus an object of respect and, so far, restricts all [arbitrary] choice. Such beings are not merely subjective ends whose existence as a result of our action has a worth for us, but are objective ends, i.e., beings whose existence in itself is an end. Such an end is one for which no other end can be substituted, to which these beings should serve merely as means. For, without them, nothing of absolute worth could be found, and if all worth is conditional and thus contingent, no supreme practical principle for reason could be found anywhere.

Thus if there is to be a supreme practical principle and a categorical imperative for the human will, it must be one that forms an objective principle of the will from the conception of that which is necessarily an end for everyone because it is an end in itself. Hence this objective principle can serve as a universal practical law. The ground of this principle is: rational nature exists as an end in itself. Man necessarily thinks of his own existence in this way; thus far it is a subjective principle of human actions. Also every other rational being thinks of his existence by means of the same rational ground which holds also for myself; thus it is at the same time an objective principle from which, as a supreme practical ground, it must be possible to derive all laws of the will. The practical imperative, therefore, is the following: Act so that you treat humanity, whether in your own person or in that of another, always as an end and never as a means only. Let us now see whether this can be achieved.

To return to our previous examples:

First, according to the concept of necessary duty to one's self, he who contemplates suicide will ask himself whether his action can be consistent with the idea of humanity as an end in itself. If, in order to escape from burdensome circumstances, he destroys himself, he uses a person merely as a means to maintain a tolerable condition up to the end of life. Man, however, is not a thing, and thus not something to be used merely as a means; he must always be regarded in all his actions as an end in himself. Therefore, I cannot dispose of man in my own person so as to mutilate, corrupt, or kill him. (It belongs to ethics proper to define more accurately this basic principle so as to avoid all misunderstanding, e.g., as to the amputation of limbs in order to preserve myself, or to exposing my life to danger in order to save it; I must, therefore, omit them here.)

Second, as concerns necessary or obligatory duties to others, he who intends a deceitful promise to others sees immediately that he intends to use another man merely as a means, without the latter containing the end in himself at the same time. For he whom I want to use for my own purposes by means of such a promise cannot possibly assent to my mode of acting against him and cannot contain the end of this action in himself. This conflict against the principle of other men is even clearer if we cite examples of attacks on their freedom and property. For then it is clear that he who transgresses the rights of men intends to make use of the persons of others merely as a means, without considering that, as rational beings, they must always be esteemed at the same time as ends, i.e., only as beings who must be able to contain in themselves the end of the very same action.

Third, with regard to contingent (meritorious) duty to one's self, it is not sufficient that the action not conflict with humanity in our person as an end in itself; it must also harmonize with it. Now in humanity there are capacities for greater perfection which belong to the end of nature with respect to humanity in our own person; to neglect these might perhaps be consistent with the preservation of humanity as an end in itself but not with the furtherance of that end.

Fourth, with regard to meritorious duty to others, the natural end which all men have is their own happiness. Humanity might indeed exist if no one contributed to the happiness of others, provided he did not intentionally detract from it; but this harmony with humanity as an end in itself is only negative rather than positive if everyone does not also endeavor, so far as he can, to further the ends of others. For the ends of any person, who is an end in himself, must as far as possible also be my end, if that conception of an end in itself is to have its full effect on me.

This principle of humanity and of every rational creature as an end in itself is the supreme limiting condition on freedom of the actions of each man. It is not borrowed from experience, first, because of its universality, since it applies to all rational beings generally and experience does not suffice to determine anything about them; and, secondly, because in experience humanity is not thought of (subjectively) as the end of men, i.e., as an object which we of ourselves really make our end. Rather it is thought of as the objective end which should constitute the supreme limiting condition of all subjective ends, whatever they may be. Thus this principle must arise from pure reason. Objectively the ground of all practical legislation lies (according to the first principle) in the rule and in the form of universality, which makes it capable of being a law (at most a natural law); subjectively, it lies in the end. But the subject of all ends is every rational being as an end in itself (by the second principle); from this there follows the third practical principle of the will as the supreme condition of its harmony with universal practical reason, viz., the idea of the will of every rational being as making universal law.

By this principle all maxims are rejected which are not consistent with the universal lawgiving of will. The will is thus not only subject to the law but subject in such a way that it must be regarded also as self-legislative and only for this reason as being subject to the law (of which it can regard itself as the author). . . .

If we now look back upon all previous attempts which have ever been undertaken to discover the principle of morality, it is not to be wondered at that they all had to fail. Man was seen to be bound to laws by his duty, but it was not seen that he is subject only to his own, yet universal, legislation, and that he is only bound to act in accordance with his own will, which is, however, designed by nature to be a will giving universal laws. For if one thought of him as subject only to a law (whatever it may be), this necessarily implied some interest as a stimulus or compulsion to obedience because the law did not arise from his will. Rather, his will was constrained by something else according to a law to act in a certain way. By this strictly necessary consequence, however, all the labor of finding a supreme ground for duty was irrevocably lost, and one never arrived at duty but only at the necessity of action from a certain interest. This might be his own interest or that of another, but in either case the imperative always had to be conditional and could not at all serve as a moral command. This principle I will call the principle of *autonomy* of the will in contrast to all other principles which I accordingly count under *heteronomy*.

The concept of each rational being as a being that must regard itself as giving universal law through all the maxims of its will, so that it may judge itself and its actions from this standpoint, leads to a very fruitful concept, namely, that of a *realm of ends*.

By "realm" I understand the systematic union of different rational beings through common laws. Because laws determine ends with regard to their universal validity, if we abstract from the personal difference of rational beings and thus from all content of their private ends, we can think of a whole of all ends in systematic connection, a whole of rational beings as ends in themselves as well as of the particular ends which each may set for himself. This is a realm of ends, which is possible on the aforesaid principles. For all rational beings stand under the law that each of them should treat himself and all others never merely as means but in every case also as an end in himself. Thus there arises a systematic union of rational beings through common objective laws. This is a realm which may be called a realm of ends (certainly only an ideal), because what these laws have in view is just the relation of these beings to each other as ends and means.

A rational being belongs to the realm of ends as a member when he gives universal laws in it while also himself subject to these laws. He belongs to it as sovereign when he, as legislating, is subject to the will of no other. The rational being must regard himself always as legislative in a realm of ends possible through the freedom of the will, whether he belongs to it as member or as sovereign. He cannot maintain the latter position merely through the maxims of his will but only when he is a completely independent being without need and with power adequate to his will.

Morality, therefore, consists in the relation of every action to that legislation through which alone a realm of ends is possible. This legislation, however, must be found in every rational being. It must be able to arise from his will, whose principle then is to take no action according to any maxim which would be inconsistent with its being a universal law and thus to act only so that the will through its maxims could regard itself at the same time as universally lawgiving. If now the maxims do not by their nature already necessarily conform to this objective principle of rational beings as universally lawgiving, the necessity of acting according to that principle is called practical constraint, i.e., duty. Duty pertains not to the sovereign in the realm of ends, but rather to each member, and to each in the same degree.

The practical necessity of acting according to this principle, i.e., duty, does not rest at all on feelings, impulses, and inclinations; it rests merely on the relation of rational beings to one another, in which the will of a rational being must always be regarded as legislative, for otherwise it could not be thought of as an end in itself. Reason, therefore, relates every maxim of the will as giving universal laws to every other will and also to every action toward itself; it does so not for the sake of any other practical motive or future advantage but rather from the idea of the dignity of a rational being who obeys no law except that which he himself also gives.

In the realm of ends everything has either a *price* or a *dignity*. Whatever has a price can be replaced by something else as its equivalent; on the other hand, whatever is above all price, and therefore admits of no equivalent, has a dignity.

That which is related to general human inclinations and needs has a *market price*. That which, without presupposing any need, accords with a certain taste, i.e., with pleasure in the mere purposeless play of our faculties, has an *affective price*. But that which constitutes the condition under which alone something can be an end in itself does not have mere relative worth, i.e., a price, but an intrinsic worth, i.e., *dignity*.

Now morality is the condition under which alone a rational being can be an end in itself, because only through it is it possible to be a legislative member in the realm of ends. Thus morality and humanity, so far as it is capable of morality, alone have dignity. Skill and diligence in work have a market value; wit, lively imagination, and humor have an affective price; but fidelity in promises and benevolence on principle (not from instinct) have intrinsic worth. . . .

And what is it that justifies the morally good disposition or virtue in making such lofty claims? It is nothing less than the participation it affords the rational being in giving universal laws. He is thus fitted to be a member in a possible realm of ends to which his own nature already destined him. For, as an end in himself, he is destined to be legislative in the realm of ends, free from all laws of nature and obedient only to those which he himself gives. Accordingly, his maxims can belong to a universal legislation to which he is at the same time also subject. A thing has no worth other than that determined for it by the law. The legislation which determines all worth must therefore have a dignity, i.e., unconditional and incomparable worth. For the esteem which a rational being must have for it, only the word "respect" is a suitable expression. Autonomy is thus the basis of the dignity of both human nature and every rational nature. . . .

From what has just been said, it can easily be explained how it happens that, although in the concept of duty we think of subjection to law, we do nevertheless ascribe a certain sublimity and dignity to the person who fulfills all his duties. For though there is no sublimity in him in so far as he is subject to the moral law, yet he is sublime in so far as he is legislative with reference to the law and subject to it only for this reason. We have also shown above how neither fear of nor inclination to the law is the incentive which can give a moral worth to action; only respect for it can do so. Our own will, so far as it would act only under the condition of a universal legislation rendered possible by its maxims—this will, ideally possible for us, is the proper object of respect, and the dignity of humanity consists just in its capacity of giving universal laws, although with the condition that it is itself subject to the same legislation.

Respect for Persons

Alan Donagan

Both Jewish and Christian thinkers have always held that the numerous specific precepts of morality are all derivable from a few substantive general principles. . . . The principle that good is to be done and sought, and evil avoided, is not primarily moral. It defines the fundamental condition that any movement or abstention from movement must satisfy if it is to be accounted an action at all. For no bodily movement can intelligibly be called an action unless it is presented as seeking or attempting some good, or shunning some evil. Even actions contrary to practical reason require "at least a remote basis" in it. Wrong actions, so far as they are actions at all, are done in pursuit of something that seems good to the agent. However, any human being who thinks clearly must recognize that there are certain goods fundamental to human flourishing—to a full human life as a rational being: they include life itself, communicable knowledge, and friendship. With regard to human beings, whether oneself or another, the principle that good is to be pursued and evil shunned first of all forbids any action whatever directed against those fundamental goods; secondarily, it commands every human being, as far as he reasonably can, to promote human good generally, both directly (by actions good in themselves, such as acquiring knowledge) and indirectly (by producing the means for human flourishing, such as growing food). But the disposition to act and abstain from action in accordance with these commands and prohibitions is what loving yourself and others consists in. Hence the primary and common principle of the natural law may also be formulated as: *Act so that the fundamental human goods, whether in your own person or in that of another, are promoted as may be possible, and under no circumstances violated.* It is a principle of what Kant thought of as respect, but of respect for certain fundamental goods. And, so interpreted, it plainly follows immediately from the first principle of practical reason. . . .

Our task is to inquire into the meaning of the primary and common principle, understood as knowable by ordinary human reason. . . . In what follows, therefore, I take the fundamental principle of that part of traditional morality which is independent of any theological presupposition to have been expressed in the scriptural commandment, "Thou shalt love thy neighbor as thyself," understanding one's neighbor to be any fellow human being, and love to be a matter, not of feeling, but of acting in ways in which human beings as such can choose to act. The philosophical sense of this commandment was correctly expressed by Kant in his formula that one act so that one treats humanity always as an end and never as a means only. . . .

Since treating a human being, in virtue of its rationality, as an end in itself, is the same as respecting it as a rational creature, Kant's formula of the fundamental principle may be restated in a form more like that of the scriptural commandment that is its original: *Act always so that you respect every human being, yourself or another, as being a rational creature.* And, since it will be convenient that the fundamental principle of the system to be developed be formulated in terms of the concept of permissibility analysed in the preceding section, the canonical form in which that principle will hereafter be cited is: *It is impermissible not to respect every human being, oneself or any other, as a rational creature.*

The structure of any system of morality whose sole first principle is that which has been identified in the preceding section must be logically very simple.

It cannot be an axiomatic system; for in axiomatic systems a body of theorems is rigorously derived from a small set of unproved propositions, the "axioms," which are stated by means of a few primitive terms. Except for additional terms introduced as abbreviations, and which therefore could be dispensed with, neither theorems nor demonstrations contain any term not mentioned in the axioms. The primitive terms remain uninterpreted at the end, as they were at the beginning. Such systems explore what follows on the assumption that their axioms hold true for everything that satisfies their primitive terms.

The structure of the fundamental principle is itself simple. It contains only one concept peculiar to moral thought, that of (moral) permissibility. And its sense is that no action which falls under the concept of not respecting some human being as a rational creature can fall under the concept of being permissible. The second concept it contains, that of (not) respecting some human being as a rational creature, is not peculiar to moral thinking. It has a place in descriptions of human conduct in anthropology and psychology, and of course in everyday descriptive discourse.

Of those precepts derivable from the first principle which are needed for the solution of serious moral problems, virtually all turn on the concept of respecting a human being as a rational creature, and virtually none on the concept of permissibility. . . .

One strategy for indirectly establishing specificatory premises, which will be adopted in a number of cases that follow, ought to be described in advance. Often direct analysis is not the most effective way to establish a specificatory premise; for the problem is that, while it is evident that certain kinds of action in most cases fall under a certain concept (for example, killing people in most cases is failing to respect them as rational beings), in some cases they do not, or are thought not to (for example, killing in self-defense is not failing to respect the person killed). How is a moralist to determine what the fundamental principle requires with respect to such kinds of action?

A natural approach is to begin by showing that it is impermissible to perform actions of that kind at will, and then to go on to determine the kinds of cases in which it is permissible. Accordingly, with respect to killing human beings, one would begin by establishing that:

(K1) To kill another human being *merely at will* is not to respect every human being (in particular, the one killed) as a rational creature.

This would not be denied by any Jewish or Christian moralist. And now an attempt is made to find in what kinds of cases killing another human being is legitimate. For example, it might be argued that:

(K2) To kill another human being who is attacking you, and concerning whom you reasonably judge that he may well kill or seriously injure you, and that his attack can only be stopped by killing him, is not to fail in respect to another human being as a rational creature, even to the one killed.

To the extent that it is possible to be assured that a complete list of such cases has been found, it will be possible to infer that:

(K3) To kill another human being, except under the circumstances specified in (K2) and the other propositions obtained from the search, is to kill him merely at will.

From (K1) and (K3) it follows that, except under specified circumstances, killing a human being is impermissible. And this conclusion is equivalent, as an appropriate definition will show, to a prohibition of murder.

The chief weakness of this strategy is that it is seldom possible to eliminate all doubts of the completeness of the survey. How can we assure ourselves beyond doubt that no significant case has been overlooked? Nozick goes so far as to state that many who have ceased to assent to "any or very many exceptionless moral principles" although at one time they did so—by which I take him to refer, among others, to the many who have repudiated the traditional morality in which they were brought up—have done so because "more and more complicated cases" forced them into what seemed an interminable process of revision.[1] And he ventures the suggestion that such a history would be common among lawyers, who know by experience how difficult it is to devise, in advance, rules adequate to "all the bizarre, unexpected, arcane, and complicated cases which actually arise."[2]

This misplaces the difficulty by comparing a moralist's task to that of a legislative draftsman, to which its resemblance . . . is slight. The task of legislative draftsmen is seldom to formulate specific precepts derived from a fundamental legal principle: almost always it is to contrive a set of regulations to further the complex and politically determined objects of public policy. Thus they attempt to solve such problems as how to frame legislation by which the rich will not be able to escape income tax, but also by which municipalities may continue to raise money by selling bonds at low interest, given that the established method, exempting such interest from income tax, enables the rich to avoid income tax. Moralists and judges do not have tasks of this kind. Their business is not to contrive ways of furthering a variety of ends, many of them hard to reconcile, and all of them subject to change; they have only to work out what rationally justifiable moral and legal principles really do require, however disconcerting the result may be.

The difficulties that arise for moralists in any tradition mostly consist of discrepancies between precepts derived by established methods from their first principle or principles, and what seem to be intuitively evident applications of those first principles to cases falling under those precepts. To invert the example given above: it is an established doctrine in the Hebrew-Christian tradition that it is permissible to kill another human being in self-defense; but to some, for example Quakers, killing another human being seems to be quite evidently incompatible with respecting his humanity. Such problems have arisen, as a matter of history, far less often from "bizarre, unexpected, arcane, and complicated cases," than from deeper reflection on cases already considered in what is now a very long tradition. And that is why Nozick seems to have exaggerated as well as misplaced the difficulty of surveying all the possible kinds of circumstances in which an action, impermissible if done merely at will, is permissible. Unusual and unexpected cases are unlikely to make much difference. The chief source of doubt is the suspicion of having overlooked the significance of some feature of a case already known.

Although the first-order precepts to be derived may be classified in a number of ways, for reasons to be given I have divided them into three groups, according as they have to do with: (1) the duties of each human being to himself or herself; (2) the duties of each human being to other human beings as such; (3) duties arising out of participation in human institutions. Those of the third group are further subdivided, according as the institutions giving rise to them either *(a)* are among the varieties of purely voluntary contract or *(b)* are in one way or another imposed on individuals by the civil or noncivil societies of which they are members. To the last of these groups belong the precepts arising out of possession of property and out of membership in a family or in a civil society.

DUTIES OF HUMAN BEINGS TO THEMSELVES

That each human being has duties to himself follows immediately from the fundamental principle; for if it is impermissible not to respect every human being as a rational creature, it is impermissible not to respect oneself as such. As we shall see, the relations which human beings can have to one another are more complex than those they can have to themselves. But they can injure or hurt themselves; and they can take care of themselves, and cultivate their various capacities. Their duties to themselves are classifiable by reference to these powers.

The worst physical injury anybody can do to himself is to kill himself, that is, to commit suicide. Yet there are reasons for which people do kill themselves; and an important question in common morality is whether it is permissible to do so. A possible view, which the Stoics maintained with respect to sages, is that any human being may quit life as he or she pleases. So stated, it is untenable. It seems evident that if one is to respect oneself as a rational creature, one may not hold one's life cheap, as something to be taken at will. Here the Jewish and Christian repudiation of the Stoic position is plainly correct. Conceding, then, that *it is impermissible for any human being to take his own life at will,* it is necessary to inquire whether there are any circumstances at all in which it is permissible. . . .

A preponderance of Jewish discussions of this subject acknowledge the permissibility of killing oneself when an external force one is powerless to resist either (1) imposes on one a choice between denying one's fundamental practical allegiance (in particular, one's religious faith) and suffering death or unendurable torture,[3] or (2) credibly threatens to force one into a life unfitting to a rational creature, such as a life of enforced prostitution, or of any other form of dehumanizing slavery.[4] There appears to be no reason to conclude that, in circumstances of either kind, killing oneself would fail to respect oneself as a rational creature. On the contrary, not to kill oneself would be either heroic or cowardly.

Suicide has also been held to be permissible when it is either (1) to ensure the lives or the fundamental well-being of others, or (2) to escape a condition of natural dehumanization.

Three kinds of case[s] in which suicide appears to be necessary to ensure the lives of others may be mentioned. (i) Those represented by the memorable Stoic example of an overloaded boat, which will sink unless some of its load is jettisoned but the entire load of which is innocent human beings.[5] If nobody can be saved unless somebody goes overboard, and if to go overboard would be suicide, then suicide in such circumstances would certainly not be contrary to the respect due to humanity as such. (ii) Those in which a disease makes a man dangerous to others, whether by infection or by making him insanely violent. Kant describes a case of the latter kind.

A man who had been bitten by a mad dog already felt hydrophobia, and he explained, in a letter he left, that since, so far as he knew, the disease was incurable, he killed himself lest he harm others as well in his madness, the onset of which he already felt.[6]

While Kant was presumably sceptical of the assertion that only by suicide could the hydrophobic have secured others from harm, situations seem perfectly possible in which there would be no other way; and others could obviously occur in connection with infectious diseases. (iii) Those in which suicide relieves others of a duty which they cannot carry out and survive. The suicide of Captain Oates, in Scott's antarctic expedition, in order not to retard his companions as they struggled back to their depot, is rightly considered an act of charity as well as of courage.

In addition, suicide has been justified simply as sparing others excessive burdens. For example, the care of a relative who has contracted an illness or suffered an injury, which incapacitates him for normal life, may call for very great sacrifices by whoever undertakes it. Suppose the sufferer to know that, although those sacrifices are supererogatory, somebody will either make them cheerfully or be coerced by family pressure into making them resentfully. In circumstances of either kind, to describe his suicide as wanting in the respect due to humanity would be questionable.

Kant's example of hydrophobia incidentally illustrates a final ground upon which suicide may be held to be permissible: namely, to obtain release from a life that has become, not merely hard to bear, but utterly dehumanized. Supposing hydrophobia to be incurable and its inevitable course to be one of extreme torment, culminating in madness and death: does respect for himself as rational compel a man to submit to it, and not escape by suicide? Or suppose that a man is trapped in a burning vehicle, without hope of getting out: does respect for himself as rational require him to let himself be burned to death, rather than commit suicide?[7] In my own judgement, suicide is in both cases entirely legitimate. The problem is to draw the line between despairing of human life in adversity and perceiving that, owing to illness or injury, the possibility of a genuinely human life will cease before biological death. When that line is crossed, the case for the permissibility of suicide is strong.

Since a man is a rational creature who is a rational animal, respect for man as the rational creature he is implies respect for the integrity and health of his body. Hence *it is impermissible, according to the first principle, for anybody to mutilate himself at will, or to do at will anything that will impair his health.* It may be doubted whether anybody has ever mutilated himself for the sake of the thing; but Kant was distressed by the thought of people selling their teeth, and appears to have believed that there were those who had themselves castrated "in order to make a more comfortable living" as singers.[8] Setting aside such cases, on the ground that those who offer inducements to anybody to submit to mutilation commit a grave wrong, the only conditions on which most people would be inclined to submit to it coincide with those in which it is permissible according to the first principle to do so. Surgical operations such as amputation, for example, are permissible for the sake of the health of the body as a whole. And, despite Kant, it is generally and reasonably allowed to be legitimate to give a bodily organ such as an eye or a kidney for transplantation, in order to save a faculty, or the life, of another. Yet this must not be at the cost of that faculty in the giver, or of his life. One may not blind oneself to save another from blindness.

As for impairment of health, the requirements of common morality are much less stringent than those of the respectable part of contemporary culture. For morality, the conditions of human life are to be accepted: risk is a part of normal life, even risks taken solely for the sake of enjoyment and recreation. As the history of both Judaism and Christianity shows, horror at the use of drugs and intoxicants as such is characteristic of fanatical sects rather than of orthodoxy. It is not inspired by common morality. Nor, as the tolerance of tobacco by both Judaism and Christianity shows, has addiction to a drug been traditionally considered unfitting to a human being. Inasmuch as the relief and enjoyment afforded by a drug compensate for any ill effects it may have, then it is permissible to use it. But it is contrary to the precept forbidding the impairment of health so to use drugs as to incapacitate oneself for the ordinary business of life. And, perhaps more importantly, it is contrary to the fundamental principle itself to allow the use of a drug to become the main point of life. For anybody to place any kind of drug-induced enjoyment before the full use of his capacities as a rational creature, is a plain case of failure to respect himself as the kind of being he is. The objection is not to the enjoyment in itself but to the inordinate value set upon it. . . .

In addition to the precepts forbidding anybody to kill or injure himself, except in certain specifiable situations, common morality demands of every human being that he *adopt some coherent plan of life according to which, by morally permissible actions, his mental and physical powers may be developed*. Not to adopt such a plan is impermissible, as wanting in respect to himself as a rational creature capable of developing such powers.

Adopting Paton's term for its Kantian equivalent, I shall refer to this precept as the "principle of culture."[9] Obviously, it entails certain prohibitions, such as that *it is impermissible for anybody to neglect his health or his education*. But in what it requires to be done, it allows large scope for choice. Most human beings are capable of mastering, to some degree, any one of a number of different branches of knowledge and skill, but not of mastering more than a few of them together. As long as a man does not neglect the fundamentals of mental and physical development, without which he cannot follow any coherent plan of self-cultivation, it is up to him to decide which of the different possibilities open to him he will choose: whether, say, to be a farmer, or a soldier, or a philosopher. Given that he has the capacity to be any one of the three, and the opportunity, common morality leaves the choice to him. And having chosen, say, to be a soldier, he does not violate the principle of culture by not developing his powers as a philosopher as far as he might have done had he chosen philosophy as his profession.

The principle of culture, as has been remarked, entails that a man must not neglect his health. This subordinate precept must be interpreted in the light of the principle itself, which requires that a man live according to some coherent plan of life. Most plans of life demand, at various junctures, that risks be taken, or that physical and emotional resources be spent. A man does not violate the principle of culture by risking his life in the pursuit of his calling, or by undermining his health with hard work and with anxieties inseparable from his responsibilities.

NONINSTITUTIONAL DUTIES TO OTHERS

The first set of noninstitutional duties to others to be considered are those having to do with force and violence. Since respect for human beings as rational creatures entails, in general, treating every normal adult as responsible for the conduct of his own affairs, to interfere by force with anybody else's conduct of his life, unless there is a special and adequate reason, is not to respect him as a rational creature. The principle may therefore be laid down that *it is impermissible for anybody at will to use force upon another*.

Not all human beings are normal, however, and not all are adult. The insane, who cannot wholly take care of themselves, must be looked after; and, if it is necessary for their well-being, may be constrained to do various things they would not do if they had their own way. The question of how far a man's insanity gives those charged with looking after him the right of coercion is a difficult one, which I shall not pursue. The general principle, however, is clear: since a madman is a rational creature whose reason is impaired, he is entitled to the respect due to a normal rational creature except to the extent that the impairment of his reason makes it necessary to prevent him from harming himself or others, and to bring him to undergo treatment which it is reasonable to think may benefit him, provided that it is neither cruel nor offensive.

Children also are rational creatures, whose reason is in process of development. Although it must be recognized that the power of normal children to look after themselves is constantly growing, while they remain children they are not fully capable of doing so: and, in a measure as they are not, those in charge of them may forcibly prevent them from harming themselves or others, and may compel them to submit to education reasonably thought to be of benefit to them.

The question of when a given human being's life as an individual begins is of great importance in the Hebrew-Christian system. The duties of human beings to others are duties to them as human beings, that is, as rational creatures of a certain kind. The forms which may be taken by the fundamental moral duty of respect for a rational creature as such will vary with the degree to which that creature is actually in possession of the reason a mature creature of that kind would normally possess; but such variations in no way annul the duty. In simpler ages, it was practically sufficient to treat duties to others as beginning with their birth. However, as medical knowledge has grown, and as techniques have been developed by which the unborn can be both benefited and injured, the theoretical issue cannot be set aside on the ground of practical unimportance.

The question of when the life of a human being begins is a biological one, since human beings are rational *animals;* and biology answers it simply and unequivocally: a human life begins at conception, when the new being receives the genetic code. Although a zygote does not, even when made visible through a microscope, look like a human being, and although adult human beings cannot have the kind of relations with it that they can have to other adults, or even to children, its status as a rational creature is in no way compromised. Attempts to deny the humanity of zygotes, by declaring that humanity begins at birth, or at viability (that is, at the point when an unborn child, extruded from the womb, could be kept alive) are scientifically obscurantist. An eight-month-old premature baby is biologically less mature than an eight-and-three-quarter-month-old unborn one; and viability has no biological significance. Whether an unborn child is viable or not depends on the state of medical technology. It is reasonable to forecast that, in a century or so, a zygote will be viable.

It follows that the principle *it is impermissible for anybody at will to use force upon another* applies to adult and child alike, to born and unborn. . . .

Three precepts are readily derivable from the general prohibition of the use of force: that *no man may at will kill another;* that *no man may at will inflict bodily injury or hurt on another;* and that *no man may hold another in slavery.* . . .

Although there are no circumstances in which slavery is sanctioned by the Hebrew-Christian first principle, there are circumstances in which the use of force upon others is. Violence—the exercise of physical force so as to inflict injury on persons and damage to property—is common among human beings, even though respect for man as rational forbids using force at will upon others. Yet the immunity to violence to which everybody consequently has a moral right is obviously conditional; and perhaps its most obvious condition is that one not further one's own ends by resorting to violence or threatening it. If anybody, in furthering his own ends, resorts to violence or threatens it, he ceases to satisfy the condition of his right to immunity and may be forcibly withstood. By violating the immunity of others, he forfeits his own. In general: *It is permissible for any human being to use force upon another in such measure as may be necessary to defend rational creatures from the other's violence.*

In this matter, common morality is not content with a permissive precept. But to appreciate the nature of its mandatory precept, it is necessary first to consider the general precept from which it is derived, and which I shall refer to as the "principle of beneficence." If a man respects other men as rational creatures, not only will he not injure them, he will necessarily also take satisfaction in their achieving the well-being they seek, and will further their efforts as far as he prudently can. In short, he will observe the general precept: *It is impermissible not to promote the well-being of others by actions in themselves permissible, inasmuch as one can do so without proportionate inconvenience.*

The duty to promote the well-being of others derives from their character as rational creatures, not from their desert. However, human well-being is a matter of human flourishing: that is, of the development and exercise of human potentialities. In a reasonably just society, human adults in good health normally can and do support themselves, either independently or in families. Hence the well-being of others can be successfully promoted only if they do their part: little can be done for the well-being of anybody who will not cultivate and exert the powers he has.

Promoting the well-being of others most conspicuously consists in: (1) contributing to the upbringing and education of those who are not adults, especially of orphans; (2) helping those who have duties which, owing to bereavement, injury, illness, or desertion, they can perform only with help; (3) restoring to a condition of independence those who have been incapacitated by illness, accident, or injury; and (4) caring for those who are crippled, deaf, or blind, or are chronically ill or senile. But it also comprises such less conspicuous activities as preventing what might harm others or frustrate their permissible projects, and abstaining from actions that would foreseeably elicit responses by which others would be injured. . . .

CONTRACTS

The most elementary institution that gives rise to moral obligations is that of contract. A contract exists when two parties, each of which must be a rational creature or an organized group of rational creatures, enter into the following relation: one of the parties, the promiser, addresses to the other a statement that he will do a certain thing, intending his statement to be understood as binding him to do that thing, provided that the party addressed should understand it as intended, and accept it; the other, the promisee, understands the promiser's statement as it was intended to be understood, and indicates his acceptance of the promiser's utterance as binding him to do what he said he would. These conditions imply the existence of an institution, because they imply that the utterance by the promiser of a statement that he will do a certain thing is accepted by both parties as the creation of a bond. Taken literally, what is uttered is a statement about the future, a statement that may turn out to be either true or false.

That there is a contract consists in the fact that both parties accept that utterance, not as a statement about the future, but as the giving of the utterer's word to see to it that his statement proves true.

What a promiser gives his word to do may be either conditional or unconditional; and the conditions may be either expressed or unexpressed. Obviously, the normal conditions of the existence of a contract are not fulfilled if the promisee misunderstands what the promiser intends. With regard to legally enforceable contracts, different conventions are adopted in different legal systems. Apart from legal contract, a promiser is morally bound to perform whatever he believed his promisee to have understood him to promise. He cannot reasonably do less; for he should have corrected any misunderstanding he was aware of. And not even his promisee can fairly claim that he has knowingly bound himself to do more.

It may be objected that this description of the institution of contract attributes a false belief to promiser and promisee alike; namely, that merely by uttering certain words a man can directly create a moral bond. Moral bonds cannot be directly created, since they exist, when they do, by virtue of a moral agent's situation and his nature as a rational being. Nobody is morally bound to do anything merely because he decides or declares that he is. . . . There is nothing intrinsically moral about the institution of contract. This is shown by the fact that it is possible to promise to do wrong. It would be absurd to suppose that, by promising to commit a murder, a member of a criminal gang can place himself under a moral obligation to commit it, or even give himself a *prima facie* reason for committing it. Yet the institution of contract may be held in high regard by members of criminal gangs: a man's reputation as a member of the team may depend on his keeping his word to the others; and for him to break it may be considered not merely to be shameful but to be a serious grievance to the promisee.

The moral question, then, is this. Given that the nonmoral institution of contract exists, and given that contracts can be made, and are made, which have no moral force whatever, does the institutional bond between promiser and promisee ever constitute a moral bond?

The chief premise of the answer to this question is that, although contracts may be made which it would be wrong to keep, in itself the institution of contract is morally legitimate. And, given that the institution is legitimate, then to break a freely made promise to do something morally permissible would be wrong for a reason related to the reason why it is wrong to lie.

Yet a man's promising to do a certain thing must not be confounded with his expressing the opinion that he will do it. It is an undertaking, not a prediction. Such undertakings, like predictions, may be lies: like predictions, they are lies if they falsely represent the minds of their makers when they make them. A lying promise falsely represents its maker's intention, as a lying prediction falsely represents its maker's opinion: and lying promises are wrong for exactly the same reasons as lying expressions of opinion. Hence breaking a promise must be distinguished from lying in making it. A promiser breaks a promise only if he fails to fulfil it, even though it is in his power to fulfil it. But a lying promise is not necessarily broken; for, circumstances not having turned out as the lying promiser expected, he may change his mind and do what he promised.

Breaking a promise nevertheless resembles lying. The institution of promising enables a moral agent to make himself responsible for his failure in the future to do what it will be in his power to do. It thereby extends from the past and present to the future the range of his acts of will, and hence of his voluntary actions, about which a man can give assurances to others. It also extends his power to deceive. For by not keeping his word he will deceive the promisee about what he will choose to do, even if he had no intention of deceiving him when he gave it. Such a deception, of a promisee who has forfeited no rights, plainly fails to respect him as a rational creature. *It is* therefore *impermissible for anybody to break a freely made promise to do something in itself morally permissible.* . . .

NOTES

1 Robert Nozick, *Anarchy, Utopia and the State* (1968), p. 5.

2 Ibid., p. 5.

3 2 Maccabees, 14:41–42. For the commandment forbidding compliance, see Maimonides, *Mishneh Torah,* I, 1, 5, 2 (Hyamson, p. 40a) and I, 1, 5, 7 (Hyamson, p. 40b).

4 *Babylonian Talmud,* Gittim, p. 57b.

5 Cicero, *De Officiis,* III, 23.

6 Kant, *Met. der Sitten,* pt. 2, 74 (pp. 423–24).

7 I heard R. M. Hare discuss cases of this kind in a lecture at the University of Notre Dame in summer 1973.

8 Kant, *Met. der Sitten,* pt. 2, 73 (p. 423).

9 Paton, *Categorical Imperative,* pp. 155, 173.

Servility and Self-Respect

Thomas E. Hill, Jr.

Several motives underlie this paper. In the first place, I am curious to see if there is a legitimate source for the increasingly common feeling that servility can be as much a vice as arrogance. There seems to be something morally defective about the Uncle Tom and the submissive housewife; and yet, on the other hand, if the only interests they sacrifice are their own, it seems that we should have no right to complain. Secondly, I have some sympathy for the now unfashionable view that each person has duties to himself as well as to others. It does seem absurd to say that a person could literally violate his own rights or owe himself a debt of gratitude, but I suspect that the classic defenders of duties to oneself had something different in mind. If there are duties to oneself, it is natural to expect that a duty to avoid being servile would have a prominent place among them. Thirdly, I am interested in making sense of Kant's

Reprinted by permission from vol. 57, no. 1 of *The Monist,* LaSalle, Illinois 61301.

puzzling, but suggestive, remarks about respect for persons and respect for the moral law. On the usual reading, these remarks seem unduly moralistic; but, viewed in another way, they suggest an argument for a kind of self-respect which is incompatible with a servile attitude. . . .

I

Three examples may give a preliminary idea of what I mean by *servility*. Consider, first, an extremely deferential black, whom I shall call the *Uncle Tom*. He always steps aside for white men; he does not complain when less qualified whites take over his job; he gratefully accepts whatever benefits his all-white government and employers allot him, and he would not think of protesting its insufficiency. He displays the symbols of deference to whites, and of contempt towards blacks: he faces the former with bowed stance and a ready 'sir' and 'Ma'am'; he reserves his strongest obscenities for the latter. Imagine, too, that he is not playing a game. He is not the shrewdly prudent calculator, who knows how to make the best of a bad lot and mocks his masters behind their backs. He accepts without question the idea that, as a black, he is owed less than whites. He may believe that blacks are mentally inferior and of less social utility, but that is not the crucial point. The attitude which he displays is that what he values, aspires for, and can demand is of less importance than what whites value, aspire for, and can demand. He is far from the picture book's carefree, happy servant, but he does not feel that he has a right to expect anything better.

Another pattern of servility is illustrated by a person I shall call the *Self-Deprecator*. Like the Uncle Tom, he is reluctant to make demands. He says nothing when others take unfair advantage of him. When asked for his preferences or opinions, he tends to shrink away as if what he said should make no difference. His problem, however, is not a sense of racial inferiority but rather an acute awareness of his own inadequacies and failures as an individual. These defects are not imaginary: he has in fact done poorly by his own standards and others'. But, unlike many of us in the same situation, he acts as if his failings warrant quite unrelated maltreatment even by strangers. His sense of shame and self-contempt make him content to be the instrument of others. He feels that nothing is owed him until he has earned it and that he has earned very little. He is not simply playing a masochist's game of winning sympathy by disparaging himself. On the contrary, he assesses his individual merits with painful accuracy.

A rather different case is that of the *Deferential Wife*. This is a woman who is utterly devoted to serving her husband. She buys the clothes *he* prefers, invites the guests *he* wants to entertain, and makes love whenever *he* is in the mood. She willingly moves to a new city in order for him to have a more attractive job, counting her own friendships and geographical preferences insignificant by comparison. She loves her husband, but her conduct is not simply an expression of love. She is happy, but she does not subordinate herself as a means to happiness. She does not simply defer to her husband in certain spheres as a trade-off for his deference in other spheres. On the contrary, she tends not to form her own interests, values, and ideals; and, when she does, she counts them as less important than her husband's. She readily responds to appeals from Women's Liberation that she agrees that women are mentally and physically equal, if not superior, to men. She just believes that the proper role for a woman is to serve her family. As a matter of fact, much of her happiness derives from her belief that she fulfills this role very well. No one is trampling on her rights, she says; for she is quite glad, and proud, to serve her husband as she does.

Each one of these cases reflects the attitude which I call servility. It betrays the absence of a certain kind of self-respect. What I take this attitude to be, more specifically, will become clearer later on. It is important at the outset, however, not to confuse the three cases sketched above with other, superficially similar cases. In particular, the cases I have sketched are not simply cases in which someone refuses to press his rights, speaks disparagingly of himself, or devotes himself to another. A black, for example, is not necessarily servile because he does not demand a just wage; for, seeing that such a demand would result in his being fired, he might forbear for the sake of his children. A self-critical person is not necessarily servile by virtue of bemoaning his faults in public; for his behavior may be merely a complex way of satisfying his own inner needs quite independent of a willingness to accept abuse from others. A woman need not be servile whenever she works to make her husband happy and prosperous; for she might freely and knowingly choose to do so from love or from a desire to share the rewards of his success. If the effort did not require her to submit to humiliation or maltreatment, her choice would not mark her as servile. There may, of course, be grounds for objecting to the attitudes in these cases; but the defect is not servility of the sort I want to consider. It should also be noted that my cases of servility are not simply instances of deference to superior knowledge or judgment. To defer to an expert's judgment on matters of fact is not to be servile; to defer to his every wish and whim is. Similarly, the belief that one's talents and achievements are comparatively low does not, by itself, make one servile. It is no vice to acknowledge the truth, and one may in fact have achieved less, and have less ability, than others. To be servile is not simply to hold certain empirical beliefs but to have a certain attitude concerning one's rightful place in a moral community.

II

Why, then, is servility a moral defect? The first part of this answer must be an attempt to isolate the objectionable features of the servile person; later we can ask why these features are objectionable. As a step in this direction, let us examine again our three paradigm cases. The moral defect in each case, I suggest, is a failure to understand and acknowledge one's own moral rights. I assume, without argument here, that each person has moral rights. Some of these rights may be basic human rights; that is, rights for which a person needs only to be human to qualify. Other rights will be derivative and contingent upon his special commitments, institutional affiliations, etc. Most rights will be prima facie ones; some may be absolute. Most can be waived under appropriate conditions; perhaps some cannot. Many rights can be forfeited; but some, presumably, cannot. The servile person does not, strictly speaking, violate his own rights. At least in our paradigm cases he fails to acknowledge fully his own moral status because he does not fully understand what his rights are, how they can be waived, and when they can be forfeited.

The defect of the Uncle Tom, for example, is that he displays an attitude that denies his moral equality with whites. He does not realize, or apprehend in an effective way, that he has as much right to a decent wage and a share of political power as any comparable white. His gratitude is misplaced; he accepts benefits which are his by right as if they were gifts. The Self-Deprecator is servile in a more complex way. He acts as if he has forfeited many important rights which in fact he has not. He does not understand, or fully realize in his own case, that certain rights to fair and decent treatment do not have to be earned. He sees his merits clearly enough, but he fails to see that what he can expect from others is not merely a function of his merits. The Deferential Wife *says* that she understands her rights vis-à-vis her husband, but what she fails to appreciate is that her consent to serve him is a valid waiver of her rights only under certain conditions. If her consent is coerced, say, by the lack of viable options for women in her society, then her consent is worth little. If socially fostered ignorance of her own talents and alternatives is responsible for her consent, then her consent should not count as a fully legitimate waiver of her right to equal consideration within the marriage. All the more, her consent to defer constantly to her husband is not a legitimate setting aside of her rights if it results from her mistaken belief that she has a moral duty to do so. (Recall: "The *proper* role for a woman is to serve her family.") If she believes that she has a *duty* to defer to her husband, then, whatever she may say, she cannot fully understand that she has a *right* not to defer to him. When she says that she freely gives up such a right, she is confused. Her confusion is rather like that of a person who has been persuaded by an unscrupulous lawyer that it is legally incumbent on him to refuse a jury trial but who nevertheless tells the judge that he understands that he has a right to a jury trial and freely waives it. He does not really understand what it is to have and freely give up the right if he thinks that it would be an offense for him to exercise it.

Insofar as servility results from moral ignorance or confusion, it need not be something for which a person is to blame. Even self-reproach may be inappropriate; for at the time a person is in ignorance he cannot feel guilty about his servility, and later he may conclude that his ignorance was unavoidable. In some cases, however, a person might reasonably believe that he should have known better. If, for example, the Deferential Wife's confusion about her rights resulted from a motivated resistance to drawing the implications of her own basic moral principles, then later she might find some ground for self-reproach. Whether blameworthy or not, servility could still be morally objectionable at least in the sense that it ought to be discouraged, that social conditions which nourish it should be reformed, and the like. Not all morally undesirable features of a person are ones for which he is responsible, but that does not mean that they are defects merely from an esthetic or prudential point of view.

In our paradigm cases, I have suggested, servility is a kind of deferential attitude towards others resulting from ignorance or misunderstanding of one's moral rights. A sufficient remedy, one might think, would be moral enlightenment. Suppose, however, that our servile persons come to know their rights but do not substantially alter their behavior. Are they not still servile in an objectionable way? One might even think that reproach is more appropriate now because they know what they are doing.

The problem, unfortunately, is not as simple as it may appear. Much depends on what they tolerate and why. Let us set aside cases in which a person merely refuses to *fight* for his rights, chooses not to exercise certain rights, or freely waives many rights which he might have insisted upon. Our problem concerns the previously servile person who continues to display the same marks of deference even after he fully knows his rights. Imagine, for example, that even after enlightenment our Uncle Tom persists in his old pattern of behavior, giving all the typical signs of believing that the injustices done to him are not really wrong. Suppose, too, that the newly enlightened Deferential Wife continues to defer to her husband, refusing to disturb the old way of life by introducing her new ideas. She acts as if she accepts the idea that she is merely doing her duty though actually she no longer believes it. Let us suppose, further, that the Uncle Tom and the Deferential Wife are not merely generous with their time and property; they also accept without protest, and even appear to sanction, treatment which is humiliating and degrading. That is, they do not simply consent to waive mutually acknowledged rights; they tolerate violations of their rights with apparent approval. They pretend to give their permission for subtle humiliations which they really believe no permission can make legitimate. Are such persons still servile despite their moral knowledge?

The answer, I think, should depend upon why the deferential role is played. If the motive is a morally commendable one, or a desire to avert dire consequences to oneself, or even an ambition to set an oppressor up for a later fall, then I would not count the role player as servile. The Uncle Tom, for instance, is not servile in my sense if he shuffles and bows to keep the Klan from killing his children, to save his own skin, or even to buy time while he plans the revolution. Similarly, the Deferential Wife is not servile if she tolerates an abusive husband because he is so ill that further strain would kill him, because protesting would deprive her of her only means of survival, or because she is collecting atrocity stories for her book against marriage. If there is fault in these situations, it seems inappropriate to call it *servility*. The story is quite different, however, if a person continues in his deferential role just from laziness, timidity, or a desire for some minor advantage. He shows too little concern for his moral status as a person, one is tempted to say, if he is willing to deny it for a small profit or simply because it requires some effort and courage to affirm it openly. A black who plays the Uncle Tom merely to gain an advantage over other blacks is harming them, of course; but he is also displaying disregard for his own moral position as an equal among human beings. Similarly, a woman throws away her rights too lightly if she continues to play the subservient role because she is used to it or is too timid to risk a change. A Self-Deprecator who readily accepts what he knows are violations of his rights may be indulging his peculiar need for punishment at the expense of denying something more valuable. In these cases, I suggest, we have a kind of servility independent of any ignorance or confusion about one's rights. The person who has it may or may not be blameworthy, depending on many factors; and the line between servile and nonservile role playing will often be hard to draw. Nevertheless, the objectionable feature is perhaps clear enough for present purposes: it is a willingness to disavow one's moral status, publicly and systematically, in the absence of any strong reason to do so.

My proposal, then, is that there are at least two types of servility: one resulting from misunderstanding of one's rights and the other from placing a comparatively low value on them. In either case, servility manifests the absence of a certain kind of self-respect. The respect which is missing is not respect for one's merits but respect for one's rights. The servile person displays this absence of respect not directly by acting contrary to his own rights but indirectly by acting as if his rights were nonexistent or insignificant. An arrogant person ignores the rights of others, thereby arrogating for himself a higher status than he is entitled to; a servile person denies his own rights, thereby assuming a lower position than he is entitled to. Whether rooted in ignorance or simply lack of concern for moral rights, the attitudes in both cases may be incompatible with a proper regard for morality. That this is so is obvious in the case of arrogance; but to see it in the case of servility requires some further argument.

III

The objectionable feature of the servile person, as I have described him, is his tendency to disavow his own moral rights either because he misunderstands them or because he cares little for them. The question remains: why should anyone regard this as a moral defect? After all, the rights which he denies are his own. He may be unfortunate, foolish, or even distasteful; but why *morally* deficient? . . . The argument which I have in mind is prompted by Kant's contention that respect for persons, strictly speaking, is respect for moral law. If taken as a claim about all sorts of respect, this seems quite implausible. If it means that we respect persons only for their moral character, their capacity for moral conduct, or their status as "authors" of the moral law, then it seems unduly moralistic. My strategy is to construe the remark as saying that at least one sort of respect for persons is respect for the rights which the moral law accords them. If one respects the moral law, then one must respect one's own moral rights; and this amounts to having a kind of self-respect incompatible with servility.

The premises for the Kantian argument, which are all admittedly vague, can be sketched as follows:

First, let us assume, as Kant did, that all human beings have equal basic human rights. Specific rights vary with different conditions, but all must be justified from a point of view under which all are equal. Not all rights need to be earned, and some cannot be forfeited. Many rights can be waived but only under certain conditions of knowledge and freedom. These conditions are complex and difficult to state; but they include something like the condition that a person's consent releases others from obligation only if it is autonomously given, and consent resulting from underestimation of one's moral status is not autonomously given. Rights can be objects of knowledge, but also of ignorance, misunderstanding, deception, and the like.

Second, let us assume that my account of servility is correct; or, if one prefers, we can take it as a definition. That is, in brief, a servile person is one who tends to deny or disavow his own moral rights because he does not understand them or has little concern for the status they give him.

Third, we need one formal premise concerning moral duty, namely, that each person ought, as far as possible, to respect the moral law. In less Kantian language, the point is that everyone should approximate, to the extent that he can, the ideal of a person who fully adopts the moral point of view. Roughly, this means not only that each person ought to do what is morally required and refrain from what is morally wrong but also that each person should treat all the provisions of morality as valuable—worth preserving and prizing as well as obeying. One must, so to speak, take up the spirit of morality as well as meet the letter of its requirements. To keep one's promises, avoid hurting others, and the like, is not sufficient; one should also take an attitude of respect towards the principles, ideals, and goals of morality. A respectful attitude towards a system of rights and duties consists of more than a disposition to conform to its definite rules of behavior; it also involves holding the system in esteem, being unwilling to ridicule it, and being reluctant to give up one's place in it. The essentially Kantian idea here is that morality, as a system of equal fundamental rights and duties, is worthy of respect, and hence a completely moral person would respect it in word and manner as well as in deed. And what a completely moral person would do, in Kant's view, is our duty to do so far as we can.

The assumptions here are, of course, strong ones, and I make no attempt to justify them. They are, I suspect, widely held though rarely articulated. In any case, my present purpose is not to evaluate them but to see how, if granted, they constitute a case against servility. The objection to the servile person, given our premises, is that he does not satisfy the basic requirement to respect morality. A person who fully respected a system of moral rights would be disposed to learn his proper place in it, to affirm it proudly, and not to tolerate abuses of it lightly. This is just the sort of disposition that the servile person lacks. If he does not understand the system, he is in no position to respect it adequately. This lack of respect may be no fault of his own, but it is still a way in which he falls short of a moral ideal. If, on the other hand, the servile person knowingly disavows his moral rights by pretending to approve of violations of them, then, barring special explanations, he shows an indifference to whether the provisions of morality are honored and publicly acknowledged. This avoidable display of indifference, by our Kantian premises, is contrary to the duty to respect morality. The disrespect in this second case is somewhat like the disrespect a religious believer might show towards his religion if, to avoid embarrassment, he laughed congenially while nonbelievers were mocking the beliefs which he secretly held. In any case, the servile person, as such, does not express disrespect for the system of moral rights in the obvious way by violating the rights of others. His lack of respect is more subtly manifested by his acting before others as if he did not know or care about his position of equality under that system.

The central idea here may be illustrated by an analogy. Imagine a club, say, an old German dueling fraternity. By the rules of the club, each member has certain rights and responsibilities. These are the same for each member regardless of what titles he may hold outside the club. Each has, for example, a right to be heard at meetings, a right not to be shouted down by the others. Some rights cannot be forfeited: for example, each may vote regardless of whether he has paid his dues and satisfied other rules. Some rights cannot be waived: for example, the right to be defended when attacked by several members of the rival fraternity. The members show respect for each other by respecting the status which the rules confer on each member. Now one new member is careful always to allow the others to speak at meetings; but when they shout him down, he does nothing. He just shrugs as if to say, 'Who am I to complain?' When he fails to stand up in defense of a fellow member, he feels ashamed and refuses to vote. He does not deserve to vote, he says. As the only commoner among illustrious barons, he feels that it is his place to serve them and defer to their decisions. When attackers from the rival fraternity come at him with swords drawn, he tells his companions to run and save themselves. When they defend him, he expresses immense gratitude—as if they had done him a gratuitous favor. Now one might argue that our new member fails to show respect for the fraternity and its rules. He does not actually violate any of the rules by refusing to vote, asking others not to defend him, and deferring to the barons, but he symbolically disavows the equal status which the rules confer on him. If he ought to have respect for the fraternity, he ought to change his attitude. Our servile person, then, is like the new member of the dueling fraternity in having insufficient respect for a system of rules and ideals. The difference is that everyone ought to respect morality whereas there is no comparable moral requirement to respect the fraternity.

The conclusion here is, of course, a limited one. Self-sacrifice is not always a sign of servility. It is not a duty always to press one's rights. Whether a given act is evidence of servility will depend not only on the attitude of the agent but also on the specific nature of his moral rights, a matter not considered here. Moreover, the extent to which a person is responsible, or blameworthy, for his defect remains an open question. Nevertheless, the conclusion should not be minimized. In order to avoid servility, a person who gives up his rights must do so with a full appreciation for what they are. A woman, for example, may devote herself to her husband if she is uncoerced, knows what she is doing, and does not pretend that she has no decent alternative. A self-contemptuous person may decide not to press various unforfeited rights but only if he does not take the attitude that he is too rotten to deserve them. A black may demand less than is due to him provided he is prepared to acknowledge that no one has a right to expect this of him. Sacrifices of this sort, I suspect, are extremely rare. Most people, if they fully acknowledged their rights, would not autonomously refuse to press them.

An even stronger conclusion would emerge if we could assume that some basic rights cannot be waived. That is, if there are some rights that others are bound to respect regardless of what we say, then, barring special explanation, we would be obliged not only to acknowledge these rights but also to avoid any appearance of consenting to give them up. To act as if we could release others from their obligation to grant these rights, apart from special circumstances, would be to fail to respect morality. Rousseau held, for example, that at least a minimal right to liberty cannot be waived. A man who consents to be enslaved, giving up liberty without *quid pro quo,* thereby displays a conditioned slavish mentality that renders his consent worthless. Similarly, a Kantian might argue that a person cannot release others from the obligation to refrain from killing him: consent is no defense against the charge of murder. To accept principles of this sort is to hold that rights to life and liberty are, as Kant believed, rather like a trustee's rights to preserve something valuable entrusted to him: he has not only a right but a duty to preserve it.

Even if there are no specific rights which cannot be waived, there might be at least one formal right of this sort. This is the right to some minimum degree of respect from others. No matter how willing a person is to submit to humiliation by others, they ought to show him some respect as a person. By analogy with self-respect, as presented here, this respect owed by others would consist of a willingness to acknowledge fully, in word as well as action, the person's basically equal moral status as defined by his other rights. To the extent that a person gives even tacit consent to humiliations incompatible with this respect, he will be acting as if he waives a right which he cannot in fact give up. To do this, barring special explanations, would mark one as servile.

IV

Kant held that the avoidance of servility is a duty to oneself rather than a duty to others. Recent philosophers, however, tend to discard the idea of a duty to oneself as a conceptual confusion. Although admittedly the analogy between a duty to oneself and a duty to others is not perfect, I suggest that something important is reflected in Kant's contention.

Let us consider briefly the function of saying that a duty is *to* someone. *First,* to say that a duty is *to* a given person sometimes merely indicates who is the object of that duty. That is, it tells us that the duty is concerned with how that person is to be treated, how his interests and wishes are to be taken into account, and the like. Here we might as well say that we have a duty *towards,* or *regarding* that person. Typically the person in question is the beneficiary of the fulfillment of the duty. For example, in this sense I have a duty to my children and even a duty to a distant stranger if I promised a third party that I would help that stranger. Clearly a duty to avoid servility would be a duty to oneself at least in this minimal sense, for it is a duty to avoid, so far as possible, the denial of one's own moral status. The duty is concerned with understanding and affirming one's rights, which are, at least as a rule, for one's own benefit.

Second, when we say that a duty is *to* a certain person, we often indicate thereby the person especially entitled to complain in case the duty is not fulfilled. For example, if I fail in my duty to my colleagues, then it is they who can most appropriately reproach me. Others may sometimes speak up on their behalf, but, for the most part, it is not the business of strangers to set me straight. Analogously, to say that the duty to avoid servility is a duty to oneself would indicate that, though sometimes a person may justifiably reproach himself for being servile, others are not generally in the appropriate position to complain. Outside encouragement is sometimes necessary, but, if any blame is called for, it is primarily self-recrimination and not the censure of others.

Third, mention of the person to whom a duty is owed often tells us something about the source of that duty. For example, to say that I have a duty to another person may indicate that the argument to show that I have such a duty turns upon a promise to that person, his authority over me, my having accepted special benefits from him, or, more generally, his rights. Accordingly, to say that the duty to avoid servility is a duty to oneself would at least imply that it is not entirely based upon promises to others, their authority, their beneficence, or an obligation to respect their rights. More positively, the assertion might serve to indicate that the source of the duty is one's own rights rather than the rights of others, etc. That is, one ought not to be servile because, in some broad sense, one ought to respect one's own rights as a person. There is, to be sure, an asymmetry: one has certain duties to others because one ought not to violate their rights, and one has a duty to oneself because one ought to affirm one's own rights. Nevertheless, to dismiss duties to oneself out of hand is to overlook significant similarities. . . .

My argument against servility may prompt some to say that the duty is "to morality" rather than "to oneself". All this means, however, is that the duty is derived from a basic requirement to respect the provisions of morality; and in this sense every duty is a duty "to morality". My duties to my children are also derivative from a general requirement to respect moral principles, but they are still duties *to* them.

Kant suggests that duties to oneself are a precondition of duties to others. On our account of servility, there is at least one sense in which this is so. Insofar as the servile person is ignorant of his own rights, he is not in an adequate position to appreciate the rights of others. Misunderstanding the moral basis for his equal status with others, he is necessarily liable to underestimate the rights of those with whom he classifies himself. On the other hand, if he plays the servile role knowingly, then, barring special explanation, he displays a lack of concern to see the principles of morality acknowledged and respected and thus the absence of one motive which can move a moral person to respect the rights of others. In either case, the servile person's lack of self-respect necessarily puts him in a less than ideal position to respect others. Failure to fulfill one's duty to oneself, then, renders a person liable to violate duties to others. This, however, is a consequence of our argument against servility, not a presupposition of it.

Reasonable Progress and Self-Respect

Virginia Held

How long is it reasonable to expect the victims of gross social inequality to wait for the redress of their grievances? Clearly, if *no* aspect of a gradual improvement is going to benefit a given individual in that individual's lifetime, it is not in the interest of that individual to wait for the fruits of that improvement. On the other hand, if equality can be achieved quickly only at the price of much pain and destruction, should an individual accept progressive rather than immediate solutions?

I shall try to consider in this paper some aspects of what might be thought of as "reasonable progress" toward equality, progress that would not be so gradual as to require the violation of a person's self-respect. I shall try to suggest, at least at an abstract level, some grounds on which an aggrieved individual might, with self-respect, reasonably accept a given rate of progress as satisfactory, or reject it as unsatisfactory. . . .

Reprinted by permission from vol. 57, no. 1 of *The Monist*, LaSalle, Illinois 61301.

EQUALITY, JUSTICE, AND OCCUPATIONAL OPPORTUNITIES

. . . I shall assume that on any plausible account of the meanings or principles of justice and equality, and of the connection between them, one aspect of injustice in an advanced society is the large-scale failure to provide what I shall call "an equal opportunity for occupational attainment." For any individual faced with such failure, the question will arise: what should be done to deal with this injustice, and are there principles which should guide a reasonable person in deciding? I will take for granted that it is eminently reasonable for any member of an advanced and economically, politically and legally substantial social system, to expect equal occupational opportunities. And I will take for granted that a society failing to provide such opportunities is, in that respect, unjust. . . . As one gazes about at the leading institutions—political, economic, academic—of the society around us, the virtual exclusion of women and nonwhites from their leading positions is too clearly visible to require comment. . . .

A lack of "equal opportunity for occupational attainment" involves more than overt discrimination at the point of hiring or promotion, although evidence of even this is widespread and well known. Background conditions, such as unequal treatment relating to occupational preparation and expectations, in the course of childhood upbringing and education, ego development, psychological counseling, technical and higher education, etc., which would make it more difficult for women and nonwhites as a group than for white males as a group to succeed occupationally, are factors contributing to the denial of equal opportunities for occupational attainment. Expectations that other obligations, such as those of caring for children, automatically fall more heavily on mothers as a group than they do on fathers as a group, or on society at large, contribute to the denial of equal opportunities because they make attainment of even the lower occupational levels, and to a greater extent the levels above the lower ones, more difficult for women as a group than for men as a group. Of course there will be difficulties in determining which background conditions are significant and relevant and which are unavoidable or trivial. Still, where the discussion concerns the lack of occupational equality for a group defined by such completely basic characteristics as sex and race, avoidable background conditions which can be judged to make occupational attainments for members of such groups more difficult merely by their possession of these characteristics can be taken to be factors contributing to a lack of equal opportunities for occupational attainments.

Certainly, equality of opportunity is not enough. Even if everyone in a given group had an equal opportunity for, say, economic reward, we should still be repelled by an outcome such that some groan in hunger while others drown in superfluity. A society that provided equal opportunities for occupational attainment might be highly and unjustifiably inegalitarian if the gap between the satisfactions of and powers attached to these occupations were unduly wide, or if the total number of positions available—of all kinds or of any given kind—were unjustifiably limited. Here, however, I shall concentrate on equality of opportunity for participation in a given total of occupational activity, however unjustifiably limited, or unjustifiably rewarded or structured. Admittedly, this is one small part only of the wider question of just occupational arrangements. . . .

The terms in which new policies offering equal opportunities are usually considered are those of new policies for new jobs. When a job becomes available or a new vacancy in an existing position occurs, those who would have been privileged under previous arrangements will now be asked to face competition from others on a basis of equality in hiring and promotion. But those persons already safely occupying secure positions are not asked to yield any of their privileges, either the privileges of occupancy or of enjoying the present rewards and powers attached to such occupancy. If voluntarily resigning one position is going to require the formerly privileged to suffer the exposure of equal competition, persons in secure positions are not likely to leave one position unless they have another secured that is as satisfactory; this is to exchange one privileged position for another, not to yield privilege. . . .

Many persons now favoring progress toward equal opportunity imagine such policies to be adequate. But is it reasonable to expect the victims of embedded injustices to accept such terms for improvement?

Let us try to consider some aspects and implications of these issues by abstracting the following model from some situations now faced by those who are denied equal opportunities for occupational attainments:

Imagine an organization in which there are one hundred positions paying more than $15,000 a year. Many of these pay considerably more than this, and involve greater influence, and there are an indefinite number of positions in this organization which pay less than this. Following current averages, ninety-six of the one hundred positions in question are occupied by white males, two by women, two by nonwhites. I shall take becoming a member of the class of those with such positions as equivalent in this model to having an opportunity to go further in one's occupational attainments in this organization over a future period of some length. Some of those entering this class will drop out of it, some will remain at the level of entry, some will attain higher levels, some far higher ones. If we assume that disparity would be the result of lack of equal opportunity and its causes rather than because of a disparity in wholly free choices not to seek occupational attainments, then equal opportunity between groups for further attainments in this organization would require equal representation among those becoming members of this class.

Suppose that under normal conditions of growth, turnover, and retirement, one new position paying more than $15,000 a year (in constant dollars) is created by this organization each year, and four positions are vacated by turnover, retirement, etc. Let us say, then, that the five positions open each year are filled on a basis of equality. To simplify the problem I shall calculate the expectations for women only although comparable calculations could be made for nonwhites. Due to past inequalities at lower and wider levels, the supply of candidates for these positions would be, let us say, averaged over the span of time involved, four male to one female. Given the fair application of criteria requiring equality in filling these positions, let us say that one additional woman per year would succeed in entering the class of those with positions earning more than $15,000, while there would be no loss in the number of women already holding such positions.

At this rate, it would take some ninety-four years for women to achieve equal occupational opportunities to go further in this organization. If we revise the four to one figure, given the changes that might occur over so long a period, we might assume it to be as nearly equal as three male to two female, with two women per year entering the class of those able to continue to progress. It would still take some forty-seven years for women to achieve equal opportunities for occupational attainments in this organization, never mind what persons with equal opportunities would be able to do in advancing further, once they had entered the class in question.

Obviously, no one can have any plausible interest in waiting ninety-four years for equality. Nor can anyone have a serious interest in waiting forty-seven years, since those embarking upon an occupation even at as early an age as twenty will have passed the normal point of retirement before attaining it.

A scheme in which no one now holding a privileged position will be asked to relinquish anything, and only such vacancies as occur through death, retirement, and the creation of new positions will be filled on a basis of equal opportunity, is hardly in the interests of all those who will gain nothing from such a change. Can an individual person justifiably accept such a policy, which will very slightly increase the possibilities of equal opportunity for occupational attainment for any given victim of past injustice, but which will leave the vast majority of victims now seeking equal opportunities no better off than they were before? If we label progress of this kind "gradual improvement" . . . the victims of inequality have good reason to find it thoroughly unacceptable. . . .

RIGHTS, INTERESTS AND SELF-RESPECT

If we abandon . . . the illusion that equality can be attained with no loss to anyone, we may ask who should be asked to lose how much, and what interests must be taken into account. Justice does not depend on such calculations of interest; justice confers rights. It is clear that women and nonwhites have rights to equal opportunities for occupational attainments based on the concepts of justice and equality I have assumed. But the issue here involves their interests in alternative approaches to achieving these rights in practice, rights the realization of which they are at present being denied in avoidable ways. In considering this question, we are dealing with the justifiability of alternative courses of action. And we might seem, in this transitional period, to have to consider the interests of one group in realizing its members' rights and the interests of another group in preventing this realization. Such a conflict ought not to arise; where it does it ought to be settled on grounds of rights, not interests. And yet it is not being so settled, and those whose rights are being thwarted must choose, if they can, justifiable courses of action to take in such circumstances. On what grounds can such a choice be made? In considering this question, it may be helpful to try to delineate the requirements of self-respect.

When rights conflict, it may happen that some rights are unavoidably denied to some persons. If we consider not a right to compete on equal terms for a given job, but, say, a right to a job, we may say that where persons have the positions they do as a result of the fair application of justifiable procedures, there may be a conflict between the rights of these persons to their jobs, and the rights of other persons to comparable jobs. The solution might then be to increase the total number of jobs, and by an adequate effort of the society to redistribute resources towards the provision of employment and away from other things, to provide for the realization of both sets of rights.

But where persons have acquired their positions as a result of unjustifiable procedures, we can conclude that although they may have interests in maintaining these positions, they do not have rights to do so. And if their maintaining these positions prevents the realization of the rights of others, we can conclude that the rights of these others are being avoidably denied.

Avoidably to deny to persons their rights is an affront to their self-respect. For persons to acquiesce in the avoidable denial of their own rights is to lack self-respect. As between forms of nonacquiescence, it is reasonable for persons whose rights are being avoidably denied to act fully in accordance with their interests, without regard to the interests of others in denying them such rights; then, for them voluntarily to yield their own interests in securing their rights to the interests of others in thwarting them is incompatible with their self-respect.

To act without regard for the interests of those with superior power is to court disaster and to risk various aspects of destruction on both sides. But if anything less is incompatible with self-respect, could any alternative be acceptable? Are there moral obligations, perhaps, which supercede self-respect? Perhaps the victims of injustice have an obligation to future generations to temper the pursuit of their interests in realizing their rights and to avoid the risks of destruction and institutional breakdown, so that although they themselves will gain nothing from a slow improvement, their children will enjoy its benefits. But this consideration seems balanced or outweighed by the wrongness of allowing the present beneficiaries of unjust privileges to continue their victimization undisturbed.

THE RISKS OF IMMEDIATE EQUALITY

Let us return to our previous model in which we can view some relevant choices at an abstract level. Let us consider an alternative under which all positions based on privilege in this organization would be suddenly vacated and let us label it "immediate equality." Of course in reality not all white males are in the same situation: some may themselves have suffered from an inequality of occupational opportunity, some may occupy their positions by right rather than privilege. But if in our model we suppose that all the occupied positions in this organization are reopened and refilled through selection procedures providing equality of opportunity, this should not disturb those who rightfully hold their positions, since they will regain them.

Assuming that such a transformation could be brought about somehow (a huge assumption, of course, but not one to be dealt with here) either by organized boycotts, by strikes, by disruptions, by political pressure leading to legislation, or by judicial decision, it would require a kind of destruction of the organizational supports of the class of persons holding positions of power in this organization, and might seem plausibly, in this context, an overthrow of an existing arrangement. It would not result in immediate equality of opportunity as defined in this model, because the supply of candidates would remain artificially unequal for at least a short period of time, but it would result in a dramatically rapid rate of progress: on the first candidate ratio assumed above, already highly optimistic for this context, if the privileged positions would be reopened annually, equal opportunity could be achieved in little more than three years.

If one could suppose that the organization, and the occupational positions being sought, would remain virtually intact, and that the only change would be for the privileged class of persons now to face competition for their positions on a basis of equality, every victim of past injustice would have an overwhelming interest in "immediate equality." In justifiably pursuing his or her own interests in realizing his or her rights, the only problem would be to weigh huge gains immediately against the same gains in the far distant future, and the solution would be obvious.

But we would have little basis for such a supposition. Some of those actually occupying established positions are rightfully there, and most seem to have an entrenched belief, which they would not be willing to test, that they belong to this group. Privileged classes can probably not be expected to yield to even the most just demands without resistance. Hence, a more plausible assumption for this model would be that many of the privileged would resist the sudden overthrow of the organizational supports of their positions even to the point of the destruction of the organization and the occupational activities within it, and that many others would be willing to accept the risks of such resistance.

So we might have to suppose that the immediate realization of equal opportunities for occupational attainments in this organization would lead to the breakdown of the organization and its positions. In that case, opportunities for the formerly privileged and the formerly victimized would be equal only because they were, in this organization, nil for both. And in that case the former victims would gain nothing from "immediate equality" as they would gain nothing from "gradual improvement," and the history of victimization would continue in either case.

Neither course of action would be in the interests of those seeking the realization of their rights. And yet, there is a difference between the two forms of defeat as here outlined. If the victims of inequality choose "immediate equality" in this context, they *risk* defeat; if they choose "gradual improvement" in this context, they accept defeat as certain. *Given such a choice, the former seems compatible with self-respect in a way in which the latter does not.*

Of course the supposition that there might be collective action on the part of the victims to bring about change is open to question. The more likely prospect might remain individual defiance of the organization denying equality of opportunity, and defeat of the defiant individual by the organization's privileged members. But even at the individual level, to risk defeat in attaining equality is compatible with self-respect in a way in which acquiescing in certain defeat is not. And recognition of this might plausibly bring the argument back to a consideration of the collective policy which would be justifiable, and which would, if anything could, reduce the likelihood of defeat.

ALTERNATIVES TO DEFEAT

Other alternatives than these two forms of defeat should of course be considered. Instead of supposing certain defeat through "gradual improvement" and a risk of defeat through "immediate equality," predictions of our actual situation might be such as to indicate certain defeat through "immediate equality," and only probable defeat through "gradual improvement." This is the picture which established organizations have an interest in promoting: they suggest that if those who have suffered injustices will be patient, attitudes will change, and the rate of improvement will increase. But for this assertion to be plausible, there would have to be evidence of an increase in the rate of equalization. . . there is no reason to suppose any such increase to be likely. Clarity about the actual yields to be produced by given rates of progress can do much to dispel illusions on these matters.

From what has been said before, we can conclude that for a person to accept the certain defeat of his or her interests in realizing a right is incompatible with that person's self-respect. For a person to risk the probable defeat of these interests may be compatible with self-respect, when these are the only choices, but it may be personally as well as socially destructive. We can add that for an organization to try to buy off selected individuals by offering them a personal increase in the probabilities of their own opportunities for occupational attainments only at the expense of a decrease in the probabilities for other victims, is to make an unjust and probably coercive offer incompatible with the self-respect of all the victims.

CHAPTER 8

RIGHTS

We hold these truths to be self-evident, that all men are created equal, that they are endowed by their Creator with certain unalienable Rights, that among these are Life, Liberty and the pursuit of Happiness.

With these words the thirteen English colonies in North America set forth the moral argument for revolution. Since England had violated these rights, the colonies ought to be a free and independent nation. A doctrine of rights inspired the birth of the United States, and much of our history is an account of the struggle to live up to the ideal. A civil war ended slavery. Women obtained the right to vote. Martin Luther King's civil rights marches and the violent responses these marches evoked combined to shock and inspire Americans to insist that segregation of races be brought to an end.

Of course, a concern with rights did not originate in America. But the concept of rights is the contribution of the English-speaking world to moral philosophy. The Greeks had no well-developed concept of individual rights. The Stoics and the medievals had a concept of natural law, but any concept of a natural right was largely undeveloped. The English philosopher John Locke did have a theory of natural rights. Locke was concerned with the problem that had troubled his predecessor Thomas Hobbes, the function of the state and limitations that individual citizens should place upon it. Locke argued that in a state of nature (a condition with no governmental institutions) men had rights to life, liberty, and property. Any state action which infringes on these rights is illegitimate.

But what arguments did Locke have to back up his claim that men had rights to life, liberty, and property? Locke's arguments for the rights to life and liberty were based on theology, specifically on the "fact" that all humans are God's children. Today Locke's arguments for the rights to life and liberty are largely forgotten; however, his argument for the right to property is far better known and continues to inspire the work of some contemporary philosophers—especially libertarians such as Robert Nozick.

Locke's argument was based on the labor theory of value. What is it that produces the goods and services we consume? Surely it is labor. Until land has been cleared, a crop planted and harvested, there is no food. Even the berries in the woods need to be picked before they can be eaten. To produce value, humans mix their labor with nature, and because they so mix their labor, they have a right to own what they produce. By labor, humans have a right to the products of their labor.

Many have argued that Locke's philosophy is based on an outdated view of the possibilities people have to labor. Locke's arguments may seem plausible in a frontier society, where there is plenty of land to be appropriated. But in contemporary society, where so many sell their labor to others (work for a corporation), Locke's theory seems simplistic. If I own the factory and you mix your labor with my machines, how much of the product do you have a right to? The problem becomes more complicated when there are few factory owners and many laborers. Most laborers either work for a factory owner or starve. Locke did have a proviso that a person's right to property was limited by the condition that there be enough left for others. The problem is in deciding how much is enough. Did the factory owners leave enough for others? These kinds of issues receive considerable attention in courses in social and political philosophy. Since the right to property is so controversial, it cannot serve as a model of a right, and hence there is little discussion of property rights in this chapter.

How rights claims are justified is an extremely important issue, however. The very success of the language of rights is leading to some real difficulties. The United Nations adopted the Universal Declaration of Human Rights, which specifies a large number of rights to which all citizens of the member states are entitled. However, many member states may not have the resources to provide these rights. The right to a vacation with pay is one often-cited example. And although the concept of moral rights has won the endorsement of the international community, just what that endorsement amounts to is a matter of some controversy. Americans emphasize political rights, but not all countries—including many of our allies—do. President Jimmy Carter tried to make the conduct of other states with respect to rights relevant in American foreign policy decisions. However, both the realities of foreign policy and some confusion as to what constituted legitimate rights thwarted Carter's efforts.

Meanwhile in our own country rights claims have reached a fever pitch. Those opposing abortion speak of the right to life. Those favoring abortion speak of a woman's right over her own body. Rights claims are made on behalf of gays, the handicapped, the aged, short people, and even on behalf of those who are less physically attractive. Employers insist on their rights; employees on theirs. Do employers have a right to hire or fire anyone they want to? Do employees have a right to their jobs so long as they perform satisfactorily? Do employees have a right to be told about the dangers associated with their jobs, whether or not they ask about those dangers? Can an employee refuse a job assignment on the grounds that it is too dangerous? Are there welfare rights, and if so what is their scope? Americans have adopted the language of rights, but there is little consensus as to which rights are basic, which rights have priority, and how rights conflicts are to be resolved. Many of these issues are treated in this chapter.

Perhaps the best way to begin the discussion is to focus on the role rights serve in moral theory. The selections by Joel Feinberg and Richard Wasserstrom address this important issue. To make his point Feinberg asks us to consider a country, Nowheresville, which is very much like our own except in one crucial respect—Nowheresville is a country where there is no concept of a moral right. Hence what is so noticeable in Nowheresville is that people do not make moral claims of entitlement. Wasserstrom agrees totally with Feinberg. To see what both authors are driving at, consider a college or university where students do not have a right to know the basis for their grade. Students can ask, beg, or cajole. Professors might, out of the goodness of their hearts, out of pity, or out of benevolence, give the basis for their grades. However, the students have no right to know the basis for the grades, and the professors have no duty to provide it. Isn't such a world morally impoverished? Doesn't a situation where students have no right to know the basis for their grades diminish the students—take away from their self-respect or humanity? Rights enable people to stand on their own feet—to make demands and claims. This is the idea behind Feinberg's notion that rights are essential moral furniture.

Let us take it as established that the concept of rights has a useful role to play in moral language. What rights do we have, and what arguments can be given on behalf of them? First, it is important to realize that there are many classifications of rights. Many rights are conventional; they are created by social institutions. If you want to know your legal rights, consult a lawyer. Conventional rights are of limited interest to the moral philosopher. Human rights are rights that people claim simply in virtue of being human. Traditionally these rights were called "natural rights," but the association of natural rights with natural-law theology led many philosophers to substitute the term "human rights." The important feature of human rights is that they are entitlements we have independent of our standing in social institutions. Indeed, since social institutions should respect and/or provide human rights, human rights constitute a test of social institutions. An institution is judged to be adequate or inadequate, good or bad, in terms of its support of human rights. Jimmy Carter examined a number of our allies on this basis and found them wanting. The issues discussed in this chapter are pretty much limited to human rights.

Moral rights are claims we make on moral grounds. Human rights are moral rights because the arguments made on behalf of them are moral arguments. These arguments are often based on the notion of self-respect, which was the focus of the previous chapter. However, a legal right can also be a moral right if the legal institutions of society pass the moral tests. My right to a jury trial is both a legal right and, under certain descriptions, a moral right.

The human rights which have received the most attention by philosophers are the rights to liberty (freedom) and well-being. Wasserstrom strengthens an argument by Gregory Vlastos (see Chapter 10) which appeals to the equal intrinsic value of freedom and well-being. Wasserstrom thinks that appeal can succeed only because freedom and well-being are the things we must have to develop our capabilities as human beings. Those things which are necessary for our development as human beings are the things to which we have human rights. What makes that right equal is the kind of argument used so effectively by Kant. This argument contends that there is no rational ground for simply preferring one person's well-being or liberty to another's. Simply preferring is arbitrary, while providing a defense is accomplished by appealing to reasons—to something nonarbitrary.

A similar strategy for defending human rights to freedom and well-being is adopted by Alan Gewirth. Gewirth asks what are the necessary conditions for human purposive actions. Answer: Freedom and well-being are necessary. Gewirth then uses the Kantian strategy to show that my concern with my own freedom and well-being logically commits me to be concerned with the freedom and well-being of all purposive agents. What justifies my concern with freedom/well-being is that these items are necessary for any purpose I undertake. Generic rights are the rights which I have to the items necessary for any purpose I undertake. However, what is true of my situation is true of any purposive agent. Therefore we must adopt what Gewirth calls the "principle of generic consistency," which says: Act in accord with the generic rights of your recipients as well as of yourself. This logical requirement provides the basis for the assertion that rights to freedom and well-being are justifiably claimed by all—hence the rights to freedom and well-being are equal rights.

Philosophers who subscribe to a theory of human rights include the right to liberty as one of those rights. However, not all philosophers include the right to well-being as a human right. A number of arguments have been given for excluding the right to well-being. One of the standard ways to develop the argument is to draw a distinction between positive and negative rights where the right to well-being is a positive right and the right to liberty is a negative right. The right to liberty is a negative right because no one has to do anything to honor it. All you have to do to honor negative rights is to leave people alone. That's not always true with respect to positive rights. To honor those, on occasion, someone has to provide something. If a person has a human right to well-being and is starving, then someone has a duty to provide that person with food.

If this distinction is adopted, those who would include a right to well-being on the list of human rights would argue that the duty to provide for positive rights falls on the state. In some cases, the state is unable to provide for the right; the state lacks the requisite resources. In other cases the state could provide for the right, but that would give the state too much power. This increased power would lead to undesirable consequences, including the consequence of violating the citizen's right to liberty; e.g., through taxation to pay for a welfare program. Another criticism is that, since rights to well-being apply only to people in specific situations, such rights lack the universality required of human rights. For example, the right to a vacation with pay applies only to workers; it would not apply to retired persons. But negative rights apply to everyone. The right to liberty does not depend on social circumstances.

This last objection is based on a confusion between basic rights and rights which implement basic rights. One way of implementing the right to liberty (the classic example of a negative right) is to allow people to vote. The fact that some people—

nonresidents, children, and criminals—are not allowed to vote does not show that the right to liberty isn't universal. Similarly the fact that retired people don't receive vacations with pay doesn't show that the right to well-being isn't universal. A human right can be implemented in different ways depending on the circumstances of the individual involved.

Moreover, the distinction between negative and positive rights has come under sharp attack. In his paper, Henry Shue demolishes the distinction by showing that honoring negative rights does, indeed, require positive action, and that honoring positive rights often requires that some cease and desist from harming another. Hence, if Shue is correct, there are at least two basic human rights of equal value—i.e., a right to liberty and a right to a minimum level of well-being.

Once you have more than one basic human right there is always the possibility of a conflict between them. One common way to generate the conflict between the two rights is to show how an income tax to provide for the basic needs of others conflicts with the right to personal property. However, given the questionable status of property rights, it might be more appropriate to generate the conflict by considering the right to vote, to be eligible for political office, and to enact one's program if duly elected. Suppose members of a political party campaign on a platform committed to (1) denial of welfare benefits to those who can work but don't, and (2) removal of children from mothers who are on welfare but continue to have children. These candidates are subsequently elected and enact their campaign platform. Surely point 1 of their platform creates a conflict between the right to liberty and the right to well-being, and point 2 creates conflicts among liberties. However one chooses to set up the problem, most philosophers agree that there is at least an appearance of conflict between the human right to liberty and the human right to well-being.

What the existence of these conflicts shows is that rights play a very important but still limited role in ethical decision-making. Ethical decision-making cannot be based solely on a theory of rights. Actually this should come as no surprise. Ethical decision-making isn't simply a matter of rules, nor is it simply a matter of honoring rights. Nonetheless, if rights aren't the only moral furniture, they are moral furniture. No theory of ethical decision-making would be adequate that did not provide an account of rights.

The Nature and Value of Rights

Joel Feinberg

1

I would like to begin by conducting a thought experiment. Try to imagine Nowheres-ville—a world very much like our own except that no one, or hardly any one (the qualification is not important), has *rights*. If this flaw makes Nowheresville too ugly to hold very long in contemplation, we can make it as pretty as we wish in other moral respects. We can, for example, make the human beings in it as attractive and virtuous as possible without taxing our conceptions of the limits of human nature. In particular, let the virtues of moral sensibility flourish. Fill this imagined world with as much benevolence, compassion, sympathy, and pity as it will conveniently hold without strain. Now we can imagine men helping one another from compassionate motives merely, quite as much or even more than they do in our actual world from a variety of more complicated motives. . . .

Let us then introduce duties into Nowheresville, but only in the sense of actions that are, or are believed to be, morally mandatory, but not in the older sense of actions that are due others and can be claimed by others as their right. Nowheresville now can have duties of the sort imposed by positive law. A legal duty is not something we are implored or advised to do merely; it is something the law, or an authority under the law, *requires* us to do whether we want to or not, under pain of penalty. When traffic lights turn red, however, there is no determinate person who can plausibly be said to claim our stopping as his due, so that the motorist owes it to *him* to stop, in the way a debtor owes it to his creditor to pay. In our own actual world, of course, we sometimes owe it to our *fellow motorists* to stop; but that kind of right-correlated duty does not exist in Nowheresville. There, motorists "owe" obedience to the Law, but they owe nothing to one another. When they collide, no matter who is at fault, no one is morally accountable to anyone else, and no one has any sound grievance or "right to complain."

When we leave legal contexts to consider moral obligations and other extra-legal duties, a greater variety of duties-without-correlative-rights present themselves. Duties of charity, for example, require us to contribute to one or another of a large number of eligible recipients, no one of whom can claim our contribution from us as his due. Charitable contributions are more like gratuitous services, favors, and gifts than like repayments of debts or reparations; and yet we do have duties to be charitable. Many persons, moreover, in our actual world believe that they are required by their own consciences to do more than that "duty" that *can* be demanded of them by their prospective beneficiaries. I have quoted elsewhere the citation from H. B. Acton of a character in a Malraux novel who "gave all his supply of poison to his fellow prisoners to enable them by suicide to escape the burning alive which was to be their

Joel Feinberg, "The Nature and Value of Rights," *The Journal of Value Inquiry*, vol. 4, Winter 1970, pp. 243–257.

fate and his." This man, Acton adds, "probably did not think that [the others] had more of a right to the poison than he had, though he thought it his duty to give it to them."[1] I am sure that there are many actual examples, less dramatically heroic than this fictitious one, of persons who believe, rightly or wrongly, that they *must do* something (hence the word "duty") for another person in excess of what that person can appropriately demand of him (hence the absence of "right").

Now the digression is over and we can return to Nowheresville and summarize what we have put in it thus far. We now find spontaneous benevolence in somewhat larger degree than in our actual world, and also the acknowledged existence of duties of obedience, duties of charity, and duties imposed by exacting private consciences, and also, let us suppose, a degree of conscientiousness in respect to those duties somewhat in excess of what is to be found in our actual world. . . . I will now introduce two further moral practices into Nowheresville that will make . . . it appear more familiar to us. These are the practices connected with the notions of *personal desert* and what I call a *sovereign monopoly of rights*.

When a person is said to deserve something good from us what is meant in part is that there would be a certain propriety in our giving that good thing to him in virtue of the kind of person he is, perhaps, or more likely, in virtue of some specific thing he has done. The propriety involved here is a much weaker kind than that which derives from our having promised him the good thing or from his having qualified for it by satisfying the well-advertised conditions of some public rule. In the latter case he could be said not merely to deserve the good thing but also to have a *right* to it, that is to be in a position to demand it as his due; and of course we will not have that sort of thing in Nowheresville. That weaker kind of propriety which is mere desert is simply a kind of *fittingness* between one party's character or action and another party's favorable response, much like that between humor and laughter, or good performance and applause.

The following seems to be the origin of the idea of deserving good or bad treatment from others: A master or lord was under no obligation to reward his servant for especially good service; still a master might naturally feel that there would be a special fittingness in giving a gratuitous reward as a grateful response to the good service (or conversely imposing a penalty for bad service). Such an act while surely fitting and proper was entirely supererogatory. The fitting response in turn from the rewarded servant should be gratitude. If the deserved reward had not been given him he should have had no complaint, since he only *deserved* the reward, as opposed to having a *right* to it, or a ground for claiming it as his due. . . .

In Nowheresville, nevertheless, we will have only the original weak kind of desert. Indeed, it will be impossible to keep this idea out if we allow such practices as teachers grading students, judges awarding prizes, and servants serving benevolent but class-conscious masters. Nowheresville is a reasonably good world in many ways, and its teachers, judges, and masters will generally try to give students, contestants, and servants the grades, prizes, and rewards they deserve. For this the recipients will be grateful; but they will never think to complain, or even feel aggrieved, when expected responses to desert fail. The masters, judges, and teachers don't *have* to do good things, after all, for *anyone*. One should be happy that they *ever* treat us well, and not grumble over their occasional lapses. Their hoped for responses, after all, are *gratuities,* and there is no wrong in the omission of what is merely gratuitous. Such is the response of persons who have no concept of *rights,* even persons who are proud of their own deserts.

Surely, one might ask, rights have to come in somewhere, if we are to have even moderately complex forms of social organization. Without rules that confer rights and impose obligations, how can we have ownership of property, bargains and deals, promises and contracts, appointments and loans, marriages and partnerships? Very well, let us introduce all of these social and economic practices into Nowheresville, but *with one big twist.* With them I should like to introduce the curious notion of a "sovereign right-monopoly." You will recall that the subjects in Hobbes's *Leviathan* had no rights whatever against their sovereign. He could do as he liked with them, even gratuitously harm them, but this gave them no valid grievance against him. The sovereign, to be sure, had a certain duty to treat his subjects well, but this duty was owed not to the subjects directly, but to God, just as we might have a duty to a person to treat his property well, but of course no duty to the property itself but only to its owner. Thus, while the sovereign was quite capable of *harming* his subjects, he could commit no wrong against them that they could complain about, since they had no prior claims against his conduct. The only party *wronged* by the sovereign's mistreatment of his subjects was God, the supreme lawmaker. . . .

Even in the *Leviathan,* however, ordinary people had ordinary rights *against one another*. They played roles, occupied offices, made agreements, and signed contracts. In a genuine "sovereign right-monopoly," as I shall be using that phrase, they will do all those things too, and thus incur genuine obligations toward one another; but the obligations (here is the twist) will not be owed directly *to* promisees, creditors, parents, and the like, but rather to God alone, or to the members of some elite, or to a single sovereign under God. Hence, the rights correlative to the obligations that derive from these transactions are all owned by some "outside" authority. . . .

In our actual world, very few . . . conceive of their mutual obligations in this way; but their small children, at a certain stage in their moral upbringing, are likely to feel precisely this way toward *their* mutual obligations. If Billy kicks Bobby and is punished by Daddy, he may come to feel contrition for his naughtiness induced by his painful estrangement from the loved parent. He may then be happy to make amends and sincere apology *to Daddy;* but when Daddy insists that he apologize to his wronged brother, that is another story. A direct apology to Billy would be a tacit recognition of Billy's status as a right-holder against him, some one he can wrong as well as harm, and someone to whom he is directly accountable for his wrongs. This is a status Bobby will happily accord Daddy; but it would imply a respect for Billy that he does not presently feel, so he bitterly resents according it to him. . . .

There will, of course, be delegated authorities in the imaginary world, empowered to give commands to their underlings and to punish them for their disobedience. But the commands are all given in the name of the right-monopoly who in turn are the only persons to whom obligations are owed. Hence, even intermediate superiors do not have claim-rights against their subordinates but only legal *powers* to create obligations in the subordinates *to* the monopolistic right-holders, and also the legal *privilege* to impose penalties in the name of that monopoly.

2

So much for the imaginary "world without rights." If some of the moral concepts and practices I have allowed into that world do not sit well with one another, no matter. Imagine Nowheresville with all of these practices if you can, or with any harmonious subset of them, if you prefer. The important thing is not what I've let into it, but what I have kept out. The remainder of this paper will be devoted to an analysis of what precisely a world is missing when it does not contain rights and why that absence is morally important.

The most conspicuous difference, I think, between the Nowheresvillians and our-selves has something to do with the activity of *claiming*. Nowheresvillians, even when they are discriminated against invidiously, or left without the things they need, or otherwise badly treated, do not think to leap to their feet and make righteous demands against one another, though they may not hesitate to resort to force and trickery to get what they want. They have no notion of rights, so they do not have a notion of what is their due; hence they do not claim before they take. . . .

To claim that one has rights is to make an assertion that one has them, and to make it in such a manner as to demand or insist that they be recognized. In this sense of "claim" many things in addition to rights can be claimed, that is, many other kinds of proposition can be asserted in the claiming way. I can claim, for example, that you, he, or she has certain rights, or that Julius Caesar once had certain rights; or I can claim that certain statements are true, or that I have certain skills, or accomplish-ments, or virtually anything at all. I can claim that the earth is flat. What is essential to *claiming that* is the manner of assertion. One can assert without even caring very much whether any one is listening, but part of the point of propositional claiming is to *make sure* people listen. . . . Not every truth is properly assertable, much less claimable, in every context. To claim that something is the case in circumstances that justify no more than calm assertion is to behave like a boor. (This kind of boorishness, I might add, is probably less common in Nowheresville.) But not to claim in the appropriate circumstances that one has a right is to be spiritless or foolish. A list of "appropriate circumstances" would include occasions when one is challenged, when one's possession is denied, or seems insufficiently acknowledged or appreciated; and of course even in these circumstances, the claiming should be done only with an appropriate degree of vehemence.

Even if there are conceivable circumstances in which one would admit rights dif-fidently, there is no doubt that their characteristic use and that for which they are distinctively well suited, is to be claimed, demanded, affirmed, insisted upon. They are especially sturdy objects to "stand upon," a most useful sort of moral furniture. Having rights, of course, makes claiming possible; but it is claiming that gives rights their special moral significance. This feature of rights is connected in a way with the customary rhetoric about what it is to be a human being. Having rights enables us to "stand up like men," to look others in the eye, and to feel in some fundamental way the equal of anyone. To think of oneself as the holder of rights is not to be unduly but properly proud, to have that minimal self-respect that is necessary to be worthy of the love and esteem of others. Indeed, respect for persons (this is an intriguing idea) may simply be respect for their rights, so that there cannot be the one without the other; and what is called "human dignity" may simply be the recognizable capacity to assert claims. To respect a person then, or to think of him as possessed of human dignity, simply *is* to think of him as a potential maker of claims. Not all of this can be packed into a definition of "rights;" but these are *facts* about the possession of rights that argue well their supreme moral importance. More than anything else I am going to say, these facts explain what is wrong with Nowheresville. . . .

In brief conclusion: To have a right is to have a claim against someone whose recognition as valid is called for by some set of governing rules or moral principles. To have a *claim* in turn, is to have a case meriting consideration, that is, to have reasons or grounds that put one in a position to engage in performative and propositional claiming. The activity of claiming, finally, as much as any other thing, makes for self-respect and respect for others, gives a sense to the notion of personal dignity, and distinguishes this otherwise morally flawed world from the even worse world of Nowheresville.

NOTE

[1] H. B. Acton, "Symposium on 'Rights'," *Proceedings of the Aristotelian Society,* Supplementary Volume 24 (1950), pp. 107–108.

Human Rights

Richard Wasserstrom

I

If there are any such things as human rights, they have certain important characteristics and functions just because rights themselves are valuable and distinctive moral "commodities." This is, I think, a point that is all too often overlooked whenever the concept of a right is treated as a largely uninteresting, derivative notion—one that can be taken into account in wholly satisfactory fashion through an explication of the concepts of duty and obligation.

Now, it is not my intention to argue that there can be rights for which there are no correlative duties, nor that there can be duties for which there are no correlative rights— although I think that there are, e.g., the duty to be kind to animals or the duty to be charitable. Instead, what I want to show is that there are important differences between rights and duties, and, in particular, that rights fulfill certain functions that neither duties (even correlative duties) nor any other moral or legal concepts can fulfill.

Perhaps the most obvious thing to be said about rights is that they are constitutive of the domain of entitlements. They help to define and serve to protect those things concerning which one can make a very special kind of claim—a claim of right. To

Richard Wasserstrom, "Rights, Human Rights, and Racial Discrimination," in *The Journal of Philosophy,* vol. LXI, no. 20, Oct. 29, 1964.

claim or to acquire anything as a matter of right is crucially different from seeking or obtaining it as through the grant of a privilege, the receipt of a favor, or the presence of a permission. To have a right to something is, typically, to be entitled to receive or possess or enjoy it now, and to do so without securing the consent of another. As long as one has a right to anything, it is beyond the reach of another properly to withhold or deny it. In addition, to have a right is to be absolved from the obligation to weigh a variety of what would in other contexts be relevant considerations; it is to be entitled to the object of the right—at least *prima facie*—without any more ado. To have a right to anything is, in short, to have a very strong moral or legal claim upon it. It is the strongest kind of claim that there is.

Because this is so, it is apparent, as well, that the things to which one is entitled as a matter of right are not usually trivial or insignificant. The objects of rights are things that matter.

Another way to make what are perhaps some of the same points is to observe that rights provide special kinds of grounds or reasons for making moral judgments of at least two kinds. First, if a person has a right to something, he can properly cite that right as the *justification* for having acted in accordance with or in the exercise of that right. If a person has acted so as to exercise his right, he has, without more ado, acted rightly—at least *prima facie*. To exercise one's right is to act in a way that gives appreciable assurance of immunity from criticism. Such immunity is far less assured when one leaves the areas of rights and goes, say, to the realm of the permitted or the nonprohibited.

And second, just as exercising or standing upon one's rights by itself needs no defense, so invading or interfering with or denying another's rights is by itself appropriate ground for serious censure and rebuke. Here there is a difference in emphasis and import between the breach or neglect of a duty and the invasion of or interference with a right. For to focus upon duties and their breaches is to concentrate necessarily upon the person who has the duty; it is to invoke criteria by which to make moral assessments of his conduct. Rights, on the other hand, call attention to the injury inflicted; to the fact that the possessor of the right was adversely affected by the action. Furthermore, the invasion of a right constitutes, as such, a special and independent injury, whereas this is not the case with less stringent claims.

Finally, just because rights are those moral commodities which delineate the areas of entitlement, they have an additional important function: that of defining the respects in which one can reasonably entertain certain kinds of expectations. To live in a society in which there are rights and in which rights are generally respected is to live in a society in which the social environment has been made appreciably more predictable and secure. It is to be able to count on receiving and enjoying objects of value. Rights have, therefore, an obvious psychological, as well as moral, dimension and significance.

II

If the above are some of the characteristics and characteristic functions of rights in general, what then can we say about human rights? More specifically, what is it for a right to be a human right, and what special role might human rights play?

Probably the simplest thing that might be said of a human right is that it is a right possessed by human beings. To talk about human rights would be to distinguish those rights which humans have from those which nonhuman entities, e.g., animals or corporations, might have.

It is certain that this is not what is generally meant by human rights. Rather than constituting the genus of all particular rights that humans have, human rights have almost always been deemed to be one species of these rights. If nothing else about the subject is clear, it is evident that one's particular legal rights, as well as some of one's moral rights, are not among one's human rights. If any right is a *human* right, it must, I believe, have at least four very general characteristics. First, it must be possessed by all human beings, as well as only by human beings. Second, because it is the same right that all human beings possess, it must be possessed equally by all human beings. Third, because human rights are possessed by all human beings, we can rule out as possible candidates any of those rights which one might have in virtue of occupying any particular status or relationship, such as that of parent, president, or promisee. And fourth, if there are any human rights, they have the additional characteristic of being assertable, in a manner of speaking, "against the whole world." That is to say, because they are rights that are not possessed in virtue of any contingent status or relationship, they are rights that can be claimed equally against any and every other human being.

Furthermore, to repeat, if there are any human *rights,* they also have certain characteristics as rights. Thus, if there are any human rights, these constitute the strongest of all moral claims that all men can assert. They serve to define and protect those things which all men are entitled to have and enjoy. They indicate those objects toward which and those areas within which every human being is entitled to act without securing further permission or assent. They function so as to put certain matters beyond the power of anyone else to grant or to deny. They provide every human being with a ready justification for acting in certain ways, and they provide each person with ready grounds upon which to condemn any interference or invasion. And they operate, as well, to induce well-founded confidence that the values or objects protected by them will be readily and predictably obtainable. If there are any human rights, they are powerful moral commodities.

Finally, it is, perhaps, desirable to observe that there are certain characteristics I have not ascribed to these rights. In particular, I have not said that human rights need have either of two features: absoluteness and self-evidence. . . . I have not said that human rights are absolute in the sense that there are no conditions under which they can properly be overridden, although I have asserted—what is quite different—that they are absolute in the sense that they are possessed equally without any special, additional qualification by all human beings.

Neither have I said (nor do I want to assert) that human rights are self-evident in any sense. Indeed, I want explicitly to deny that a special manner of knowing or a specific epistemology is needed for the development of a theory of human rights. I want to assert that there is much that can be said in defense or support of the claim that a particular right is a human right. And I want to insist, as well, that to adduce reasons for human rights is consistent with their character as human, or natural, rights. Nothing that I have said about human rights entails a contrary conclusion.

III

To ask whether there are any human, or natural rights is to pose a potentially misleading question. Rights of any kind, and particularly natural rights, are not like chairs or trees. One cannot simply look and see whether they are there. There are, though, at least two senses in which rights of all kinds can be said to exist. There is first the sense in which we can ask and answer the empirical question of whether in a given society there is intellectual or conceptual acknowledgment of the fact that persons or other entities have rights at all. We can ask, that is, whether the persons in that society "have" the concept of a right (or a human right), and whether they regard that concept as meaningfully applicable to persons or other entities in that society. And there is, secondly, the sense in which we can ask the question, to what extent, in a society that acknowledges the existence of rights, is there general respect for, protection of, or noninterference with the exercise of those rights.

These are not, though, the only two questions that can be asked. For we can also seek to establish whether any rights, and particularly human rights, ought to be both acknowledged and respected. I want now to begin to do this by considering the way in which an argument for human rights might be developed.

It is evident, I think, that almost any argument for the acknowledgment of any rights as human rights starts with the factual assertion that there are certain respects in which all persons are alike or equal. The argument moves typically from that assertion to the conclusion that there are certain human rights. What often remains unclear, however, is the precise way in which the truth of any proposition about the respects in which persons are alike advances an argument for the acknowledgment of human rights. And what must be supplied, therefore, are the plausible intermediate premises that connect the initial premise with the conclusion.

One of the most careful and complete illustrations of an argument that does indicate some of these intermediate steps is that provided by Gregory Vlastos in an article entitled, "Justice and Equality."[1] Our morality, he says, puts an equal intrinsic value on each person's well-being and freedom. In detail, the argument goes like this:

There is, Vlastos asserts, a wide variety of cases in which all persons are capable of experiencing the same values.

> Thus, to take a perfectly clear case, no matter how A and B might differ in taste and style of life, they would both crave relief from acute physical pain. In that case we would put the same value on giving this to either of them, regardless of the fact that A might be a talented, brilliantly successful person, B "a mere nobody". . . . [I]n all cases where human beings are capable of enjoying the same goods, we feel that the intrinsic value of their enjoyment is the same. In just this sense we hold that (1) *one man's well-being is as valuable as any other's*. . . . [Similarly] we feel that choosing for oneself what one will do, believe, approve, say, read, worship, has its own intrinsic value, the same for all persons, and quite independently of the value of the things they happen to choose. Naturally we hope that all of them will make the best possible use of their freedom of choice. But we value their exercise of the freedom, regardless of the outcome; and we value it equally for all. For us (2) *one man's freedom is as valuable as any other's*. . . . [Thus], since we do believe in equal value as to human well-being and freedom, we should also believe in the *prima facie* equality of men's *right* to well-being and to freedom (51–52).

As it is stated, I am not certain that this argument answers certain kinds of attack.

In particular, there are three questions that merit further attention. First, why should anyone have a right to the enjoyment of any goods at all, and, more specifically, well-being and freedom? Second, for what reasons might we be warranted in believing that the intrinsic value of the enjoyment of such goods is the same for all persons? And third, even if someone ought to have a right to well-being and freedom and even if the intrinsic value of each person's enjoyment of these things is equal, why should all men have the equal right—and hence the human right—to secure, obtain, or enjoy these goods?

I think that the third question is the simplest of the three to answer. If anyone has a right to well-being and freedom and if the intrinsic value of any person's enjoyment of these goods is equal to that of any other's, then all men do have an equal right—and hence a human right—to secure, obtain, or enjoy these goods, just because it would be irrational to distinguish among persons as to the possession of these rights. That is to say, the principle that no person should be treated differently from any or all other persons unless there is some general and relevant reason that justifies this difference in treatment is a fundamental principle of morality, if not of rationality itself. Indeed, although I am not certain how one might argue for this, I think it could well be said that all men do have a "second-order" human right—that is, an absolute right—to expect all persons to adhere to this principle.

This principle, or this right, does not by itself establish that there are any specific human rights. But either the principle or the right does seem to establish that well-being and freedom are human rights if they are rights at all and if the intrinsic value of each person's enjoyment is the same. For, given these premises, it does appear to follow that there is no relevant and general reason to differentiate among persons as to the possession of this right.

I say "seem to" and "appear to" because this general principle of morality may not be strong enough. What has been said so far does not in any obvious fashion rule out the possibility that there is some general and relevant principle of differentiation. It only, apparently, rules out possible variations in intrinsic value as a reason for making differentiations.

The requirement of *relevance* does, I think, seem to make the argument secure. For, if *the reason* for acknowledging in a person a right to freedom and well-being is the intrinsic value of his enjoyment of these goods, then the nature of the intrinsic value of any other person's enjoyment is the only relevant reason for making exceptions or for differentiating among persons as to the possession of these rights.

As to the first question, that of whether a person has a right to well-being and freedom, I am not certain what kind of answer is most satisfactory. If Vlastos is correct in asserting that these enjoyments are *values,* then that is, perhaps, answer enough. That is to say, if enjoying well-being is something *valuable*—and especially if it is intrinsically valuable—then it seems to follow that this is the kind of thing to which one ought to have a right. For if anything ought to be given the kind of protection afforded by a right, it ought surely be that which is valuable. Perhaps, too, there is nothing more that need be said other than to point out that we simply do properly value well-being and freedom.

I think that another, more general answer is also possible. Here I would revert more specifically to my earlier discussion of some of the characteristics and functions of rights. There are two points to be made. First, if we are asked, why ought anyone have a right to anything? or why not have a system in which there are not rights at all? the answer is that such a system would be a morally impoverished one. It would prevent persons from asserting those kinds of claims, it would preclude persons from having those types of expectations, and it would prohibit persons from making those kinds of judgments which a system of rights makes possible.

Thus, if we can answer the question of why have rights at all, we can then ask and answer the question of what things—among others—ought to be protected by *rights*. And the answer, I take it, is that one ought to be able to claim as entitlements those minimal things without which it is impossible to develop one's capabilities and to live a life as a human being. Hence, to take one thing that is a precondition of well-being, the relief from acute physical pain, this is the kind of enjoyment that ought to be protected as a right of some kind just because without such relief there is precious little that one can effectively do or become. And similarly for the opportunity to make choices, examine beliefs, and the like.

To recapitulate. The discussion so far has indicated two things: (1) the conditions under which any specific right would be a human right, and (2) some possible grounds for arguing that certain values or enjoyments ought to be regarded as matters of right. The final question that remains is whether there are any specific rights that satisfy the conditions necessary to make them human rights. Or, more specifically, whether it is plausible to believe that there are no general and relevant principles that justify making distinctions among persons in respect to their rights to well-being and freedom.

Vlastos has it that the rights to well-being and freedom do satisfy these conditions, since he asserts that we, at least, do regard each person's well-being and freedom as having equal intrinsic value. If this is correct, if each person's well-being and freedom does have *equal* intrinsic value, then there is no general and relevant principle for differentiating among persons as to these values and, hence, as to their rights to secure these values. But this does not seem wholly satisfactory. It does not give us any reason for supposing that it is plausible to ascribe equal intrinsic value to each person's well-being and freedom.

The crucial question, then, is the plausibility of ascribing equal intrinsic value to each person's well-being and freedom. There are, I think, at least three different answers that might be given.

First, it might be asserted that this ascription simply constitutes another feature of our morality. The only things that can be done are to point out that this is an assumption that we do make and to ask persons whether they would not prefer to live in a society in which such an assumption is made.

While perhaps correct and persuasive, this does not seem to me to be all that can be done. In particular, there are, I think, two further arguments that may be made.

The first is that there are cases in which all human beings *equally* are capable of enjoying the same goods, e.g., relief from acute physical pain, or that they are capable of deriving equal enjoyment from the same goods. If this is true, then if anyone has a right to this enjoyment, that right is a human right just because there is no rational ground for preferring one man's enjoyment to another's. For, if all persons do have equal capacities of these sorts and if the existence of these capacities is the reason for ascribing these rights to anyone, then all persons ought to have the right to claim equality of treatment in respect to the possession and exercise of these rights.

The difficulty inherent in this argument is at the same time the strength of the next one. The difficulty is simply that it does seem extraordinarily difficult to know how one would show that all men are equally capable of enjoying any of the same goods, or even how one might attempt to gather or evaluate relevant evidence in this matter. In a real sense, interpersonal comparisons of such a thing as the ability to bear pain seems to be logically as well as empirically unobtainable. Even more unobtainable, no doubt, is a measure of the comparative enjoyments derivable from choosing for oneself. These are simply enjoyments the comparative worths of which, as different persons, there is no way to assess. If this is so, then this fact gives rise to an alternative argument.

We do know, through inspection of human history as well as of our own lives, that the denial of the opportunity to experience the enjoyment of these goods makes it impossible to live either a full or a satisfying life. In a real sense, the enjoyment of these goods differentiates human from nonhuman entities. And therefore, even if we have no meaningful or reliable criteria for comparing and weighing capabilities for enjoyment or for measuring their quantity or quality, we probably know all we need to know to justify our refusal to attempt to grade the value of the enjoyment of these goods. Hence, the dual grounds for treating their intrinsic values as equal for all persons: either these values are equal for all persons, or, if there are differences, they are not in principle discoverable or measurable. Hence, the argument, or an argument, for the human rights to well-being and freedom.

NOTE

[1] In Richard B. Brandt, ed., *Social Justice* (Englewood Cliffs, N.J.: Prentice-Hall, 1962), pp. 31–72.

The Basis and Content of Human Rights

Alan Gewirth

Despite the great practical importance of the idea of human rights, some of the most basic questions about them have not yet received adequate answers. We may assume, as true by definition, that human rights are rights that all persons have simply insofar as they are human. But are there any such rights? How, if at all, do we know that there are? What is their scope or content, and how are they related to one another? Are any of them absolute, or may each of them be overridden in certain circumstances? . . .

Reprinted by permission of New York University Press from *Human Rights:* NOMOS XXIII, edited by J. Roland Pennock and John W. Chapman. Copyright © 1981 by New York University.

I

Let us . . . begin to develop answers to these questions about human rights. First, since these rights derive from a valid moral criterion or principle, we must consider . . . the context or subject matter of morality. . . . Amid the various divergent moralities with their conflicting substantive and distributive criteria, a certain core meaning may be elicited. According to this, a morality is a set of categorically obligatory requirements for actions that are addressed at least in part to every actual or prospective agent, and that are intended to further the interests, especially the most important interests, of persons or recipients other than or in addition to the agent or the speaker. . . .

As we have seen, moralities differ with regard to what interests of which persons they view as important and deserving of support. But amid these differences, all moralities have it in common that they are concerned with actions. For all moral judgments, including right-claims, consist directly or indirectly in precepts about how persons ought to act toward one another. The specific contents of these judgments, of course, vary widely and often conflict with one another. But despite these variations and conflicts, they have in common the context of the human actions that they variously prescribe or prohibit and hence view as right or wrong. It is thus this context which constitutes the general subject matter of all morality.

How does the consideration of human action serve to ground or justify the ascription and content of human rights? . . .

As we have seen, all moral precepts, regardless of their varying specific contents, are concerned directly or indirectly with how persons ought to act. This is also true of most if not all other practical precepts. Insofar as actions are the possible objects of any such precepts, they are performed by purposive agents. Now, every agent regards his purposes as good according to whatever criteria (not necessarily moral ones) are involved in his acting to fulfill them. This is shown, for example, by the endeavor or at least intention with which each agent approaches the achieving of his purposes. Hence, . . . he also, as rational, regards as necessary goods the proximate general necessary conditions of his acting to achieve his purposes. For without these conditions he either would not be able to act for any purposes or goods at all or at least would not be able to act with any chance of succeeding in his purposes. These necessary conditions of his action and successful action are freedom and well-being, where freedom consists in controlling one's behavior by one's unforced choice while having knowledge of relevant circumstances, and well-being consists in having the other general abilities and conditions required for agency. The components of such well-being fall into a hierarchy of three kinds of goods: basic, nonsubtractive, and additive. These will be analyzed more fully below.

In saying that every rational agent regards his freedom and well-being as necessary goods, I am primarily making . . . a dialectically necessary point about what is logically involved in the structure of action. Since agents act for purposes they regard as worth pursuing—for otherwise they would not control their behavior by their unforced choice with a view to achieving their purposes—they must, insofar as they are rational, also regard the necessary conditions of such pursuit as necessary goods. . . . I shall call freedom and well-being the *generic features* of action, since they characterize all action or at least all successful action in the respect in which action has been delimited above.

It is from the consideration of freedom and well-being as the necessary goods of action that the ascription and contents of human rights follow. The main point is that with certain qualifications to be indicated below, there is a logical connection between necessary goods and rights. . . . The reason for this is that rights involve *normative necessity*. One way to see this is through the correlativity of rights and strict "oughts" or duties. The judgment "A has a right to X" both entails and is entailed by, "All other persons ought at least to refrain from interfering with A's having (or doing) X," where this "ought" includes the idea of something due or owed to A. Under certain circumstances, including those where the subject or right-holder A is unable to have X by his own efforts, the rights-judgment also entails and is entailed by, "Other persons ought to assist A to have X," where again the "ought" includes the idea of something due or owed to A. Now, these strict "oughts" involve normative necessity; they state what, as of right, other persons *must* do. Such necessity is also involved in the frequently noted use of "due" and "entitlement" as synonyms or at least as components of the substantive use of "right." A person's rights are what belong to him as his due, what he is entitled to, hence what he can rightly demand of others. In all these expressions the idea of normative necessity is central.

This necessity is an essential component in the ascription of rights, but it is not sufficient to logically ground this ascription. Let us recur to freedom and well-being as the necessary goods of action. From "X is a necessary good for A" does it logically follow that "A has a right to X"? To understand this question correctly, we must keep in mind that "necessary good" is here used in a rational and invariant sense. It does not refer to the possibly idiosyncratic and unfounded desires of different protagonists, as when someone asserts, "I must have a Florida vacation (or a ten-speed bicycle); it is a necessary good for me." Rather, a "necessary good" is here confined to the truly grounded requirements of agency; hence, it correctly characterizes the indispensable conditions that all agents must accept as needed for their actions. . . .

For the concept of necessary goods logically to generate the concept of rights, both concepts must figure in judgments made by the agent or right-holder himself in accordance with the dialectically necessary method. It will be recalled that this method begins from statements or judgments that are necessarily made or accepted by protagonists or agents, and the method then traces what these statements or judgments logically imply. Thus, in the present context of action, the method requires that the judgments about necessary goods and rights be viewed as being made by the agent himself from within his own internal, conative standpoint in purposive agency.

When this internal, conative view is taken, the logical gaps indicated above between judgments about necessary goods and ascriptions of rights are closed. The agent is now envisaged as saying, "My freedom and well-being are necessary goods." From this there does logically follow his further judgment, "I have rights to freedom and well-being." For the assertion about necessary goods is now not a mere factual means-end statement; on the contrary, because it is made by the agent himself from within his own conative standpoint in purposive agency, it carries his advocacy or endorsement. In effect, he is saying, "I must have freedom and well-being in order to pursue by my actions any of the purposes I want and intend to pursue." Thus his statement is prescriptive.

By the same token, his statement carries the idea of something that is his due, to which he is entitled. It must be kept in mind that these concepts do not have only moral or legal criteria; they may be used with many different kinds of criteria, including intellectual, aesthetic, and prudential ones. In the present context the agent's criterion is prudential: the entitlement he claims to freedom and well-being is grounded in his own needs as an agent who wants to pursue his purposes. He is saying that he has rights to freedom and well-being because these goods are due to him from within his own standpoint as a prospective purposive agent, since he needs these goods in order to act either at all or with the general possibility of success.

This consideration also shows how, from the agent's judgment "My freedom and well-being are necessary goods," there also logically follows a claim on his part against other persons. For he is saying that because he must have freedom and well-being in order to act, he must have whatever further conditions are required for his fulfilling these needs; and these further conditions include especially that other persons at least refrain from interfering with his having freedom and well-being. Thus, the agent's assertion of his necessary needs of agency entails a claim on his part to the noninterference of other persons and also, in certain circumstances, to their help. . . .

II

Thus far I have shown that rights and right-claims are necessarily connected with action, in that every agent, on pain of self-contradiction, must hold or accept that he has rights to the necessary conditions of action. I shall henceforth call these *generic rights,* since freedom and well-being are the generic features of action. As so far presented, however, they are only prudential rights but not yet moral ones, since their criterion, as we have seen, is the agent's own pursuit of his purposes. In order to establish that they are also moral and human rights, we must show that each agent must admit that all other humans also have these rights. For in this way the agent will be committed to take favorable account of the purposes or interests of other persons besides himself. Let us see why he must take this further step.

This involves the question of the ground or sufficient reason or sufficient condition on the basis of which any agent must hold that he has the generic rights. Now, this ground is not subject to his optional or variable decisions. There is one, and only one, ground that every agent logically must accept as the sufficient justifying condition for his having the generic rights, namely, that he is a prospective agent who has purposes he wants to fulfill. Suppose some agent A were to hold that he has these rights only for some more restrictive necessary and sufficient reason R. This would entail that in lacking R he would lack the generic rights. But if A were to accept this conclusion, that he may not have the generic rights, he would contradict himself. For we saw above that it is necessarily true of every agent that he must hold or accept at least implicitly that he has rights to freedom and well-being. Hence, A would be in the position of both affirming and denying that he has the generic rights: affirming it because he is an agent, denying it because he lacks R. To avoid this contradiction, every agent must hold that being a prospective purposive agent is a sufficient reason or condition for having the generic rights.

Because of this sufficient reason, every agent, on pain of self-contradiction, must also accept the generalization that all prospective purposive agents have the generic rights. . . . If any agent A were to deny or refuse to accept this generalization in the case of any other prospective purposive agent, A would contradict himself. For he would be in the position of saying that being a prospective purposive agent both is and is not a sufficient justifying condition for having the generic rights. Hence, on pain of self-contradiction, every agent must accept the generalization that all prospective purposive agents have the generic rights.

Thus, we have now arrived at the basis of human rights. For the generic rights to freedom and well-being are moral rights, since they require of every agent that he take favorable account of the most important interests of all other prospective agents, namely, the interests grounded in their needs for the necessary conditions of agency. And these generic rights are also human rights, since every human being is an actual, prospective, or potential agent. I shall discuss the distribution of these rights among humans more fully below. But first I must also establish that the generic rights are human rights in the further respect indicated above, namely, that they are grounded in or justified by a valid moral criterion or principle.

The above argument for the generic rights as moral rights has already provided the full basis for deriving a supreme moral principle. We have seen that every agent, on pain of self-contradiction, must accept the generalization that all prospective purposive agents have the generic rights to freedom and well-being. From this generalization, because of the correlativity of rights and strict "oughts," it logically follows that every person ought to refrain from interfering with the freedom and well-being of all other persons insofar as they are prospective purposive agents. It also follows that under certain circumstances every person ought to assist other persons to have freedom and well-being, when they cannot have these by their own efforts and he can give them such assistance without comparable cost to himself, although more usually such assistance must operate through appropriate institutions. Since to refrain and to assist in these ways is to act in such a way that one's actions are in accord with the generic rights of one's recipients, every agent is logically committed, on pain of self-contradiction, to accept the following precept: *Act in accord with the generic rights of your recipients as well as of yourself*. I shall call this the *Principle of Generic Consistency (PGC)*, since it combines the formal consideration of consistency with the material consideration of the generic features and rights of agency. To act in accord with someone's right to freedom is, in part, to refrain from coercing him; to act in accord with someone's right to well-being is, in part, to refrain from harming him by adversely affecting his basic, nonsubtractive, or additive goods. In addition, to act in accord with these rights may also require positive assistance. These rights, as thus upheld, are now moral ones because they are concerned to further the interests or goods of persons other than or in addition to the agent. The *PGC*'s central moral requirement is the *equality of generic rights,* since it requires of every agent that he accord to his recipients the same rights to freedom and well-being that he necessarily claims for himself. . . .

III

There remain two broad questions about human rights as so far delineated. First, the rights to freedom and well-being are very general. What more specific contents do they have, and how are these contents related to one another? Second, human rights are often thought of in terms of political effectuation and legal enforcement. How does this relation operate in the case of the generic rights? Should all of them be legally enforced or only some, and how is this to be determined?

To answer the first question we must analyze the components of well-being and of freedom. It was noted above that well-being, viewed as the abilities and conditions required for agency, comprises three kinds of goods: basic, nonsubtractive, and additive. Basic goods are the essential preconditions of action, such as life, physical integrity, and mental equilibrium. Thus, a person's basic rights—his rights to basic goods—are violated when he is killed, starved, physically incapacitated, terrorized, or subjected to mentally deranging drugs. The basic rights are also violated in such cases as where a person is drowning or starving and another person who, at no comparable cost to himself, could rescue him or give him food knowingly fails to do so.

Nonsubtractive goods are the abilities and conditions required for maintaining undiminished one's level of purpose-fulfillment and one's capabilities for particular actions. A person's nonsubtractive rights are violated when he is adversely affected in his abilities to plan for the future, to have knowledge of facts relevant to his projected actions, to utilize his resources to fulfill his wants, and so forth. Ways of undergoing such adversities include being lied to, cheated, stolen from, or defamed; suffering broken promises; or being subjected to dangerous, degrading, or excessively debilitating conditions of physical labor or housing or other strategic situations of life when resources are available for improvement.

Additive goods are the abilities and conditions required for increasing one's level of purpose-fulfillment and one's capabilities for particular actions. A person's additive rights are violated when his self-esteem is attacked, when he is denied education to the limits of his capacities, or when he is discriminated against on grounds of race, religion, or nationality. This right is also violated when a person's development of the self-regarding virtues of courage, temperance, and prudence is hindered by actions that promote a climate of fear and oppression, or that encourage the spread of physically or mentally harmful practices such as excessive use of drugs, or that contribute to misinformation, ignorance, and superstition, especially as these bear on persons' ability to act effectively in pursuit of their purposes. When a person's right to basic well-being is violated, I shall say that he undergoes basic harm; when his rights to nonsubtractive or additive well-being are violated, I shall say that he undergoes specific harm.

Besides these three components of the right to well-being, the human rights also include the right to freedom. This consists in a person's controlling his actions and his participation in transactions by his own unforced choice or consent and with knowledge of relevant circumstances, so that his behavior is neither compelled nor prevented by the actions of other persons. Hence, a person's right to freedom is violated if he is subjected to violence, coercion, deception, or any other procedures that attack or remove his informed control of his behavior by his own unforced choice. This right includes having a sphere of personal autonomy and privacy whereby one is let alone by others unless and until he unforcedly consents to undergo their action.

In general, whenever a person violates any of these rights to well-being or freedom, his action is morally wrong and he contradicts himself. For he is in the position of saying or holding that a right he necessarily claims for himself insofar as he is a prospective purposive agent is not had by some other person, even though the latter, too, is a prospective purposive agent. Hence, all such morally wrong actions are rationally unjustifiable.

It must also be noted, however, that these rights to freedom and well-being may conflict with one another. For example, the right to freedom of one person A may conflict with the right to well-being of another person B when A uses his freedom to kill, rob, or insult B. Here the duty of other persons to refrain from interfering with A's control of his behavior by his unforced choice may conflict with their duty to prevent B from suffering basic or specific harm when they can do so at no comparable cost to themselves. In addition, different persons' rights to well-being may conflict with one another, as when C must lie to D in order to prevent E from being murdered, or when F must break his promise to G in order to save H from drowning. Moreover, a person's right to freedom may conflict with his own right to well-being, as when he commits suicide or ingests harmful drugs. Here the duty of other persons not to interfere with his control of his behavior by his unforced choice may conflict with their duty to prevent his losing basic goods when they can do so at no comparable cost to themselves.

These conflicts show that human rights are only *prima facie,* not absolute, in that under certain circumstances they may justifiably be overridden. . . . But although human rights may be overridden, this still leaves the Principle of Generic Consistency as an absolute or categorically obligatory moral principle. For the *PGC* sets the criteria for the justifiable overriding of one moral right by another and hence for the resolution of conflicts among rights. The basis of these criteria is that the *PGC* is both a formal and a material principle concerned with transactional consistency regarding the possession and use of the necessary conditions of action. The criteria stem from the *PGC*'s central requirement that there must be mutual respect for freedom and well-being among all prospective purposive agents. Departures from this mutual respect are justified only where they are required either to prevent or rectify antecedent departures, or to avoid greater departures, or to comply with social rules that themselves reflect such respect in the ways indicated in the procedural and instrumental applications of the *PGC*. Thus the criteria for resolving conflicts of rights or duties fall under three headings of progressively lesser importance.

The Bogus Distinction—"Negative" Rights and "Positive" Rights

Henry Shue

I

Many Americans would probably be initially inclined to think that rights to subsistence are at least slightly less important than rights to physical security, even though subsistence is at least as essential to survival as security is and even though questions of security do not even arise when subsistence fails. Much official U.S. government rhetoric routinely treats all "economic rights," among which basic subsistence rights are buried amidst many non-basic rights, as secondary and deferrable. . . . Now that the same argument in favor of basic rights to both aspects of personal survival, subsistence and security, is before us, we can examine critically some of the reasons why it sometimes appears that although people have basic security rights, the right, if any, to even the physical necessities of existence like minimal health care, food, clothing, shelter, unpolluted water, and unpolluted air is somehow less urgent or less basic.

Frequently it is asserted or assumed that a highly significant difference between rights to physical security and rights to subsistence is that they are respectively "negative" rights and "positive" rights. This position, which I will now try to refute, is considerably more complex than it at first appears. I will sometimes refer to it as the position that subsistence rights are *positive* and *therefore secondary*. Obviously taking the position involves holding that subsistence rights are positive in some respect in which security rights are negative and further claiming that this difference concerning positive/negative is a good enough reason to assign priority to negative rights over positive rights. I will turn shortly to the explanation of this assumed positive/negative distinction. But first I want to lay out all the premises actually needed by the position that subsistence rights are positive and therefore secondary, although I need to undercut only some—strictly speaking, only one—of them in order to cast serious doubt upon the position's conclusions.

The alleged lack of priority for subsistence rights compared to security rights assumes:

1 The distinction between subsistence rights and security rights is (a) sharp and (b) significant.

2 The distinction between positive rights and negative rights is (a) sharp and (b) significant.

3 Subsistence rights are positive.

4 Security rights are negative.

I am not suggesting that anyone has ever laid out this argument in all the steps it actually needs. On the contrary, a full statement of the argument is the beginning of its refutation—this is an example of the philosophical analogue of the principle that sunlight is the best antiseptic. . . .

I will concentrate on establishing that premises 3 and 4 are both misleading. Then I will suggest a set of distinctions among duties that accurately transmits the insight distorted by 3 and 4. Insofar as 3 and 4 are inaccurate, considerable doubt is cast upon 2, although it remains possible that someone can specify some sharply contrasting pair of rights that actually are examples of 2. I will not directly attack premise 1.

Now the basic idea behind the general suggestion that there are positive rights and negative rights seems to have been that one kind of rights (the positive ones) require other people to act positively—to "do something"—whereas another kind of rights (the negative ones) require other people merely to refrain from acting in certain ways—to do nothing that violates the rights. For example, according to this picture, a right to subsistence would be positive because it would require other people, in the last resort, to supply food or clean air to those unable to find, produce, or buy their own; a right to security would be negative because it would require other people merely to refrain from murdering or otherwise assaulting those with the right. The underlying distinction, then, is between acting and refraining from acting; and positive rights are those with correlative duties to act in certain ways and negative rights are those with correlative duties to refrain from acting in certain ways. Therefore, the moral significance, if any, of the distinction between positive rights and negative rights depends upon the moral significance, if any, of the distinction between action and omission of action.

The ordinarily implicit argument for considering rights to subsistence to be secondary would, then, appear to be basically this. Since subsistence rights are positive and require other people to do more than negative rights require—perhaps more than people can actually do—negative rights, such as those to security, should be fully guaranteed first. Then, any remaining resources could be devoted, as long as they lasted, to the positive—and perhaps impossible—task of providing for subsistence. Unfortunately for this argument, neither rights to physical security nor rights to subsistence fit neatly into their assigned sides of the simplistic positive/negative dichotomy. We must consider whether security rights are purely negative and then whether subsistence rights are purely positive. I will try to show (1) that security rights are more "positive" than they are often said to be, (2) that subsistence rights are more "negative" than they are often said to be, and given (1) and (2), (3) that the distinctions between security rights and subsistence rights, though not entirely illusory, are too fine to support any weighty conclusions, especially the very weighty conclusion that security rights are basic and subsistence rights are not.

In the case of rights to physical security, it may be possible *to avoid violating* someone's rights to physical security yourself by merely refraining from acting in any of the ways that would constitute violations. But it is impossible *to protect* anyone's rights to physical security without taking, or making payments toward the taking of, a wide range of positive actions. For example, at the very least the protection of rights to physical security necessitates police forces; criminal courts; penitentiaries; schools for training police, lawyers, and guards; and taxes to support an enormous system for the prevention, detection, and punishment of violations of personal security. All these activities and institutions are attempts at providing social guarantees for individuals' security so that they are not left to face alone forces that they cannot handle on their own. How much more than these expenditures one thinks would be necessary in order for people actually to be reasonably secure (as distinguished from merely having the cold comfort of knowing that the occasional criminal is punished after someone's security has already been violated) depends on one's theory of violent crime, but it is not unreasonable to believe that it would involve extremely expensive, "positive" programs. Probably no one knows how much positive action would have to be taken in a contemporary society like the United States significantly to reduce the levels of muggings, rapes, murders, and other assaults that violate personal security, and in fact to make people reasonably secure.

Someone might suggest that this blurs rights to physical security with some other type of rights, which might be called rights-to-be-protected-against-assaults-upon-phys-ical-security. According to this distinction, rights to physical security are negative, requiring others only to refrain from assaults, while rights-to-be-protected-against-assaults-upon-physical-security are positive, requiring others to take positive steps to prevent assaults.

Perhaps if one were dealing with some wilderness situation in which individuals' encounters with each other were infrequent and irregular, there might be some point in noting to someone: I am not asking you to cooperate with a system of guarantees to protect me from third parties, but only to refrain from attacking me yourself. But in an organized society, insofar as there were any such things as rights to physical security that were distinguishable from some other rights-to-be-protected-from-as-saults-upon-physical-security, no one would have much interest in the bare rights to physical security. What people want and need . . . is the protection of their rights. Insofar as this frail distinction holds up, it is the rights-to-be-protected-against-assaults that any reasonable person would demand from society. A demand for physical security is not normally a demand simply to be left alone, but a demand to be protected against harm. It is a demand for positive action, or, in the words of our initial account of a right, a demand for social guarantees against at least the standard threats.

So it would be very misleading to say simply that physical security is a negative matter of other people's refraining from violations. Ordinarily it is instead a matter of some people refraining from violations and of third parties being prevented from violations by the positive steps taken by first and second parties. The "negative" refraining may in a given case be less significant than the "positive" preventing—it is almost never the whole story. The end-result of the positive preventative steps taken is of course an enforced refraining from violations, not the performance of any positive action. The central core of the right is a right that others not act in certain ways. But the mere core of the right indicates little about the social institutions needed to secure it, and the core of the right does not contain its whole structure. The protection of "negative rights" requires positive measures, and therefore their actual enjoyment requires positive measures. In any imperfect society enjoyment of a right will depend to some extent upon protection against those who do not choose not to violate it.

Rights to subsistence too are in their own way considerably more complex than simply labeling them "positive" begins to indicate. In fact, their fulfillment involves at least two significantly different types of action. On the one hand, rights to subsistence sometimes do involve correlative duties on the part of others to provide the needed commodities when those in need are helpless to secure a supply for themselves, as, for example, the affluent may have a duty to finance food supplies and transportation and distribution facilities in the case of famine. Even the satisfaction of subsistence rights by such positive action, however, need not be any more expensive or involve any more complex governmental programs than the effective protection of security rights would. A food stamp program, for example, could be cheaper or more expensive than, say, an anti-drug program aimed at reducing muggings and murders by addicts. Which program was more costly or more complicated would depend upon the relative dimensions of the respective problems and would be unaffected by any respect in which security is "negative" and subsistence is "positive." Insofar as any argument for giving priority to the fulfillment of "negative rights" rests on the assumption that actually securing "negative rights" is usually cheaper or simpler than securing "positive rights," the argument rests on an empirical speculation of dubious generality.

The other type of action needed to fulfill subsistence rights is even more difficult to distinguish sharply from the action needed to fulfill security rights. Rights to physical subsistence often can be completely satisfied without the provision by others of any commodities to those whose rights are in question. All that is sometimes necessary is to protect the persons whose subsistence is threatened from the individuals and institutions that will otherwise intentionally or unintentionally harm them. A demand for the fulfillment of rights to subsistence may involve not a demand to be provided with grants of commodities but merely a demand to be provided some opportunity for supporting oneself. The request is not to be supported but to be allowed to be self-supporting on the basis of one's own hard work.

What is striking is the similarity between protection against the destruction of the basis for supporting oneself and protection against assaults upon one's physical security. We can turn now to some examples that clearly illustrate that the honoring of subsistence rights sometimes involves action no more positive than the honoring of security rights does. Some cases in which all that is asked is protection from harm that would destroy the capacity to be self-supporting involve threats to subsistence of a complexity that is not usually noticed with regard to security, although the adequate protection of security would involve analyses and measures more complex than a preoccupation with police and prisons. The complexity of the circumstances of subsistence should not, however, be allowed to obscure the basic fact that essentially all that is being asked in the name of subsistence rights in these examples is protection from destructive acts by other people.

II

. . . Suppose the largest tract of land in the village was the property of the descendant of a family that had held title to the land for as many generations back as anyone could remember. By absolute standards this peasant was by no means rich, but his land was the richest in the small area that constituted the universe for the inhabitants of this village. He grew, as his father and grandfather had, mainly the black beans that are the staple (and chief—and adequate—source of protein) in the regional diet. His crop usually constituted about a quarter of the black beans marketed in the village. Practically every family grew part of what they needed, and the six men he hired during the seasons requiring extra labor held the only paid jobs in the village—everyone else just worked his own little plot.

One day a man from the capital offered this peasant a contract that not only guaranteed him annual payments for a 10-year lease on his land but also guaranteed him a salary (regardless of how the weather, and therefore the crops, turned out—a great increase in his financial security) to be the foreman for a new kind of production on his land. The contract required him to grow flowers for export and also offered him the opportunity, which was highly recommended, to purchase through the company, with payments in installments, equipment that would enable him to need to hire only two men. The same contract was offered to, and accepted by, most of the other larger landowners in the general region to which the village belonged.

Soon, with the sharp reduction in supply, the price of black beans soared. Some people could grow all they needed (in years of good weather) on their own land, but the families that needed to supplement their own crop with purchases had to cut back their consumption. In particular, the children in the four families headed by the laborers who lost their seasonal employment suffered severe malnutrition, especially since the parents had originally worked as laborers only because their own land was too poor or too small to feed their families.

Now, the story contains no implication that the man from the capital or the peasants-turned-foremen were malicious or intended to do anything worse than single-mindedly pursue their own respective interests. But the outsider's offer of the contract was one causal factor, and the peasant's acceptance of the contract was another causal factor, in producing the malnutrition that would probably persist, barring protective intervention, for at least the decade the contract was to be honored. If the families in the village had rights to subsistence, their rights were being violated. Society, acting presumably by way of the government, ought to protect them from a severe type of active harm that eliminates their ability even to feed themselves.

But was anyone actually harming the villagers, or were they simply suffering a regrettable decline in their fortunes? If someone was violating their rights, who exactly was the violator? Against whom specifically should the government be protecting them? For, we normally make a distinction between violating someone's rights and allowing someone's rights to be violated while simply minding our own business. It makes a considerable difference—to take an example from another set of basic rights—whether I myself assault someone or I merely carry on with my own affairs while allowing a third person to assault someone when I could protect the victim and end the assault. Now, I may have a duty not to allow assaults that I can without great danger to myself prevent or stop, as well as a duty not to assault people myself, but there are clearly two separable issues here. And it is perfectly conceivable that I might have the one duty (to avoid harming) and not the other (to protect from harm by third parties), because they involve two different types of action.

The switch in land-use within the story might then be described as follows. Even if one were willing to grant tentatively that the villagers all seemed to have rights to subsistence, some of which were violated by the malnutrition that some suffered after the switch in crops, no individual or organization can be identified as the violator: not the peasant-turned-foreman, for example, because—let us assume—he did not foresee the "systemic" effects of his individual choice; not the business representative from the capital because—let us assume—although he was knowledgeable enough to know what would probably happen, it would be unrealistically moralistic to expect him to forgo honest gains for himself and the company he represented because the gains had undesired, even perhaps regretted, "side-effects"; not any particular member of the governmental bureaucracy because—let us assume—no one had been assigned responsibility for maintaining adequate nutrition in this particular village. The local peasant and the business representative were both minding their own business in the village, and no one in the government had any business with this village. The peasant and the representative may have attended to their own affairs while harm befell less fortunate villagers, but allowing harm to occur without preventing it is not the same as directly inflicting it yourself. The malnutrition was just, literally, unfortunate: bad luck, for which no one could fairly be blamed. The malnutrition was, in effect, a natural disaster—was, in the obnoxious language of insurance law, an act of God. Perhaps the village was, after all, becoming overpopulated.

But, of course, the malnutrition resulting from the new choice of crop was not a natural disaster. The comforting analogy does not hold. The malnutrition was a social disaster. The malnutrition was the product of specific human decisions permitted by the presence of specific social institutions and the absence of others, in the context of the natural circumstances, especially the scarcity of land upon which to grow food, that were already given before the decisions were made. The harm in question, the malnutrition, was not merely allowed to happen by the parties to the flower-growing contract. The harm was partly caused by the requirement in the contract for a switch away from food, by the legality of the contract, and by the performance of the required switch in crops. If there had been no contract or if the contract had not required a switch away from food for local consumption, there would have been no malnutrition as things were going. In general, when persons take an action that is sufficient in some given natural and social circumstances to bring about an undesirable effect, especially one that there is no particular reason to think would otherwise have occurred, it is perfectly normal to consider their action to be one active cause of the harm. The parties to the contract partly caused the malnutrition.

But the society could have protected the villagers by countering the initiative of the contracting parties in any one of a number of ways that altered the circumstances, and the absence of the appropriate social guarantees is another cause of the malnutrition.

Such contracts could, for example, have already been made illegal. Or they could have been allowed but managed or taxed in order to compensate those who would otherwise predictably be damaged by them. Exactly what was done would be, *for the most part,* an economic and political question. But it is possible to have social guarantees against the malnutrition that is repeatedly caused in such standard, predictable ways.

Is a right to subsistence in such a case, then, a positive right in any important ways that a right to security is not? Do we actually find a contrast of major significance? No. As in the cases of the threats to physical security that we normally consider, the threat to subsistence is human activity with largely predictable effects. Even if, as we tend to assume, the motives for deprivations of security tend to be vicious while the motives for deprivations of subsistence tend to be callous, the people affected usually need protection all the same. The design, building, and maintenance of institutions and practices that protect people's subsistence against the callous—and even the merely over-energetic—is no more and no less positive than the conception and execution of programs to control violent crimes against the person. It is not obvious which, if either, it is more realistic to hope for or more economical to pursue. It is conceivable, although I doubt if anyone really knows, that the two are more effectively and efficiently pursued together. Neither looks simple, cheap, or "negative."

This example of the flower contract is important in part because, at a very simple level, it is in fact typical of much of what is happening today among the majority of the people in the world, who are poor and rural, and are threatened by forms of "economic development" that lower their own standard of living. But it is also important because, once again in a very simple way, it illustrates the single most critical fact about rights to subsistence; where subsistence depends upon tight supplies of essential commodities (like food), a change in supply can have, often by way of intermediate price effects, an indirect but predictable and devastating effect on people's ability to survive. A change in supply can transport self-supporting people into helplessness and, if no protection against the change is provided, into malnutrition or death. Severe harm to some people's ability to maintain themselves can be caused by changes in the use to which other people put vital resources (like land) they control. In such cases even someone who denied that individuals or organizations have duties to supply commodities to people who are helpless to obtain them for themselves, might grant that the government ought to execute the society's duty of protecting people from having their ability to maintain their own survival destroyed by the actions of others. If this protection is provided, there will be much less need later to provide commodities themselves to compensate for deprivations.

What transmits the effect in such cases is the local scarcity of the vital commodity. Someone might switch thousands of acres from food to flowers without having any effect on the diet of anyone else where the supply of food was adequate to prevent a significant price rise in response to the cut in supply. And it goes without saying that the price rises are vitally important only if the income and wealth of at least some people is severely limited, as of course it is in every society, often for the rural majority. It is as if an abundant supply sometimes functions as a sponge to absorb the otherwise significant effect on other people, but a tight supply (against a background of limited income and wealth) sometimes functions as a conductor to transmit effects to others, who feel them sharply.

It is extremely difficult merely to mind one's own business amidst a scarcity of vital commodities. It is illusory to think that this first commandment of liberalism can always be obeyed. The very scarcity draws people into contact with each other, destroys almost all area for individual maneuver, and forces people to elbow each other in order to move forward. The tragedy of scarcity, beyond the deprivations necessitated by the scarcity itself, is that scarcity tends to make each one's gain someone else's loss. One can act for oneself only by acting against others, since there is not enough for all. Amidst abundance of food a decision to grow flowers can be at worst a harmless act and quite likely a socially beneficial one. But amidst a scarcity of food, due partly to a scarcity of fertile land, an unmalicious decision to grow flowers can cause death—unless there are social guarantees for adequate nutrition. A call for social guarantees for subsistence in situations of scarcity is not a call for intervention in what were formerly private affairs. . . .

I believe the whole notion that there is a morally significant dichotomy between negative rights and positive rights is intellectually bankrupt—that premise 2, as stated in the first section of this [paper] is mistaken. The cases we have considered establish at the very least that the dichotomy distorts when it is applied to security rights and subsistence rights—that premises 3 and 4 were mistaken. The latter is all that needed to be shown.

III

Still, it is true that sometimes fulfilling a right does involve transferring commodities to the person with the right and sometimes it merely involves not taking commodities away. Is there not some grain of truth obscured by the dichotomy between negative and positive rights? Are there not distinctions here that it is useful to make?

The answer, I believe, is: yes, there are distinctions, but they are not distinctions between rights. The useful distinctions are among duties, and there are no one-to-one pairings between kinds of duties and kinds of rights. The complete fulfillment of each kind of right involves the performance of multiple kinds of duties. . . . In the remainder of this [paper] I would like to tender a very simple tripartite typology of duties. For all its own simplicity, it goes considerably beyond the usual assumption that for every right there is a single correlative duty, and suggests instead that for every basic right—and many other rights as well—there are three types of duties, all of which must be performed if the basic right is to be fully honored but not all of which must necessarily be performed by the same individuals or institutions. This latter point opens the possibility of distributing each of the three kinds of duty somewhat differently and perhaps confining any difficulties about the correlativity of subsistence rights and their accompanying duties to fewer than all three kinds of duties.

So I want to suggest that with every basic right, three types of duties correlate:

I Duties to *avoid* depriving.
II Duties to *protect* from deprivation.
III Duties to *aid* the deprived.

This may be easier to see in the case of the more familiar basic right, the right to physical security (the right not to be tortured, executed, raped, assaulted, etc.). For every person's right to physical security, there are three correlative duties:

I Duties not to eliminate a person's security—duties to *avoid* depriving.
II Duties to protect people against deprivation of security by other people—duties to *protect* from deprivation.
III Duties to provide for the security of those unable to provide for their own—duties to *aid* the deprived.

Similarly, for every right to subsistence there are:

I Duties not to eliminate a person's only available means of subsistence—duties to *avoid* depriving.
II Duties to protect people against deprivation of the only available means of subsistence by other people—duties to *protect* from deprivation.
III Duties to provide for the subsistence of those unable to provide for their own—duties to *aid* the deprived.

If this suggestion is correct, the common notion that *rights* can be divided into rights to forbearance (so-called negative rights), as if some rights have correlative duties only to avoid depriving, and rights to aid (so-called positive rights), as if some rights have correlative duties only to aid, is thoroughly misguided. This misdirected simplification is virtually ubiquitous among contemporary North Atlantic theorists and is, I think, all the more pernicious for the degree of unquestioning acceptance it has now attained. It is duties, not rights, that can be divided among avoidance and aid, and protection. And—this is what matters—every basic right entails duties of all three types. Consequently the attempted division of rights, rather than duties, into forbearance and aid (and protection, which is often understandably but unhelpfully blurred into avoidance, since protection is partly, but only partly, the enforcement of avoidance) can only breed confusion.

It is impossible for any basic right—however "negative" it has come to seem—to be fully guaranteed unless all three types of duties are fulfilled. The very most "negative"-seeming right to liberty, for example, requires positive action by society to protect it and positive action by society to restore it when avoidance and protection both fail. This by no means implies, as I have already mentioned, that all three types of duties fall upon everyone else or even fall equally upon everyone upon whom they do fall.

CHAPTER 9

VIRTUE

Suppose someone remarked at a party that you were a virtuous person. Would you feel complimented or a little uneasy? You wouldn't feel uneasy if someone said that you were respectful, thoughtful, kind, courageous, or intelligent. Yet each of these traits is or has been considered a virtue. What may account for any possible uneasiness about being called virtuous in general is the fact that the term "virtuous" seldom arises in ordinary conversation. Until very recently it was not much discussed by ethical theorists either. Talk about virtue was considered out of fashion. Perhaps the connotations of the word, which linked it with sexual purity, made reference to virtue especially out of place during the sexual revolution of the 1960s and 1970s. Few today believe that the essential characteristic of the virtuous person is sexual restraint or chastity. Moreover, traditional philosophical discussions of virtue, which go back to the early Greeks, did not emphasize the virtue of chastity.

However, to abandon talk about the virtues is to ignore a central ingredient in the moral life. The proper focus of ethics is on the moral agent—the person who makes moral decisions. Even if you believed that your chief responsibility in making moral decisions was to focus on the rules, you would, as a moral agent, need a set of attitudes and beliefs, a certain personality, or character to discover the appropriate rules and to act on them. You would need to exhibit certain virtues. Possessing virtue promotes both the quality of our ethical decisions and our ability to withstand temptation and act morally. One of the more interesting developments in current ethical theory is the rediscovery of the importance of virtue. Professor Alasdair MacIntyre's book *After Virtue* has served as the catalyst for the rediscovery.

The classical view of virtue is found in Aristotle. Aristotle distinguished intellectual virtues from moral ones. Aristotle's analysis of intellectual virtue is a paradigm of his functional thinking. He identifies five ways that we can know something, and there is a corresponding intellectual virtue for these five ways of knowing. One of the chief characteristics distinguishing intellectual virtues from moral ones is the fact that moral virtues represent a mean between excess and deficiency; intellectual virtues do not have this characteristic. Intellectual virtues do not have excesses; you can't have too much wisdom.

More attention has been directed to Aristotle's account of the moral virtues. You may have heard that Aristotle's theory of virtue is the theory of the golden mean. Suitably understood and limited, this characterization of Aristotle's philosophy is correct. With respect to moral virtues, Aristotle's theory of virtue is corrective. Virtues are habits which enable us to avoid overdoing and underdoing. How do we correct the tendency to drink too much or to overeat? Develop the virtue of temperance. How do we get the strength to stand up for our rights? Develop the virtue of courage. Temperance is the mean between the excess *profligacy* and the deficiency *insensibility*. (Aristotle admits that you don't find many people with the vice of insensibility.) Courage is the mean between *cowardice* and *recklessness*. Aristotle works out in great detail the means, excesses, and deficiencies for all the moral virtues. The extent of Aristotle's labors is exhibited in the following table.

Activity	Vice (*Excess*)	Virtue (*Mean*)	Vice (*Deficit*)
Facing death	Too much fear (i.e., cowardice)	Right amount of fear (i.e., courage)	Too little fear (i.e., foolhardiness)
Bodily actions (eating, drinking, sex, etc.)	Profligacy	Temperance	No name for this state, but it may be called "insensitivity"
Giving money	Prodigality	Liberality	Illiberality
Large-scale giving	Vulgarity	Magnificence	Meanness
Claiming honors	Vanity	Pride	Humility
Social intercourse	Obsequiousness	Friendliness	Sulkiness
According honors	Injustice	Justice	Injustice
Retribution for wrongdoing	Injustice	Justice	Injustice

Source: W. T. Jones, *The Classical Mind*, Harcourt, Brace, & World, New York, 1952, 1969, p. 268.

Although the characterization of the virtues as the mean between excess and deficiency represents Aristotle's main contribution to a theory of virtue, he addresses several other topics which a complete theory of virtue must address. Plato posed the question as to whether virtue could be taught. Since virtuous parents sometimes seemed to raise rather unvirtuous children, Plato had rather grave doubts that virtue could be taught. Virtue certainly couldn't be taught by many of those who claimed to teach it—by lawyers and politicians, for example. If a virtue could be taught—and experts disagree as to Plato's actual opinion on this matter—it could only be taught by philosophers. Aristotle's answer to Plato's question was not oblique. The intellectual virtues are taught; the moral virtues are in us potentially as a result of our human nature and are developed by habit. We become morally virtuous by practicing the moral virtues. Aristotle's advice is not empty. If you get used to being honest or courageous, then each subsequent act of honesty or courage is easier. That's why it is important to give children the opportunity to practice virtue. Presumably it is easier to be honest in situations where honesty is less in danger of being compromised than when it is easy to compromise. Courage on the football field makes it easier to show courage on the battlefield.

As virtuous behavior becomes a habit we have an important resource for making ethical decisions. This theme is developed in Warnock's article, "Moral Virtues." In his discussion Warnock considers one of the more interesting problems in ethical decision-making—the problem of weakness of will. Weakness of will occurs when we know what is morally required but we don't do it. Studying is put off so that you can spend an evening with your friends at the pub. As the exam arrives and an opportunity to cheat occurs you take it. You know you did wrong, and you knew it when you did it. Why did you do it? You had "weakness of will." Possessing virtue gives you willpower; it enables you to overcome weakness of will. Warnock argues that genuinely moral virtues are dispositions which help us overcome weakness of will with respect to our treatment of others. These moral virtues, for Warnock, are four in number—nonmaleficence, fairness, beneficence, and nondeception.

Peter Geach's "Why We Need the Virtues" provides another perspective on the role the virtues play in the moral life. Geach's approach is based on a teleological, or functional, analysis. In that respect his approach to the virtues is in the tradition of the early Greek moral philosophers. As you recall, something is good if it performs its function. To know whether something is good, we have to know something about the purpose, or function, of the thing. Of course, statements about function may be of different types. What is the function of a knife? an ear? a person? a state? Those questions look alike but they may not be. Geach begins with the question, "What are people for?" Now Geach admits that the answer to this question is not the same as the answer to a question like "What is the heart for?" After all people may not have an end or a purpose. Merely the fact that people have ends or purposes would be enough to establish that they need the virtues. What is sufficient for a proper understanding of the virtues is that many (most) important human goals or purposes involve cooperation with other persons—including persons with whom we might have considerable disagreement. Despite this disagreement, however, we do cooperate, and this cooperation is only possible against a background of some fundamental agreement including a commitment to the four cardinal virtues of wisdom, temperance, justice, and courage. The function of the virtues is to make life in the human community possible.

This line of argument that virtue is necessarily tied to successful cooperative human action receives its full development in MacIntyre's account. Since MacIntyre's discussion is fairly complicated, we will have to move slowly. MacIntyre begins with the notion of an action and ends with the concept of a tradition. All human actions are not equal; they are not all of the same type. Of particular interest to MacIntyre are those actions which take place within a practice. Such cooperative actions are important because practices involve the attempt to attain goods which are valuable in terms of the practice themselves rather than merely the attempt to attain goods which are outside or external to the practice. In addition, a practice is governed by standards of excellence, and success in the practice reflects on what it means for human beings to achieve excellence. MacIntyre gives chess, medicine, and physics as examples of practices. The concept of practice plays a very important role in MacIntyre's thought. To engage in the practice of professional baseball, as opposed to merely playing professional baseball, you can't be in it solely for the money. You must be willing to accept the authority of more expert teachers, and you must be willing to try to excel (give it your best). MacIntyre then argues that virtues are necessary for the effective exercise of practices. For instance, practices cannot be sustained without truthfulness, justice, and courage.

However, there is such a multitude of human practices that persons must choose among competing practices and set priorities among the practices they participate in. More important, a human life must be structured into a unified whole. If you didn't unify your life, attempting to engage in competing practices would be self-defeating. The second step in MacIntyre's argument is to explain what it means for human actions to be intelligible and for a human life to be unified. Ultimately human lives are both intelligible and unified in terms of traditions. Explaining how a human life becomes unified in terms of a tradition is the third step in MacIntyre's argument. Our life then fits in with other unified lives.

But traditions can be corrupted and destroyed, with disastrous consequences. What sustains and enriches a tradition? Virtuous behavior. Hence, for MacIntyre, virtues have a very central role indeed in the moral life. By sustaining and enriching traditions, the practice of the virtues enables us to unify our lives. The practice of the virtues enables us to make sense of our lives. An understanding of the virtues is essential in enabling us to answer that much maligned question, "What is the meaning of life?"

Although MacIntyre's work will set the standard for discussions of virtue for many years, most philosophers would agree that MacIntyre has not said the last word on the issue. MacIntyre's *After Virtue* was written in response to what MacIntyre sees as an ethical crisis: there are no standards in ethics. But what account of objectivity has he provided? After all, there are a multitude of traditions. To say that the virtues are necessary to prevent the destruction of a tradition hardly provides objectivity. "What traditions should survive?" is the appropriate ethical question. The traditions of nationalism, the use of force to settle disputes, and male superiority are traditions that ought to be destroyed. What is needed are some objective criteria which will tell us which traditions ought to be sustained and enriched and which should be overthrown. Perhaps the virtues might provide such criteria. Only those traditions which can be sustained by the virtues are traditions that ought to be enriched and sustained. However, the virtue of courage sustains war as a means of settling international disputes. Hence it surely isn't self-evident that the traditional virtues can supply the criteria we need. The other possibility is to develop a theory of what it means to be a fully integrated, self-realized human being. Aristotle had such a theory, but MacIntyre does not. In the absence of further analysis, MacIntyre's theory of the virtues cannot make the claim to objectivity that a theory like Kant's can. Nonetheless, MacIntyre's reintroduction of the virtues into discussions of ethics is an important contribution. A theory of virtue is required if we are to have a complete understanding of the nature of an ethical decision.

Virtue

Aristotle

1

There are, then, two sorts of virtue; intellectual and moral. Intellectual virtue is mostly originated and promoted by teaching, which is why it needs experience and time. Moral virtue is produced by habit, which is why it is called "moral," a word only slightly different from our word for habit.

It is quite plain that none of the moral virtues is produced in us by nature, since none of the things with natural properties can be trained to acquire a different property. For example, the stone, which has a natural downward motion, cannot be trained to move upwards, not even if one "trains" it by countless upward throws. Similarly, fire cannot be trained to move downwards. In general, none of the things with a given natural property can be trained to acquire another.

The virtues, then, are neither innate nor contrary to nature. They come to be because we are fitted by nature to receive them; but we perfect them by training or habit.

Further, in the case of all our natural faculties, we have them first potentially, but it is only later on that we make them fully active. This is clear in the case of the senses: we do not acquire our senses as a result of innumerable acts of seeing or hearing, but the opposite is the case. We have them, and then make use of them; we do not come to get them by making use of them. However, we do acquire the virtues by first making use of them in acts, as is also the case with techniques. Where doing or making is dependent on knowing how, we acquire the know-how by actually doing. For example, people become builders by actually building, and the same applies to lyre players. In the same way, we become just by doing just acts; and similarly with "temperate" and "brave." There is further evidence in contemporary institutions: legislators make citizens good by training them. Indeed, all legislators aim at that, and those who do it incorrectly miss their objective. That is the point of difference between the institutions of a good and of a bad community. . . .

2

Since the present inquiry is not "theoretical" like the rest—we are not studying in order to know what virtue is, but to become good, for otherwise there would be no profit in it—we must consider the question of how we ought to act. Action is lord and master of the kind of resulting disposition, as we said. Action should be in accordance with right reason; that is true of all actions, and it will serve as our basis. (We shall define right reason later on, and state its relation to the other virtues.) Before going on, it must be agreed that all our statements about action have to be general, not exact. The point is, as we said at the start, that the type of answer turns upon the kind of subject matter, and matters dealing with action and questions of expediency are always changing like the circumstances that promote health. Since this is true in general, it is still truer to say that answers about particular issues cannot be exact. These issues cannot be dealt with by a single technique or a set of rules; those who are engaged in action must study the special circumstances, as in the case of medicine and navigation.

But although the present discussion is of this type, we must try to help. Let us consider this first: it is in the nature of things for the virtues to be destroyed by excess and deficiency, as we see in the case of health and strength—a good example, for we must use clear cases when discussing abstruse matters. Excessive or insufficient training destroys strength, just as too much or too little food and drink ruins health. The right amount, however, brings health and preserves it. So this applies to moderation, bravery, and the other virtues. The man who runs away from everything in fear, and faces up to nothing, becomes a coward; the man who is absolutely fearless, and will walk into anything, becomes rash. It is the same with the man who gets enjoyment from all pleasures, abstaining from none: he is immoderate; whereas he who avoids all pleasures, like a boor, is a man of no sensitivity. Moderation and bravery are destroyed by excess and deficiency, but are kept flourishing by the mean. . . .

3

Now, we must consider what virtue is. There are three things in the soul: emotions, capacities, and dispositions. Virtue must be one of these.

By emotions I mean appetite, anger, fear, confidence, envy, joy, friendliness, hatred, desire, emulation, pity—in short, everything that is accompanied by pleasure and pain.

By capacities I mean our ability to experience the emotions—for instance, the capacity of feeling anger, pain, and pity.

Disposition describes how we react—well or badly—toward the emotions, e.g., feeling anger. If the reaction is either excessive or insufficient, we are bad; if moderate, good; and so with other feelings.

Neither the virtues nor the vices are emotions. It is not our emotions that decide whether we are called good or bad, but our virtues and vices. We are not praised or blamed for our emotions (men are not praised for feeling fear or anger, nor does feeling anger as such get blamed, but feeling anger in a certain way), whereas we are for our virtues and vices. Another point: we feel anger and fear without choosing to, whereas the virtues are a sort of choice, or at least not possible without choice. In addition, the emotions are said to "move" us whereas in respect to the virtues and vices, we are said not to be moved, but to be in a certain state.

For this reason, the virtues are not capacities either. We are not called good or bad merely because we have a capacity for feeling, nor are we praised or blamed for that reason. Also, we have capacities by nature, but we are not good or bad by nature. . . . If, therefore, virtue is neither emotion nor capacity, it must, by elimination, be disposition. This is a statement as to the generic meaning of virtue.

We must not leave it at that—just "disposition"; we must also say what kind. It should be said that all virtue, whatever it belongs to, renders that thing good and makes it function well. The virtue of the eye makes the eye good and makes it function well, since it is by the virtue of the eye that we have good sight. Similarly, the virtue or excellence of a horse makes the horse good, good at running and at carrying its rider and at facing the enemy. Now, if this is always the case, the virtue of man will be the disposition through which he becomes a good man and through which he will do his job well. How that will come about, we have already said, but it will be still clearer if we examine the nature of this virtue.

Of every continuous—that is, divisible thing—one can take more or less or the equal amount; and these divisions can be made either by reference to the thing itself as standard, or relatively to us. Equal is the mean between excess and deficiency. What is the mean relative to the thing? It is that which is equidistant from each end, which is one and the same for all. The mean relative to us is that which is neither too much nor too little; and this is not one and the same for all. If ten is a lot and two a little, then six is the mean relative to the thing: six exceeds two by the same amount that it is exceeded by ten; it is the mean by proportion. The mean relative to us should not be interpreted like that. If ten pounds are a lot for a man to eat, whereas two are too little, the trainer will not order six. Perhaps that will be too much or too little for the particular man: too little for Milo, but too much for the man who is just starting to train. Similarly with running and wrestling.

In this same way, everyone who knows, in any field, avoids excess and deficiency; he looks for the mean and chooses the mean, not the mean according to the thing, but the mean relative to us. Every art does its job well in this way, by looking to the mean and leading its products toward it—which is why people say of things well done that you cannot add anything or take anything away, since "well done" is ruined by excess and deficiency and achieved by the mean; and good craftsmen, as we were saying, work with their eye on the mean. To resume: if virtue, like nature, requires more accuracy and is better than any art, then it will aim at the mean. I speak here of moral virtue, since that is concerned with emotions and actions; and excess, deficiency, and the mean occur in these. In feeling fear, confidence, desire, anger, pity, and in general pleasure and pain, one can feel too much or too little; and both extremes are wrong. The mean and the good is feeling at the right time, about the right things, in relation to the right people, and for the right reason; and the mean and the good are the task of virtue. Similarly, in regard to actions, there are excess, deficiency, and the mean.

Virtue is concerned with emotions and actions, where excess is wrong, as is deficiency, but the mean is praised and is right. Both being praised and being right belong to virtue. So virtue is a kind of mean, since it does at least aim at the mean. Also, going wrong happens in many ways (for bad belongs to the unlimited . . . and good to the limited), whereas doing right happens in one way only. That is why one is easy, the other difficult: missing the target is easy, but hitting it is hard. For these reasons, excess and deficiency belong to evil, the mean to good:

"There is only one kind of good man, but many kinds of bad."

Virtue, then, is a disposition involving choice. It consists in a mean, relative to us, defined by reason and as the reasonable man would define it. It is a mean between two vices—one of excess, the other of deficiency. Also, virtue discovers and chooses the mean, whereas the vices exceed or fall short of the essential, in the spheres of both emotions and acts. . . .

4

We must not only put this in general terms but also apply it to particular cases. In statements concerning acts, general statements cover more ground, but statements on a specified point are more accurate. Acts are concerned with particulars, after all; and theory should agree with particular facts. Let us, then, take these particular virtues from our table.

Now, courage is the mean in matters of fearing and feeling brave. The man who exceeds in fearlessness has no special name (there are many vices and virtues that have no names). He who exceeds in confidence is overconfident, whereas the man who exceeds in feeling fear and falls short in confidence is a coward.

Concerning pleasures and pains (not all are involved, and indeed pains are less so), the mean is temperance, and the excess profligacy. As for falling short in connection with pleasures, there are hardly any such people, and that is why they, too (compare the instances above), do not have a name. But let us call them "insensible."

As regards giving and taking money the mean is liberality, whereas the excess and the deficiency are, in order, spendthriftness and illiberality. In this case, excess and deficiency work in opposite ways. The spendthrift exceeds in spending and falls short in taking, whereas the illiberal man exceeds in taking and falls short in spending. . . .

As for honor and dishonor, the mean is grandeur of soul, whereas the excess is a sort of vanity, and the deficiency meanness of soul. We said above that liberality differs from magnificence in the minor scale of its operation. Similarly, there is a minor virtue related to grandeur of soul; whereas the latter has great honor as its object, this one is concerned with small honors. It is possible to strive for honor in the right way, and also more or less than one should: he who strives too much is called ambitious, he who falls short unambitious, and the man in the middle has no name. There are no names for the dispositions, except for ambition—which is why the extremes lay claim to the middle territory, so that there are times when we call the mean "ambitious" and other times when we call it "unambitious"; and sometimes we praise the one, at other times the other. Why we do this will be explained later; but now let us speak about the rest of the dispositions in the manner indicated.

In connection with anger also, there are excess, deficiency, and the mean, although they have no established names. But let us call the middle man good-tempered and speak of the mean as good temper. Now for the extremes: he who exceeds is quick tempered, and the corresponding vice is quick temper; but the man who falls short is without temper, and the deficiency is an absence of temper.

There are also three other means. They have a certain resemblance to one another, but they do differ. All are concerned with human relations in word and action. The difference, however, is that one is concerned with truth, the others with pleasure, pleasure being here of two sorts, one in the sphere of amusement, the other in all matters that have to do with life.

We must discuss these, too, to see more clearly that the mean is always praiseworthy, and the extremes neither praiseworthy nor right, but blameworthy. Most of these, too, have no name, but we must try to coin names for them, as we did before, for the sake of clarity and ease of understanding.

Let us take truth. The man who exemplifies the mean is the truthful man, and the mean should be called truthfulness; pretence of this virtue by way of excess is boastfulness, and the corresponding man boastful; but pretence by way of deficiency is false modesty.

Now, for pleasure by way of amusement. The middle man is the wit, and his disposition wittiness; the excess is buffoonery, and the man a buffoon; the deficiency is boorishness, and the man a boor. As for the other sorts of pleasure in life, the man who pleases in the right way is a friend, and the mean is friendship. The man who exceeds this, if he does so for no ulterior motive, is obsequious, but if it is for his own advantage, he is a flatterer. He who falls short and never gives pleasure is quarrelsome and a surly fellow.

There are means, too, in the sphere of the feelings. Shame is not a virtue, but the man who is modest is praised. In this case, too, we speak of the mean (the man mentioned above) and of the excess: the man who feels shame about everything is cowed, whereas the man who falls short, or feels no shame at all, is shameless. The mean, again, is the man who is modest.

Indignation is the mean between envy and malice. These concern the pleasure and pain experienced over what happens to neighbors. The indignant man feels pain when people prosper without deserving to; the envious man, who exceeds the former, feels pain at all good fortune; whereas the malicious man, so far from feeling pain, actually feels pleasure. . . .

Moral Virtues

G. J. Warnock

One might begin by saying that, if things are to go better . . . if, that is, people's needs and interests, and some at least of their wants, are to be more fully satisfied than they otherwise might be—one very basic *desideratum* would surely be greater resources from which to satisfy them. This is obviously true in a sense; but it is as well to be clear in what sense. . . . In all our undertakings we must make do, in one way or another, with what there is; we cannot add to the stock of what there is *ex nihilo*. Thus the case is that, in the relevant sense, increasing the resources available for the satisfaction of people's needs, wants, and interests is a matter of making better use for that purpose of the resources, in a more basic sense, which are already available but cannot be increased by our own efforts. It is a matter, one might say, of turning unusable resources into usable ones, or of putting what there is into usable forms.

G. J. Warnock, *The Object of Mortality*, Methuen & Co., Ltd., London, 1971. Reprinted by permission.

And if that is to be done, one thing that is obviously and essentially required is knowledge—in the first place information about the environment, its contents and potentialities, and in the second place the vast variety of technical skills involved in its transformation into usable forms. Such knowledge must be acquired, preserved, disseminated, and transmitted.

Continuing at the same level of monstrous generality, one might mention next the obvious need for organization. It is perfectly obvious that very little of any sort would ever be done, if every individual attempted to do everything on his own, or merely in such more or less fortuitous groups as might be formed *ad hoc* from time to time by individual initiative. For vastly many purposes, the long-run co-operation of many individuals is absolutely necessary; and if such co-operation is to be effective, it must be somehow directed—there must be some way of determining objectives, and of regulating more or less closely what the roles of individuals are to be in the co-operative undertaking. It is of course largely at any rate from this necessity that there come to exist what may generally be called 'institutions'—tribes, national states, federations of states, clubs, associations and parties of all kinds, firms, trade unions, armies, universities, the Mafia, and so on. It need not be maintained that the formation and character of such more or less co-operative institutions is fully determined by strictly practical ends; some may be in part just 'natural', like the family perhaps in its more general aspects, though not in details, and some may be wholly or in part, as one might say, for fun, for the sake of the pleasures of association in itself. But that there *is* a practical necessity here is indisputable; there are countless things that we want and need that we could not possibly get, even if it were known how they could be got, without the organized, institutionalized co-operation of many individuals, and for that matter also of institutions with other institutions.

That, then, which is of course a very great deal, is obviously part of what is required if amelioration of the human predicament, or perhaps merely the avoidance of its excessive deterioration, is to be practically possible; if we have the requisite information and technical skills, and if there are institutional forms for bringing about the application of knowledge and skills in directed co-operative undertakings, then many things towards human betterment *can* be done. But this of course does not ensure that they will be. That is a problem of a totally different kind.

Well, at least one idea for its solution comes readily to mind. If, as has been suggested, humans have, placed as they are, a certain inherent propensity to act to the disadvantage or detriment of other humans, and even of themselves, then, if they are not to do so, they can be *made* not to do so. If, for instance, they are prone to be a good deal less concerned with the wants, needs, and interests of others than with their own, then, if they are to act in some other or in the general interest rather than purely in their own, they can be made so to act. What is required, one may reason, for the suitable modification of the patterns of behaviour towards which people are 'naturally' prone, may thus be some suitably designed system of coercion. People must be given an interest, which they do not just naturally have, in doing things which they are not just naturally inclined towards doing; and this is exactly what a system of coercion can supply.

Now there is every reason to think that this is part of the answer; but there is also every reason to think that it is not and could not be, as perhaps Hobbes thought it was, the sole and whole answer. Part of the answer, certainly: taking things as they are and have been and are likely to continue to be, it is not deniable that there are people who are deflected from acting damagingly to others, or even to themselves, solely or mainly by the anticipation of consequences disagreeable to themselves if they so act—consequences liable to be deliberately imposed on them by others, by whom to that extent they can be said to be coerced. No doubt the most conspicuous example here is law. . . .

However, it is not true, and scarcely could be true, that people are brought to abstain from acting damagingly to others, or even to themselves, solely by coercion or by coercive deterrence. There is a practical point here, and also, I think, a kind of logical point. In the first place, if nothing but coercion kept people in order, then the machinery of coercion would have to be very vast—police, say, might have to equal in number the rest of the population, or at any rate somehow be ubiquitous and powerful enough for their surveillance to be pretty continuous and continuously effective. In practice this seems, in most societies, not in fact to be necessary for the purpose. . . . But it seems a point of no less importance that coercion is itself something that people do; such a system is directed and executed, after all, by people. If it is to do any good, or to do good rather than harm, then it must be directed and executed (let us say vaguely) properly; and it seems that it could not solely be coercion that brought this about. If coercion is ever to operate, except by pure chance, in any general interest, it seems reasonable to hold that there must be some persons, indeed many persons, prepared to act in that general interest without themselves being coerced into doing so. . . . As things are and long have been and are likely to continue to be, it is reasonable to say that the beneficent operation of any coercive system requires that there should be, at least sometimes and in some people, some propensity to act beneficently without being made to do so. Of course I am not suggesting for a moment that all coercive systems actually are beneficent.

We thus come to what seems clearly most important in the present connection. If any of those things towards the amelioration of the human predicament which can be done are to be done in fact, then not only must people sometimes be *made* to do things which they are not just naturally disposed to do anyway; they must also sometimes voluntarily, without coercion, act otherwise than people are just naturally disposed to do. It is necessary that people should acquire, and should seek to ensure that others acquire, what may be called *good dispositions*—that is, some readiness on occasion voluntarily to do desirable things which not all human beings are just naturally disposed to do anyway, and similarly not to do damaging things. . . .

We have already found . . . some reason for thinking that, of the limitations which constitute (in a sense) the human predicament, the most important are those that might be called most 'internal' to human beings—that is, limitations of rationality and sympathy. It may now seem to be the case that, essentially for just the same reasons, what is crucial for betterment is the promotion of 'good dispositions'. All the other things—acquiring, disseminating, preserving, and transmitting knowledge, setting up and maintaining organizations and institutions, devising and operating means of making people do things—all of these things are things that people do; so that everything in the end depends on their readiness to do them, and to do them at least some of the time without being compelled to do so. . . . What matters most is what, of the things we can do, we choose to do; if this goes wrong, then everything goes wrong, and only more wrong, the more efficiently it goes.

There comes into view, then, among very general *desiderata* for the betterment of the human predicament, a distinction which seems to be of great and (I hope) of obvious importance—a distinction, namely, between what makes betterment possible, and what tends to bring it about that it actually occurs; roughly, between means available to people for the improvement of their lot, and the disposition to make beneficial use of those means. Moreover, if we now look again at this topic of human dispositions, it seems possible to discern here also a similar distinction—between, as one may put it, those dispositions whose tendency is to increase the effectiveness, or capacity, of a person, and those which tend to determine to what uses his capacities will be put.

The dispositions I have in mind under the first head may all be regarded, I think, as different varieties of the disposition to accept, or tolerate, or endure what, in various ways, may in itself be disagreeable. Pertinacious exertion, whether physical or mental, is often—not always—in itself somewhat disagreeable; there is some natural inclination to abandon what is found laborious; and the propensity, on appropriate occasions, not to do so, is rightly and for clear reasons regarded as a desirable disposition. The prospect or presence of danger is disagreeable; but it is very plainly desirable that a person should not always indulge his natural inclination to escape or avoid it. Somewhat similarly, there is an endless range and variety of discomforts which it is both disagreeable and often necessary to incur, and an endless range and variety of satisfactions or indulgences which it is both unpleasant but often highly desirable not to pursue. And in the 'good dispositions' which consist in such readinesses to endure the disagreeable we have, as will readily be seen, a large number of generally recognized and familiar virtues—conspicuously, industriousness, courage, and self-control; but many others also.

Now as to these I offer the suggestion— . . . that, while there is clear and good reason to regard these dispositions as virtues, it would not be unreasonable to hold that they are not *moral* virtues. They may be, indeed in some degree they certainly are, necessary conditions of the effective exercise of moral virtues, as indeed of effective action of any kind; but one may still wish to say that they *are* not moral virtues. Whether this suggestion is acceptable or not, let me at any rate offer forthwith my reasons for making it. It seems to me that there would be two good reasons for wishing to say this, or perhaps one reason put in two rather different ways. In the first place these virtues, while of course they are not necessarily, yet they may be exclusively and entirely, what might be called self-profiting. That is, the acquisition and exercise of these virtues is not only typically essential to, but could in principle be wholly directed to, the attainment of an agent's personal interests or ends—possibly, indeed, of ends of his to the gross damage or neglect of the interests of others. If, for instance, the dominant object of my life is to maintain, by fair means or foul, my personal power and ascendancy over some group, or party, or gang, or country, or empire, I may well display, and need to display, exceptional industry in maintaining and de-

fending my system of despotism, great courage in resisting the pressures and mach-
inations of my opponents and enemies, and marked self-control in adhering, perhaps
sometimes in the teeth of great temptation and difficulty, to the sagacious promotion
of my long-run interests, undistracted by impulse, self-indulgence, passion, or pleasure.
Courage, asceticism, iron self-control, resolution in the face of hardship or danger or
difficulty—these are almost standard equipment for the really major destroyers, whether
military, political, or criminal, or all three at once. Thus, while the dispositions here
in question are undoubted virtues, they are virtues all of which a very bad man might
have; and while probably such qualities are admirable even in a bad man, he is not,
it seems to me quite reasonable to maintain, *morally* the better for his possession of
those admirable qualities.

Second, while these dispositions certainly do tend to countervail, as it were, something in the human predicament which contributes importantly to its natural tendency
to turn out rather badly, they do not tend quite directly to countervail that in the
predicament which there seems reason to regard, both in fact and moral theory, as
really central. For these dispositions tend to countervail, and are genuinely admirable
in so far as they do so, what might be called natural human *weaknesses*—varieties,
that is, of the natural inclination to evade or avoid, in its various forms, the burdensome
or disagreeable. But they have in themselves no tendency at all to counteract the
limitation of human sympathies; and this is really just another way of saying that, as
I mentioned a moment ago, they may be wholly self-profiting, and even very damaging
to others than the agent himself.

This, then, invites the suggestion, which I am perfectly ready to make, that the
paradigmatic *moral* virtues may be, not these, but rather those good dispositions whose
tendency is directly to countervail the limitation of human sympathies, and whose
exercise accordingly is essentially—though indeed not, by itself, necessarily effectively—good *for* persons other than the agent himself. Let us see what profit we can
extract from this proposition.

What questions are they, then, that can appropriately be put to the hypothesis that
we now have in view? We are operating with the idea that, 'good dispositions' being
crucially important to abatement of the ills inherent in the human predicament, one
might with reason regard as specifically *moral virtues* those which, not being essentially, or even potentially, exclusively self-profiting, would tend to countervail those
particular ills liability to which is to be laid at the door of the limitedness of human
sympathies. So, if we seek further light on what these good dispositions would be,
we need now to consider in a little more detail what those particular ills are—that is,
in what ways, in consequence of the limitedness of human sympathies, people are
typically *liable* to act so as to worsen, or not to act so as to ameliorate, the predicament.

The first step on this path, at any rate, seems an easy one to take. If I am exclusively,
or even predominantly, concerned with the satisfaction of my own wants, interests,
or needs, or of those of some limited group such as my family, or friends, or tribe,
or country, or class, with whose interests and ends I am naturally disposed to sympathize, then I, other members of that group, or the group as a whole, may be naturally
prone to act directly to the detriment of other persons, non-members of the group, or
of other groups. I may be inclined, from competitiveness or mere indifference or even

active malevolence, to do positive harm to others, whether in the form of actual injury to them, or of frustration and obstruction of the satisfaction of their wants, interests, and needs. There is here, that is to say, a liability to act simply *maleficently*—harmfully, damagingly—to others, quite directly, either out of sheer unconcern with the damage so inflicted, or even out of a positive taste for the infliction of damage on persons or groups outside the circle of one's sympathies. That being so, it can scarcely seem controversial to say that *one* of the 'good dispositions' we are in search of will be the disposition to abstain from (deliberate, unjustified) maleficence. Of course, if we nominate this disposition as one of the moral virtues, it may reasonably be remarked that it is not, in a sense, very much of a virtue; a disposition, that is to say, not to act deliberately maleficently towards other persons, from sheer unconcern for or active malevolence towards them, is, one may hopefully suppose, just normally to be expected in normal persons, who accordingly come up for commendation on this account only if their nonmaleficence is exceptional in degree, or maintained in the face of exceptional temptation, or provocation, or difficulty. However, the propensity *not* to act injuriously towards others whenever one has, or might have, some 'natural' inclination to do so, while perhaps not specially creditable in ordinary circumstances, is still very clearly of fundamental importance; for it is obvious what a gangster's world we should find ourselves in without it—and indeed do find ourselves in, when and so far as this disposition is absent.

The next step seems also, in general terms, scarcely more problematic. If we need, and if humans in general do not just naturally, regularly, and reliably have, the disposition of non-maleficence, just the same can plainly be said of the disposition towards positive beneficence. The limitedness of sympathies tends often to make it not just natural to interest oneself directly in another's good; there is need, then, for cultivation of the disposition to do so, which will very often take the particular form of readiness to give *help* to others in their activities. It seems reasonable to hold, and indeed practically impossible not to hold, that responsibility for pursuit of an individual's good is primarily his own—partly for the reason that it is primarily for him to say (though of course he cannot say infallibly) what that good is, and partly for the plain, practical reason that, in normal circumstances, if everyone embroils himself persistently, however well-meaningly, in other people's concerns rather than his own, a considerable measure of chaos and cross-purposes is likely to ensue. There are, however, many ends a person may have which cannot be secured by his own efforts alone. There are common ends, to be secured only by the co-operation of many. There are some persons who have particular claims upon the beneficence of particular other persons. And there are some persons who, though perhaps without any special claims, should be helped because their need of help is exceptionally great, or their ability to help themselves exceptionally restricted. Not much more than this could be said in quite general terms. People and societies clearly differ a good deal, for a variety of reasons, in their assessment of the proportion of time, talents, efforts, and resources that an individual should devote to ends and interests other than his own; moreover, what is required in this way, what there is scope for, depends very much on the organization and institutions of particular societies. How far, for instance, there is need and room for private charity will depend on the extent to which public provision is made for the relief of indigence. But it is worth remarking, I think, that disagreement on this issue is often disagreement on the facts, at least in part. It was once held, notoriously, that it is *in fact* most advantageous for everybody that each, by and large, should pursue and promote his own interests single-mindedly; and though this thesis no doubt was often disingenuously asserted by those who fancied their chances in the envisaged free-for-all, and indeed is certainly not true without qualification, it is still, I suppose, a question of fact, and an unsettled question, in what ways and to what extent it needs to be qualified. In any case we are not attempting to settle here exactly what, in one case or another, the proper exercise of this virtue would actually consist in; what here matters, and what in general terms seems scarcely disputable, is that, along with non-maleficence, it *is* a virtue.

What else? Well, so far we have laid at the door of 'limited sympathies', and accordingly have affirmed the need to countervail, the inclination to act damagingly to others towards whom one is not 'naturally' sympathetic, and not to act beneficently when such action is needed or claimed. I believe that we should now add, as an independent requirement, the disposition not to *discriminate,* as surely most humans have some natural propensity to do, to the disadvantage of those outside the limited circle of one's natural concern. If, for instance, twenty people have a claim upon, or are substantially in need of, some service or benefit that I can provide, it seems not enough merely to say that I should not refuse it; it must be added that I should not help or benefit some of them *less* merely because, for instance, I may happen to like them less, or be less well-disposed towards them. The general name for this good disposition is, I take it, fairness. Of course it is commonly supposed, and indeed it would be unrealistically inhuman not to suppose, that actual sympathies and natural ties quite often justify discriminatory treatment; nevertheless, it must be observed that these should issue in discriminatory treatment only when, as is not always the case, they do actually justify it. Once again it would be inappropriate and probably quite unprofitable to try here to specify in any detail what, in this case or that, the exercise of this good disposition would actually consist in; what matters here is merely the very general proposition that, as an essential corrective to the arbitrariness and ine-quality and deprivation liable otherwise to result from the haphazard incidence of limited sympathies, it surely *is* a 'good disposition' to be ready, on appropriate oc-casions, to recognize the need for or claims to good, or to relief from ill, of those in whose good or ill one may have no natural concern whatever. And we may add that the importance of this virtue of fairness tends, evidently but interestingly, to increase with the increase of scope and occasions for its exercise. For very many people, after all, their power to help or harm others is actually so limited as probably to be confined, on most occasions, to persons who may well be within the circle of their natural concern; but as such power increases, it is increasingly likely to expand its scope over persons to whom one may personally be wholly indifferent, or even of whom one may know nothing at all. This is to say, surely truly, that the virtue of fairness—or, more formally, justice—is a more important virtue in, for instance, political rulers, judicial functionaries, commanders of armies, heads of institutions, and so on, than it is in the case of relatively obscure private persons, whose circumstances may confront them with relatively little occasion to exercise it.

Then one more thing. If we consider the situation of a person, somewhat prone by nature to an exclusive concern with his own, or with some limited range of, interests and needs and wants, living among other persons more or less similarly constituted, we see that there is one device in particular, very often remarkably easy to employ, by which he may be naturally more or less inclined to, so to speak, carve out his egoistical way to his own, and if necessary at the expense of other, ends; and that is *deception*. It is possible for a person, and often very easy, by doing things, and especially in the form of saying things, to lead other persons to the belief that this or that is the case; and one of the simplest and most seductive ways of manipulating and maneuvering other persons for the sake of one's own ends is that of thus operating self-interestedly upon their beliefs. Clearly this is not, necessarily, directly damaging. We all hold from time to time an immense range and variety of false beliefs, and very often are none the worse for doing so; we are the worse for it only if, as is often not the case, our false belief leads or partly leads us actually to act to our detriment in some way. Thus, I do not necessarily do you any harm at all if, by deed or word, I induce you to believe what is not in fact the case; I may even do you good, possibly by way, for example, of consolation or flattery. Nevertheless, though deception is thus not necessarily directly damaging, it is easy to see how crucially important it is that the natural inclination to have recourse to it should be counteracted. It is, one might say, not the implanting of false beliefs that is damaging, but rather the generation of the suspicion that they may be being implanted. For this undermines trust; and, to the extent that trust is undermined, all co-operative undertakings, in which what one person can do or has reason to do is dependent on what others have done, are doing, or are going to do, must tend to break down. I cannot reasonably be expected to go over the edge of a cliff on a rope, for however vital an object, if I cannot trust you to keep hold of the other end of it; there is no sense in my asking you for your opinion on some point, if I do not suppose that your answer will actually express your opinion. (Verbal communication is doubtless the most important of all our co-operative undertakings.) The crucial difficulty is precisely, I think, that deception is so easy. Deliberately saying, for instance, what I do not believe to be true is just as easy as saying what I do believe to be true, and may not be discriminable from it by even the most practised and expert of observers; thus, uncertainty as to the credentials of *any* of my performances in this respect is inherently liable to infect *all* my performances—there are, so to speak, no 'natural signs', or there may be none, by which the untrustworthy can be distinguished from the veracious, so that, if any may be deceptive, all may be. Nor, obviously, would it be any use merely to devise some special formula for the purpose of explicitly signalling non-deceptive performance; for, if the performance may be deceptive, so also might be the employment of any such formula—it is easy to say 'I really mean it', not really meaning it, and hence to say 'I really mean it' without thereby securing belief. Even *looking* sincere and ingenuous, though perhaps slightly more difficult than simply saying that one is, is an art that can be learned. In practice, of course, though there may be very few persons indeed whom we take to be non-deceptive on all occasions, we do manage, and rightly, to trust quite a lot of the people quite a lot of the time; but this depends on the supposition that, while sometimes they may have special reasons, which with luck and experience and judgement we may come to understand, for resorting to deceptive performance on some occasions, they do not do so simply *whenever* it suits their book. If one could not make even this milder supposition, then co-operative involvement among persons would become, if not impossible, at any rate more or less useless and unreasonable—like political agreements between bourgeois politicians and Marxists.

Parenthetically, I should like to mention here, though not to discuss, the curious case, which does also occur, of persons who, while seldom or perhaps even never deliberately speaking or acting, to suit their book, contrary to their real beliefs, seem to have the knack of so tailoring their beliefs as to suit their book. This singular propensity is, in a way, even more damaging than that of the common-or-garden liar; it is compatible, for one thing, with extreme self-righteousness; but, more importantly, while the liar for his own ends misrepresents the way things are, he may perfectly retain the capacity to realize how they are, and may thus be thought to be, in a sense, more redeemable than one whose capacity to see straight is itself corrupted. But we impinge here on self-deception, a complex topic.

We suggest, then, that, in the general context of the human predicament, there are these four (at least) distinguishable damaging, or non-ameliorative, types of propensity which tend naturally to emanate directly from 'limited sympathies'—those of malef-icence, non-beneficence, unfairness, and deception. If now we apply the supposition that the 'object' of morality is to make the predicament less grim than, in a quasi-Hobbesian state of nature, it seems inherently liable to be, and to do so specifically by seeking to countervail the deleterious liabilities inherent in 'limited sympathies', we seem to be led to four (at least) general types of good disposition as those needed to countervail the above-mentioned four types of propensity; and these dispositions will be, somewhat crudely named, those of non-maleficence, fairness, beneficence, and non-deception. We venture the hypothesis that these (at least) are fundamental *moral virtues*. . . .

Why We Need the Virtues

Peter Geach

The definite article in my title is significant. I am concerned with why [we] need the seven virtues to which tradition gives pre-eminence: the theological virtues of faith, hope, and charity, and the cardinal virtues of prudence, temperance, justice, and courage. I commit myself to the thesis that all of these *are* virtues: and I shall argue that this thesis cannot rationally be doubted so far as the four cardinal virtues are concerned. . . .

We are familiar with the type of reasoning which starts from some aim or policy laid down as a premise and proceeds step by step to infer the means of securing the aim, carrying out the policy. The logical structure of such reasoning, and its relation

Peter Geach, *The Virtues: The Stanton Lectures 1973–4*. Cambridge, England, Cambridge University Press, 1977. Reprinted by permission.

to the structure of deductive propositional reasoning, is not yet fully a matter of agreement, but we may reasonably hope that the matter will be cleared up. Aristotle's doctrine of teleology is that if we speak as if Nature had aims or policies we may work out what happens in the world by constructing reasonings formally parallel to human practical deliberations. Because most of his examples, even in biology, can be faulted for inadequate natural knowledge, the Aristotelian doctrine has been much blown upon. All the same, I think, it can be strongly defended, and the common attacks upon it are quite worthless.

It should be clear from the way I have stated it that an Aristotelian teleological explanation does not ascribe either something like desire to inanimate natural agents, or a contrivance of means for ends to Almighty God. Hobbes's witticisms about how a pane of glass, if it knew what it would be at, would stay in the window and not fall into the street, may have hit at the doctrine of his contemporaries, but leave Aristotle untouched. . . .

Nor are teleological explanations barren or scientifically useless. They often have heuristic value in biology: quite recently, J. Z. Young explained the present role of the human pineal gland by making the heuristic assumption that it wouldn't be there ('evolution' wouldn't have 'let' it survive!) if it had no function.

Lastly, teleology is not straightforwardly incompatible with mechanism. An old-fashioned mechanical clock is a paradigm both of Newtonian explicability by efficient causes and of explicability in terms of what it is for—to tell the time—and of the way its parts subserve this end. This would of course still be true of a clock we unexpectedly found on arrival in the sandy desert of Mars; we need no information or conjecture about the existence and nature of Martians in order to satisfy ourselves that the clock is a complex mechanism *de facto* describable by elaborating a teleological analysis of its structure and movements. . . .

I maintain then that this teleological way of thinking, conducted on essentially Aristotelian principles but without his obsolete natural science, is intellectually respectable. And in that way of thinking it makes good sense to ask 'What are men for?' We may not be so ready with an answer, even a partial answer, as when we ask 'What are hearts for?' 'What are teeth for?'; but Aristotle is right to my mind in [hoping to attain] an answer—the success in bringing men's partial organs and activities under a teleological account should encourage us to think that some answer may be found. But not as quickly as Aristotle thought: it does not show straight off what men are for if we know that men and men only are capable of theoretical discourse.

But in order to show that men need virtues to effect whatever men are for, it may turn out unnecessary to determine the end and the good of man. For people whose first practical premises, formulating their ultimate ends, are not only divergent but irreconcilable may nevertheless agree on bringing about some situation which is an indispensable condition of either end's being realized, or on avoiding some situation which would prevent the realization of either end. That is what compromise means, that is what diplomacy is in aid of.

Consider the fact that people of different religions or of no religion at all can agree to build and run a hospital, and agree broadly on what shall be done in the hospital. There will of course be marginal policy disagreements, e.g. about abortion operations and the limits of experimentation on human beings. But there can be agreement on fighting disease, because disease impedes men's efforts towards most goals.

Of course such compromise agreement can be achieved only so long as there is not too violent disagreement about ultimate ends. A Christian Scientist would not agree about the hospital. But then, if a Christian Scientist takes his religion seriously, he must disagree about a great deal that the rest of us believe about how things are in the world. . . .

The thesis of the intractable nature of disputes about values, and of radical difference between these and disputes about facts, is often supported by a curiously circular argument; I believe Alan Gewirth was the first to notice this. When we say everybody agrees on some proposition of physics, we know very well, if we will clear our mind of cant, that 'everybody' is a mere figure of speech; huge numbers of people on Earth will have heard of the matter, but among those who have only a minority are really competent to form an opinion, the rest accept it on authority. This holds good even for such notorious facts as that the Earth is round and the Sun a huge ball millions of miles away. But when it is a matter of practical judgment, then, some philosophers would have us think, anybody's and everybody's opinion must be fairly polled; we must consult the Christian Scientists, the Azande, the Trobriand Islanders, Herr Hitler, old Uncle Joe Stalin and all. It is not at all surprising that there is a very different result of the poll when a very different lot of people are being polled. . . .

I peremptorily exclude from discussion sufficiently crazy moral views, on the same footing as sufficiently crazy theoretical views. There is a sufficiency of theoretical and practical consensus between men, these exclusions once made, for people of diverse opinions to cooperate in building houses and roads and railways and hospitals, running universities, and so on. And on the basis of this consensus we can see the need of the four cardinal virtues to men: these virtues are needed for any large-scale worthy enterprise, just as health and sanity are needed. We need prudence or practical wisdom for any large-scale planning. We need justice to secure cooperation and mutual trust among men, without which our lives would be nasty, brutish, and short. We need temperance in order not to be deflected from our long-term and large-scale goals by seeking short-term satisfactions. And we need courage in order to persevere in face of setbacks, weariness, difficulties, and dangers. . . .

I have tried to expound [our] need of the virtues in terms of what [people] are for, their inbuilt teleology. One reply to this might be 'What of it? You have only described what by metaphor may be called Nature's intentions for man. But why should we care about these if they conflict with our intentions and our freely adopted values? Nature, as the Victorian radical Place put it, is a dirty old toad.'

Of course a [person] is free to 'know good and evil' in what I am told is the sense of Genesis; to lay down his own standards, regardless of his inbuilt teleologies. The trouble is that it will not work out. Nature is such that one living thing lives by destroying and consuming other life, and of course this is one of the things that make all men call Nature a dirty old toad or the like. But if someone decided to be a conscientious objector to this arrangement, he would soon have to choose whether to endure the pangs of conscience or of hunger. If this objection went so far as stopping the phagocytes in his blood from destroying alien life, he would die quickly and nastily. Other moral standards at odds with what by nature [people] are for would lead to disaster less quickly and less dramatically but no less surely. This, in Biblical language, is the wrath of God coming upon the children of disobedience: which is not a matter of an irascible Nobodaddy above the clouds, but of the daily experience that fools who persist in their folly are not spared the natural consequences, though by God's mercy the disaster may be delayed.

The Nature of the Virtues

Alasdair MacIntyre

I

. . . In the Homeric account of the virtues—and in heroic societies more generally— the exercise of a virtue exhibits qualities which are required for sustaining a social role and for exhibiting excellence in some well-marked area of social practice: to excel is to excel at war or in the games, as Achilles does, in sustaining a household, as Penelope does, in giving counsel in the assembly, as Nestor does, in the telling of a tale, as Homer himself does. When Aristotle speaks of excellence in human activity, he sometimes though not always, refers to some well-defined type of human practice: flute-playing, or war, or geometry. I am going to suggest that this notion of a particular type of practice as providing the arena in which the virtues are exhibited and in terms of which they are to receive their primary, if incomplete, definition is crucial to the whole enterprise of identifying a core concept of the virtues. . . .

By a 'practice' I am going to mean any coherent and complex form of socially established cooperative human activity through which goods internal to that form of activity are realised in the course of trying to achieve those standards of excellence which are appropriate to, and partially definitive of, that form of activity, with the result that human powers to achieve excellence, and human conceptions of the ends and goods involved, are systematically extended. Tic-tac-toe is not an example of a practice in this sense, nor is throwing a football with skill; but the game of football is, and so is chess. Bricklaying is not a practice; architecture is. Planting turnips is not a practice; farming is. So are the enquiries of physics, chemistry and biology, and so is the work of the historian, and so are painting and music. In the ancient and

Alasdair MacIntyre, *After Virtue: A Study in Moral Theory*. Gerald Duckworth & Co., Ltd., London. © 1981 by Alasdair MacIntyre. Reprinted by permission of University of Notre Dame Press.

medieval worlds the creation and sustaining of human communities—of households, cities, nations—is generally taken to be a practice in the sense in which I have defined it. Thus the range of practices is wide: arts, sciences, games, politics in the Aristotelian sense, the making and sustaining of family life, all fall under the concept. But the question of the precise range of practices is not at this stage of the first importance. Instead let me explain some of the key terms involved in my definition, beginning with the notion of goods internal to a practice.

Consider the example of a highly intelligent seven-year-old child whom I wish to teach to play chess, although the child has no particular desire to learn the game. The child does however have a very strong desire for candy and little chance of obtaining it. I therefore tell the child that if the child will play chess with me once a week I will give the child 50¢ worth of candy; moreover I tell the child that I will always play in such a way that it will be difficult, but not impossible, for the child to win and that, if the child wins, the child will receive an extra 50¢ worth of candy. Thus motivated the child plays and plays to win. Notice however that, so long as it is the candy alone which provides the child with a good reason for playing chess, the child has no reason not to cheat and every reason to cheat, provided he or she can do so successfully. But, so we may hope, there will come a time when the child will find in those goods specific to chess, in the achievement of a certain highly particular kind of analytical skill, strategic imagination and competitive intensity, a new set of reasons, reasons now not just for winning on a particular occasion, but for trying to excel in whatever way the game of chess demands. Now if the child cheats, he or she will be defeating not me, but himself or herself.

There are thus two kinds of good possibly to be gained by playing chess. On the one hand there are those goods externally and contingently attached to chess-playing and to other practices by the accidents of social circumstance—in the case of the imaginary child candy, in the case of real adults such goods as prestige, status and money. There are always alternative ways for achieving such goods, and their achievement is never to be had *only* by engaging in some particular kind of practice. On the other hand there are the goods internal to the practice of chess which cannot be had in any way but by playing chess or some other game of that specific kind. We call them internal for two reasons: first, as I have already suggested, because we can only specify them in terms of chess or some other game of that specific kind and by means of examples from such games (otherwise the meagerness of our vocabulary for speaking of such goods forces us into such devices as my own resort to writing of 'a certain highly particular kind of'); and secondly because they can only be identified and recognised by the experience of participating in the practice in question. Those who lack the relevant experience are incompetent thereby as judges of internal goods. . . .

A practice involves standards of excellence and obedience to rules as well as the achievement of goods. To enter into a practice is to accept the authority of those standards and the inadequacy of my own performance as judged by them. It is to subject my own attitudes, choices, preferences and tastes to the standards which currently and partially define the practice. Practices of course . . . have a history: games, sciences and arts all have histories. Thus the standards are not themselves immune from criticism, but none the less we cannot be initiated into a practice without accepting the authority of the best standards realised so far. If, on starting to listen to music, I do not accept my own incapacity to judge correctly, I will never learn to hear, let alone to appreciate, Bartok's last quartets. If, on starting to play baseball, I do not accept that others know better than I when to throw a fast ball and when not, I will never learn to appreciate good pitching let alone to pitch. In the realm of practices the authority of both goods and standards operates in such a way as to rule out all subjectivist and emotivist analyses of judgment. De gustibus *est* disputandum.

We are now in a position to notice an important difference between what I have called internal and what I have called external goods. It is characteristic of what I have called external goods that when achieved they are always some individual's property and possession. Moreover characteristically they are such that the more someone has of them, the less there is for other people. This is sometimes necessarily the case, as with power and fame, and sometimes the case by reason of contingent circumstance as with money. External goods are therefore characteristically objects of competition in which there must be losers as well as winners. Internal goods are indeed the outcome of competition to excel, but it is characteristic of them that their achievement is a good for the whole community who participate in the practice. So when Turner transformed the seascape in painting or W.G. Grace advanced the art of batting in cricket in a quite new way their achievement enriched the whole relevant community.

But what does all or any of this have to do with the concept of the virtues? It turns out that we are now in a position to formulate a first, even if partial and tentative definition of a virtue: *A virtue is an acquired human quality the possession and exercise of which tends to enable us to achieve those goods which are internal to practices and the lack of which effectively prevents us from achieving any such goods*. Later this definition will need amplification and amendment. But as a first approximation to an adequate definition it already illuminates the place of the virtues in human life. For it is not difficult to show for a whole range of key virtues that without them the goods internal to practices are barred to us, but not just barred to us generally, barred in a very particular way.

It belongs to the concept of a practice as I have outlined it—and as we are all familiar with it already in our actual lives, whether we are painters or physicists or quarterbacks or indeed just lovers of good painting or first-rate experiments or a well-thrown pass—that its goods can only be achieved by subordinating ourselves to the best standard so far achieved, and that entails subordinating ourselves within the practice in our relationship to other practitioners. We have to learn to recognise what is due to whom; we have to be prepared to take whatever self-endangering risks are demanded along the way; and we have to listen carefully to what we are told about our own inadequacies and to reply with the same carefulness for the facts. In other words we have to accept as necessary components of any practice with internal goods and standards of excellence the virtues of justice, courage and honesty. For not to accept these, to be willing to cheat as our imagined child was willing to cheat in his or her early days at chess, so far bars us from achieving the standards of excellence or the goods internal to the practice that it renders the practice pointless except as a device for achieving external goods.

We can put the same point in another way. Every practice requires a certain kind of relationship between those who participate in it. Now the virtues are those goods by reference to which, whether we like it or not, we define our relationships to those other people with whom we share the kind of purposes and standards which inform practices. Consider an example of how reference to the virtues has to be made in certain kinds of human relationship. . . .

Just as, so long as we share the standards and purposes characteristic of practices, we define our relationships to each other, whether we acknowledge it or not, by reference to standards of truthfulness and trust, so we define them too by reference to standards of justice and of courage. If A, a professor, gives B and C the grades that their papers deserve, but grades D because he is attracted by D's blue eyes or is repelled by D's dandruff, he has defined his relationship to D differently from his relationship to the other members of the class, whether he wishes it or not. Justice requires that we treat others in respect of merit or desert according to uniform and impersonal standards; to depart from the standards of justice in some particular instance defines our relationship with the relevant person as in some way special or distinctive.

The case with courage is a little different. We hold courage to be a virtue because the care and concern for individuals, communities and causes which is so crucial to so much in practices requires the existence of such a virtue. If someone says that he cares for some individual, community or cause, but is unwilling to risk harm or danger on his, her or its own behalf, he puts in question the genuineness of his care and concern. Courage, the capacity to risk harm or danger to oneself, has its role in human life because of this connection with care and concern. This is not to say that a man cannot genuinely care and also be a coward. It is in part to say that a man who genuinely cares and has not the capacity for risking harm or danger has to define himself, both to himself and to others, as a coward.

I take it then that from the standpoint of those types of relationship without which practices cannot be sustained truthfulness, justice and courage—and perhaps some others—are genuine excellences, are virtues in the light of which we have to characterise ourselves and others, whatever our private moral standpoint or our society's particular codes may be. For this recognition that we cannot escape the definition of our relationships in terms of such goods is perfectly compatible with the acknowledgment that different societies have and have had different codes of truthfulness, justice and courage. Lutheran pietists brought up their children to believe that one ought to tell the truth to everybody at all times, whatever the circumstances or consequences, and Kant was one of their children. Traditional Bantu parents brought up their children not to tell the truth to unknown strangers, since they believed that this could render the family vulnerable to witchcraft. In our culture many of us have been brought up not to tell the truth to elderly great-aunts who invite us to admire their new hats. But each of these codes embodies an acknowledgment of the virtue of truthfulness. So it is also with varying codes of justice and of courage.

Practices then might flourish in societies with very different codes; what they could not do is flourish in societies in which the virtues were not valued, although institutions and technical skills serving unified purposes might well continue to flourish. . . . For the kind of cooperation, the kind of recognition of authority and of achievement, the kind of respect for standards and the kind of risk-taking which are characteristically involved in practices demand for example fairness in judging oneself and others . . . of fairness absent in my example of the professor, a ruthless truthfulness without which fairness cannot find application . . . and willingness to trust the judgments of those whose achievement in the practice give them an authority to judge which presupposes fairness and truthfulness in those judgments, and from time to time the taking of self-endangering, reputation-endangering and even achievement-endangering risks. It is no part of my thesis that great violinists cannot be vicious or great chess-players mean-spirited. Where the virtues are required, the vices also may flourish. It is just that the vicious and mean-spirited necessarily rely on the virtues of others for the practices in which they engage to flourish and also deny themselves the experience of achieving those internal goods which may reward even not very good chess-players and violinists.

To situate the virtues any further within practices it is necessary now to clarify a little further the nature of a practice by drawing two important contrasts. The discussion so far I hope makes it clear that a practice, in the sense intended, is never just a set of technical skills, even when directed towards some unified purpose and even if the exercise of those skills can on occasion be valued or enjoyed for their own sake. What is distinctive of a practice is in part the way in which conceptions of the relevant goods and ends which the technical skills serve—and every practice does require the exercise of technical skills—are transformed and enriched by these extensions of human powers and by that regard for its own internal goods which are partially definitive of each particular practice or type of practice. Practices never have a goal or goals fixed for all time—painting has no such goal nor has physics—but the goals themselves are transmuted by the history of the activity. It therefore turns out not to be accidental that every practice has its own history and a history which is more and other than that of the improvement of the relevant technical skills. This historical dimension is crucial in relation to the virtues.

To enter into a practice is to enter into a relationship not only with its contemporary practitioners, but also with those who have preceded us in the practice, particularly those whose achievements extended the reach of the practice to its present point. It is thus the achievement, and *a fortiori* the authority, of a tradition which I then confront and from which I have to learn. And for this learning and the relationship to the past which it embodies the virtues of justice, courage and truthfulness are prerequisite in precisely the same way and for precisely the same reasons as they are in sustaining present relationships within practices.

It is not only of course with sets of technical skills that practices ought to be contrasted. Practices must not be confused with institutions. Chess, physics and medicine are practices; chess clubs, laboratories, universities and hospitals are institutions. Institutions are characteristically and necessarily concerned with what I have called external goods. They are involved in acquiring money and other material goods; they are structured in terms of power and status, and they distribute money, power and status as rewards. Nor could they do otherwise if they are to sustain not only themselves, but also the practices of which they are the bearers. For no practices can survive for any length of time unsustained by institutions. Indeed so intimate is the relationship of practices to institutions—and consequently of the goods external to the goods internal to the practices in question—that institutions and practices characteristically form a single causal order in which the ideals and the creativity of the practice are always vulnerable to the acquisitiveness of the institution, in which the cooperative care for common goods of the practice is always vulnerable to the competitiveness of the institution. In this context the essential function of the virtues is clear. Without them, without justice, courage and truthfulness, practices could not resist the corrupting power of institutions.

Yet if institutions do have corrupting power, the making and sustaining of forms of human community—and therefore of institutions—itself has all the characteristics of a practice, and moreover of a practice which stands in a peculiarly close relationship to the exercise of the virtues in two important ways. The exercise of the virtues is itself apt to require a highly determinate attitude to social and political issues; and it is always within some particular community with its own specific institutional forms that we learn or fail to learn to exercise the virtues. There is of course a crucial difference between the way in which the relationship between moral character and political community is envisaged from the standpoint of liberal individualist modernity and the way in which that relationship was envisaged from the standpoint of the type of ancient and medieval tradition of the virtues. . . . For liberal individualism a community is simply an arena in which individuals each pursue their own self-chosen conception of the good life, and political institutions exist to provide that degree of order which makes such self-determined activity possible. Government and law are, or ought to be, neutral between rival conceptions of the good life for man, and hence, although it is the task of government to promote law-abidingness, it is on the liberal view no part of the legitimate function of government to inculcate any one moral outlook.

By contrast, on the particular ancient and medieval view . . . political community not only requires the exercise of the virtues for its own sustenance, but it is one of the tasks of government to make its citizens virtuous, just as it is one of the tasks of parental authority to make children grow up so as to be virtuous adults. The classical statement of this analogy is by Socrates in the *Crito*. It does not of course follow from an acceptance of the Socratic view of political community and political authority that we ought to assign to the modern state the moral function which Socrates assigned to the city and its laws. Indeed the power of the liberal individualist standpoint partly derives from the evident fact that the modern state is indeed totally unfitted to act as moral educator of any community. But the history of how the modern state emerged is of course itself a moral history. If my account of the complex relationship of virtues to practices and to institutions is correct, it follows that we shall be unable to write a true history of practices and institutions unless that history is also one of the virtues and vices. For the ability of a practice to retain its integrity will depend on the way in which the virtues can be and are exercised in sustaining the institutional forms which are the social bearers of the practice. The integrity of a practice causally requires the exercise of the virtues by at least some of the individuals who embody it in their activities; and conversely the corruption of institutions is always in part at least an effect of the vices. . . .

II

I have defined the virtues partly in terms of their place in practices. But surely, it may be suggested, some practices—that is, some coherent human activities which answer to the description of what I have called a practice—are evil. So in discussions by some moral philosophers of this type of account of the virtues it has been suggested that torture and sado-masochistic sexual activities might be examples of practices. But how can a disposition be a virtue if it is the kind of disposition which sustains practices and some practices issue in evil? My answer to this objection falls into two parts.

First I want to allow that there *may* be practices—in the sense in which I understand the concept—which simply *are* evil. I am far from convinced that there are, and I do not in fact believe that either torture or sado-masochistic sexuality answer to the description of a practice which my account of the virtues employs. But I do not want to rest my case on this lack of conviction, especially since it is plain that as a matter of contingent fact many types of practice may on particular occasions be productive of evil. For the range of practices includes the arts, the sciences and certain types of intellectual and athletic game[s]. And it is at once obvious that any of these may under certain conditions be a source of evil: the desire to excel and to win can corrupt, a man may be so engrossed by his painting that he neglects his family, what was initially an honourable resort to war can issue in savage cruelty. But what follows from this? . . .

That the virtues need initially to be defined and explained with reference to the notion of a practice . . . in no way entails approval of all practices in all circumstances. That the virtues—as the objection itself presupposed—*are* defined not in terms of good and right practices, but of practices, does not entail or imply that practices as actually carried through at particular times and places do not stand in need of moral criticism. And the resources for such criticism are not lacking. There is in the first place no inconsistency in appealing to the requirements of a virtue to criticise a practice. Justice may be initially defined as a disposition which in its particular way is necessary to sustain practices; it does not follow that in pursuing the requirements of a practice violations of justice are not to be condemned. Moreover . . . a morality of virtues requires as its counterpart a conception of moral law. Its requirements too have to be met by practices. But, it may be asked, does not all this imply that more needs to be said about the place of practices in some larger moral context? Does not this at least suggest that there is more to the core concept of a virtue than can be spelled out in terms of practices? I have after all emphasised that the scope of any virtue in human life extends beyond the practices in terms of which it is initially defined. What then is the place of the virtues in the larger arenas of human life? . . .

III

Any contemporary attempt to envisage each human life as a whole, as a unity, whose character provides the virtues with an adequate *telos* encounters two different kinds of obstacle, one social and one philosophical. The social obstacles derive from the way in which modernity partitions each human life into a variety of segments, each with its own norms and modes of behaviour. So work is divided from leisure, private life from public, the corporate from the personal. So both childhood and old age have been wrenched away from the rest of human life and made over into distinct realms. And all these separations have been achieved so that it is the distinctiveness of each and not the unit of the life of the individual who passes through those parts in terms of which we are taught to think and to feel.

The philosophical obstacles derive from two distinct tendencies, one chiefly, though not only, domesticated in analytical philosophy and one at home in both sociological theory and in existentialism. The former is the tendency to think atomistically about human action and to analyse complex actions and transactions in terms of simple components. Hence the recurrence in more than one context of the notion of 'a basic action'. That particular actions derive their character as parts of larger wholes is a point of view alien to our dominant ways of thinking and yet one which it is necessary at least to consider if we are to begin to understand how a life may be more than a sequence of individual actions and episodes.

Equally the unity of a human life becomes invisible to us when a sharp separation is made . . . between the individual and the roles that he or she plays. . . . For a self separated from its roles in the Sartrian mode loses that arena of social relationships in which the Aristotelian virtues function if they function at all. The patterns of a virtuous life would fall under those condemnations of conventionality which Sartre put into the mouth of Antoine Roquentin in *La Nausée* and which he uttered in his own person in *L'Etre et le néant*. Indeed the self's refusal of the inauthenticity of conventionalised social relationships becomes what integrity is diminished into in Sartre's account.

At the same time the liquidation of the self into a set of demarcated areas of role-playing allows no scope for the exercise of dispositions which could genuinely be accounted virtues in any sense remotely Aristotelian. For a virtue is not a disposition that makes for success only in some one particular type of situation. What are spoken of as the virtues of a good committee man or of a good administrator or of a gambler or a pool hustler are professional skills professionally deployed in those situations where they can be effective, not virtues. Someone who genuinely possesses a virtue can be expected to manifest it in very different types of situation, many of them situations where the practice of a virtue cannot be expected to be effective in the way that we expect a professional skill to be. Hector exhibited one and the same courage in his parting from Andromache and on the battlefield with Achilles; Eleanor Marx exhibited one and the same compassion in her relationship with her father, in her work with trade unionists and in her entanglement with Aveling. And the unity of a virtue in someone's life is intelligible only as a characteristic of a unitary life, a life that can be conceived and evaluated as a whole. Hence just as in the discussion of the changes in and fragmentation of morality which accompanied the rise of modernity in the earlier parts of this book, each stage in the emergence of the characteristically modern views of the moral judgment was accompanied by a corresponding stage in the emergence of the characteristically modern conceptions of selfhood; so now, in defining the particular pre-modern concept of the virtues with which I have been preoccupied, it has become necessary to say something of the concomitant concept of selfhood, a concept of a self whose unity resides in the unity of a narrative which links birth to life to death as narrative beginning to middle to end. . . .

It is a conceptual commonplace, both for philosophers and for ordinary agents, that one and the same segment of human behaviour may be correctly characterised in a number of different ways. To the question 'What is he doing?' the answers may with equal truth and appropriateness be 'Digging', 'Gardening', 'Taking exercise', 'Preparing for winter' or 'Pleasing his wife'. Some of these answers will characterise the agent's intentions, others unintended consequences of his actions, and of these unintended consequences some may be such that the agent is aware of them and others not. What is important to notice immediately is that any answer to the questions of how we are to understand or to explain a given segment of behaviour will presuppose some prior answer to the question of how these different correct answers to the question 'What is he doing?' are related to each other. For if someone's primary intention is to put the garden in order before the winter and it is only incidentally the case that in so doing he is taking exercise and pleasing his wife, we have one type of behaviour to be explained; but if the agent's primary intention is to please his wife by taking exercise, we have quite another type of behaviour to be explained and we will have to look in a different direction for understanding and explanation. . . .

Where intentions are concerned, we need to know which intention or intentions were primary, that is to say, of which it is the case that, had the agent intended otherwise, he would not have performed that action. Thus if we know that a man is gardening with the self-avowed purposes of healthful exercise and of pleasing his wife, we do not yet know how to understand what he is doing until we know the answer to such questions as whether he would continue gardening if he continued to believe that gardening was healthful exercise, but discovered that his gardening no longer pleased his wife, *and* whether he would continue gardening, if he ceased to believe that gardening was healthful exercise, but continued to believe that it pleased his wife, *and* whether he would continue gardening if he changed his beliefs on both points. That is to say, we need to know both what certain of his beliefs are and which of them are causally effective; and, that is to say, we need to know whether certain contrary-to-fact hypothetical statements are true or false. And until we know this, we shall not know how to characterise correctly what the agent is doing. . . .

Consider what the argument so far implies about the interrelationships of the intentional, the social and the historical. We identify a particular action only by invoking two kinds of context, implicitly if not explicitly. We place the agent's intentions, I have suggested, in causal and temporal order with reference to their role in his or her history; and we also place them with reference to their role in the history of the setting or settings to which they belong. In doing this, in determining what causal efficacy the agent's intentions had in one or more directions, and how his short-term intentions succeeded or failed to be constitutive of long-term intentions, we ourselves write a further part of these histories. Narrative history of a certain kind turns out to be the basic and essential genre for the characterisation of human actions. . . .

At the beginning . . . I argued that in successfully identifying and understanding what someone else is doing we always move towards placing a particular episode in the context of a set of narrative histories, histories both of the individuals concerned and of the settings in which they act and suffer. It is now becoming clear that we render the actions of others intelligible in this way because action itself has a basically historical character. It is because we all live out narratives in our lives and because we understand our own lives in terms of the narratives that we live out that the form of narrative is appropriate for understanding the actions of others. Stories are lived before they are told—except in the case of fiction. . . .

A central thesis then begins to emerge: man is in his actions and practice, as well as in his fictions, essentially a story-telling animal. He is not essentially, but becomes through his history, a teller of stories that aspire to truth. But the key question for men is not about their own authorship; I can only answer the question 'What am I to do?' if I can answer the prior question 'Of what story or stories do I find myself a part?' We enter human society, that is, with one or more imputed characters—roles into which we have been drafted—and we have to learn what they are in order to be able to understand how others respond to us and how our responses to them are apt to be construed. It is through hearing stories about wicked stepmothers, lost children, good but misguided kings, wolves that suckle twin boys, youngest sons who receive no inheritance but must make their own way in the world and eldest sons who waste their inheritance on riotous living and go into exile to live with the swine, that children learn or mislearn both what a child and what a parent is, what the cast of characters may be in the drama into which they have been born and what the ways of the world are. Deprive children of stories and you leave them unscripted, anxious stutterers in their actions as in their words. Hence there is no way to give us an understanding of any society, including our own, except through the stock of stories which constitute its initial dramatic resources. Mythology, in its original sense, is at the heart of things. Vico was right and so was Joyce. And so too of course is that moral tradition from heroic society to its medieval heirs according to which the telling of stories has a key part in educating us into the virtues. . . .

What the narrative concept of selfhood requires is . . . twofold. On the one hand, I am what I may justifiably be taken by others to be in the course of living out a story that runs from my birth to my death; I am the *subject* of a history that is my own and no one else's, that has its own peculiar meaning. When someone complains—as do some of those who attempt or commit suicide—that his or her life is meaningless, he or she is often and perhaps characteristically complaining that the narrative of [his or her] life has become unintelligible . . . , that it lacks any point, any movement towards a climax or a *telos*. Hence the point of doing any one thing rather than another at crucial junctures in [his or her life] seems to such a person to have been lost.

To be the subject of a narrative that runs from one's birth to one's death is . . . to be accountable for the actions and experiences which compose a narratable life. It is, that is, to be open to being asked to give a certain kind of account of what one did or what happened to one or what one witnessed at any earlier point in one's life the time at which the question is posed. Of course someone may have forgotten or suffered brain damage or simply not attended sufficiently at the relevant times to be able to give the relevant account. But to say of someone under some one description ('The prisoner of the Chateau d'If') that he is the same person as someone characterised quite differently ('The Count of Monte Cristo') is precisely to say that it makes sense to ask him to give an intelligible narrative account enabling us to understand how he could at different times and different places be one and the same person and yet be so differently characterised. Thus personal identity is just that identity presupposed by the unity of the character which the unity of a narrative requires. Without such unity there would not be subjects of whom stories could be told.

The other aspect of narrative selfhood is correlative: I am not only accountable, I am one who can always ask others for an account, who can put others to the question. I am part of their story, as they are part of mine. The narrative of any one life is part of an interlocking set of narratives. Moreover this asking for and giving of accounts itself plays an important part in constituting narratives. Asking you what you did and why, saying what I did and why, pondering the differences between your account of what I did and my account of what I did, and *vice versa,* these are essential constituents of all but the very simplest and barest of narratives. Thus without the accountability of the self those trains of events that constitute all but the simplest and barest of narratives could not occur; and without that same accountability narratives would lack that continuity required to make both them and the actions that constitute them intelligible. . . .

It is now possible to return to the question from which this enquiry into the nature of human action and identity started: In what does the unity of an individual life consist? The answer is that its unity is the unity of a narrative embodied in a single life. To ask 'What is the good for me?' is to ask how best I might live out that unity and bring it to completion. To ask 'What is the good for man?' is to ask what all answers to the former question must have in common. But now it is important to emphasize that it is the systematic asking of these two questions and the attempt to answer them in deed as well as in word which provide the moral life with its unity. The unity of a human life is the unity of a narrative quest. Quests sometimes fail, are frustrated, abandoned or dissipated into distractions; and human lives may in all these ways also fail. But the only criteria for success or failure in a human life as a whole are the criteria of success or failure in a narrated or to-be-narrated quest. A quest for what?

Two key features of the medieval conception of a quest need to be recalled. The first is that without some at least partly determinate conception of the final *telos* there could not be any beginning to a quest. Some conception of the good for man is required. Whence is such a conception to be drawn? Precisely from those questions which led us to attempt to transcend that limited conception of the virtues which is available in and through practices. It is in looking for a conception of *the* good which will enable us to order other goods, for a conception of *the* good which will enable us to extend our understanding of the purpose and content of the virtues, for a conception of *the* good which will enable us to understand the place of integrity and constancy in life, that we initially define the kind of life which is a quest for the good. But secondly it is clear the medieval conception of a quest is not at all that of a search for something already adequately characterised, as miners search for gold or geologists for oil. It is in the course of the quest and only through encountering and coping with the various particular harms, dangers, temptations and distractions which provide any quest with its episodes and incidents that the goal of the quest is finally to be understood. A quest is always an education both as to the character of that which is sought and in self-knowledge.

The virtues therefore are to be understood as those dispositions which will not only sustain practices and enable us to achieve the goods internal to practices, but which will also sustain us in the relevant kind of quest for the good, by enabling us to overcome the harms, dangers, temptations and distractions which we encounter, and which will furnish us with increasing self-knowledge and increasing knowledge of the good. The catalogue of the virtues will therefore include the virtues required to sustain the kind of households and the kind of political communities in which men and women can seek for the good together and the virtues necessary for philosophical enquiry about the character of the good. We have then arrived at a provisional conclusion about the good life for man: the good life for man is the life spent in seeking for the good life for man, and the virtues necessary for the seeking are those which will enable us to understand what more and what else the good life for man is. We have also completed the second stage in our account of the virtues, by situating them in relation to the good life for man and not only in relation to practices. But our enquiry requires a third stage.

For I am never able to seek for the good or exercise the virtues only *qua* individual. This is partly because what it is to live the good life concretely varies from circumstance to circumstance even when it is one and the same conception of the good life and one and the same set of virtues which are being embodied in a human life. What the good life is for a fifth-century Athenian general will not be the same as what it was for a medieval nun or a seventeenth-century farmer. But it is not just that different individuals live in different social circumstances; it is also that we all approach our own circumstances as bearers of a particular social identity. I am someone's son or daughter, someone else's cousin or uncle; I am a citizen of this or that city, a member of this or that guild or profession; I belong to this clan, that tribe, this nation. Hence what is good for me has to be the good for one who inhabits these roles. As such, I inherit from the past of my family, my city, my tribe, my nation, a variety of debts, inheritances, rightful expectations and obligations. These constitute the given of my life, my moral starting point. This is in part what gives my life its own moral particularity.

This thought is likely to appear alien and even surprising from the standpoint of modern individualism. From the standpoint of individualism I am what I myself choose to be. I can always, if I wish to, put in question what are taken to be the merely contingent social features of my existence. I may biologically be my father's son; but I cannot be held responsible for what he did unless I choose implicitly or explicitly to assume such responsibility. I may legally be a citizen of a certain country; but I cannot be held responsible for what my country does or has done unless I choose implicitly or explicitly to assume such responsibility. Such individualism is expressed by those modern Americans who deny any responsibility for the effects of slavery upon black Americans, saying 'I never owned any slaves'. It is more subtly the standpoint of those other modern Americans who accept a nicely calculated responsibility for such effects measured precisely by the benefits they themselves as individuals have indirectly received from slavery. In both cases 'being an American' is not in itself taken to be part of the moral identity of the individual. And of course there is nothing peculiar to modern Americans in this attitude: the Englishman who says, '*I* never did any wrong to Ireland; why bring up that old history as though it had something to do with *me?*' or the young German who believes that being born after 1945 means that what Nazis did to Jews has no moral relevance to his relationship to his Jewish contemporaries, exhibit the same attitude, that according to which the self is detachable from its social and historical roles and statuses. And the self so detached is of course a self very much at home in either Sartre's or Goffman's perspective, a self that can have no history. The contrast with the narrative view of the self is clear. For the story of my life is always embedded in the story of those communities from which I derive my identity. I am born with a past; and to try to cut myself off from that past, in the individualist mode, is to deform my present relationships. The possession of an historical identity and the possession of a social identity coincide. Notice that rebellion against my identity is always one possible mode of expressing it.

Notice also that the fact that the self has to find its moral identity in and through its membership in communities such as those of the family, the neighbourhood, the city and the tribe does not entail that the self has to accept the moral *limitations* of the particularity of those forms of community. Without those moral particularities to begin from there would never be anywhere to begin; but it is in moving forward from such particularity that the search for the good, for the universal, consists. Yet particularity can never be simply left behind or obliterated. The notion of escaping from it into a realm of entirely universal maxims which belong to man as such, whether in its eighteenth-century Kantian form or in the presentation of some modern analytical moral philosophies, is an illusion and an illusion with painful consequences. When men and women identify what are in fact their partial and particular causes too easily and too completely with the cause of some universal principle, they usually behave worse than they would otherwise do.

What I am, therefore, is in key part what I inherit, a specific past that is present to some degree in my present. I find myself part of a history and that is generally to say, whether I like it or not, whether I recognise it or not, one of the bearers of a tradition. It was important when I characterised the concept of a practice to notice that practices always have histories and that at any given moment what a practice is depends on a mode of understanding it which has been transmitted often through many generations. And thus, insofar as the virtues sustain the relationships required for practices, they have to sustain relationships to the past—and to the future—as well as in the present. But the traditions through which particular practices are transmitted and reshaped never exist in isolation for larger social traditions. . . .

So when an institution—a university, say, or a farm, or a hospital—is the bearer of a tradition of practice or practices, its common life will be partly, but in a centrally important way, constituted by a continuous argument as to what a university is and ought to be or what good farming is or what good medicine is. Traditions, when vital, embody continuities of conflict. . . .

A living tradition then is an historically extended, socially embodied argument, and an argument precisely in part about the goods which constitute that tradition. Within a tradition the pursuit of goods extends through generations, sometimes through many generations. Hence the individual's search for his or her good is generally and characteristically conducted within a context defined by those traditions of which the individual's life is a part, and this is true both of those goods which are internal to practices and of the goods of a single life. Once again the narrative phenomenon of embedding is crucial: the history of a practice in our time is generally and characteristically embedded in and made intelligible in terms of the larger and longer history of the tradition through which the practice in its present form was conveyed to us; the history of each of our own lives is generally and characteristically embedded in and made intelligible in terms of the larger and longer histories of a number of traditions. I have to say 'generally and characteristically' rather than 'always', for traditions decay, disintegrate and disappear. What then sustains and strengthens traditions? What weakens and destroys them?

The answer in key part is: the exercise or the lack of exercise of the relevant virtues. The virtues find their point and purpose not only in sustaining those relationships necessary if the variety of goods internal to practices are to be achieved and not only in sustaining the form of an individual life in which that individual may seek out his or her good as the good of his or her whole life, but also in sustaining those traditions which provide both practices and individual lives with their necessary historical context. Lack of justice, lack of truthfulness, lack of courage, lack of the relevant intellectual virtues—these corrupt traditions, just as they do those institutions and practices which derive their life from the traditions of which they are the contemporary embodiments. To recognise this is of course also to recognise the existence of an additional virtue, one whose importance is perhaps most obvious when it is least present, the virtue of having an adequate sense of the traditions to which one belongs or which confront one. . . . An adequate sense of tradition manifests itself in a grasp of those future possibilities which the past has made available to the present. Living traditions, just because they continue a not-yet-completed narrative, confront a future whose determinate and determinable character, so far as it possesses any, derives from the past. . . .

FOUR

ETHICAL DECISIONS IN A SOCIAL CONTEXT

10

JUSTICE AND EQUALITY

One of the most common moral criticisms that we make of our circumstances in life is that they are unjust. A child will protest against a parental directive, "It's not fair." Or perhaps we complain that the teacher isn't fair; the test isn't fair. President John Kennedy once remarked that life wasn't fair. In this chapter we will be discussing the notion of fairness and the closely related notion of justice.

One of the earliest analyses of justice was by the Greek philosopher Plato. Justice is a matter of giving each person his or her due. Of course the next question is obvious. What constitutes a person's due? Plato's theory was tied to the Greek idea of function. Everything has its function, and when everything is performing its function, the world is in order and everything is receiving its due. Consider a human being. Although we are composed of several faculties, such as reason, appetites, and will, reason is the ruler of the human being. When reason is in control, humans behave justly. If reason is not in control, our desires are not properly ordered and we behave unjustly.

For Plato, what is true of a human being is true of the state as well. A state is composed of various classes, with the business class, the military, and the ruling class figuring prominently in Plato's discussion. These three classes are analogous to the three parts of the human soul. So long as each class performs its appropriate function, all the citizens receive their due and justice results. For Plato justice results when everything is in its proper place and performing its proper function. Actually the term "receiving its due" is somewhat misleading. Most of Plato's examples of justice represent just behavior in terms of people performing their due rather than receiving their due.

You will notice that there is nothing egalitarian or democratic about Plato's account. Slaves receive their due when they are treated like slaves. Kings receive their due when they are treated like kings. The first link between equality and justice occurs in the thought of Plato's student Aristotle. Aristotle identified justice as one of the moral virtues and hence as a mean between two extremes. Aristotle distinguished the unjust as the unlawful from the unjust as the unfair. This latter notion has captured the interest of later philosophers. For Aristotle unfairness results when departures are made from either distributive justice or rectifying justice. Distributive justice occurs when equals are treated equally according to merit. Distributive justice is justice according to equal proportions. If Judy shows twice as much courage in battle as Jim, then Judy deserves twice as much praise. With respect to rectifying justice someone has gained at someone else's expense. If Judy robs John of $100, Judy has gained $100 at the expense of John. Rectifying justice requires that the $100 be returned to John. Of course with physical or psychological injury, rectifying the unjust gain is a complicated matter, but it should be noted that such rectification is not identical with the philosophy of "an eye for an eye and a tooth for a tooth." Judges need not resort to this kind of reciprocal justice in order to provide rectifying justice. The important task is to return to a state of equality by compensating the victim for the loss.

Both distributive justice and rectifying justice take place against a social background. With distributive justice, there are certain standards of merit which provide the basis of the distribution. With rectifying justice we are restoring a status quo; we are taking from the perpetrator of the injustice an amount equal to the loss of the victim. The equality involved is to return just that amount which brings the state of affairs back to a specified starting point. But are the criteria for merit just, and was the initial starting point which is being rectified just? Aristotle focused on justice between individuals, but what about the justice of the institutions the individuals participate in?

The focus of the selection by John Rawls is on just institutions. As with Aristotle, Rawls provides a link between justice and equality. Just institutions must be in conformity with the fundamental principles of justice. These principles of justice are the principles that free and equal moral persons would adopt if they were to meet as hypothetical institutional planners. For Rawls the principles of justice are determined as part of a social contract where everyone affected by social institutions is a contractor. Moreover, to prevent people from adopting a bias, people must pretend to be ignorant of all idiosyncrasies, such as level of income, the job skills one has, and level of educational attainment. By eliminating those individual characteristics which provide merit within social institutions from having any impact when institutions are being designed, Rawls is an egalitarian in a fairly fundamental sense. What justified giving each person affected by social institutions an equal voice in the design of social institutions? Rawls argues that there are no criteria which make some people more worthy to society than others. Rawls maintains that you can talk about the worth of an individual to an institution within society, but you cannot talk about the worth of an individual to society as a whole.

Rawls recognizes that social life is a cooperative enterprise, but given that individual interests conflict, he also regards social life as a competitive enterprise that needs rules. A theory of justice makes social interactions fair. In fact, Rawls called one of his early papers on justice, "Justice as Fairness." The social contract constrained in the manner described by Rawls is a fair procedure for determining the principles of justice. Social institutions which behave in conformity with the principles of justice are fair.

Another significant feature of Rawls's approach to justice is his emphasis on procedures. Since Rawls is primarily concerned with the justice of social institutions, this emphasis may not be surprising. Rawls's distinction among the various types of procedural justice has implications for the practice of justice in an imperfect world. In an ideal world, both just procedures and just results would exist. In an ideal world, the criminal-justice system would convict all the guilty but only the guilty. No guilty person would be found innocent, and no innocent person would be found guilty. In this ideal world, the criminal-justice system would exhibit the characteristic of perfect procedural justice. Alas, we do not live in an ideal world. Our criminal-justice system must be constructed in conformity with the view that it is more important not to convict an innocent person than it is to allow a guilty person to go free. In an imperfect world, the operating principle is to err on the side of protecting the innocent. Hence in an imperfect world such as our own, the criminal-justice system may be governed by principles different from those that govern the criminal-justice system in the ideal world. In the imperfect world, the criminal-justice system exhibits the characteristic of imperfect procedural justice.

There is a third kind of procedural justice, which is exemplified by a fair lottery. So long as the dice aren't loaded, the results of a game of chance are fair whatever the outcome. It doesn't matter whether the winners are rich or poor. So long as the game of chance was carried on in accordance with fair rules, the results are just. Situations like the game of chance are called instances of "pure procedural justice." Rawls seems to believe that a society where the social institutions are in conformity with the principles of justice is a society that exhibits pure procedural justice. What changes, if any, would the social contractors make in the principles of justice if the principles were used to design social institutions in an imperfect world?

To ask whether a society or even an individual action is just, we now realize, is to ask a complicated question. To determine whether a society is just, we need to know the principles which govern its institutions. Would such principles pass the tests of justice? Are the procedures embodied in the social institutions just? Is there an appropriate match between theoretical justice and the realities of the social situation? To answer these questions other ethical concepts must come into play. Does the society honor individual human rights? A society which doesn't couldn't be a just society. In this regard it is interesting to note that Rawls's two principles of justice embody liberty and a standard of well-being—the two goods which are emphasized by human-rights theorists.

One of the most entrenched American beliefs is that the just society is in some important sense an equal society. Aristotle defined justice in terms of equality, and Rawls insisted that all persons affected by a social practice should have an equal say in designing the practice. Since we have already encountered several senses in which a society can be equal, the assertion that demands for equality must be specified should come as no surprise. To condemn a society because it denies equality is inadequate. The important question to ask is whether existing inequalities are justified or unjustified.

There is a formal sense of equality which is required of all societies. The formal principle of equality is: treat equals equally and unequals unequally. But that formal requirement is nothing more than a requirement of consistency. If I call this object a "chair," then I must call other objects relevantly similar (equal) to it "chairs" as well.

The formal principle of equality is a principle of rationality; as such it applies to morality but extends to any other rational endeavor as well. Of course, sometimes an appeal to consistency takes you a long way. Recall how Kant used the notion of consistency to develop his notion of the categorical imperative.

Some egalitarian principles are more than just formal but are nonetheless too general. Both the Platonic and Aristotelian principles of equality suffer from that defect. Aristotle's proportional equality, for example, requires a theory of merit. The moral of this discussion is that "equality" is a context-dependent concept. The notion of equality is only useful in making moral decisions tied to some other notion, such as rights.

Gregory Vlastos in his article "Justice and Equality" defends a theory of justice based on a theory of equal rights to well-being and liberty. In the course of his analysis he clears up several confusions which often plague egalitarian theories. For instance, a vivid example concerning the pursuit of a victim by Murder Inc. shows why a commitment to equality often requires very unequal distributions. Moreover, the unequal distributions are not earned (merited). The potential victim of Murder Inc. does not merit the extra police protection but rather is entitled to it as a member of the community with equal rights. In passing, it is worth noting that Vlastos's argument for the rights to liberty and well-being is based on the ultimate value of human beings as such and the equal worth of their experience of liberty and well-being. A review of the essentials of Vlastos's argument is beneficial because it uses the basic concepts of several recent chapters and shows how these concepts can be tied together as an aid to making moral decisions.

1 All human beings have equal intrinsic value—Kant's argument based on the second formulation of the categorical imperative.

2 Since human beings have equal human value, their experiences of liberty and well-being have equal value.

3 Human beings have equal rights to liberty and well-being.

4 Justice is done when the equal rights of liberty and well-being are protected and sustained.

5 Protecting and sustaining equal rights to liberty and well-being often require unequal distributions of goods and resources.

There may well be some gaps in the argument, but that is not the important point. Vlastos has tied together the fundamental principle of respect for persons and an egalitarian theory of justice grounded on equal human rights to tell us how society should respond to a threat to one of its members by Murder Inc.

Recall that the introduction to Chapter 8 concluded with the pessimistic conclusion that there are basic conflicts between the right to liberty and the right to well-being. Perhaps there is some egalitarian theory which could resolve any conflicts between these two basic rights. Perhaps the solution is to find an ultimate egalitarian right which would settle any conflicts. In his essay Ronald Dworkin provides such a right. The egalitarian tradition in the United States and many other countries emphasizes the right of each individual to equal concern and respect. However, as Dworkin points out, this right to equal concern and respect can be interpreted in two ways—as a right to equal treatment or as a right to treatment as an equal. Dworkin rejects the latter interpretation in favor of the former. The problem with the treatment-as-an-equal interpretation is that individuals can be treated as equals and still have their interests sacrificed for the public good. Since treatment as an equal in the political sphere *is* the right to have your interest taken into account, you can vote, and hence your interest is taken into account, but nonetheless your interest is sacrificed if it is in the minority. Now, Dworkin argues that a genuine right cannot be sacrificed for consideration of the public good (utilitarian considerations), hence the only acceptable interpretation of a right to equal concern and respect is as a right to equal treatment. Furthermore, a right to equal treatment is a right to an equal distribution of some good or commodity. The final step in the argument is to show how many of the traditional liberties can be grounded in or derived from a right to equal treatment. In this way, Dworkin tries to show how equality can function as a primary moral concept. The just society is that society which honors and implements the right to equal treatment.

Justice

Aristotle

With regard to justice and injustice we must consider (1) what kind of actions they are concerned with, (2) what sort of mean justice is, and (3) between what extremes the just act is intermediate. Our investigation shall follow the same course as the preceding discussions.

We see that all men mean by justice that kind of state of character which makes people disposed to do what is just and makes them act justly and wish for what is just; and similarly by injustice that state which makes them act unjustly and wish for what is unjust. . . .

Let us take as a starting-point, then, the various meanings of 'an unjust man'. Both the lawless man and the grasping and unfair man are thought to be unjust, so that evidently both the law-abiding and the fair man will be just. The just, then, is the lawful and the fair, the unjust the unlawful and the unfair. . . .

Since the lawless man was seen to be unjust and the law-abiding man just, evidently all lawful acts are in a sense just acts; for the acts laid down by the legislative art are lawful, and each of these, we say, is just. Now the laws in their enactments on all subjects aim at the common advantage either of all or of the best or of those who hold power, or something of the sort; so that in one sense we call those acts just that tend to produce and preserve happiness and its components for the political society. And the law bids us do both the acts of a brave man (e.g. not to desert our post nor take to flight nor throw away our arms), and those of a temperate man (e.g. not to commit adultery nor to gratify one's lust), and those of a good-tempered man (e.g. not to strike another nor to speak evil), and similarly with regard to the other virtues and forms of wickedness, commanding some acts and forbidding others; and the rightly-framed law does this rightly, and the hastily conceived one less well.

This form of justice, then, is complete virtue, but not absolutely, but in relation to our neighbour. And therefore justice is often thought to be the greatest of virtues, and 'neither evening nor morning star' is so wonderful; and proverbially 'in justice is every virtue comprehended.' And it is complete virtue in its fullest sense, because it is the actual exercise of complete virtue. It is complete because he who possesses it can exercise his virtue not only in himself but towards his neighbour also; for many men can exercise virtue in their own affairs, but not in their relations to their neighbour. This is why the saying of Bias is thought to be true, that 'rule will show the man'; for a ruler is necessarily in relation to other men and a member of a society. For this same reason justice, alone of the virtues, is thought to be 'another's good', because it is related to our neighbour; for it does what is advantageous to another, either a ruler or a copartner. Now the worst man is he who exercises his wickedness both towards himself and towards his friends, and the best man is not he who exercises his virtue towards himself but he who exercises it towards another; for this is a difficult

"Nicomachean Ethics," trans. W.D. Ross, from *The Oxford Translation of Aristotle*, ed. W.D. Ross, vol. 9 (1925). Reprinted by permission of Oxford University Press.

task. Justice in this sense, then, is not part of virtue but virtue entire, nor is the contrary injustice a part of vice but vice entire. What the difference is between virtue and justice in this sense is plain from what we have said; they are the same but their essence is not the same; what, as a relation to one's neighbour, is justice is, as a certain kind of state without qualification, virtue. . . .

The unjust has been divided into the unlawful and the unfair, and the just into the lawful and the fair. To the unlawful answers the afore-mentioned sense of injustice. But since the unfair and the unlawful are not the same, but are different as a part is from its whole (for all that is unfair is unlawful, but not all that is unlawful is unfair), the unjust and injustice in the sense of the unfair are not the same as but different from the former kind, as part from whole; for injustice in this sense is a part of injustice in the wide sense, and similarly justice in the one sense of justice in the other. Therefore we must speak also about particular justice and particular injustice, and similarly about the just and the unjust. . . .

Of particular justice and that which is just in the corresponding sense, (A) one kind is that which is manifested in distributions of honour or money or the other things that fall to be divided among those who have a share in the constitution (for in these it is possible for one man to have a share either unequal or equal to that of another), and (B) one is that which plays a rectifying part in transactions between man and man. . . .

(A) We have shown that both the unjust man and the unjust act are unfair or unequal; now it is clear that there is also an intermediate between the two unequals involved in either case. And this is the equal; for in any kind of action in which there is a more and a less there is also what is equal. If, then, the unjust is unequal, the just is equal, as all men suppose it to be, even apart from argument. And since the equal is intermediate, the just will be an intermediate. Now equality implies at least two things. The just, then, must be both intermediate and equal and relative (i.e. for certain persons). And *qua* intermediate it must be between certain things (which are respectively greater and less); *qua* equal, it involves *two* things; *qua* just, it is for certain people. The just, therefore, involves at least four terms; for the persons for whom it is in fact just are two, and the things in which it is manifested, the objects distributed, are two. And the same equality will exist between the persons and between the things concerned; for as the latter—the things concerned—are related, so are the former; if they are not equal, they will not have what is equal, but this is the origin of quarrels and complaints—when either equals have and are awarded unequal shares, or unequals equal shares. Further, this is plain from the fact that awards should be 'according to merit'; for all men agree that what is just in distribution must be according to merit in some sense, though they do not all specify the same sort of merit, but democrats identify it with the status of freeman, supporters of oligarchy with wealth (or with noble birth), and supporters of aristocracy with excellence.

The just, then, is a species of the proportionate (proportion being not a property only of the kind of number which consists of abstract units, but of number in general). For proportion is equality of ratios, and involves four terms at least; . . . . and the just, too, involves at least four terms, and the ratio between one pair is the same as that between the other pair; for there is a similar distinction between the persons and between the things. As the term A, then, is to B, so will C be to D, and therefore, *alternando,* as A is to C, B will be to D. . . . The conjunction, then, of the term A with C and of B with D is what is just in distribution, and this species of the just is intermediate, and the unjust is what violates the proportion; for the proportional is intermediate, and the just is proportional. (Mathematicians call this kind of proportion geometrical; for it is in geometrical proportion that it follows that the whole is to the whole as either part is to the corresponding part.) . . .

This, then, is what the just is—the proportional; the unjust is what violates the proportion. Hence one term becomes too great, the other too small, as indeed happens in practice; for the man who acts unjustly has too much, and the man who is unjustly treated too little, of what is good. In the case of evil the reverse is true; for the lesser evil is reckoned a good in comparison with the greater evil, since the lesser evil is rather to be chosen than the greater, and what is worthy of choice is good, and what is worthier of choice a greater good.

This, then, is one species of the just.

(B) The remaining one is the rectificatory, which arises in connexion with transactions both voluntary and involuntary. This form of the just has a different specific character from the former. For the justice which distributes common possessions is always in accordance with the kind of proportion mentioned above; . . . and the injustice opposed to this kind of justice is that which violates the proportion. But the justice in transactions between man and man is a sort of equality indeed, and the injustice a sort of inequality; not according to that kind of proportion, however, but according to arithmetical proportion. For it makes no difference whether a good man has defrauded a bad man or a bad man a good one, nor whether it is a good or a bad man that has committed adultery; the law looks only to the distinctive character of the injury, and treats the parties as equal, if one is in the wrong and the other is being wronged, and if one inflicted injury and the other has received it. Therefore, this kind of injustice being an inequality, the judge tries to equalize it; for in the case also in which one has received and the other has inflicted a wound, or one has slain and the other been slain, the suffering and the action have been unequally distributed; but the judge tries to equalize things by means of the penalty, taking away from the gain of the assailant. . . . Now the judge restores equality; it is as though there were a line divided into unequal parts, and he took away that by which the greater segment exceeds the half, and added it to the smaller segment. And when the whole has been equally divided, then they say they have 'their own'—i.e. when they have got what is equal. The equal is intermediate between the greater and the lesser line according to arithmetical proportion. . . .

We have now defined the unjust and the just. These having been marked off from each other, it is plain that just action is intermediate between acting unjustly and being unjustly treated; for the one is to have too much and the other to have too little. Justice is a kind of mean, but not in the same way as the other virtues, but because it relates to an intermediate amount, while injustice relates to the extremes. And justice is that in virtue of which the just man is said to be a doer, by choice, of that which is just, and one who will distribute either between himself and another or between two others not so as to give more of what is desirable to himself and less to his neighbour (and conversely with what is harmful), but so as to give what is equal in accordance with proportion; and similarly in distributing between two other persons. Injustice on the other hand is similarly related to the unjust, which is excess and defect, contrary to proportion, of the useful or hurtful. For which reason injustice is excess and defect, viz. because it is productive of excess and defect—in one's own case excess of what is in its own nature useful and defect of what is hurtful, while in the case of others it is as a whole like what it is in one's own case, but proportion may be violated in either direction. In the unjust act to have too little is to be unjustly treated; to have too much is to act unjustly.

Let this be taken as our account of the nature of justice and injustice, and similarly of the just and the unjust in general. . . .

Just Institutions

John Rawls

I

An important assumption of my book *A Theory of Justice*[1] is that the basic structure of society is the primary subject of justice. By the basic structure is meant the way in which the major social institutions fit together into one system, and how they assign fundamental rights and duties and shape the division of advantages that arises through social cooperation. Thus the political constitution, the legally recognized forms of property, and the organization of the economy, all belong to the basic structure. I held that the first test of a conception of justice is whether its principles provide reasonable guidelines for the classical questions of social justice in this case.

In my book I did not consider in any detail why the basic structure is to be taken as the primary subject. I left this to be gathered from various remarks made while discussing other matters. Here I shall try to remedy this lack. Of course, it is perfectly legitimate at first to restrict inquiry to the basic structure. We must begin somewhere, and this starting point may turn out to be justified by how everything works out. But certainly we would like to find a more illuminating answer than this; and moreover one that draws upon the special features of the basic structure in contrast with other social arrangements, and connects these features with the particular role and content of the principles of justice themselves. I aim to present an explanation that meets these conditions.

John Rawls, "The Basic Structure as Subject," in the *American Philosophical Quarterly,* vol. 14, no. 2, April 1977. Edited by Nicholas Rescher. Published in Oxford by Basil Blackwell. Paper presented at the 51st Annual Meeting of the American Philosophical Association, Pacific Division, Portland, Oregon, March 1977.

Now a social contract is an agreement (1) between all rather than some members of society, and it is (2) between them as members of society (as citizens) and not as individuals who hold some particular position or role within it. In the Kantian form of this doctrine, of which the conception of justice as fairness is an example, (3) the parties are regarded as, and also regard themselves as, free and equal moral persons; and (4) the content of the agreement is the first principles that are to regulate the basic structure. We take as given a short list of conceptions of justice developed by the tradition of moral philosophy and then ask which of these the parties would acknowledge, when the alternatives are thus restricted. Assuming that we have a clear enough idea of the circumstances necessary to insure that any agreement reached is fair, the content of justice for the basic structure can be ascertained, or at least approximated, by the principles that would be agreed to. (Of course, this presupposes the reasonableness of the tradition; but where else can we start?) Thus pure procedural justice is invoked at the highest level; the fairness of the circumstances transfers to fairness of the principles adopted.

I wish to suggest the following: first that once we think of the parties to a social contract as free and equal (and rational) persons, then it is natural to take the basic structure as the primary subject. Second, that in view of the distinctive features of this structure, the initial agreement, and the conditions under which it is made, must be understood in a special way that distinguishes this agreement from all others; and doing this allows a Kantian view to take account of the fully social nature of human relationships. And finally, that while a large element of pure procedural justice transfers to the principles of justice, these principles must embody an ideal form for the basic structure in the light of which ongoing institutional processes are to be constrained and the accumulated results of individual transactions continually corrected.

II

Several lines of reasoning point to the basic structure as the primary subject of justice. One is the following: suppose we begin with the initially attractive idea that society should develop over time in accordance with free agreements fairly arrived at and fully honored. Straightway we need an account of when agreements are free and the social circumstances under which they are reached are fair. In addition, while these conditions may be fair at an earlier time, the accumulated results of many separate ostensibly fair agreements, together with social and historical contingencies, are likely as time passes to alter institutions and opportunities so that the conditions for free and fair agreements no longer hold. The role of the basic structure is to secure just background conditions against which the actions of individuals and associations take place. Unless this structure is appropriately regulated and corrected, the social process will cease to be just, however free and fair particular transactions may look when viewed by themselves.

We recognize this fact when we say, for example, that the distribution resulting from voluntary market transactions (even should all the ideal conditions for competitive efficiency obtain) is not, in general, fair unless the antecedent distribution of income and wealth as well as the structure of the system of markets is fair. The existing wealth must have been properly acquired and all must have had fair opportunities to earn income, to learn wanted skills, and so on. Again, the conditions necessary for background justice can be undermined, even though nobody acts unfairly or is aware of how the conjunction of contingencies affects the opportunities of others. There are no feasible rules that it is practicable to impose on economic agents that can prevent these undesirable consequences. These consequences are often so far in the future, or so indirect, that the attempt to forestall them by restrictive rules that apply to individuals would be an excessive if not impossible burden. Thus we start with the basic structure and try to see how this system itself should make the corrections necessary to preserve background justice.

III

A second reflection points in the same direction. Consider the situation of individuals engaged in market transactions. We have seen that certain background conditions are necessary for these transactions to be fair. But what about the nature of individuals themselves: how did they get to be what they are? A theory of justice cannot take their final aims and interests, their attitude to themselves and their life, as given. Everyone recognizes that the form of society affects its members and determines in large part the kind of persons they want to be as well as the kind of persons they are. It also limits people's ambitions and hopes in different ways, for they will with reason view themselves in part according to their place in it and take account of the means and opportunities they can realistically expect. Thus an economic regime is not only an institutional scheme for satisfying existing desires and aspirations but a way of fashioning desires and aspirations in the future.

Nor, similarly, can we view the abilities and talents of individuals as fixed natural gifts, even if there is an important genetic component. These abilities and talents cannot come to fruition apart from social conditions and as realized they always take but one of many possible forms. An ability is not, for example, a computer in the head with a definite measurable capacity unaffected by social circumstances. Among the elements affecting the realization of natural capacities are social attitudes of encouragement and support and the institutions concerned with their training and use. Thus even a potential ability at any given time is not something unaffected by existing social forms and particular contingencies over the course of life up to that moment. So not only our final ends and hopes for ourselves but our realized abilities and talents reflect, to a large degree, our personal history, opportunities, and social position. What we might have been had these things been different, we cannot know.

Finally, both of the preceding considerations are strengthened by the fact that the basic structure most likely contains significant social and economic inequalities. These I assume to be necessary, or else highly advantageous, in maintaining effective social cooperation; presumably there are various reasons for this, among which the need for incentives is but one. Even if these inequalities are not very great, they seem bound to have a considerable effect and so to favor some over others depending upon their social origins, their realized natural endowments, and the chance coincidences and opportunities that have come their way. The basic structure includes inequalities between certain starting-places, so to speak, and this feature, together with the earlier observations, prompts us to take this structure as the primary subject.

IV

In the conception of justice as fairness the institutions of the basic structure are viewed as just provided they (reasonably) satisfy the principles that free and equal moral persons, in a situation that is fair between them, would adopt for the purpose of regulating that structure. The main two principles read as follows: (1) Each person has an equal right to the most extensive scheme of equal basic liberties compatible with a similar scheme of liberties for all. (2) Social and economic inequalities are permissible provided that (a) they are to the greatest expected benefit of the least advantaged; and (b) attached to positions and offices open to all under conditions of fair equality of opportunity.

Let us consider how the special features of the basic structure affect the conditions of the initial agreement and hence the content of these principles. Now by assumption the basic structure is the all-inclusive social system that determines background justice; so any fair situation between individuals conceived as free and equal moral persons must be one that suitably evens out the contingencies within this system. Agreements reached when people know their present place in an ongoing society would be influenced by disparate social and natural contingencies. The principles adopted would then be selected by the historical course of events that took place within that structure. We would not have gotten beyond social happenstance in order to find an independent standard.

It is also clear why, when we interpret the parties as free and equal moral persons, they are to reason as if they know very little about themselves (referring here to the restrictions of the veil of ignorance). For to proceed otherwise is still to allow the disparate and deep contingent effects of the social system to influence the principles adopted; and this is true even if the parties have no particular information about themselves but only general facts about their own society (which is perhaps all that a condition of impartiality requires). When we as contemporaries are influenced by a general description of the present state of society in agreeing how we are to treat each other, and those generations that come after us, we have not yet left out of account the accidents of the basic structure. And so one arrives at the thicker rather than the thinner veil of ignorance: the parties are to be understood so far as possible solely as moral persons, that is, in abstraction from all those contingencies that the basic structure over time has shaped and influenced; and to be fair between them, the initial situation must situate them equally for as moral persons they are equal: the same essential properties qualify each.

Finally, the social contract must be regarded as hypothetical. Of course, any actual agreement is liable to the distortions just noted; but in any case, historically valid compacts, were such to exist, would have but limited force and could not serve as the basis of a general theory. Equally decisive is the fact that society is a system of cooperation that extends over time: it is cooperation between generations and not just cooperation among contemporaries. If we are to account for the duties and obligations between generations, there is no clear way to do this in a contract view without interpreting the initial agreement as hypothetical. The correct principles for the basic structure are those that the members of any generation (and hence all generations) would agree to as the ones their generation is to follow and as the principles they would want other generations to have followed and to follow subsequently, no matter how far back or forward in time.

Once we note the distinctive role of the basic structure and abstract from the various contingencies within it to find an appropriate conception of justice to regulate it, something like the notion of the original position seems inevitable. It is a natural extension of the idea of the social contract when the basic structure is taken as the primary subject of justice.

V

The essential point is the distinctive role of the basic structure: we must distinguish between particular agreements made and associations formed within this structure, and the initial agreement and membership in society as a citizen. Consider first particular agreements: typically these are based on the parties' known (or probable) assets and abilities, opportunities and interests, as these have been realized within background institutions. We may assume that each party, whether an individual or an association, has various alternatives open to them, that they can compare the likely advantages and disadvantages of these alternatives, and act accordingly. Under certain conditions someone's contribution to a joint venture, or to an on-going association, can be estimated: one simply notes how the venture or association would fare without that person's joining, and the difference measures their worth to the venture or association. The attractiveness of joining to the individual is similarly given by a comparison with their opportunities. Thus particular agreements are reached within the context of existing and foreseeable configurations of relationships as these have been and most likely will be realized within the basic structure; and it is these configurations that give meaning to contractual calculations.

The context of a social contract is strikingly different, and must allow for three facts, among others: namely, that membership in our society is given, that we cannot know what we would have been like had we not belonged to it (perhaps the thought itself lacks a sense), and that society as a whole has no ends or ordering of ends in the sense that associations and individuals do. The bearing of these facts is clear once we try to view the social contract as an ordinary agreement and ask how deliberations leading up to it would proceed. Since membership in their society is given, there is no question of the parties comparing the attractions of other societies. Moreover, there is no way to identify potential contribution to society as an individual not yet a member of it; for this potentiality cannot be known and is, in any case, irrelevant to their present situation. Not only this, but from the standpoint of society as a whole *vis-á-vis* any one member, there is no set of agreed ends by reference to which the potential social contributions of an individual could be assessed. Associations and individuals have such ends, but not a well-ordered society; although it has the aim of giving justice to all its citizens, this is not an aim that ranks their expected contributions and on that basis determines their social role. The notion of an individual's contribution to society as itself an association falls away. It is necessary, therefore, to construe the social contract in a special way that distinguishes it from other agreements.

In the conception of justice as fairness this is done by constructing the notion of the original position. This construction must reflect the fundamental contrasts just noted and it must supply the missing elements so that an appropriate agreement may be reached. Consider in turn the points in the preceding paragraph. First, the parties in the original position suppose that their membership in the society is given. This presumption reflects the fact that we are born into our society and within its framework realize but one of many possible forms of our person; the question of entering another society does not arise. The task is to agree on principles for the basic structure of the society of one's birth. Second, the veil of ignorance not only establishes fairness between equal moral persons, but by excluding information about the parties' actual interests and abilities, it represents the fact that apart from our place and history in a society, even our potential abilities cannot be known and our interests and character are still to be formed. Thus, the initial situation suitably recognizes that our nature apart from society is but a potential for a whole range of possibilities. Third and finally, there is no social end except that established by the principles of justice themselves, or else authorized by them; but these principles have yet to be adopted.

Nevertheless, although the calculations that typically influence agreements within society have no place, other aspects of the original position provide the setting for rational deliberation. Thus the alternatives are not opportunities to join other societies, but instead a list of conceptions of justice to regulate the basic structure of one's own society. The parties' interests and preferences are given by their desire for primary goods. Their particular final ends and aims indeed are already formed, although not known to them; and it is these already formed interests that they seek to protect by ranking conceptions on the basis of their preference (in the original position) for primary goods. Finally, the availability of general social theory gives a sufficient basis for estimating the feasibility and consequences of the various conceptions of justice. These aspects of the original position allow us to carry through the idea of the social contract despite the unusual nature of this agreement.

VI

I now point out three ways in which the social aspect of human relationships is reflected in the content of the principles of justice themselves. First, the difference principle (which governs economic and social inequalities) does not distinguish between what is acquired by individuals as members of society and what would have been acquired by them had they not been members. Indeed, no sense can be made of the notion of that part of an individual's social benefits that exceed what would have been their situation in another society or in a state of nature. We can, if we like, in setting up the arguments from the original position, introduce the state of nature in relation to the so-called no-agreement point.[2] This point can be defined as general egoism and its consequences, and this can serve as the state of nature. But these conditions do not identify a definite state. All that is known in the original position is that each of the conceptions of justice available to the parties has consequences superior to general egoism. There is no question of determining anyone's contribution to society, or how much better off each is than they would have been had they not belonged to society and then adjusting the social benefits of citizens by reference to these estimates. Although we may draw this kind of distinction for agreements made within society, the requisite calculations for principles holding for the basic structure itself have no foundation. Neither our situation in other societies, nor in a state of nature, has any role in comparing conceptions of justice. And clearly these notions have no relevance at all in the application of the principles of justice.

Second, and related to the preceding, the two principles of justice regulate how entitlements are acquired in return for contributions to associations, or to other forms of cooperation, within the basic structure. As we have seen, these contributions are estimated on the basis of particular configurations of contingencies, which are influenced in part by individual efforts and achievements, in part by social accident and happenstance. Contributions can only be locally defined as contributions to this or that association in this or that situation. Such contributions reflect an individual's worth (marginal usefulness) to some particular group. These contributions are not to be mistaken for contributions to society itself, or for the worth to society of its members as citizens. The sum of an individual's entitlements, or even of their uncompensated contributions to associations within society, is not to be regarded as a contribution to society. To this kind of contribution we can give no meaning; there is no clear or useful notion of an individual's contribution to society that parallels the idea of individual contributions to associations within society. Insofar as we compare the worth of citizens at all, their worth in a well-ordered society is always equal; and this equality is reflected in the system of basic equal liberties and fair opportunities, and in the operations of the difference principle.

Third and last, recall that in a Kantian view the parties are regarded as free and equal moral persons. Now freedom means a certain form of social institutions, namely, a certain pattern of rights and liberties; and equality in turn means, for example, that certain basic liberties and opportunities are equal and that social and economic inequalities are regulated by principles suitably expressive of equality. Moral persons are those with a conception of the good (a system of final ends) and a capacity to understand a conception of justice and to follow it in their life. Of course, we cannot define free and equal moral persons as those whose social relations answer to precisely the principles that are agreed to in the social contract. For then we should have no argument for these principles. But it is no accident that once the parties are described in terms that require some social expression, the first principles of justice are themselves institutional and apply to the public structure of society. The content of the two principles fulfills this expectation. And this is in contrast, for example, with utilitarianism which takes as basic the capacity for pleasure and pain, or for certain valuable experiences. Nevertheless, the social manner in which the parties are described does not mean a lapse into some kind of holism; what results is a conception of a well-ordered society regulated by the two principles of justice.

VII

Now I come to the last point: namely, why it is that, although society may reasonably rely on a large element of pure procedural justice in determining distributive shares, a conception of justice must incorporate an ideal form for the basic structure in the light of which the accumulated results of on-going social processes are to be limited and corrected.

First a remark about pure procedural justice: the two principles make considerable use of this notion. They apply to the basic structure and its system for acquiring entitlements; within appropriate limits, whatever distributive shares result are just. A fair distribution can be arrived at only by the actual working of a fair social process over time in the course of which, in accordance with publicly announced rules, entitlements are earned and honored. These features define pure procedural justice. Therefore, if it is asked in the abstract whether one distribution of a given stock of things to definite individuals with known desires and preferences is more just than another, then there is simply no answer to this question.[3]

Thus the principles of justice, in particular the difference principle, apply to the main public principles and policies that regulate social and economic inequalities. They are used to adjust the system of entitlements and earnings and to balance the familiar everyday standards and precepts which this system employs. The difference principle holds, for example, for income and property taxation, for fiscal and economic policy. It applies to the announced system of public law and statutes and not to particular transactions or distributions, nor to the decisions of individuals and associations, but rather to the institutional background against which these take place. There are no unannounced and unpredictable interferences with citizens' expectations and acquisitions. Entitlements are earned and honored as the public system of rules declares. Taxes and restrictions are all in principle foreseeable, and holdings are acquired on the known condition that certain corrections will be made. The objection that the difference principle enjoins continuous and capricious interference with private transactions is based on a misunderstanding.

Again, the two principles of justice do not insist that the actual distribution reflect any observable pattern, say equality, nor any measure computed from the distribution, such as a certain Gini coefficient (as a measure of the degree of equality). What is enjoined is that (permissible) inequalities make a certain functional contribution over time to the expectations of the least favored. The aim, however, is not to eliminate the various contingencies from social life, for some such contingencies seem inevitable. Thus even if an equal distribution of natural assets seemed more in keeping with the equality of free persons, the question of redistributing these assets (were this conceivable) does not arise, since it is incompatible with the integrity of the person. Nor need we make any specific assumptions about how great these natural variations are; we only suppose that, as realized in later life, they are influenced by many kinds of contingencies. Institutions must organize social cooperation so that they encourage constructive efforts. We have a right to our natural abilities and a right to whatever we become entitled to by taking part in a fair social process. The two principles of justice define the relevant fair process and so whatever distributive shares result are fair.

At the same time, these principles specify an ideal form for the basic structure in the light of which pure procedural processes are constrained and corrected. Among these constraints are the limits on the accumulation of property (especially if private property in productive assets exists) that derive from the requirements of the fair value of political liberty and fair equality of opportunity, and the limits based on considerations of stability and excusable envy, both of which are connected to the essential primary good of self-respect.[4] We need such an ideal to guide the corrections necessary to preserve background justice. As we have seen, even if everyone acts fairly as defined by rules that it is both reasonable and practicable to impose on individuals, the upshot of many separate transactions will undermine background justice. This is obvious once we view society, as we must, as involving cooperation over generations. Thus even in a well-ordered society, adjustments in the basic structure are always necessary. What we have, in effect, is an institutional division of labor between the basic structure and rules applying directly to particular transactions. Individuals and associations are left free to advance their ends more effectively within the framework of the basic structure secure in the knowledge that elsewhere in the social system the necessary corrections to preserve background justice are being made.

The essential point, then, is that the need for a structural ideal to specify constraints and to guide corrections does not depend upon injustice. Even with strict compliance with all reasonable and practical rules, such adjustments are continually required. The fact that actual political and social life is often pervaded by much injustice merely underlines this necessity. A procedural theory that contains no structural principles for a just social order would be of no use in our world, where the political goal is to eliminate injustice and steer change towards a fair basic structure. The notion of a well-ordered society provides the requisite structural principles and specifies the overall direction of political action. There is no rational basis for preventing or eliminating injustice if such an ideal form for background institutions is rejected.

NOTES

1 Cambridge, Mass., 1971.
2 See *A Theory of Justice (op. cit.)*, pp. 136, 147; see also p. 80.
3 On pure procedural justice, see *ibid.*, pp. 64, 66, 72ff, 79, 84–89, 274–280, 305–315.
4 See *ibid.*, pp. 224–227, 227f; 534–537, 543–546.

Justice and Equality

Gregory Vlastos

I

The close connection between justice and equality is manifest in both history and language. The great historic struggles for social justice have centered about some demand for equal rights: the struggle against slavery, political absolutism, economic exploitation, the disfranchisement of the lower and middle classes and the disfranchisement of women, colonialism, racial oppression. On the linguistic side let me mention a curiosity that will lead us into the thick of our problem. When Aristotle in Book V of the *Nicomachean Ethics* comes to grips with distributive justice, almost

Adapted from "Justice and Equality" by Gregory Vlastos from the book *Social Justice* edited by Richard B. Brandt. © 1962 by Prentice-Hall, Inc. Published by Prentice-Hall, Inc., Englewood Cliffs, N.J. 07632.

the first remark he has to make is that "justice is equality, as all men believe it to be, quite apart from any argument." . . . But it so happens that Aristotle, like Plato and others before him, believed firmly that a just distribution is in general an unequal one. And to say this, if "equal" is your word for "just," you would have to say that an "equal" distribution is an *unequal* one. . . . This tour de force must have provoked many an honest man at the time. . . . We may view it more dispassionately as classical testimony to the strength of the tie between equality and justice: even those who meant to break the conceptual link could not, or would not, break the verbal one. The meritarian view of justice paid reluctant homage to the equalitarian one by using the vocabulary of equality to assert the justice of inequality.

But when the equalitarian has drawn from this what comfort he may, he still has to face the fact that the expropriation of his word "equality" could be carried through so reputably and so successfully that its remote inheritance has made it possible for us to speak now in a perfectly matter of fact way of "equitable inequalities" or "inequitable equalities." This kind of success cannot be wholly due to the tactical skill of those who carried out the original maneuver; though one may envy the virtuosity with which Plato disposes of the whole notion of democratic equality in a single sentence (or rather less, a participial clause) when he speaks of democracy as "distributing an odd sort of equality to equals and unequals."[1] The democrats themselves would have been intellectually defenseless against that quip. Their faith in democracy had no deep roots in any concept of human equality; the *isonomia* (equality of law) on which they prided themselves was the club-privilege of those who had had the good judgment to pick their ancestors from free Athenian stock of the required purity of blood. But even if we could imagine a precocious humanitarian in or before Plato's time, founding the rights of the citizen on the rights of man, it is not clear that even he would be proof against Plato's criticism. For what Plato would like to know is whether his equalitarian opponent really means to universalize equality: would he, would anyone, wish to say that there are no just inequalities? That there are no rights in respect of which men are unequal?

One would think that this would be among the first questions that would occur to equalitarians, and would have had long since a clear and firm answer. Strange as it may seem, this has not happened. The question has been largely evaded. Let me give an example: Article I of the Declaration of Rights of Man and Citizen (enacted by the Constituent Assembly of the First French Republic in 1791) reads: "Men are born and remain free and equal in rights. Social distinctions can be based only upon public utility." Bentham takes the first sentence to mean that men are equal in *all* rights. One would like to think that this was a wilful misunderstanding. For it would be only too obvious to the drafters of the Declaration that those "social distinctions" of which they go on to speak would entail many inequalities of right. Thus the holder of a unique political office (say, the president of a republic) would not be equal in all rights to all other men or even to one other man: no other man would have equal right to this office, or to as high an office; and many would not have equal right to any political office, even if they had, as they would according to the republican constitution, equal rights of eligibility to all offices. But if this is in the writers' minds, why don't they come out and say that men are born and remain equal in some rights, but are either not born or do not remain equal in a great many others? They act as though they were afraid to say the latter on this excessively public occasion, lest their public construe the admission of some unequal rights as out of harmony with the ringing commitment to human rights which is the keynote of the Declaration. What is this? Squeamishness? Confusion? Something of both? Or has it perhaps a sound foundation and, if so, in what? Plato's question is not answered. It is allowed to go by default. . . .

II

Let me begin with the . . . maxim of distributive justice: "To each according to his need." Since needs are often unequal, this looks like a precept of unequal distribution. But this is wrong. It is in fact *the most perfect form of equal distribution.* To explain this let me take one of the best established rights in the natural law tradition: the right to the security of life and person. Believing that this is an equal right, what do we feel this means in cases of special need?

Suppose, for instance, New Yorker X gets a note from Murder Inc., that looks like business. To allocate several policemen and plainclothesmen to guard him over the next few weeks at a cost a hundred times greater than the per capita cost of security services to other citizens during the same period, is surely *not* to make an exception to the equal distribution required by the equal right of all citizens to the security of their life and person; it is not done on the assumption that X has a greater right to security or a right to greater security. If the visitor from Mars drew this conclusion from the behavior of the police, he would be told that he was just mistaken. The greater allocation of community resources in X's favor, we would have to explain, is made precisely *because* X's security rights are equal to those of other people in New York. This means that X is entitled to the same level of police-made security as is maintained for other New Yorkers. Hence in these special circumstances, where his security level would drop to zero without extra support, he should be given this to bring his security level nearer the normal. I say "nearer," not "up to" the normal, because I am talking of New York as of 1961. If I were thinking of New York with an ideal municipal government, ideally supplied with police resources, I *would* say "up to the normal," because that is what equality of right would ideally mean. But as things are, perhaps the best that can be done for X without disrupting the general level of security maintained for all the other New Yorkers is to decrease his chances of being bumped off in a given week to, say, one to ten thousand, while those of ordinary citizens, with ordinary protection are, say, one to ten million—no small difference. Now if New York were more affluent, it would be able to buy more equality of security for its citizens (as well as more security): by getting more, and perhaps also better paid, policemen, it would be able to close the gap between security maintained for people in ordinary circumstances and that supplied in cases of special need, like that of X in his present jam. Here we stumble on something of considerable interest: that approximation to the goal of completely equal security benefits for all citizens is a function of two variables: first, and quite obviously, of the pattern of distribution of the resources; second, and less obviously, of their size. If the distributable resources are so meager that they are all used up to maintain a general level barely sufficient for ordinary needs, their reallocation to meet exceptional need will look too much like robbing Peter to pay Paul. In such conditions there is likely to be little, if any, provision for extremity of need and, what is more, the failure to meet the extremity will not be felt as a social injustice but as a calamity of fate. . . .

So we can see why distribution according to personal need, far from conflicting with the equality of distribution required by a human right, is so linked with its very meaning that under ideal conditions equality of right would coincide with distribution according to personal need. Our visitor misunderstood the sudden mobilization of New York policemen in favor of Mr. *X,* because he failed to understand that it is benefits to persons, not allocation of resources as such, that are meant to be made equal; for then he would have seen at once that unequal distribution of resources would be required to equalize benefits in cases of unequal need. But if he saw this he might then ask, "But why do you want this sort of equality?" My answer would have to be: Because the human worth of all persons is equal, however unequal may be their merit. To the explanation of this proposition I shall devote the balance of this Section.

By "merit" I shall refer throughout this essay to all the kinds of valuable qualities or performances in respect of which persons may be graded. The concept will not be restricted to moral actions or dispositions. Thus wit, grace of manner, and technical skill count as meritorious qualities fully as much as sincerity, generosity, or courage. Any valuable human characteristic, or cluster of characteristics, will qualify, provided only it is "acquired," i.e., represents what its possessor has himself made of his natural endowments and environmental opportunities. Given the immense variety of individual differences, it will be commonly the case that of any two persons either may excel the other in respect of different kinds or sub-kinds of merit. Thus if *A* and *B* are both clever and brave men, *A* may be much the cleverer as a business man, *B* as a literary critic, and *A* may excel in physical, *B* in moral, courage. It should be clear from just this that to speak of "a person's merit" will be strictly senseless except insofar as this is an elliptical way of referring to that person's merits, i.e., to those specifiable qualities or activities in which he rates well. So if there is a value attaching to the person himself as an integral and unique individual, *this* value will not fall under merit or be reducible to it. For it is of the essence of merit, as here defined, to be a grading concept; and there is no way of grading individuals as such. We can only grade them with respect to their qualities, hence only by abstracting from their individuality. If *A* is valued for some meritorious quality, *m,* his individuality does not enter into the valuation. As an individual he is then dispensable; his place could be taken without loss of value by any other individual with as good an *m*-rating. Nor would matters change by multiplying and diversifying the meritorious qualities with which *A* is endowed. No matter how enviable a package of well-rounded excellence *A* may represent, it would still follow that, if he is valued only for his merit, he is not being valued as an individual. To be sure individuals *may* be valued only for their merits. This happens all too commonly. *A* might be valued in just this way by *P,* the president of his company, for whom *A,* highly successful vice-president in charge of sales, amusing dinner-guest, and fine asset to the golf club, is simply high-grade equipment in various complexes of social machinery which *P* controls or patronizes. On the other hand, it is possible that, much as *P* prizes this conjunct of qualities *(M),* he values *A* also as an individual. *A* may be his son, and he may be genuinely fond of him. If so, his affection will be for *A*, not for his *M*-qualities. The latter *P* approves, admires, takes pride in, and the like. But his affection and good will are for *A*, and *not only because*, or *insofar as*, *A* has the *M*-qualities. For *P* may be equally fond of another son who rates well below *A* in *P*'s scoring system. Moreover, *P*'s affection for *A*, as distinct from his approval or admiration of him, need not fluctuate with the ups and downs in *A*'s achievements. Perhaps *A* had some bad years after graduating from college, and it looked then as though his brilliant gifts would be wasted. It does not follow that *P*'s love for *A* then lapsed or even ebbed. Constancy of affection in the face of variations of merit is one of the surest tests of whether or not a parent does love a child. If he feels fond of it only when it performs well, and turns coldly indifferent or hostile when its achievements slump, then his feeling for the child can scarcely be called *love*. There are many relations in which one's liking or esteem for a person are strictly conditional on his measuring up to certain standards. But convincing evidence that the relation is of this type is no evidence that the relation is one of parental love or any other kind of love. It does nothing to show that one has this feeling, or any feeling, for an *individual*, rather than for a place-holder of qualities one likes to see instantiated by somebody or other close about one.

Now if this concept of value attaching to a person's individual existence, over and above his merit—"individual worth," let me call it—were applicable *only* in relations of personal love, it would be irrelevant for the analysis of justice. To serve our purpose its range of application must be coextensive with that of justice. It must hold in all human relations, including (or rather, especially in) the most impersonal of all, those to total strangers, fellow-citizens or fellow-men. I must show that the concept of individual worth does meet this condition.

Consider its role in our political community, taking the prescriptions of our laws for the treatment of persons as the index to our valuations. For merit (among other reasons) persons may be appointed or elected to public office or given employment by state agencies. For demerit they may lose licences, jobs, offices; they may be fined, jailed, or even put to death. But in a large variety of law-regulated actions directed to individuals, either by private persons or by organs of the state, the question of merit and demerit does not arise. The "equal protection of the laws" is due to persons not to meritorious ones, or to them in some degree above others. So too for the right to vote. One does not have it for being intelligent and public-spirited, or lose it for being lazy, ignorant, or viciously selfish. One is entitled to exercise it as long as, having registered, one manages to keep out of jail. This kind of arrangement would look like whimsy or worse, like sheer immoralism, if the only values recognized in our political community were those of merit. For obviously there is nothing compulsory about our political system; we would certainly devise, if we so wished, workable alternatives which would condition fundamental rights on certain kinds of merit. For example, we might have three categories of citizenship. The top one might be for those who meet high educational qualifications and give definite evidence of responsible civic interest, e.g., by active participation in political functions, tenure of public office, record of leadership in civic organizations and support to them, and the like. People in this *A*-category might have multiple votes in all elections and exclusive eligibility for the more important political offices; they might also be entitled to a higher level of protection by the police and to a variety of other privileges and immunities. At the other end there would be a *C*-category, disfranchised and legally underprivileged, for those who do not meet some lower educational test or have had a record of law-infraction or have been on the relief rolls for over three months. In between would be the *B*'s with ordinary suffrage and intermediate legal status.

This "*M*-system" would be more complicated and cumbersome than ours. But something like it could certainly be made to work if we were enamoured of its peculiar scheme of values. Putting aside the question of efficiency, it gives us a picture of a community whose political valuations, conceived entirely in terms of merit, would never be grounded on individual worth, so that this notion would there be politically useless. For us, on the other hand, it is indispensable. We have to appeal to it when we try to make sense of the fact that our legal system accords to all citizens an identical status, carrying with it rights such as the *M*-system reserves to the *B*'s or the *A*'s, and some of which (like suffrage or freedom of speech) have been denied even to the nobility in some caste-systems of the past. . . .

Consider finally the role of the same value in the moral community. Here differences of merit are so conspicuous and pervasive that we might even be tempted to *define* the moral response to a person in terms of moral approval or disapproval of his acts or disposition, i.e., in terms of the response to his moral merit. But there are many kinds of moral response for which a person's merit is as irrelevant as is that of New Yorker *X* when he appeals to the police for help. If I see someone in danger of drowning I will not need to satisfy myself about his moral character before going to his aid. I owe assistance to any man in such circumstances, not merely to good men. Nor is it only in rare and exceptional cases, as this example might suggest, that my obligations to others are independent of their moral merit. To be sincere, reliable, fair, kind, tolerant, unintrusive, modest in my relations with my fellows is not due them because they have made brilliant or even passing moral grades, but simply because they happen to be fellow-members of the moral community. . . .

Here, then, as in the single-status political community, we acknowledge personal rights which are not proportioned to merit and could not be justified by merit. Their only justification could be the value which persons have simply because they are persons: their "intrinsic value as individual human beings," as Frankena calls it; the "infinite value" or the "sacredness" of their individuality, as others have called it. I shall speak of it as "individual human worth"; or "human worth," for short. What these expressions stand for is also expressed by saying that men are "ends in themselves." This latter concept is Kant's. Some of the kinks in his formulation of it can be straightened out by explaining it as follows: Everything other than a person can only have value *for* a person. This applies not only to physical objects, natural or manmade, which have only instrumental value, but also to those products of the human spirit which have also intrinsic , no less than extrinsic, value: an epic poem, a scientific theory, a legal system, a moral disposition. Even such things as these will have value only because they can be (a) experienced or felt to be valuable by human beings and (b) chosen by them from competing alternatives. Thus of everything without exception it will be true to say: if *x* is valuable and is not a person, then *x* will have value for some individual other than itself. Hence even a musical composition or a courageous deed, valued for their own sake, as "ends" not as means to anything else, will still fall into an entirely different category from that of the *valuers,* who do not need to be valued as "ends" by someone else in order to have value. In just this sense persons, and only persons, are "ends in themselves."

The two factors in terms of which I have described the value of the valuer—the capacities answering to (a) and (b) above—may not be exhaustive. But their conjunction offers a translation of "individual human worth" whose usefulness for working purposes will speak for itself. To (a) I might refer as "happiness," if I could use this term as Plato and Aristotle used *eudaimonia,* i.e., without the exclusively hedonistic connotations which have since been clamped on it. It will be less misleading to use "well-being" or "welfare" for what I intend here; that is, the enjoyment of value in all the forms in which it can be experienced by human beings. To (b) I shall refer as "freedom," bringing under this term not only conscious choices and deliberate decisions but also those subtler modulations and more spontaneous expressions of individual preference which could scarcely be called "choices" or "decisions" without some forcing of language. So understood, a person's well-being and freedom are aspects of his individual existence as unique and unrepeatable as is that existence itself: If A and B are listening to the same symphony with similar tastes and dispositions, we may speak of their enjoying the "same" good, or having the "same" enjoyment, and say that each has made the "same" choice for this way of spending his time and money. But here "same" will mean no more than "very similar"; the two enjoyments and choices, occurring in the consciousness of A and B respectively, are absolutely unique. So in translating "A's human worth" into "the worth of A's well-being and freedom" we are certainly meeting the condition that the former expression is to stand for whatever it is about A which, unlike his merit, has *individual* worth.

We are also meeting another condition: that the equality of human worth be justification, or ground, of equal human rights. I can best bring this out by reverting to the visitor from Mars who had asked a little earlier why we want equalization of security benefits. Let us conjure up circumstances in which his question would spring, not from idle curiosity, but from a strong conviction that this, or any other, right entailing such undiscriminating equality of benefits, would be entirely *un*reasonable. Suppose then that he hails from a strict meritarian community, which maintains the M-system in its political life and analogous patterns in other associations. And to make things simpler, let us also suppose that he is shown nothing in New York or elsewhere that is out of line with our formal professions of equality, so that he imagines us purer, more strenuous, equalitarians than we happen to be. The pattern of valuation he ascribes to us then seems to him fantastically topsy-turvy. He can hardly bring himself to believe that rational human beings should want equal personal rights, legal and moral, for their "riff-raff" and their élites. Yet neither can he explain away our conduct as pure automatism, a mere fugue of social habit. "These people, or some of them," he will be saying to himself, "must have some reasons for this incredible code. What could these be?" If we volunteered an answer couched in terms of human worth, he might find it hard to understand us. Such an answer, unglossed, would convey to him no more than that we recognize something which is highly and equally valuable in all persons, but has nothing to do with their merit, and constitutes the ground of their equal rights. But this might start him hunting—snark-hunting—for some special quality named by "human worth" as honesty is named by "honesty" and kindness by "kindness," wondering all the while how it could have happened that he and all his tribe have had no inkling of it, if all of them have always had it.

But now suppose that we avail ourselves of the aforesaid translation. We could then tell him: "To understand our code you should take into account how very different from yours is our own estimate of the relative worth of the welfare and freedom of different individuals. We agree with you that not all persons are capable of experiencing the same values. But there is a wide variety of cases in which persons are capable of this. Thus, to take a perfectly clear case, no matter how *A* and *B* might differ in taste and style of life, they would both crave relief from acute physical pain. In that case we would put the same value on giving this to either of them, regardless of the fact that *A* might be a talented, brilliantly successful person, *B* 'a mere nobody.' On this we would disagree sharply. You would weigh the welfare of members of the élite more highly than that of 'riff-raff,' as you call them. We would not. If *A* were a statesman, and giving him relief from pain enabled him to conclude an agreement that would benefit millions, while *B*, an unskilled laborer, was himself the sole beneficiary of the like relief, we would, of course, agree that the *instrumental* value of the two experiences would be vastly different—but not their *intrinsic* value. In all cases where human beings are capable of enjoying the same goods, we feel that the intrinsic value of their enjoyment is the same. In just this sense we hold that (1) *one man's well-being is as valuable as any other's*. And there is a parallel difference in our feeling for freedom. You value it only when exercised by good persons for good ends. We put no such strings on its value. We feel that choosing for oneself what one will do, believe, approve, say, see, read, worship, has its own intrinsic value, the same for all persons, and quite independently of the value of the things they happen to choose. Naturally, we hope that all of them will make the best possible use of their freedom of choice. But we value their exercise of that freedom, regardless of the outcome; and we value it equally for all. For us (2) *one man's freedom is as valuable as any other's*."

This sort of explanation, I submit, would put him in a position to resolve his dilemma. For just suppose that, taking this homily at face-value, he came to think of us as believing (1) and (2). No matter how unreasonable he might think of us he would feel it entirely reasonable that, since we do believe in equal *value* of human well-being and freedom, we should also believe in the *prima facie* equality of men's *right* to well-being and to freedom. He would see the former as a good reason for the latter; or, more formally, he could think of (1) and (2) respectively as the crucial premises in justification arguments whose respective conclusions would be: (3) One man's *(prima facie)* right to well-being is equal to that of any other, and (4) One man's *(prima facie)* right to freedom is equal to that of any other. Then, given (4), he could see how this would serve as the basis for a great variety of rights to specific kinds of freedom: freedom of movement, of association, of suffrage, of speech, of thought, of worship, of choice of employment, and the like. For each of these can be regarded as simply a specification of the general right to freedom, and would thus be covered by the justification of the latter. Moreover, given (3), he could see in it the basis for various welfare-rights, such as the right to education, medical care, work under decent conditions, relief in periods of unemployment, leisure, housing, etc. Thus to give him (1) and (2) as justification for (3) and (4) would be to give him a basis for every one of the rights which are mentioned in the most complete of currently authoritative declarations of human rights, that passed by the Assembly of the United Nations in 1948. Hence to tell him that we believe in the equal worth of individual freedom and happiness would be to answer, in terms he can understand, his question, "What is your reason for your equalitarian code?"

Nowhere in this defense of the translation of "equal human worth" into "equal worth of human well-being and freedom" have I claimed that the former can be *reduced* to the latter. I offered individual well-being and freedom simply as two things which do satisfy the conditions defined by individual human worth. Are there others? For the purposes of this essay this may be left an open question. For if there are, they would provide, at most, additional grounds for human rights. The ones I have specified are grounds enough. They are all I need for the analysis of equalitarian justice as, I trust, will appear directly.

III

I offer the following definition: An action is *just* if, and only if, it is prescribed exclusively by regard for the rights of all whom it affects substantially. . . .

A major feature of my definition of "just" is that it makes the answer to "Is x just?" (where x is any action, decision, etc.) strictly dependent on the answer to another question: "What are the rights of those who are substantially affected by x?" The definition cannot, and does not pretend that it can, give the slightest help in answering the latter question, with but one exception: it does tell us that the substantially affected rights, whatever they may be, should all be impartially respected. Thus it does disclose one right, though a purely *formal* one: the right to have one's *other* rights respected as impartially as those of any other interested party. But what are these other rights? Are they equal or unequal? On this the definition is silent. It is thus completely neutral in the controversy between meritarians and equalitarians, and should prove equally acceptable to either party. Its neutralism should not be held against it. The words "just" and "unjust" are not the private property of the equalitarians; they may be used as conscientiously by those who reject, as by those who share, their special view of justice. We are not compelled to provide for this in our definitions; but there are obvious advantages in doing so. For we thereby offer our opponents common ground on which they too may stand while making their case. We allow Aristotle, for instance, to claim, without misusing language, that slavery and the disfranchisement of manual workers are just institutions. It allows us to rebut his claim, not by impugning its linguistic propriety, but by explaining that we affirm what his claim implicitly denies: that all human beings have the right to personal and political freedom.

It should now be plain to the reader why I have been so heavily preoccupied with the question of human rights throughout the first half of this essay, and content to write most of Section II without even mentioning the word "justice." I have done so precisely because my purpose in this essay is not to discuss justice in general, but equalitarian justice. As should now be obvious, had I tried to reason from the concept of justice to that of equalitarian justice I would have been reasoning in a circle. I did allude at the start to important historical and linguistic ties of justice with equality. But these, while perfectly relevant, are obviously not conclusive. They would be dismissed by a determined and clear-headed opponent, like Plato, as mere evidences of a widespread *mis*conception of justice. I am not suggesting that we should yield him this point or that, conversely, there is any good reason to think that he would come around to our view if we presented him with the argument of Section II (or a stronger one to the same effect). My contention is rather that we would be misrepresenting our view of justice if we were to give him the idea that it is susceptible of proof by that kind of historical and linguistic evidence. To explain our position to him so that, quite apart from his coming to agree with it, he would at least have the chance to *understand* it, one thing would matter above all: to show that we believe in human rights, and why.

That is why the weight of the argument in the preceding Section II fell so heavily on the notion of human worth, understood to mean nothing less than the equal worth of the happiness and freedom of all persons. Given this, we have equal welfare-rights and freedom-rights; and this puts us in a position to cover the full range of human rights which the natural rights tradition left so perplexingly indeterminate. . . .

NOTE

1 *Rep.* 558c; and cf. *Laws* 757a: "For when equality is given to unequals the result is inequality, unless due measure is applied."

The Priority of Equality

Ronald Dworkin

I

Do we have a right to liberty? Thomas Jefferson thought so, and since his day the right to liberty has received more play than the competing rights he mentioned to life and the pursuit of happiness. Liberty gave its name to the most influential political movement of the last century, and many of those who now despise liberals do so on the ground that they are not sufficiently libertarian. Of course, almost everyone concedes that the right to liberty is not the only political right, and that therefore claims to freedom must be limited, for example, by restraints that protect the security or property of others. Nevertheless the consensus in favor of some right to liberty is a vast one, though it is, as I shall argue in this paper, misguided.

Ronald Dworkin, *Taking Rights Seriously,* Harvard University Press, Cambridge, Mass. © 1977 by Ronald Dworkin.

The right to liberty is popular all over this political spectrum. The rhetoric of liberty fuels every radical movement from international wars of liberation to campaigns for sexual freedom and women's liberation. But liberty has been even more prominent in conservative service. Even the mild social reorganizations of the anti-trust and union-ization movements, and of the early New Deal, were opposed on the grounds that they infringed the right to liberty, and just now efforts to achieve some racial justice in America through techniques like the busing of black and white schoolchildren, and social justice in Britain through constraints in private education are bitterly opposed on that ground.

It has become common, indeed, to describe the great social issues of domestic politics, and in particular the racial issue, as presenting a conflict between the demands of liberty and equality. It may be, it is said, that the poor and the black and the uneducated and the unskilled have an abstract right to equality, but the prosperous and the whites and the educated and the able have a right to liberty as well and any efforts at social reorganization in aid of the first set of rights must reckon with and respect the second. Everyone except extremists recognizes, therefore, the need to compromise between equality and liberty. Every piece of important social legislation, from tax policy to integration plans, is shaped by the supposed tension between these two goals.

I have this supposed conflict between equality and liberty in mind when I ask whether we have a *right* to liberty, as Jefferson and everyone else has supposed. That is a crucial question. If freedom to choose one's schools, or employees, or neighbor-hood is simply something that we all want, like air conditioning or lobsters, when we are not entitled to hang on to these freedoms in the face of what we concede to be the rights of others to an equal share of respect and resources. But if we can say, not simply that we want these freedoms, but that we are ourselves entitled to them, then we have established at least a basis for demanding a compromise. . . .

I have in mind the traditional definition of liberty as the absence of constraints placed by a government upon what a man might do if he wants to. . . . This conception of liberty as license is neutral amongst the various activities a man might pursue, the various roads he might wish to walk. It diminishes a man's liberty when we prevent him from talking or making love as he wishes, but it also diminishes his liberty when we prevent him from murdering or defaming others. These latter constraints may be justifiable, but only because they are compromises necessary to protect the liberty or security of others, and not because they do not, in themselves, infringe the independent value of liberty. Bentham said that any law whatsoever is an 'infraction' of liberty, and though some such infractions might be necessary, it is obscurantist to pretend that they are not infractions after all. In this neutral, all embracing sense of liberty as license, liberty and equality are plainly in competition. Laws are needed to protect equality and laws are inevitably compromises of liberty.

Liberals like Berlin are content with this neutral sense of liberty, because it seems to encourage clear thinking. It allows us to identify just what is lost, though perhaps unavoidably, when men accept constraints on their actions for some other goal or value. It would be an intolerable muddle, on this view, to use the concept of liberty or freedom in such a way that we counted a loss of freedom only when men were prevented from doing something that we thought they ought to do. It would allow totalitarian governments to masquerade as liberal, simply by arguing that they prevent men from doing only what is wrong. Worse, it would obscure the most distinctive point of the liberal tradition, which is that interfering with a man's free choice to do what he might want to do is in and of itself an insult to humanity, a wrong that may be justified but can never be wiped away by competing considerations. For a true liberal, any constraint upon freedom is something that a decent government must regret, and keep to the minimum necessary to accommodate the other rights of its constituents.

In spite of this tradition, however, the neutral sense of liberty seems to me to have caused more confusion than it has cured, particularly when it is joined to the popular and inspiring idea that men and women have a right to liberty. For we can maintain that idea only by so watering down the idea of a right that the right to liberty is something hardly worth having at all.

The term 'right' is used in politics and philosophy in many different senses, some of which I have tried to disentangle elsewhere. In order sensibly to ask whether we have a right to liberty in the neutral sense, we must fix on some one meaning of 'right'. . . . A successful claim of right . . . has this consequence. If someone has a right to something, then it is wrong for the government to deny it to him even though it would be in the general interest to do so. This sense of a right (which might be called the anti-utilitarian concept of a right) seems to me very close to the sense of right principally used in political and legal writing and argument in recent years. It marks the distinctive concept of an individual right against the State which is the heart, for example, of constitutional theory in the United States.

I do not think that the right to liberty would come to very much, or have much power in political argument, if it relied on any sense of the right any weaker than that. If we settle on this concept of a right, however, then it seems plain that there exists no general right to liberty as such. I have no political right to drive up Lexington Avenue. If the government chooses to make Lexington Avenue one-way down town, it is a sufficient justification that this would be in the general interest, and it would be ridiculous for me to argue that for some reason it would nevertheless be wrong. The vast bulk of the laws which diminish my liberty are justified on utilitarian grounds, as being in the general interest or for the general welfare; if, as Bentham supposes, each of these laws diminishes my liberty, they nevertheless do not take away from me anything that I have a right to have. It will not do, in the one-way street case, to say that although I have a right to drive up Lexington Avenue, nevertheless the government for special reasons is justified in overriding that right. That seems silly because the government needs no special justification—but only *a* justification—for this sort of legislation. So I can have a political right to liberty, such that every act of constraint diminishes or infringes that right, only in such a weak sense of right that the so called right to liberty is not competitive with strong rights, like the right to equality, at all. In any strong sense of right, which would be competitive with the right to equality, there exists no general right to liberty at all. . . .

If we want to argue for a right to certain liberties, therefore, we must find another ground. We must argue on grounds of political morality that it is wrong to deprive individuals of these liberties, for some reason, apart from direct psychological damage, in spite of the fact that the common interest would be served by doing so. I put the matter this vaguely because there is no reason to assume, in advance, that only one kind of reason would support that moral position. It might be that a just society would recognize a variety of individual rights, some grounded on very different sorts of moral considerations from others. In what remains of this chapter I shall try to describe only one possible ground for rights. It does not follow that men and women in civil society have only the rights that the argument I shall make would support; but it does follow that they have at least these rights, and that is important enough.

II

The central concept of my argument will be the concept not of liberty but of equality. I presume that we all accept the following postulates of political morality. Government must treat those whom it governs with concern, that is, as human beings who are capable of suffering and frustration, and with respect, that is, as human beings who are capable of forming and acting on intelligent conceptions of how their lives should be lived. Government must not only treat people with concern and respect, but with equal concern and respect. It must not distribute goods or opportunities unequally on the ground that some citizens are entitled to more because they are worthy of more concern. It must not constrain liberty on the ground that one citizen's conception of the good life of one group is nobler or superior to another's. These postulates, taken together, state what might be called the liberal conception of equality; but it is a conception of equality, not of liberty as license, that they state.

The sovereign question of political theory, within a state supposed to be governed by the liberal conception of equality, is the question of what inequalities in goods, opportunities and liberties are permitted in such a state, and why. The beginning of an answer lies in the following distinction. Citizens governed by the liberal conception of equality each have a right to equal concern and respect. But there are two different rights that might be comprehended by that abstract right. The first is the right to equal treatment, that is, to the same distribution of goods or opportunities as anyone else has or is given. The Supreme Court, in the Reapportionment Cases, held that citizens have a right to equal treatment in the distribution of voting power; it held that one man must be given one vote in spite of the fact that a different distribution of votes might in fact work for the general benefit. The second is the right to treatment as an equal. This is the right, not to an equal distribution of some good or opportunity, but the right to equal concern and respect in the political decision about how these goods and opportunities are to be distributed. Suppose the question is raised whether an economic policy that injures long-term bondholders is in the general interest. Those who will be injured have a right that their prospective loss be taken into account in deciding whether the general interest is served by the policy. They may not simply be ignored in that calculation. But when their interest is taken into account it may nevertheless be outweighed by the interests of others who will gain from the policy, and in that case their right to equal concern and respect, so defined, would provide no objection. In the case of economic policy, therefore, we might wish to say that those who will be injured if inflation is permitted have a right to treatment as equals in the decision whether that policy would serve the general interest, but no right to equal treatment that would outlaw the policy even if it passed that test.

I propose that the right to treatment as an equal must be taken to be fundamental under the liberal conception of equality, and that the more restrictive right to equal treatment holds only in those special circumstances in which, for some special reason, it follows from the more fundamental right, as perhaps it does in the special circumstance of the Reapportionment Cases. I also propose that individual rights to distinct liberties must be recognized only when the fundamental right to treatment as an equal can be shown to require these rights. If this is correct, then the right to distinct liberties does not conflict with any supposed competing right to equality, but on the contrary follows from a conception of equality conceded to be more fundamental.

I must now show, however, how the familiar rights to distinct liberties—those established, for example, in the United States constitution—might be thought to be required by that fundamental conception of equality. I shall try to do this, for present purposes, only by providing a skeleton of the more elaborate argument that would have to be made to defend any particular liberty on this basis, and then show why it would be plausible to expect that the more familiar political and civil liberties would be supported by such an argument if it were in fact made.

A government that respects the liberal conception of equality may properly constrain liberty only on certain very limited types of justification. I shall adopt, for purposes of making this point, the following crude typology of political justifications. There are, first, arguments of principle, which support a particular constraint on liberty on the argument that the constraint is required to protect the distinct right of some individual who will be injured by the exercise of the liberty. There are, second, arguments of policy, which support constraints on the different ground that such constraints are required to reach some overall political goal, that is, to realize some state of affairs in which the community as a whole, and not just certain individuals, are better off by virtue of the constraint. Arguments of policy might be further subdivided in this way. Utilitarian arguments of policy argue that the community as a whole will be better off because (to put the point roughly) more of its citizens will have more of what they want overall, even though some of them will have less. Ideal arguments of policy, on the other hand, argue that the community will be better off, not because more of its members will have more of what they want, but because the community will be in some way closer to an ideal community, whether its members desire the improvement in question or not.

The liberal conception of equality sharply limits the extent to which ideal arguments of policy may be used to justify any constraint on liberty. Such arguments cannot be used if the idea in question is itself controversial within the community. Constraints cannot be defended, for example, directly on the ground that they contribute to a culturally sophisticated community, whether the community wants the sophistication or not, because that argument would violate the canon of the liberal conception of equality that prohibits a government from relying on the claim that certain forms of life are inherently more valuable than others. . . .

CHAPTER 11

UTILITARIANISM

In the Broadway musical *Dreamgirls,* the lead singer, Effie, is replaced by an outsider. Although Effie has a beautiful voice and has been the mainstay of their family group, a crossover from soul to "pop" requires a dynamic, sexy lead singer. A successful crossover requires more than a beautiful voice. Needless to say, Effie is crushed; however, in a beautiful but sad ballad, she is urged to accept the change for the good of the family and the good of the group. Often we as individuals are asked to give up our own interest for the greater interest of the group. Indeed, many would argue that the correct ethical decision is that decision which contributes most to the welfare of the group. It's one thing to say that ethical decisions ought to aim for the public welfare. It is quite another to find a morally acceptable means for achieving the public welfare. This chapter provides an account of the best-known ethical theory of the public good, the theory of utilitarianism. As you may recall from the General Introduction, utilitarianism is the best-known example of consequentialism.

Utilitarian theories hold that the moral worth of actions or practices is determined solely by the consequences of the actions or practices. To understand utilitarianism, consider a person trying to decide whether to give $50 to charity or spend it on gifts for a friend. The counsel of a utilitarian would be that one ought to make one's choice on the basis of that action which would lead to the production of the best consequences for all affected. Or, consider a debate in Congress concerning whether taxes should be raised. The utilitarian would again urge that the decision be made on the basis of the greatest good for the greatest number. If raising taxes would provide the greatest increment of good throughout society, then it should be approved. Otherwise it should not be approved. Utilitarianism, then, is the view that an action or practice is right (when compared to any alternative action or practice) if it leads to the greatest possible balance of good consequences, and that the concepts of duty and right are subordinated to or determined by that which is good.

Although utilitarian views were espoused throughout the early history of ethical theory, the classical utilitarian writings are those of Jeremy Bentham (1748–1832) and John Stuart Mill (1806–1873). Bentham provides an especially appropriate example because he came to his utilitarian views as a result of his unhappiness with the British legal system and the writings of its chief apologist, William Blackstone. Bentham thought the British system for classifying crimes outdated because it was based on an abstract moral theory concerning the gravity of offenses. As an alternative, Bentham suggested that crimes be classified according to the unhappiness and misery they caused to the victims and to society. His revisions in the classification scheme were intended to bring about revisions in views on how severely certain crimes should be punished. Bentham's fundamental rule was that, while the punishment for any crime should exceed the advantage gained by committing the crime, the punishment should not be any greater than what is necessary to ensure that the crime is in the end disadvantageous for the criminal. Bentham thought that one should calculate the social benefits of rehabilitating and deterring criminals and should subtract from that figure the pain that punishment causes. One should punish up to, but should not exceed, that point where the infliction of pain brings about the greatest benefits in rehabilitation and deterrence. Prisons, then, should make sure that crime does not pay, but they should not go overboard. To provide the flavor of Bentham's analysis, some of his writings on punishment are included in the Bentham selection in this chapter.

Perhaps the most significant difference between the deontological and utilitarian theorists is that deontologists look to the past while utilitarians look to the future. Consider punishment. A deontologist will emphasize what the criminal did and hold that a just punishment is one based on merit. It should equalize or compensate for the harm. Bentham just didn't look at punishment that way. He asked such questions as whether the pain caused by the punishment outweighed the gain of the crime to the criminal, whether a specific punishment would encourage greater criminal excess, whether the punishment for any given crime could deter other crimes of this type. A utilitarian could argue, for example, that at best capital punishment is only justified for certain types of murder. To punish rape by death—a suggestion that is still heard today—would only encourage the rapist to kill the victim. Hence the death penalty for rape could not be justified on utilitarian grounds even if some deontological considerations might lead to the conclusion that the rapist deserved the death penalty. Similar considerations might lead the utilitarian to reduce the punishments for so-called crimes of passion. Given the nature of crimes of passion, extreme punishment for them has little deterrent effect. Whether the person who commits a crime of passion deserves an extreme punishment is an abstract theoretical issue that distorts the criminal-justice system. By emphasizing the question of desert, it is easy to lose sight of the public welfare. On utilitarian ground, the purpose of the criminal-justice system is to make sure that crime does not pay; it is not the purpose of the criminal-justice system to seek revenge.

In addition to the emphasis on the future, utilitarianism has several other essential characteristics. Every utilitarian is committed to the maximization of the good, since utilitarianism asserts that a correct ethical decision is one that produces the greatest balance of good over evil for all the persons affected. What divides utilitarians are differences as to what counts as good consequences and how these good consequences should be measured.

Perhaps the most common utilitarian theory of good consequences is hedonism. Good consequences are those that lead to the greatest pleasure. To fully understand utilitarianism, a distinction must be made between extrinsic goods and intrinsic goods. Extrinsic goods are simply useful as a means to an end. Money is the perfect example. Intrinsic goods are goods that are valuable in and of themselves. A hedonistic utilitarian argues that pleasure is the only intrinsic good. All other goods are extrinsic; they are goods as a means to pleasure. Bentham is a pure hedonistic utilitarian. He believed that human action was motivated by the seeking of pleasure and the avoidance of pain, and that the correct ethical decision was to provide the greatest amount of pleasure for the greatest number.

Later hedonistic utilitarians tended to substitute the term "happiness" for the term "pleasure." (Indeed some philosophers would still like to distinguish the hedonistic theory that pleasure is the sole intrinsic good from eudaemonism, or the theory that happiness is the greatest good.) The chief reason for substituting happiness for pleasure was the bad connotations of "pleasure." Bentham's view that intrinsic goodness was to be understood solely in terms of pleasure received such ridicule that his philosophy was sometimes referred to as the pig philosophy. It received this name because on hedonistic grounds it seemed better to be a satisfied pig than a dissatisfied Socrates. Less pejoratively it seems that under hedonism the pleasure of artistic creation may be no better than, or even inferior to, the pleasures of wine, women, and song, so long as the pleasure of the latter is more than the former.

John Stuart Mill was particularly sensitive to the charge that utilitarianism was a pig philosophy. He believed that utilitarianism was consistent with the commonsense view that the life of a dissatisfied Socrates was better than the life of a satisfied pig. In the selection included in this chapter, Mill introduces distinctions among pleasures so that some pleasures are higher or better than others.

With respect to the measurement of pleasure, Bentham developed a hedonic calculus. The quantitative measure of any pleasurable experience is reached by considering its intensity, duration, certainty, nearness, fecundity (its ability to produce additional pleasure), purity, and extent. Bentham's hedonic calculus provided a means for evaluating matters of policy and legislation. In facing a problem of what to do, e.g., staying with your sick mother or joining the resistance to fight the Nazis, make your decision on the basis of the greatest happiness. Use the hedonic calculus to get a quantitative figure for the happiness of all relevant individuals affected by your act. Then, after adding the happiness and subtracting the unhappiness for each alternative act, perform the act that produces the most happiness. However, Bentham's calculus was so imprecise that it never caught on—even among utilitarians.

Having introduced the distinction between higher and lower pleasures, Mill could not appeal to the hedonic calculus even if he had wanted to. The calculus contained no way for determining which pleasures were higher. Mill's device was to consult a panel of experts whose members had had the experiences in question.

To those who might retort that such a panel of experts could not take the perspective of the pig, Mill argued that humans were qualitatively different from animals. Humans have a higher capacity that prevents them from desiring a lower grade of existence even if they would be happier. Mill refers to this capacity as man's sense of dignity. This sense of dignity provides the ground for qualitative distinctions among pleasures.

Contemporary utilitarianism has developed considerably since the time of Bentham and Mill. Those students familiar with economics might know that until very recently utilitarianism provided the basis for the psychological theory underlying laissez faire economics. Some economists have maintained that the maximum amount of goods and services can be squeezed from scarce resources through a free-market, competitive economy. These economists further believed that in maximizing the production of valued goods and services, happiness was maximized as well. Utilitarian analysis provided the bridge for that conclusion. Here is a simplified example: Suppose Sam goes to the grocery store for a six-pack of beer. While there, he meets his friend Jim, who is also buying a six-pack. Since both pay $2.50 for the beer, economists assume that, other things being equal, Sam and Jim receive the same satisfaction from the beer. Suppose, however, the price of beer goes up to $2.75, and Sam shifts to wine while Jim stays with the six-pack. It is then assumed that Jim must obtain more satisfaction from a $2.75 six-pack than Sam. By replacing Bentham's categories of certainty, nearness, fecundity, etc., with the measuring rod of *price,* economists have argued that an economy constructed along the lines of the postulates of free competition maximized utility (happiness). Economic theory was thus utilitarian at its core.

Moreover, both economists and many philosophers recently have substituted individual preferences for pleasure or happiness as the intrinsic good. The concept of utility is understood from this perspective not in terms of experiences or states of affairs, but rather in terms of the actual preferences of an individual as determined by his or her behavior. Accordingly, to maximize a person's utility is to provide that which he or she has chosen or would choose from among the available alternatives that might be produced. To maximize the utility of all persons affected by an action or policy is to maximize the utility of the aggregate group. This approach is indifferent as regards hedonistic or pluralistic construals of intrinsic value. What is intrinsically valuable is what individuals prefer to obtain, and utility is thus translated into the satisfaction of those needs and desires that individuals choose to satisfy.

To many this modern approach to value seems preferable to its predecessors for two main reasons. First, it bypasses disputes as to what is intrinsically good. The conflict between hedonists and nonhedonists is resolved by appealing to preferences. Second, the approach has proved fruitful in public policy decisions. It is bound to make a strong appeal to those who are both quantitatively oriented and wedded to the view that public policies should be closely related to the subjective preferences of those served by such policies and activities.

The most significant contemporary distinction between utilitarians is between act-utilitarians and rule-utilitarians. Act-utilitarians, like Bentham, argue that one ought to do those acts that produce the greatest good for the greatest number. On an act-utilitarian view, rules are mere shorthand devices that are suitable as rules of thumb but are to be abandoned on occasions when following them would not lead to the greatest good for the greatest number.

Under rule-utilitarianism, however, rules have a very different status. On rule-utilitarianism, the appropriate answer to the questionn "What ought I to do?" is, "You ought to follow the appropriate rule for that type of situation." However, the appropriate answer to the question "What rules should one adopt?" is, "One should adopt those rules which lead to the greatest good for the greatest number." Perhaps the difference between the two types of utilitarianism can be illustrated by an example. Consider the practice of grading college students for course work. Suppose that one of the rules for a grade of A in mathematics 11 is a 90 average on quizzes and examinations. An act-utilitarian would treat the rule of 90 for an A as a rule of thumb. In circumstances where utility would be maximized, one could give an A for less than 90 or a B for a grade of 90 or better. What determines each act of grading is the consequences of giving a certain grade in that particular case. The rule of A for 90 is a guide, but it is not authoritative. For the rule-utilitarian, things are different. A student with an 85 could not argue for an A on the basis of the special circumstances of his or her case alone. Rather, the student would have to show that the grading rule of A for 90 does not provide the greatest good for the greatest number. The task of the moral philosopher, on the rule-utilitarian account, is to formulate the rules that pass the utilitarian test.

In this chapter, act-utilitarianism is represented by J. J. C. Smart, and rule-utilitarianism is represented by Richard Brandt. Although some philosophers, like David Lyons, think that ultimately act- and rule-utilitarianism come to the same thing, it is easy to see how the distinction between them arose. Act-utilitarianism had been criticized because it seemed to justify patently immoral acts. Consider a classic example. A small town has been plagued by a number of particularly vicious murders. The citizenry is near panic. Heavily armed homeowners sit behind their locked windows and doors. The local sheriff knows the identity of the killer, who has fled the country. He also knows that he will be unable to convince the local populace that the danger is over. The sheriff discovers a hobo in the freight yards. Although subsequent investigation shows that the hobo is innocent, he can be convincingly made to appear guilty. Since the hobo is without family or friends, and the situation in the town is especially grave, he can be punished with a resulting increase in utility. On act-utilitarian grounds, the punishment of the innocent in such circumstances seems morally required. But punishment of the innocent seems blatantly immoral. To save utilitarianism from such counterintuitive conclusions as the punishment of innocent persons, the rule-utilitarian requires that we look to rules or practices rather than to individual acts.

What can be said about a rule that permits punishment of the innocent in circumstances like those described above? Surely such a rule could not pass the test put forward by rule-utilitarians. Such a rule would not, when followed generally, lead to the greatest good for the greatest number. The proper use of utilitarianism is to evaluate the rules, practices, and institutions of society to make sure that they lead to the public good. However, individuals within society who are contemplating what to do should follow the rules. The test for individual action is the relevant rules or practices; and the test for rules and practices is the greatest-happiness principle of utilitarianism.

As this applies to punishment, penal officials are duty bound to follow rules that provide for a fair trial, as well as the other relevant rules of criminal justice. The rules providing for a system of punishment are themselves justified by their utilitarian results. John Rawls's "Two Concepts of Rules" (Chapter 6) took this approach.

Rule-utilitarians believe that they are able to avoid the problems associated with punishment-of-the-innocent type examples. Hence a rule-utilitarian like Brandt has devoted his efforts to determining what considerations have to be taken into account if rules are to pass the utilitarian test. In the selection included here, Brandt proposes how one establishes whether a set of rules maximizes welfare.

If rule-utilitarianism avoids a host of problems like those presented by the punishment-of-the-innocent example, what can be said on behalf of act-utilitarianism? J. J. C. Smart accuses the rule-utilitarians of rule worship. If it sometimes *really* does maximize good consequences to break a rule, why shouldn't we? Not to break the rule in such cases surely is irrational, Smart argues. Moreover, a careful act-utilitarian takes account of such notions as justice, equity, and the dangers that result from breaking rules. Normally justice should be promoted, and well-entrenched moral rules should not be broken. The rule-utilitarians are certainly correct to emphasize such matters. But a careful act-utilitarian can take account of such factors and still argue that on occasion the correct ethical decision is to break the rule. To do otherwise would be unfaithful to the fundamental demand of utilitarianism, which requires that we maximize the good. In his essay, Brandt replies to this charge of rule worship.

Contemporary utilitarianism is much more sophisticated than the classical utilitarianism of Bentham and Mill. Classical utilitarianism was criticized because it ignored many considerations which were required for making an ethical decision. Among the alleged sins of omission were: (1) neglecting rules, (2) neglecting promises, (3) neglecting virtues, (4) neglecting justice, and (5) neglecting rights. Brandt's formulation of utilitarianism illustrates the extent to which theoretical utilitarianism has tried to find a place for ordinary moral practices and well-used ethical concepts. Indeed some philosophers still look for the ethical equivalent of unified-field theory; they still hope that ultimately deontology and utilitarianism can be made consistent with each other. In fact they have tried to show how a version of Kantianism leads to the utilitarian ethic. Will this effort or similar efforts succeed? It's too early to tell. In any case utilitarian theory will continue to play a major, if not decisive, role in many types of ethical decisions.

Of the Principle of Utility

Jeremy Bentham

I

Nature has placed mankind under the governance of two sovereign masters, *pain* and *pleasure*. It is for them alone to point out what we ought to do, as well as to determine what we shall do. On the one hand the standard of right and wrong, on the other the chain of causes and effects, are fastened to their throne. They govern us in all we do, in all we say, in all we think: every effort we can make to throw off our subjection will serve but to demonstrate and confirm it. In words a man may pretend to abjure their empire: but in reality he will remain subject to it all the while. The *principle of utility* recognises this subjection, and assumes it for the foundation of that system, the object of which is to rear the fabric of felicity by the hands of reason and of law. Systems which attempt to question it, deal in sounds instead of sense, in caprice instead of reason, in darkness instead of light.

But enough of metaphor and declamation: it is not by such means that moral science is to be improved.

The principle of utility is the foundation of the present work: it will be proper therefore at the outset to give an explicit and determinate account of what is meant by it. By the principle of utility is meant that principle which approves or disapproves of every action whatsoever, according to the tendency which it appears to have to augment or diminish the happiness of the party whose interest is in question: or, what is the same thing in other words, to promote or to oppose that happiness. I say of every action whatsoever; and therefore not only of every action of a private individual, but of every measure of government.

By utility is meant that property in any object, whereby it tends to produce benefit, advantage, pleasure, good, or happiness, (all this in the present case comes to the same thing) or (what comes again to the same thing) to prevent the happening of mischief, pain, evil, or unhappiness to the party whose interest is considered: if that party be the community in general, then the happiness of the community: if a particular individual, then the happiness of that individual. . . .

An action then may be said to be conformable to the principle of utility, or, for shortness sake, to utility, (meaning with respect to the community at large) when the tendency it has to augment the happiness of the community is greater than any it has to diminish it.

A measure of government (which is but a particular kind of action, performed by a particular person or persons) may be said to be conformable to or dictated by the principle of utility, when in like manner the tendency which it has to augment the happiness of the community is greater than any which it has to diminish it . . . .

A man may be said to be a partizan of the principle of utility, when the approbation

An Introduction to the Principles of Morals and Legislation, by Jeremy Bentham, Esq., M.A. Oxford: at the Clarendon Press, London: Henry Frowde, © 1879.

or disapprobation he annexes to any action, or to any measure, is determined by and proportioned to the tendency which he conceives it to have to augment or to diminish the happiness of the community: or in other words, to its conformity or unconformity to the laws or dictates of utility.

Of an action that is conformable to the principle of utility one may always say either that it is one that ought to be done, or at least that it is not one that ought not to be done. One may say also, that it is right it should be done; at least that it is not wrong it should be done: that it is a right action; at least that it is not a wrong action. When thus interpreted, the words *ought,* and *right* and *wrong,* and others of that stamp, have a meaning: when otherwise, they have none.

Has the rectitude of this principle been ever formally contested? It should seem that it had, by those who have not known what they have been meaning. Is it susceptible of any direct proof? It should seem not: for that which is used to prove everything else, cannot itself be proved: a chain of proofs must have their commencement somewhere. To give such proof is as impossible as it is needless. . . .

II

Pleasures then, and the avoidance of pains, are the *ends* which the legislator has in view: it behoves him therefore to understand their *value*. Pleasures and pains are the *instruments* he has to work with: it behoves him therefore to understand their force, which is again, in other words, their value.

To a person considered *by himself,* the value of a pleasure or pain considered *by itself,* will be greater or less, according to the four following circumstances:

1 Its *intensity*.
2 Its *duration*.
3 Its *certainty* or *uncertainty*.
4 Its *propinquity* or *remoteness*.

These are the circumstances which are to be considered in estimating a pleasure or a pain considered each of them by itself. But when the value of any pleasure or pain is considered for the purpose of estimating the tendency of any *act* by which it is produced, there are two other circumstances to be taken into the account; these are,

5 Its *fecundity,* or the chance it has of being followed by sensations of the *same* kind: that is, pleasures, if it be a pleasure: pains, if it be a pain.

6 Its *purity,* or the chance it has of *not* being followed by sensations of the *opposite* kind: that is, pains, if it be a pleasure: pleasures, if it be a pain.

These two last, however, are in strictness scarcely to be deemed properties of the pleasure or the pain itself; they are not, therefore, in strictness to be taken into the account of the value of that pleasure or that pain. They are in strictness to be deemed properties only of the act, or other event, by which such pleasure or pain has been produced; and accordingly are only to be taken into the account of the tendency of such act or such event.

To a *number* of persons, with reference to each of whom the value of a pleasure or a pain is considered, it will be greater or less, according to seven circumstances: to wit, the six preceding ones; *viz.*

1 Its *intensity*.
2 Its *duration*.
3 Its *certainty* or *uncertainty*.
4 Its *propinquity* or *remoteness*.
5 Its *fecundity*.
6 Its *purity*.

And one other; to wit:

7 Its *extent;* that is, the number of persons to whom it *extends;* or (in other words) who are affected by it.

To take an exact account then of the general tendency of any act, by which the interests of a community are affected, proceed as follows. Begin with any one person of those whose interests seem most immediately to be affected by it: and take an account,

1 Of the value of each distinguishable *pleasure* which appears to be produced by it in the *first* instance.

2 Of the value of each *pain* which appears to be produced by it in the *first* instance.

3 Of the value of each pleasure which appears to be produced by it *after* the first. This constitutes the *fecundity* of the first *pleasure* and the *impurity* of the first *pain*.

4 Of the value of each *pain* which appears to be produced by it after the first. This constitutes the *fecundity* of the first *pain,* and the *impurity* of the first pleasure.

5 Sum up all the values of all the *pleasures* on the one side, and those of all the pains on the other. The balance, if it be on the side of pleasure, will give the *good* tendency of the act upon the whole, with respect to the interests of that *individual* person; if on the side of pain, the *bad* tendency of it upon the whole.

6 Take an account of the *number* of persons whose interests appear to be concerned; and repeat the above process with respect to each. *Sum up* the numbers expressive of the degrees of *good* tendency, which the act has, with respect to each individual, in regard to whom the tendency of it is *good* upon the whole: do this again with respect to each individual, in regard to whom the tendency of it is *good* upon the whole: do this again with respect to each individual, in regard to whom the tendency of it is *bad* upon the whole. Take the *balance;* which, if on the side of *pleasure,* will give the general *good tendency* of the act, with respect to the total number or community of individuals concerned: if on the side of pain, the general *evil tendency,* with respect to the same community.

It is not to be expected that this process should be strictly pursued previously to every moral judgment, or to every legislative or judicial operation. It may, however, be always kept in view: and as near as the process actually pursued on these occasions approaches to it, so near will such process approach to the character of an exact one. . . .

III

The general object which all laws have, or ought to have, in common, is to augment the total happiness of the community; and therefore, in the first place, to exclude, as far as may be, every thing that tends to subtract from that happiness: in other words, to exclude mischief.

But all punishment is mischief: all punishment in itself is evil. Upon the principle of utility, if it ought at all to be admitted, it ought only to be admitted in as far as it promises to exclude some greater evil.

It is plain, therefore, that in the following cases punishment ought not to be inflicted.

1 Where it is *groundless:* where there is no mischief for it to prevent; the act not being mischievous upon the whole.

2 Where it must be *inefficacious:* where it cannot act so as to prevent the mischief.

3 Where it is *unprofitable,* or too *expensive:* where the mischief it would produce would be greater than what it prevented.

4 Where it is *needless:* where the mischief may be prevented, or cease of itself, without it: that is, at a cheaper rate.

CASES IN WHICH PUNISHMENT IS GROUNDLESS

These are,

1. Where there has never been any mischief: where no mischief has been produced to any body by the act in question. Of this number are those in which the act was such as might, on some occasions, be mischievous or disagreeable, but the person whose interest it concerns gave his *consent* to the performance of it. This consent, provided it be free, and fairly obtained, is the best proof that can be produced, that, to the person who gives it, no mischief, at least no immediate mischief, upon the whole, is done. For no man can be so good a judge as the man himself, what it is gives him pleasure or displeasure.

2. Where the mischief was *outweighed:* although a mischief was produced by that act, yet the same act was necessary to the production of a benefit which was of greater value than the mischief. This may be the case with any thing that is done in the way of precaution against instant calamity, as also with any thing that is done in the exercise of the several sorts of powers necessary to be established in every community, to wit, domestic, judicial, military, and supreme.

3. Where there is a certainty of an adequate compensation: and that in all cases where the offence can be committed. This supposes two things: 1. That the offence is such as admits of an adequate compensation: 2. That such a compensation is sure to be forthcoming. Of these suppositions, the latter will be found to be a merely ideal one: a supposition that cannot, in the universality here given to it, be verified by fact. It cannot, therefore, in practice, be numbered amongst the grounds of absolute impunity. It may, however, be admitted as a ground for an abatement of that punishment, which other considerations, standing by themselves, would seem to dictate.

CASES IN WHICH PUNISHMENT MUST BE INEFFICACIOUS

These are,

1. Where the penal provision is *not established* until after the act is done. Such are the cases, 1. Of an *ex-post-facto* law; where the legislator himself appoints not a punishment till after the act is done. 2. Of a sentence beyond the law; where the judge, of his own authority, appoints a punishment which the legislator had not appointed.

2. Where the penal provision, though established, is *not conveyed* to the notice of the person on whom it seems intended that it should operate. Such is the case where the law has omitted to employ any of the expedients which are necessary, to make sure that every person whatsoever, who is within the reach of the law, be apprized of all the cases whatsoever, in which (being in the station of life he is in) he can be subjected to the penalties of the law.

3. Where the penal provision, though it were conveyed to a man's notice, *could produce no effect* on him, with respect to the preventing him from engaging in any act of the *sort* in question. Such is the case, 1. In extreme *infancy;* where a man has not yet attained that state or disposition of mind in which the prospect of evils so distant as those which are held forth by the law, has the effect of influencing his conduct. 2. In *insanity;* where the person, if he has attained to that disposition, has since been deprived of it through the influence of some permanent though unseen cause. 3. In *intoxication;* where he has been deprived of it by the transient influence of a visible cause: such as the use of wine, or opium, or other drugs, that act in this manner on the nervous system: which condition is indeed neither more nor less than a temporary insanity produced by an assignable cause.

4. Where the penal provision (although, being conveyed to the party's notice, it might very well prevent his engaging in acts of the sort in question, provided he knew that it related to those acts) could not have this effect, with regard to the *individual* act he is about to engage in: to wit, because he knows not that it is of the number of those to which the penal provision relates. This may happen, 1. In the case of *unintentionality;* where he intends not to engage, and thereby knows not that he is about to engage, in the *act* in which eventually he is about to engage. 2. In the case of *unconsciousness;* where, although he may know that he is about to engage in the *act* itself, yet, from not knowing all the material *circumstances* attending it, he knows not of the *tendency* it has to produce that mischief, in contemplation of which it has been made penal in most instances. . . .

CASES WHERE PUNISHMENT IS UNPROFITABLE

These are,

1. Where, on the one hand, the nature of the offence, on the other hand, that of the punishment, are, *in the ordinary state of things,* such, that when compared together, the evil of the latter will turn out to be greater than that of the former.

Now the evil of the punishment divides itself into four branches, by which so many different sets of persons are affected. 1. The evil of *coercion* or *restraint:* or the pain which it gives a man not to be able to do the act, whatever it be, which by the apprehension of the punishment he is deterred from doing. This is felt by those by whom the law is *observed*. 2. The evil of *apprehension:* or the pain which a man, who has exposed himself to punishment, feels at the thoughts of undergoing it. This is felt by those by whom the law has been *broken,* and who feel themselves in *danger* of its being executed upon them. 3. The evil of *sufferance:* or the pain which a man feels, in virtue of the punishment itself, from the time when he begins to undergo it. This is felt by those by whom the law is broken, and upon whom it comes actually to be executed. 4. The pain of sympathy, and the other *derivative* evils resulting to the persons who are in *connection* with the several classes of original sufferers just mentioned. Now of these four lots of evil, the first will be greater or less, according to the nature of the act from which the party is restrained: the second and third according to the nature of the punishment which stands annexed to that offence.

On the other hand, as to the evil of the offence, this will also, of course, be greater or less, according to the nature of each offence. The proportion between the one evil and the other will therefore be different in the case of each particular offence. The cases, therefore, where punishment is unprofitable on this ground, can by no other means be discovered, than by an examination of each particular offense. . . .

CASES WHERE PUNISHMENT IS NEEDLESS

These are,

Where the purpose of putting an end to the practice may be attained as effectually at a cheaper rate: by instruction, for instance, as well as by terror: by informing the understanding, as well as by exercising an immediate influence on the will. This seems to be the case with respect to all those offences which consist in the disseminating pernicious principles in matters of *duty;* of whatever kind the duty be; whether political, or moral, or religious. And this, whether such principles be disseminated *under,* or even *without,* a sincere persuasion of their being beneficial. I say, even *without:* for though in such a case it is not instruction that can prevent the writer from endeavouring to inculcate his principles, yet it may the readers from adopting them: without which, his endeavouring to inculcate them will do no harm. In such a case, the sovereign will commonly have little need to take an active part: if it be the interest of *one* individual to inculcate principles that are pernicious, it will as surely be the interest of *other* individuals to expose them. But if the sovereign must needs take a part in the controversy, the pen is the proper weapon to combat error with, not the sword.

Utilitarianism

John Stuart Mill

I

. . . The creed which accepts as the foundation of morals, Utility, or the Greatest Happiness Principle, holds that actions are right in proportion as they tend to promote happiness, wrong as they tend to produce the reverse of happiness. By happiness is intended pleasure, and the absence of pain; by unhappiness, pain, and the privation of pleasure. To give a clear view of the moral standard set up by the theory, much more requires to be said; in particular, what things it includes in the ideas of pain and pleasure; and to what extent this is left an open question. But these supplementary explanations do not affect the theory of life on which this theory of morality is grounded—namely, that pleasure, and freedom from pain, are the only things desirable as ends; and that all desirable things (which are as numerous in the utilitarian as in any other scheme) are desirable either for the pleasure inherent in themselves, or as means to the promotion of pleasure and the prevention of pain.

Now, such a theory of life excites in many minds, and among them in some of the most estimable in feeling and purpose, inveterate dislike. To suppose that life has (as they express it) no higher end than pleasure—no better and nobler object of desire and pursuit—they designate as utterly mean and groveling; as a doctrine worthy only of swine, to whom the followers of Epicurus were, at a very early period, contemptuously likened; and modern holders of the doctrine are occasionally made the subject of equally polite comparisons by its German, French, and English assailants.

When thus attacked, the Epicureans have always answered, that it is not they, but their accusers, who represent human nature in a degrading light; since the accusation supposes human beings to be capable of no pleasures except those of which swine are capable. If this supposition were true, the charge could not be gainsaid, but would then be no longer an imputation: for if the sources of pleasure were precisely the same to human beings and to swine, the rule of life which is good enough for the one would be good enough for the other. The comparison of the Epicurean life to that of beasts is felt as degrading, precisely because a beast's pleasures do not satisfy a human being's conceptions of happiness. Human beings have faculties more elevated than the animal appetites, and when once made conscious of them, do not regard anything as happiness which does not include their gratification. I do not, indeed, consider the Epicureans to have been by any means faultless in drawing out their scheme of consequences from the utilitarian principle. To do this in any sufficient manner, many Stoic, as well as Christian elements require to be included. But there is no known Epicurean theory of life which does not assign to the pleasures of the intellect, of the

Utilitarianism by John Stuart Mill. Published by Longman's, Green, and Co. © 1907 New York.

feelings and imagination, and of the moral sentiments, a much higher value as pleasures than to those of mere sensation. It must be admitted, however, that utilitarian writers in general have placed the superiority of mental over bodily pleasures chiefly in the greater permanency, safety, uncostliness, &c., of the former—that is, in their circumstantial advantages rather than in their intrinsic nature. And on all these points utilitarians have fully proved their case; but they might have taken the other, and, as it may be called, higher ground, with entire consistency. It is quite compatible with the principle of utility to recognise the fact, that some *kinds* of pleasure are more desirable and more valuable than others. It would be absurd that while, in estimating all other things, quality is considered as well as quantity, the estimation of pleasures should be supposed to depend on quantity alone.

If I am asked, what I mean by difference of quality in pleasures, or what makes one pleasure more valuable than another, merely as a pleasure, except its being greater in amount, there is but one possible answer. Of two pleasures, if there be one to which all or almost all who have experience of both give a decided preference, irrespective of any feeling of moral obligation to prefer it, that is the more desirable pleasure. If one of the two is, by those who are competently acquainted with both, placed so far above the other that they prefer it, even though knowing it to be attended with a greater amount of discontent, and would not resign it for any quantity of the other pleasure which their nature is capable of, we are justified in ascribing to the preferred enjoyment a superiority in quality, so far outweighing quantity as to render it, in comparison, of small account.

Now it is an unquestionable fact that those who are equally acquainted with, and equally capable of appreciating and enjoying both, do give a most marked preference to the manner of existence which employs their higher faculties. Few human creatures would consent to be changed into any of the lower animals, for a promise of the fullest allowance of a beast's pleasures; no intelligent human being would consent to be a fool, no instructed person would be an ignoramus, no person of feeling and conscience would be selfish and base, even though they should be persuaded that the fool, the dunce, or the rascal is better satisfied with his lot than they are with theirs. They would not resign what they possess more than he, for the most complete satisfaction of all the desires which they have in common with him. If they ever fancy they would, it is only in cases of unhappiness so extreme, that to escape from it they would exchange their lot for almost any other, however undesirable in their own eyes. A being of higher faculties requires more to make him happy, is capable probably of more acute suffering , and is certainly accessible to it at more points, than one of an inferior type; but in spite of these liabilities, he can never really wish to sink into what he feels to be a lower grade of existence. . . . Whoever supposes that this preference takes place at a sacrifice of happiness—that the superior being, in anything like equal circumstances, is not happier than the inferior—confounds the two very different ideas, of happiness, and content. It is indisputable that the being whose capacities of enjoyment are low, has the greatest chance of having them fully satisfied; and a highly-endowed being will always feel that any happiness which he can look for, as the world is constituted, is imperfect. But he can learn to bear its imperfections, if they are at all bearable; and they will not make him envy the being who is indeed unconscious of the imperfections, but only because he feels not at all the good which those imperfections qualify. It is better to be a human being dissatisfied than a pig satisfied; better to be Socrates dissatisfied than a fool satisfied. And if the fool, or the pig, is of a different opinion, it is because they only know their own side of the question. The other party to the comparison knows both sides. . . .

From this verdict of the only competent judges, I apprehend there can be no appeal. On a question which is the best worth having of two pleasures, or which of two modes of existence is the most grateful to the feelings, apart from its moral attributes and from its consequences, the judgment of those who are qualified by knowledge of both, or, if they differ, that of the majority among them, must be admitted as final. And there needs be the less hesitation to accept this judgment respecting the quality of pleasures, since there is no other tribunal to be referred to even on the question of quantity. What means are there of determining which is the acutest of two pains, or the intensest of two pleasurable sensations, except the general suffrage of those who are familiar with both? Neither pains nor pleasure are homogeneous, and pain is always heterogeneous with pleasure. What is there to decide whether a particular pleasure is worth purchasing at the cost of a particular pain, except the feelings and judgment of the experienced? . . .

II

It has already been remarked, that questions of ultimate ends do not admit of proof, in the ordinary acceptation of the term. To be incapable of proof by reasoning is common to all first principles; to the first premises of our knowledge, as well as to those of our conduct. But the former, being matters of fact, may be the subject of a direct appeal to the faculties which judge of fact—namely, our senses, and our internal consciousness. Can an appeal be made to the same faculties on questions of practical ends? Or by what other faculty is cognizance taken of them?

Questions about ends are, in other words, questions what things are desirable. The utilitarian doctrine is, that happiness is desirable, and the only thing desirable, as an end; all other things being only desirable as means to that end. What ought to be required of this doctrine—what conditions is it requisite that the doctrine should fulfil—to make good its claim to be believed?

The only proof capable of being given that an object is visible, is that people actually see it. The only proof that a sound is audible, is that people hear it: and so of the other sources of our experience. In like manner, I apprehend, the sole evidence it is possible to produce that anything is desirable, is that people do actually desire it. If the end which the utilitarian doctrine proposes to itself were not, in theory and in practice, acknowledged to be an end, nothing could ever convince any person that it was so. No reason can be given why the general happiness is desirable, except that each person, so far as he believes it to be attainable, desires his own happiness. This, however, being a fact, we have not only all the proof which the case admits of, but all which it is possible to require, the happiness is a good: that each person's happiness is a good to that person, and the general happiness, therefore, a good to the aggregate of all persons. Happiness has made out its title as *one* of the ends of conduct, and consequently one of the criteria of morality.

But it has not, by this alone, proved itself to be the sole criterion. To do that, it would seem, by the same rule, necessary to show, not only that people desire happiness, but that they never desire anything else. Now it is palpable that they do desire things which, in common language, are decidedly distinguished from happiness. They desire, for example, virtue, and the absence of vice, no less really than pleasure and the absence of pain. The desire of virtue is not as universal, but it is as authentic a fact, as the desire of happiness. And hence the opponents of the utilitarian standard deem that they have a right to infer that there are other ends of human action besides happiness, and that happiness is not the standard of approbation and disapprobation.

But does the utilitarian doctrine deny that people desire virtue, or maintain that virtue is not a thing to be desired? the very reverse. . . . The ingredients of happiness are very various, and each of them is desirable in itself, and not merely when considered as swelling an aggregate. The principle of utility does not mean that any given pleasure, as music, for instance, or any given exemption from pain, as for example, health, are to be looked upon as means to a collective something termed happiness, and to be desired on that account. They are desired and desirable in and for themselves; besides being means, they are a part of the end. Virtue, according to the utilitarian doctrine, is not naturally and originally part of the end, but it is capable of becoming so; and in those who love it disinterestedly it has become so, and is desired and cherished, not as a means to happiness, but as a part of their happiness.

To illustrate this farther, we may remember that virtue is not the only thing, originally a means, and which if it were not a means to anything else, would be and remain indifferent, but which by association with what it is a means to, comes to be desired for itself, and that too with the utmost intensity. What, for example, shall we say of the love of money? There is nothing originally more desirable about money than about any heap of glittering pebbles. Its worth is solely that of the things which it will buy; the desires for other things than itself, which it is a means of gratifying. Yet the love of money is not only one of the strongest moving forces of human life, but money is, in many cases, desired in and for itself; the desire to possess it is often stronger than the desire to use it, and goes on increasing when all the desires which point to ends beyond it, to be compassed by it, are falling off. It may then be said truly, that money is desired not for the sake of an end, but as part of the end. From being a means to happiness, it has come to be itself a principal ingredient of the individual's conception of happiness. The same may be said of the majority of the great objects of human life—power, for example, or fame; except that to each of these there is a certain amount of immediate pleasure annexed, which has at least the semblance of being naturally inherent in them; a thing which cannot be said of money. Still, however, the strongest natural attraction, both of power and of fame, is the immense aid they give to the attainment of our other wishes; and it is the strong association thus generated between them and all our objects of desire, which gives to the direct desire of them the intensity it often assumes, so as in some characters to surpass in strength all other desires. In these cases the means have become a part of the end, and a more important part of it than any of the things which they are means to. What was once desired as an instrument for the attainment of happiness, has come to be desired for its own sake. In being desired for its own sake it is, however, desired as *part* of happiness. The person is made, or thinks he would be made, happy by its mere possession; and is made unhappy by failure to obtain it. The desire of it is not a different thing from the desire of happiness, any more than the love of music, or the desire of health. They are included in happiness. They are some of the elements of which the desire of happiness is made up. Happiness is not an abstract idea, but a concrete whole; and these are some of its parts. And the utilitarian standard sanctions and approves their being so. Life would be a poor thing, very ill provided with sources of happiness, if there were not this provision of nature, by which things originally indifferent, but conducive to, or otherwise associated with, the satisfaction of our primitive desires, become in themselves sources of pleasure more valuable than the primitive pleasures, both in permanency, in the space of human existence that they are capable of covering, and even in intensity.

Virtue, according to the utilitarian conception, is a good of this description. There was no original desire of it, or motive to it, save its conduciveness to pleasure, and especially to protection from pain. But through the association thus formed, it may be felt a good in itself, and desired as such with as great intensity as any other good; and with this difference between it and the love of money, of power, or of fame, that all of these may, and often do, render the individual noxious to the other members of the society to which he belongs, whereas there is nothing which makes him so much a blessing to them as the cultivation of the disinterested love of virtue. And conse-quently, the utilitarian standard, while it tolerates and approves those other acquired desires, up to the point beyond which they would be more injurious to the general happiness than promotive of it, enjoins and requires the cultivation of the love of virtue up to the greatest strength possible, as being above all things important to the general happiness.

It results from the preceding considerations, that there is in reality nothing desired except happiness. Whatever is desired otherwise than as a means to some end beyond itself, and ultimately to happiness, is desired as itself a part of happiness, and is not desired for itself until it has become so. Those who desire virtue for its own sake, desire it either because the consciousness of it is a pleasure, or because the conscious-ness of being without it is a pain, or for both reasons united; as in truth the pleasure and pain seldom exist separately, but almost always together, the same person feeling pleasure in the degree of virtue attained, and pain in not having attained more. If one of these gave him no pleasure, and the other no pain, he would not love or desire virtue, or would desire it only for the other benefits which it might produce to himself or to persons whom he cared for.

We have now, then, an answer to the question, of what sort of proof the principle of utility is susceptible. If the opinion, which I have now stated is psychologically true—if human nature is so constituted as to desire nothing which is not either a part of happiness or a means of happiness, we can have no other proof, and we require no other, that these are the only things desirable. If so, happiness is the sole end of human action, and the promotion of it the test by which to judge of all human conduct;

from whence it necessarily follows that it must be the criterion of morality, since a part is included in the whole.

And now to decide whether this is really so; whether mankind do desire nothing for itself but that which is a pleasure to them, or of which the absence is a pain; we have evidently arrived at a question of fact and experience, dependent, like all similar questions, upon evidence. It can only be determined by practised self-consciousness and self-observation, assisted by observation of others. I believe that these sources of evidence, impartially consulted, will declare that desiring a thing and finding it pleasant, aversion to it and thinking of it as painful, are phenomena entirely inseparable, or rather two parts of the same phenomenon; in strictness of language, two different modes of naming the same psychological fact: that to think of an object as desirable (unless for the sake of its consequences), and to think of it as pleasant, are one and the same thing; and that to desire anything, except in proportion as the idea of it is pleasant, is a physical and metaphysical impossibility. . . .

Act-Utilitarianism

J. J. C. Smart

I

The system of normative ethics which I am here concerned to defend is, as I have said earlier, *act*-utilitarianism. Act-utilitarianism is to be contrasted with rule-utilitarianism. Act-utilitarianism is the view that the rightness or wrongness of an action is to be judged by the consequences, good or bad, of the action itself. Rule-utilitarianism is the view that the rightness or wrongness of an action is to be judged by the goodness and badness of the consequences of a rule that everyone should perform the action in like circumstances. . . .

I have argued elsewhere the objections to rule-utilitarianism as compared with act-utilitarianism. Briefly they boil down to the accusation of rule worship: the rule-utilitarian presumably advocates his principle because he is ultimately concerned with human happiness: why then should he advocate abiding by a rule when he knows that it will not in the present case be most beneficial to abide by it? The reply that in most cases it is most beneficial to abide by the rule seems irrelevant. And so is the reply that it would be better that everybody should abide by the rule than that nobody should. This is to suppose that the only alternative to 'everybody does A' is 'no one does A'. But clearly we have the possibility 'some people do A and some don't'. Hence to refuse to break a generally beneficial rule in those cases in which it is not most beneficial to obey it seems irrational and to be a case of rule worship.

The type of utilitarianism which I shall advocate will, then, be act-utilitarianism, not rule-utilitarianism. . . .

Utilitarianism: For and Against. J. J. C. Smart and Bernard Williams, © 1973 by Cambridge University Press, New York.

II

An act-utilitarian judges the rightness or wrongness of actions by the goodness and badness of their consequences. But is he to judge the goodness and badness of the consequences of an action solely by their pleasantness and unpleasantness? Bentham, who thought that quantity of pleasure being equal, the experience of playing pushpin was as good as that of reading poetry, could be classified as a hedonistic act-utilitarian. Moore, who believed that some states of mind, such as those of acquiring knowledge, had intrinsic value quite independent of their pleasantness, can be called an ideal utilitarian. Mill seemed to occupy an intermediate position. He held that there are higher and lower pleasures. This seems to imply that pleasure is a necessary condition for goodness but that goodness depends on other qualities of experience than pleasantness and unpleasantness. I propose to call Mill a quasi-ideal utilitarian. . . .

What Bentham, Mill and Moore are all agreed on is that the rightness of an action is to be judged solely by consequences, states of affairs brought about by the action. Of course we shall have to be careful here not to construe 'state of affairs' so widely that any ethical doctrine becomes utilitarian. For if we did so we would not be saying anything at all in advocating utilitarianism. If, for example, we allowed 'the state of having just kept a promise', then a deontologist who said we should keep promises simply because they are promises would be a utilitarian. And we do not wish to allow this.

According to the type of non-cognitivist (or subjectivist) ethics that I am assuming, the function of the words 'ought' and 'good' is primarily to express approval, or in other words, to commend. With 'ought' we commend actions. With 'good' we may commend all sorts of things, but here I am concerned with 'good' as used to commend states of affairs or consequences of actions. Suppose we could know with certainty the total consequences of two alternative actions A and B, and suppose that A and B are the only possible actions open to us. Then in deciding whether we ought to do A or B, the act-utilitarian would ask whether the total consequences of A are better than those of B, or vice versa, or whether the total consequences are equal. That is, he commends A rather than B if he thinks that the total consequences of A are better than those of B. But to say 'better' is itself to commend. So the act-utilitarian has to do a double evaluation or piece of commending. First of all he has to evaluate consequences. Then on the basis of his evaluation of consequences he has to evaluate the actions A and B which would lead to these two sets of consequences. It is easy to fail to notice that this second evaluation is needed, but we can see that it is necessary if we remind ourselves of the following fact. This is that a non-utilitarian, say a philosopher of the type of Sir David Ross, might agree with us in the evaluation of the relative merits of the total sets of consequences of the actions A and B and yet disagree with us about whether we ought to do A or B. He might agree with us in the evaluation of total consequences but disagree with us in the evaluation of possible actions. He might say: "The total consequences of A are better than the total consequences of B, but it would be *unjust* to do A, for you *promised* to do B."

My chief concern in this study is with the *second* type of evaluation: the evaluation of actions. The utilitarian addresses himself to people who very likely agree with him as to what consequences are good ones, but who disagree with him about the principle that what we ought to do is to produce the best consequences. For a reason, which will appear presently, the difference between ideal and hedonistic utilitarianism in most cases will not usually lead to a serious disagreement about what ought to be done in practice. In this section, however, I wish to clear the ground by saying something about the *first* type of evaluation, the evaluation of consequences. It is with respect to this evaluation that Bentham, Mill and Moore differ from one another. Let us consider Mill's contention that it is 'better to be Socrates dissatisfied than a fool satisfied'. Mill holds that pleasure is not to be our sole criterion for evaluating consequences: the state of mind of Socrates might be less pleasurable than that of the fool, but, according to Mill, Socrates would be happier than the fool.

It is necessary to observe, first of all, that a purely hedonistic utilitarian, like Bentham, might agree with Mill in preferring the experiences of discontented philosophers to those of contented fools. His preference for the philosopher's state of mind, however, would not be an *intrinsic* one. He would say that the discontented philosopher is a useful agent in society and that the existence of Socrates is responsible for an improvement in the lot of humanity generally. Consider two brothers. One may be of a docile and easy temperament: he may lead a supremely contented and unambitious life, enjoying himself hugely. The other brother may be ambitious, may stretch his talents to the full, may strive for scientific success and academic honours, and may discover some invention or some remedy for disease or improvement in agriculture which will enable innumerable men of easy temperament to lead a contented life, whereas otherwise they would have been thwarted by poverty, disease or hunger. Or he may make some advance in pure science which will later have beneficial practical applications. Or, again, he may write poetry which will solace the leisure hours and stimulate the brains of practical men or scientists, thus indirectly leading to an improvement in society. That is, the pleasures of poetry or mathematics may be *extrinsically* valuable in a way in which those of pushpin or sun-bathing may not be. Though the poet or mathematician may be discontented, society as a whole may be the more contented for his presence.

Again, a man who enjoys pushpin is likely eventually to become bored with it, whereas the man who enjoys poetry is likely to retain this interest throughout his life. Moreover the reading of poetry may develop imagination and sensitivity, and so as a result of his interest in poetry a man may be able to do more for the happiness of others than if he had played pushpin and let his brain deteriorate. In short, both for the man immediately concerned and for others, the pleasures of poetry are, to use Bentham's word, more *fecund* than those of pushpin. . . .

So much for the issue between Bentham and Mill. What about that between Mill and Moore? Could a pleasurable state of mind have no intrinsic value at all, or perhaps even a *negative* intrinsic value? Are there pleasurable states of mind towards which we have an unfavourable attitude, even though we disregard their consequences? In order to decide this question let us imagine a universe consisting of one sentient being only, who falsely believes that there are other sentient beings and that they are undergoing exquisite torment. So far from being distressed by the thought, he takes a great delight in these imagined sufferings. Is this better or worse than a universe containing no sentient being at all? Is it worse, again, than a universe containing only one sentient being with the same beliefs as before but who sorrows at the imagined tortures of his fellow creatures? I suggest, as against Moore, that the universe containing the deluded sadist is the preferable one. After all he is happy, and since there is no other sentient being, what harm can he do? . . .

It is difficult, I admit, not to feel an immediate repugnance at the thought of the deluded sadist. If throughout our childhood we have been given an electric shock whenever we had tasted cheese, then cheese would have become immediately distasteful to us. Our repugnance to the sadist arises, naturally enough, because in our universe sadists invariably do harm. If we lived in a universe in which by some extraordinary laws of psychology a sadist was always confounded by his own knavish tricks and invariably did a great deal of good, then we should feel better disposed towards the sadistic mentality. . . . Normally when we call a thing 'bad' we mean indifferently to express a dislike for it in itself or to express a dislike for what it leads to. When a state of mind is sometimes extrinsically good and sometimes extrinsically bad, we find it easy to distinguish between our intrinsic and extrinsic preferences for instances of it, but when a state of mind is always, or almost always, extrinsically bad, it is easy for us to confuse an extrinsic distaste for it with an intrinsic one. If we allow for this, it does not seem so absurd to hold that there are no pleasures which are intrinsically bad. Pleasures are bad only because they cause harm to the person who has them or to other people. But if anyone likes to disagree with me about this I do not feel very moved to argue the point. Such a disagreement about ultimate ends is not likely to lead to any disagreement in practice. For in all actual cases there are sufficient extrinsic reasons for abhorring sadism and similar states of mind. *Approximate* agreement about ultimate ends is often quite enough for rational and co-operative moral discourse. In practical cases the possibility of factual disagreement about what causes produce what effects is likely to be overwhelmingly more important than disagreement in ultimate ends between hedonistic and ideal utilitarians. . . .

III

Another type of ultimate disagreement between utilitarians, whether hedonistic or ideal, can arise over whether we should try to maximize the *average* happiness of human beings (or the average goodness of their states of mind) or whether we should try to maximize the *total* happiness or goodness. I have not yet elucidated the concept of total happiness, and you may regard it as a suspect notion. But for present purposes I shall put it in this way: Would you be quite indifferent between (a) a universe containing only one million happy sentient beings, all equally happy, and (b) a universe containing two million happy beings, each neither more nor less happy than any in the first universe? Or would you, as a humane and sympathetic person, give a preference to the second universe? I myself cannot help feeling a preference for the second universe. But if someone feels the other way I do not know how to argue with him. It looks as though we have yet another possibility of disagreement within a general utilitarian framework.

This type of disagreement might have practical relevance. It might be important in discussions of the ethics of birth control. This is not to say that the utilitarian who values total, rather than average, happiness may not have potent arguments in favour of birth control. But he will need more arguments to convince himself than will the other type of utilitarian.

In most cases the difference between the two types of utilitarianism will not lead to disagreement in practice. For in most cases the most effective way to increase the total happiness is to increase the average happiness, and vice versa. . . .

I shall now state the act-utilitarian doctrine. Purely for simplicity of exposition I shall put it forward in a broadly hedonistic form. If anyone values states of mind such as knowledge independently of their pleasurableness he can make appropriate verbal alterations to convert it from hedonistic to ideal utilitarianism. And I shall not here take sides on the issue between hedonistic and quasi-ideal utilitarianism. I shall concern myself with the evaluation signified by 'ought' in 'one ought to do that which will produce the best consequences', and leave to one side the evaluation signified by the word 'best'.

Let us say, then, that the only reason for performing an action A rather than an alternative action B is that doing A will make mankind (or, perhaps, all sentient beings) happier than will doing B. Here I put aside the consideration that in fact we can have only probable belief about the effects of our actions, and so our reason should be more precisely stated as that doing A will produce more probable benefit than will doing B. . . . This is so simple and natural a doctrine that we can surely expect that many of my readers will have at least some propensity to agree. For I am talking, as I said earlier, to sympathetic and benevolent men, that is, to men who desire the happiness of mankind. Since they have a favourable attitude to the general happiness, surely they will have a tendency to submit to an ultimate moral principle which does no more than express this attitude. It is true that these men, being human, will also have purely selfish attitudes. Either these attitudes will be in harmony with the general happiness (in cases where everyone's looking after his own interests promotes the maximum general happiness) or they will not be in harmony with the general happiness, in which case they will largely cancel one another out, and so could not be made the basis of an interpersonal discussion anyway. It is possible, then, that many sympathetic and benevolent people depart from or fail to attain a utilitarian ethical principle only under the stress of tradition, of superstition, or of unsound philosophical reasoning. If this hypothesis should turn out to be correct, at least as far as these readers are concerned, then the utilitarian may contend that there is no need for him to defend his position directly, save by stating it in a consistent manner, and by showing that common objections to it are unsound. After all, it expresses an ultimate attitude, not a liking for something merely as a means to something else. Save for attempting to remove confusions and discredit superstitions which may get in the way of clear moral thinking, he cannot, of course, appeal to argument and must rest his hopes on the good feeling of his readers. If any reader is not a sympathetic and benevolent man, then of course it cannot be expected that he will have an ultimate pro-attitude to human happiness in general. . . .

The utilitarian's ultimate moral principle, let it be remembered, expresses the sentiment not of altruism but of benevolence, the agent counting himself neither more nor less than any other person. Pure altruism cannot be made the basis of a universal moral discussion because it might lead different people to different and perhaps incompatible courses of action, even though the circumstances were identical. When two men each try to let the other through a door first a deadlock results. Altruism could hardly commend itself to those of a scientific, and hence universalistic, frame of mind. If you count in my calculations why should I not count in your calculations? And why should I pay more attention to my calculations than to yours? Of course we often tend to praise and honour altruism even more than generalized benevolence. This is because people too often err on the side of selfishness, and so altruism is a fault on the right side. If we can make a man try to be an altruist he may succeed as far as acquiring a generalized benevolence.

Suppose we could predict the future consequences of actions with certainty. Then it would be possible to say that the total future consequences of action A are such-and-such and that the total future consequences of action B are so-and-so. In order to help someone to decide whether to do A or to do B, we could say to him: 'Envisage the total consequences of A, and think them over carefully and imaginatively. Now envisage the total consequences of B, and think them over carefully. As a benevolent and humane man, and thinking of yourself just as one man among others, would you prefer the consequences of A or those of B? That is, we are asking for a comparison of one (present and future) *total* situation with another (present and future) *total* situation. So far we are not asking for a *summation* or *calculation* of pleasures or happiness. We are asking only for a comparison of total situations. And it seems clear that we can frequently make such a comparison and say that one total situation is better than another. For example few people would not prefer a total situation in which a million people are well-fed, well-clothed, free of pain, doing interesting and enjoyable work, and enjoying the pleasures of conversation, study, business, art, humour, and so on, to a total situation where there are ten thousand such people only, or perhaps 999,999 such people plus one man with toothache, or neurotic, or shivering with cold. In general, we can sum things up by saying that if we are humane, kindly, benevolent people, we want as many people as possible now and in the future to be as happy as possible. Someone might object that we cannot envisage the total future situation, because this stretches into infinity. In reply to this we may say that it does not stretch into infinity, as all sentient life on earth will ultimately be extinguished, and furthermore we do not normally in practice need to consider very remote consequences, as these in the end approximate rapidly to zero like the furthermost ripples on a pond after a stone has been dropped into it.

But do the remote consequences of an action diminish to zero? Suppose that two people decide whether to have a child or remain childless. Let us suppose that they decide to have the child, and that they have a limitless succession of happy descendants. The remote consequences do not seem to get less. Not at any rate if these people are Adam and Eve. The difference would be between the end of the human race and a limitless accretion of human happiness, generation by generation. The Adam and Eve example shows that the 'ripples on the pond' postulate is not needed in every case for a rational utilitarian decision. If we had some reason for thinking that every generation would be more happy than not we would not (in the Adam and Eve sort of case) need to be worried that the remote consequences of our action would be in detail unknown. The necessity for the 'ripples in the pond' postulate comes from the fact that usually we do not know whether remote consequences will be good or bad. Therefore we cannot know what to do unless we can assume that remote consequences can be left out of account. This can often be done. Thus if we consider two actual parents, instead of Adam and Eve, then they need not worry about thousands of years hence. Not, at least, if we assume that there will be ecological forces determining the future population of the world. If these parents do not have remote descendants, then other people will presumably have more than they would otherwise. And there is no reason to suppose that my descendants would be more or less happy than yours. We must note, then, that unless we are dealing with 'all or nothing' situations (such as the Adam and Eve one, or that of someone in a position to end human life altogether) we need some sort of 'ripples in the pond' postulate to make utilitarianism workable in practice. I do not know how to prove such a postulate, though it seems plausible enough. If it is not accepted, not only utilitarianism, but also deontological systems like that of Sir David Ross, who at least admits beneficence as one *prima facie* duty among the others, will be fatally affected.

Sometimes, of course, more needs to be said. For example one course of action may make some people very happy and leave the rest as they are or perhaps slightly less happy. Another course of action may make all men rather more happy than before but no one very happy. Which course of action makes mankind happier on the whole? Again, one course of action may make it highly probable that everyone will be made a little happier whereas another course of action may give us a much smaller probability that everyone will be made very much happier. In the third place, one course of action may make everyone happy in a pig-like way, whereas another course of action may make a few people happy in a highly complex and intellectual way.

It seems therefore that we have to weigh the maximizing of happiness against equitable distribution, to weigh probabilities with happiness, and to weigh the intellectual and other qualities of states of mind with their pleasurableness. Are we not therefore driven back to the necessity of some calculus of happiness? Can we just say: "envisage two total situations and tell me which you prefer"? If this were possible, of course there would be no need to talk of summing happiness or of a calculus. All we should have to do would be to put total situations in an order of preference. . . .

We have already considered the question of intellectual versus non-intellectual pleasures and activities. This is irrelevant to the present issue because there seems to be no reason why the ideal or quasi-ideal utilitarian cannot use the method of envisaging total situations just as much as the hedonistic utilitarian. It is just a matter of envisaging various alternative total situations, stretching out into the future, and saying which situation one prefers. The non-hedonistic utilitarian may evaluate the total situations differently from the hedonistic utilitarian, in which case there will be an ultimate ethical disagreement. This possibility of ultimate disagreement is always there, though we have given reasons for suspecting that it will not frequently lead to important disagreement in practice. . . .

The Concept of a Pluralistic Welfare-Maximizing Moral System

Richard B. Brandt

It is possible that a system of several moral rules, properly selected, might maximize welfare, and hence be the kind of moral system fully rational persons would support. This [paper] will explore that possibility.

Such a conception is not novel. It was put forward by Bishop Berkeley and theological utilitarians: the idea was that God wishes to maximize the happiness of sentient creation and to that end has promulgated certain laws fitted to that purpose, and has revealed them to man either in the Bible or through conscience or reason in some sense.[1] An analogue of this theological moral utilitarianism has been devised by utilitarian reformers of the criminal law including Bentham. They have thought of the ideal criminal code as a complex system of prohibitions, penalties, and procedures such that the operation of the whole system will maximize welfare.

We have, then, a general idea of such a plural moral system. This [paper] will work out some details. (1) First it will review the ways in which moral codes can differ: the various parts of a moral code which can be varied so as to get a welfare-maximizing system as a whole. (2) It will discuss in more detail how an ideal system of injunctions should be identified: what they will regulate, the level of abstraction at which they should be framed, whether and how the several rules may be assigned weights and how probability estimates might be used in applying them. It will show how historical moral codes can serve as a guide in fixing the basic rules of an 'ideal' code. All of this discussion will provide reason for thinking that the currency of a code so devised would in fact maximize social welfare. (3) It will conclude by replying to some apparently serious objections.

I. THE VARIABLE FEATURES OF PLURAL MORAL SYSTEMS

i. Intrinsic Motivation

The most important part of a moral code is the basic desires for (aversions to) certain kinds of behaviour for themselves, like the prohibitions and injunctions of the criminal and civil law. A basic aversion to some form of behaviour will, in English, normally be expressed by 'It is (prima facie) wrong to . . . ' (The words 'prima facie' indicate that the prohibition can be overridden by stronger prima facie injunctions.) These motivations can vary in three respects: the kind of behaviour involved; whether the behaviour is desired or is aversive; and the strength of the motivation. The kinds of behaviour in question need not be simple. Take promises. A code may require that promises be kept, prima facie, but only certain kinds of promise, perhaps ones not

A Theory of the Good and the Right by Richard B. Brandt (1979) pp. 286–301, 305. Reprinted by permission of Oxford University Press.

made under duress, or ones not made on the basis of a misrepresentation of facts given deliberately in order to extract the promise. Such exceptions might be made because it would be socially harmful for people to feel obligated to keep such promises.

Not all logically possible 'rules of obligation' of this sort are causally possible. Obviously the basic motivations cannot be very numerous, since they have to be instituted by a process of conditioning, or some such device (e.g. the use of prestigious persons as models). Again, the complexity of the conduct enjoined or banned is limited by the intellectual capacities of the average person. What these rules may require is limited by the strain of self-interest in everyone, and the specific desires and aversions bound to develop in nearly everyone, including some degree of benevolence; and they are also limited by the fact that these other desires are prior in the sense that the basic moral motivations can be acquired by conditioning only by building essentially on them.

ii.   Justifications

What if these basic motivations conflict in a given situation? What if the basic code prohibits both breaking promises and injuring others, but in a given case injuring another can be avoided only by breaking a promise? A complete moral system will ideally answer these questions. How can this be done? One possibility is that the particular built-in strength of each motivation decides the issue in each case in favour of the stronger: so a person 'ought' to do what he is most motivated (morally) to do. These strengths could be built in so that conflicts of obligations decided in this way would come out as the code-builder wanted; a utilitarian, for instance, might reflect on how great an injury to others might just balance the loss from a breach of promise in cases of a certain type, and set the motivation to avoid that much injury so as just to match an already set aversion to that kind of breach of promise. (Of course we can hardly in practice tune the consciences of people finely enough so that they come out exactly as we might want.) But there is a second possibility: introducing a special moral rule (motivation) restricted to conflicts of the primary rules, or at least to severe conflicts.

iii.   Guilt-Feelings, Disapproval of Others, and Excuses

Responses by guilt feeling or disapproval, to breaches of the rules of obligation, are another variable of a moral code. To some extent the responses are fixed by the basic motivations: for instance, if aversion to injuring others is built in on the basis of underlying benevolence, a person will have a tendency to feel remorse if he injures another, and to have anti-attitudes towards someone else who does. In some cases, however, the disposition to have guilt-feelings must be learned separately, and then it is variable independently of the basic motivations. Variations are also possible through cognitive changes: the intensity of a young child's guilt-feelings seems often a function of how much damage his wrong-doing caused; later by acquiring discriminations based on concepts like intention, inadvertence, and mistake, his guilt-feelings (and anti-attitudes towards others) are reduced. Persons can be trained to perceive the acts of another not in terms of the objective change he caused, but in terms of intention and motives. Evidently the relation between intrinsic motivation and the feelings of guilt or disapproval—what we may call the 'system of excuses'—is variable, just as in the criminal law the relation between commission of a forbidden act and the punishment varies.

iv. Admiration, Praise, and Pride

There is another variable. At least in the Anglo-Saxon world some types of action are not required morally, but their performance is praised and arouses respect or admiration: acts of heroism (like falling on a live hand-grenade in order to save one's comrades), or of saintliness (like caring for a cantankerous relative through a long illness, with patience and without complaint). Although admiration and respect are native responses to certain sorts of situation and are not learned by conditioning, the frequency and expression of these attitudes can be varied: people can be taught to recognize the rare, difficult, and socially beneficial traits of character which some actions normally express: and they can be taught to express favourable attitudes in praise. If people are taught to respond with praise to such actions, the actions are encouraged; and people may come to value the traits of character they express, to develop a corresponding self-ideal, and to take pride in behaving in such a manner.

This variable feature of moral codes may be of interest to a utilitarian, because he may think it beneficial to encourage such supererogatory actions, but not to require them.

2. THE CONTENT OF A WELFARE-MAXIMIZING MORAL SYSTEM

Let us confine attention to the intrinsic motivation of a moral system, the system of injunctions and prohibitions. I shall suggest some directives about how to identify welfare-maximizing injunctions and prohibitions. This will give us clues to what the rules will be; but we cannot state them precisely without a specific society and set of institutions before us.

If we assume that the rules of the code are not to be just directives to produce welfare, directly or indirectly, they must be rules enjoining or prohibiting act-types. But which ones? The most expeditious first move is to find areas of behaviour needing regulation, by consulting our actual moral code, the codes of criminal law and tort law, and so on. We can then decide which items on this list of actually regulated behaviours it would maximize utility for a moral code to prohibit, and ideas for additions may occur to us. For instance, such a survey will indicate some need for morality to regulate fulfilling contracts and promises, and risking injury to others. The older manuals of casuistry, or a treatise like Sidgwick's *Methods of Ethics,* comprise a mine of information about the structure of conscience of at least some people. These sources will not only provide suggestions about which act-types probably need regulation; they will also provide information about what exceptive clauses may be useful.

The ideal rules are presumably some not very distant variant of some present rules.

Like 'incrementalists' among political scientists we should frame our ideal code by improving the present rules. How? For one thing, some, having lost their function, should be scrapped. The present moral or legal rules may not reflect recent technological or institutional changes, and where we know such changes have occurred, reflection about the creation of quite new rules, doubtless analogous to some old ones, will be in order.

At what level of abstraction should the rules regulating act-types be framed? Should there, for instance, be a basic rule forbidding carrying a revolver? Or is it enough if there is a rule prohibiting risking injury to others? One advantage to abstract rules is increased applicability—perhaps world-wide. Abstract rules can also be few in number, and that is an advantage since the basic motivations have to be established by conditioning. On the other hand, the conditions and exceptions of the abstract rule, as well as the inference from it to the concrete application may be too complex for the average person. A reasonable compromise is to propose that the code contain fairly concrete rules for frequent situations, especially ones for which predictability of behaviour is important to many persons. For less frequent or less important matters, more abstract regulations requiring some inference may be sufficient.

These facts suggest that the moral code taught or emphasized may vary somewhat from sub-group to sub-group in a society. Children may need to be taught not to cheat in examinations and to be honest about money and perhaps to respect the morality of queues; but they need not hear about pacifism or tax-evasion. Physicians and lawyers frequently face moral problems of special and complex kinds, and possibly it is useful for them to be taught special rules about obligations to patients/clients, or at least careful accounts of the connection between general moral rules and the special situations they meet frequently: hence the need for codes of medical and legal ethics. The same for various other professions, and for business men. We can leave open the question whether these various 'ethics' for special groups can all in principle be deduced as special cases of the rules to be taught to society as a whole, or whether they must be justified by direct appeal to welfare-maximization.

If a moral code is to maximize welfare, it must be suited not only to the intellectual capacities of the average person, but also to his degree of selfishness, impulsiveness, and so on. Possibly some rules will be welfare-maximizing, not because strict adherence to them would be, but because the actual imperfect response to them will be, just as a speed limit of 55 m.p.h. is consistent with information that more benefit is gained if traffic moves at 60 m.p.h., because the thinking and habits of motorists are such that with an advertised speed limit (enforced as nearly as personnel and finances permit) of 55 m.p.h., the traffic will actually move at approximately the ideal speed.

Should, or can, a plural system of moral principles incorporate a feature, analogous to the act utilitarian injunction to maximize expectable (as contrasted with actual) utility, which allows the specific implications of the code for action to be sensitive to the fact that different actions are more or less likely to realize a desired outcome? It should, and it can. It should, because if a utility-maximizing code is devised to prevent injury to others, an expectable utility-maximizing code will also prohibit in appropriate ways the taking of risk of injury. It should, because if such a code is devised to accomplish execution of promises (to return a book, perhaps), it should direct whether the borrower must return it personally or whether he may trust it to the postal services. The moral system can incorporate such a feature, and in a fairly simple way. For subscription to a moral principle, I have argued, is essentially a matter of intrinsic motivation; and it follows from the psychological theory . . . that, given an aversion of a certain strength, the tendency to perform an action will be a multiplicative function of the strength of that aversion and the degree of expectation that the act will enable avoidance of the aversive outcome. Thus, if there is an intrinsic aversion to the failure to return a book, and posting it makes the probability of loss as high as 40 per cent, the consequent tendency to post it will be weaker than the tendency to return it personally. Similarly, if there is an aversion to injuring another person, the resulting tendency to avoid that act will be stronger than the tendency to perform an act believed to pose only a small risk of injury. (Matter will be complicated if the code contains a 'right' permitting a small risk when the cost to the agent of avoiding it is considerable. In any case, the adequate teaching of a moral code must include some teaching of probability reasoning.) To accomplish the objective of a system of principles sensitive to the above considerations, all that needs to be done is to set the degree of intrinsic motivation at an appropriate level—ideally a motivation such that the consequent tendencies to avoid acts with various degrees of risk will be at approximately welfare-maximizing strength. . . .

The above remarks on how to identify a welfare-maximizing code will give a reasonably good idea what such a system would be like. Indeed, there seems no doubt that we know what some of the relatively specific rules in such a moral system would be: rules safeguarding personal security, requiring fulfilment of contracts and promises, and so on. Our discussion does suggest that many options are open and debatable; most of these options, however, are not very different from one another, and they usually correspond to murky areas in ordinary moral thinking, where people are confused about what is right and would like the guidance of a definite principle. Nothing prevents us, however, from learning more about the optimal specific rules; philosophers, psychologists, and other social scientists could co-operate in determining what a welfare-maximizing moral code would be. Indeed, it is not clear why much greater effort is not being made in this direction.

The fact that we start with our present rules does not imply that a complete code would simply reflect our long-established 'intuitions'. On the contrary, the conception of a happiness-maximizing moral code can have rather revolutionary implications. This would be clear in any country where the moral code forbids racial intermarriage. Moreover, it is clear that there is a prima facie case against the moral code prohibiting anything—which may be quite surprising. For what someone wants to do there is (at least normally) some benefit in permitting: he will enjoy doing it, and feel frustrated in being prevented on grounds of conscience. If something is to be prohibited or enjoined, a case must be made out for the long-range benefit of restricting the freedom of individuals, making them feel guilty, and utilizing the teaching resources of the community. Without proof of long-range benefit, any restriction lacks justification.

Is there a fatal logical flaw in the present conception, set by the fact that two different moral systems might be equally beneficial? This possibility is no mere spec-ulation, for it looks very much as if two quite similar codes, say with different emphases on the obligation to keep promises, might not offer noticeably different effects on welfare. Or, different systems might adopt different ones of the options mentioned for adjudicating beween conflicting rules, or for dealing with situations not specifically mentioned in the rules; again, there might be no demonstrably different promise for welfare. Of course, it would seem that the greater the disparity, the larger the chance of demonstrating different effects on welfare. But suppose that two somewhat different codes would promise approximately equal benefits. Then we could say of some rules that they comprise part of a welfare-maximizing system, but of the others only that they comprise parts of alternative systems, each of which would do equally well in producing welfare, and better than the rest. Which one would then be taught? It would make no difference, as long as there could be agreement—just as with rules of the road. If two moral rules promised equal benefits on other grounds, the fact that one was already 'conventional' should turn the scales in its favour. Until such agreement is reached, however, there would be no definite correct answer to the question of which rule would be supported by rational persons. Individual moral deliberators would presumably emerge with different answers. But we have already learned to tolerate different people acting conscientiously on different systems of moral principles; in this situation, no one could be criticized for sticking to his favoured moral system, among the optional alternatives.

A natural mistake about the content of the 'ideal' code is to assume that the welfare-maximizing code which rational people would support would be a one-principle code after all, like act utilitarianism, just one principle: 'Do whatever would be required by the moral code the currency of which would maximize welfare.' Is this the whole moral code which rational people would support? The answer to the question is: 'No, rational persons would not support that one-principle moral code.' We can see why not if we try to spell it out. Suppose it were true that the moral code the currency of which would maximize welfare is just this one-principle code. Then what we should have to teach is: 'Do whatever would be required by the moral code, "Do what would be required by the moral code . . . " ' and so on infinitely. In other words: 'Follow the principle which is to follow the principle . . . ' Either there is some other specifiable set of rules the currency of which would maximize welfare, or there is not. If there is not, then the one-principle becomes, in the phrase of C. I. Lewis, a 'perpetual stutter'. If there is, then *it* is the set of principles rational persons would want taught, and is the moral code the currency of which would maximize welfare.

Currency of the type of plural moral code here envisaged can be shown by a cost-benefit analysis to produce more benefit, as shown by a total cost-benefit analysis, than any of the one-principle codes. . . . For a system of plural rules, specifically built in for situations of importance and frequency in the society, avoids the major difficulties of the other theories. When individuals are deciding what is the right thing to do, in the normal case they need not engage in elusive calculations which tempt them to decide in favour of what they want to do. A principle about promise-keeping, with rules about possible exceptions, is built in. The individual need not deliberate about whether in this case it would do a little more good to break the promise—and because he need not, other individuals can predict reliably what a moral man will do. Others will be able to plan on specific behaviour by moral persons. Moreover, they need not worry about the outcomes of others' moral deliberations: they will feel personally secure, and secure about promised activity taking place. Furthermore, the agent benefits from his ability to know at any time whether his role, or prior behaviour, or his general obligation to help others in severe need, places him under an obligation at any given moment. Knowing that no such obligation is undischarged, he is free to do as he pleases as long as he does not risk injury or cause inconvenience to others. For the most part he can quietly go about his business. There are nice things he can do for us, even heroic and saintly things, and if he does these things he is properly admired or even loved by others; but he is not obligated to do them.

Evidently, then, there is strong reason to think that the currency of a carefully selected plural code in a society will produce considerably more welfare or happiness, on balance, than any of the one-principle codes that historically have been advocated.

We have the conception, then of a welfare-maximizing moral code for a given society. We do not know exactly what its injunctions and prohibitions would be, but we have some guidelines for identifying it, and presumably co-operation among various disciplines would come very close to determining the ideal code which fully rational persons would support and teach, in preference to one of the one-principle codes.

3. PARADOXES FOR THE PLURAL IDEAL-CODE UTILITARIAN?

Philosophers critical of utilitarianism have usually been less unhappy with a 'rule-utilitarian' conception like the foregoing, than with the conception of an act utilitarian code for society . . . Nevertheless, many have been critical of the present conception; and some of the objections have sufficiently wide currency that it seems necessary to consider them. The objections are roughly the following: (a) that a code like the foregoing can hardly maximize welfare, and hence a person of utilitarian persuasion is defeating his own purposes if he espouses it; (b) that there are circumstances in which the following of such a code even by a good many persons in our actual society could only be harmful; and (c) that conformity to such a code would necessarily result in significant unfairness. Let us look at the reasoning.

(a) The first argument is an abstract a priori argument. It urges that if this code makes recommendations for behaviour different from AU [Act Utilitarianism]—and they must be different, or the theory loses all its claim to fame—it must be telling people to do something different from producing the very best consequences, which is what the AU code recommends. So following it must be producing less than the very best. Much the same point is made by others who say that rule-utilitarians must be rule-worshippers, since they advocate following a rule even when so doing would fail to maximize utility. . . . These points, however, rest on a confusion. For to have an AU code is to be motivated (basic motivations) to do what one thinks will have best consequences, so that doing what one is thus motivated to do is not at all necessarily to do what will have best consequences, assuming that agents are not omniscient. Whereas persons committed to the ideal code are motivated (basic motivations) to do what they think will be the keeping of a promise, the avoidance of causing injury, etc., and doing what they are thus motivated to do will be to do what in the long-run will have the best consequences, even if some such acts do not. Non-omniscient persons acting to keep their promises (of certain kinds) will actually succeed in producing more welfare than those who are aiming at maximizing welfare directly. So this first line of reasoning may be dismissed.

(b) A second argument commences by conceding that at least normally welfare is maximized by everyone following the recommendations of an ideal code. Roughly, the 'ideal' code is picked with that end in mind, so that it can be no surprise that it succeeds. But suppose the currency of a code in a certain society would maximize welfare; it does not follow that some people acting in accordance with it will maximize welfare, irrespective of what other people are doing. Consider an example: There is a society in which violence on the streets is common, everyone carries a weapon, and the ability to use it is the only guarantee of safety. In this society, universal following of the rule: 'Do not carry a weapon' would maximize benefits, but for only one person to follow such a rule would merely endanger his life.

This argument depends on an unduly simple conception of what an optimal set of rules would be like. Two points need to be made. (1) The first is that the unfortunate behaviour suggested above might be required by one rule with prima facie force, but there will usually or always be other rules. One of these might well be: 'Defend yourself and your wife and children against unjustifiable violent attack with effective means.' Both of these rules have only prima facie force, but the second might have more stringency than the first in the ideal code. If so, then, if one could not discharge the second obligation compatibly with following the first rule, one would be morally bound to infringe the rule against carrying a weapon. (2) But in any case an unrestricted prohibition against carrying weapons could hardly be even a prima facie rule of a welfare-maximizing code for that society. We must remember that an ideal moral code will be devised somehow to deal optimally with problems that actually will arise, and hence with the fact that many persons will be carrying lethal weapons in the streets. (Even if the 'rule' were for no one ever to carry a weapon, we should have to expect some weapons in the streets, for even if the rule is 'current' to the extent that the most widely accepted ones are, there will be some who do not accept it, and others who will not follow it, out of self-interest. We must recall that for a person to subscribe to a code is only for him to be motivated in the appropriate direction, not necessarily always to follow it.) One of the reasons, we recall, why the construction of an ideal code should begin with actual codes is that the latter draw attention to situations which need regulation. Now, obviously, one thing an optimal moral code would aim to avoid is moral people being the prey of unscrupulous or morally weak persons; and it would be a deterrent to potential criminals not be be sure, when attacking a moral man, that he would be defenceless. So everything considered, what kind of moral rule would be welfare-maximizing? Apparently an alternative rule, something like: 'Do not carry a weapon when there is no significant personal risk in not doing so; if there is significant personal risk, you may carry a weapon but use it only for self-protection, and meanwhile you should work to enlist co-operation in reducing violence in the streets. The currency of this rule would have virtually all the advantage of the unrestricted prohibition, and bring the further benefit that it provides for expectable contingencies.

What this example shows is that an ideal moral rule will not permit catastrophes arising (1) from the behaviour of those who do not accept the rule, or (2) from the behaviour of those who do accept it but fail to follow it because of stronger contrary motivation, or (3) from other predictable or probable situations. An ideal code might, of course, make some risky demands; if it would be welfare-maximizing for behaviour to meet a certain standard, it might be best to teach a code requiring some risk of harm, in order for the society to get started on the ascent to ideal behaviour. . . .

We have the conception, then, of a plural moral system—of basic motivations, justification, rules of excuses, and so on—subscription to which by a large majority of the adult population of a given society would result in more welfare than subscription to any other moral system. Not only do we have the idea of such a system; we know what some of its main features would be, and we know in principle how to go on to find as precise details as need be. In the preceding section I argued that, if we understand what the details of such a system really would be, we can see that only a few persons conforming to it in the society where its currency would be welfare-maximizing would almost always be doing what would produce as much good as anything they might do instead.

I have argued that fully rational persons would support such a moral system for a society in which they expected to live. But we must be careful to notice that in fact probably no one is living in a society with a moral code exactly ideal in that sense. If such a code were current in a given society, the ideal motivations etc. would be built in. As a result, if a practical problem arose for a person in that society, he would need roughly only to follow conscience (his built-in-moral motivations, responding to his intellectual analysis of his situation), perhaps assisted by a background explanation of the welfare-maximizing purpose of moral codes, in order to do the right thing. . . .

Let us look finally at how an actual agent may reasonably make a decision, if he is convinced about the above-supported general description of what he is obligated to do (say, what a welfare-maximizing system would require) but is not sure of the precise requirement of such a system for a situation he is in. He thinks, however, after careful reflection that such a system would require that he do so-and-so. For instance, suppose an agent thinks that a welfare-maximizing system would call on people to keep their promises in the kind of situations he takes himself to be in, so that, as far as he can see, justified moral principles require him to keep his promise. In that situation, given the proposed meaning for 'moral obligation' it would not be misleading for him unqualifiedly to assert: 'I am morally obligated to keep my promise.' But, if he wishes to be very circumspect, he might say 'It is possible that I am not really obligated to keep my promise, but as far as I can see, on the facts I know and in the light of the reasoning I have gone through, I am obligated.' He can say this correctly, even if in fact he is mistaken about what the principles of a welfare-maximizing moral code would require. And, if he then follows his own moral conclusion, he is morally blameless for doing the objectively wrong thing (barring some morally culpable error in his total reasoning); and if he does not follow it he morally deserves reproach, even if what he then does is objectively right. The moral status of his action would not be altered by the fact that most of the persons in his society would disagree with his conclusion and would not disapprove if he failed to keep his promise.

NOTE

[1] Berkeley gave the theory an interesting statement, supported by arguments, in 1712, in *Passive Obedience, or the Christian Doctrine of Not Resisting the Supreme Power, Proved and Vindicated upon the Principles of the Law of Nature*.

CHAPTER 12

ROLE MORALITY AND PROFESSIONAL ETHICS

One of the most common problems that any star-studded athletic team can have is that its "stars" all perform to enhance their own reputations rather than perform in the best interest of the team. In basketball, players take too many low-percentage shots. In baseball, a slugger goes for the fences when the appropriate play is to use the surprise bunt to get on base. Hence, the championship team is often not the team with the best individual players. Rather it's the team that functions best *as a team*. Since the team members are performing for the good of the team, in an important sense the team is greater than the sum of its parts.

This fact of athletic life is not without its implications for ethics. Since even nonutilitarians agree that the public interest is one consideration in making ethical decisions, both nonutilitarians and utilitarians face the problem of motivating individuals to act in the public interest. In other words, both utilitarians and nonutilitarians have problems analogous to those confronting the coach of an athletic team. The traditional device of utilitarian moral theorists is an altruistic or benevolent disposition in human nature. Hume argued that people did distinguish between self-interest and altruism and often justified their actions on altruistic grounds. Hume argued that an analysis of language reveals a distinction between the "subjective" claims of self-interest and the "objective" claims of altruism. One way of explaining this linguistic fact is to argue that human beings are able to empathize with their fellow human beings. We are sympathetic when misfortune befalls others, and as a result we try to help them. We behave altruistically. Some utilitarians believe that a sympathetic disposition is a common and natural ingredient in human behavior. Other utilitarians are more pessimistic and think that this sympathetic disposition needs rather careful and continuous nurturing.

However, neither the coach nor the ethical theorist need rely totally on human sympathy or altruism as the motivating force for team spirit or conduct in support of the public good. Another approach is simply to point out that ultimately individual success is bound up with team success (that achieving individual interests is dependent on the achievement of the public interest). A common criticism of traditional ethics in the liberal tradition is the excessive emphasis on the individual. The starting point of most Anglo-American ethical theory is the individual, and the adequacy of an ethical theory depends on its ability to accommodate individual interests and individual rights. But isn't the notion of an individual outside a social context a mere abstraction? F. H. Bradley argues that all individuals exist in a social context. Without that context individuals couldn't survive or, at the very least, they couldn't grow and develop. As an individual you are what you are because of the position you hold in society. You are a family member, an employee, a colleague, and a friend. In a very real sense these relations make you the individual you are. An individual apart from all social relations is an abstract entity. For this reason it is easy to see how to defend the view that the good of the individual is bound up with the good of society. The coach who continually points out that a collection of players wins or loses as a team has a valid philosophical point.

But how far are we willing to take the notion of collective responsibility? W. H. Walsh begins his provocative essay with a host of examples where, contrary to Chapter 3, we feel comfortable in applying moral concepts where it makes no sense to talk about individual responsibility. We either take pride in or feel ashamed of our ancestors. The behavior of parents reflects on their children, and vice versa. Our treatment of American Indians as the United States was settled and the existence of slavery cause us shame, and many white Americans, even though they are in no way responsible for what happened in pre–Civil War times, feel an obligation to compensate American Indians and black Americans.

Walsh admits that ethical analysis of the sort we have been undertaking could be used to show that these feelings and the behavior based on them are irrational. After all, one of the tasks of ethical theory is to improve our ethical decision-making. However, in this case, Walsh believes that such a move would be mistaken. Such a move is based on the principle that "a man is accountable only for what he has done himself or might have done himself." But Walsh thinks that principle is not always the correct one to apply in ethical decisions. Walsh thinks that the career of Genghis Khan does reflect badly on all human beings and that a feeling of shame on our part is appropriate. He also thinks that the contemporary English are to some extent saddled with the responsibility of their forebears' treatment of the Scots (substitute contemporary Americans are to some extent saddled with the responsibility of their forebears' treatment of the Indians).

This recognition that individuals are the individuals they are because of the social positions they hold helps us understand the concept of loyalty. Loyalty hasn't found much favor in this generation, and the concept has received little attention from contemporary philosophers. This indifference and neglect is not without reason. Nearly all the participants in the Watergate affair cited loyalty to the President and his program as the reason for their participation. Besides Watergate, a lot of evil has been done in the name of loyalty. But should loyalty be deemphasized or perhaps given up? If he were still alive the American philosopher Josiah Royce would answer that question with a resounding no. Not only is loyalty a virtue, he would argue, but loyalty is the central concept in making ethical decisions. Indeed Royce maintained that "all the commonplace virtues, in so far as they are indeed defensible and effective, are special forms of loyalty to loyalty." Since Royce was not unaware that a great deal of evil had been done in the name of loyalty, he needed to show what distinguished the moral practice of loyalty from its misuse. First, Royce accepted and defended Bradley's contention that there are no abstract individuals, that human beings are bound together in a myriad of relationships, and that in an important sense these relationships constitute who we are. This interrelationship of human beings is the basis of loyalty. However, after a certain age, either what relationships we have or the nature of the relationships we have is a responsible autonomous choice. Genuine loyalty is loyalty to a cause which is freely chosen. This attitude is consistent with what we learned in Chapter 3. But how do we distinguish good causes from bad causes? Royce seems to have two criteria for making that distinction. First, loyalty to a bad cause ultimately undermines loyalty. With respect to loyalty overall, loyalty to a bad cause is self-defeating. Second, true loyalty is loyalty to humanity. Bad causes are destructive of humanity, but loyalty in the morally acceptable sense is always supportive of humanity. Royce's first argument uses a strategy similar to Kant's. Royce's second argument rests on the unconditional value of the human being, and hence this argument too has affinities with Kant. The moral slogan for both of Royce's arguments is "Be loyal to loyalty." But what about the details of Royce's arguments? Royce's strategy is to argue that all the moral duties and virtues represent instances of loyalty because those duties and virtues support decisions and behavior which respect the ultimate dignity of human beings. If we grant this step in the argument, we can see how loyalty to a bad cause is ultimately self-defeating. A bad cause is one that undercuts or is inconsistent with our duties and the practice of virtue. Hence one can appeal to considerations brought forth by Kant or MacIntyre to establish the inconsistency.

But hasn't Royce gone around in a circle? Hasn't he answered the question "What is an ethical decision?" by saying, "Be loyal to loyalty," and hasn't he answered the question "What is loyalty to loyalty?" by saying, "Follow the constraints required for an ethical decision"? Reading the selection by Royce in this chapter might give the impression that Royce is arguing in a circle. However, so long as there is more to an ethical decision than mere loyalty, the circle is broken. Loyalty becomes an element in making an ethical decision, but only one element. Whether loyalty is morally used or morally abused depends upon whether the loyal decision is consistent with the other elements of ethical decision-making.

If Royce is understood in this way, rather than reasoning in a circle, he has provided a crucial test for evaluating not only loyal causes but any decision we make as a result of the positions or roles we hold in society. To see this, let us trace out the implications of Bradley's view that in most respects individuals are the individuals they are because of the roles they hold. If our social positions are that important, most of the ethical decisions we make will be made in the context of a role, and a role carries norms of appropriate behavior with it. Let me illustrate. One distinguishes between being a bricklayer and being a good bricklayer. Just because someone is a member of the bricklayers' union, there is nothing inconsistent in a disgruntled homeowner saying, "I don't care if Jones does have his union card, he's no bricklayer." This distinction shouldn't prove mysterious to students. All students know professors certified by their college or university as teachers but who, in the opinion of the students, aren't teachers at all. By the way, we professors apply the distinction equally well to students.

Since many of our decisions are made from the context of the roles we hold, and since roles carry with them norms for good performance, you can see why Bradley describes ethics as "my station and its duties." Indeed Bradley put his position as follows: "There is nothing better than my station and its duties, nor anything higher or more truly beautiful."

But every social position or role has moral requirements—if only requirements for good performance. One of the advantages of a complete and accurate job description is that it provides the employee with a specific standard for good performance. In the absence of a complete and accurate job description, employees don't know what they are supposed to do, and they can be fired for reasons irrelevant to job performance even though poor performance may be given as the excuse. One of the problems associated with the "my station and its duties" ethic is that the duties of the station are often neither explicit nor clear.

In principle the moral requirements of any job could be made explicit and clear. However, achievement of that goal would not end our difficulties. Since we hold so many positions and hence take on so many obligations, there are tremendous opportunities for conflicts among roles. Some conflicts arise within the role itself. For example employees often have conflicts in their role as employees. Management encourages maximum productivity, and from that perspective the best employee is the most productive employee. However, co-workers hardly ever have much praise for the extraordinarily productive worker. College students employed in summer jobs frequently discover this fact the hard way. A person who far exceeds the average is a serious threat, since it is feared that management will wonder why others can't also produce as much.

Second, there are conflicts among roles. For example, conflicts occur between one's duties to the job and to one's family, church, friends, and state. Conflicts created by job obligations are particularly acute. Until recently many corporations moved young executives from one part of the country to another every one or two years—often at great emotional cost to spouses and children. Some corporations have placed restraints on the kinds of activities employees may pursue during off-hours. These restraints can apply to either political or social activities.

But the third type of conflict involves the conflict that occurs between the moral requirements of the role and the moral requirements of society at large. This type of conflict is the focus of Richard De George's discussion of the Pinto case. Were the engineers at Ford morally remiss for not blowing the whistle or for not fighting in some other way the decision concerning the placement of the gas-tank housing on the Ford Pinto? De George advances several reasons for thinking they were not responsible for that decision. The engineers did point out that a $6.65 modification would make the car safer. But did their responsibility go any further? De George proposes three criteria which would morally permit engineers, in such situations, to blow the whistle on safety issues, and he proposes five criteria which would morally obligate engineers to go public in such cases. De George then analyzes the Pinto case in light of these criteria.

What kind of general conclusions can we draw from cases where there are conflicts either among our role-related obligations or between the requirements of a role and the requirements of conventional morality? First Bradley is right in indicating that our stations in life bring with them moral duties, and Royce is right to emphasize our duty of loyalty to those with whom we stand in relation. The duty of loyalty can be overridden by a higher duty, however. Nonetheless, since the duty of loyalty is a moral duty it can only be overridden by another moral duty; expediency or personal interest won't do. Moreover, social institutions must conform to the requirements of justice if we are to have genuine moral obligations to them. This is the significance of the point made by Rawls in Chapter 10. Ultimately social institutions and their associated duties must be in conformity with general principles of morality. The plea "I was only following orders" has limits as an excuse.

Nonetheless, De George is right in pointing out that following higher moral principles or even conforming to general societal moral principles can have tremendous personal costs for the individual. We can't expect individuals to be moral heroes. Sometimes "I was only following orders" is a legitimate excuse. Often where conflicts between the requirements of a role and the requirements of societal morality exist, the morally appropriate response is to bring the institution into conformity with the morality of society.

Pride, Shame and Responsibility

W. H. Walsh

I begin by rehearsing a number of familiar facts. There are occasions on which we take pride in, or feel shame about, things which are in no sense our personal doing. To many people the fortunes of their country and family are not only an object of lively and continuing interest, but a matter with which they find themselves to be intimately concerned. Nor is their concern in these affairs limited to the immediate present: the activities and reputation of their forbears touch them almost, if not quite, as closely as the activities and reputation of their contemporaries; they are sensitive to criticism directed against their ancestors and predecessors as they are to criticism of those with whom their own lives are immediately bound up, and conversely take pleasure when kind things are said of countrymen and relations they neither knew nor could have known. Whatever the rationale, they have a sense of belonging with past and, for that matter, future generations to unities which are larger than themselves; unities which are most readily illustrated, as above, by reference to family and country, but which can also embrace entities of many different sorts, such as a political movement, an educational organization, a church or even so unlikely a thing as the white race. It is because of this sense of belonging that they feel themselves to be in a certain way answerable not only for what they have done themselves and for the deeds and omissions of persons they either have or might have influenced (their children, their contemporaries), but also for the actions, the achievements and above all the failings of members of the same group in the past. There are few Scots who do not feel pride and satisfaction when they reflect on the battle of Bannockburn, and even Englishmen like myself will admit to a sense of unease, indeed of guilt, when they consider certain episodes in the past history of their country, episodes with which, in the nature of things, they could have had no personal connection.

In urging that what I have said so far is no more than simple fact I should not, of course, want to deny that there are all sorts of local variation in the facts. E. M. Forster once said notoriously that, if he were ever called on to choose between a friend and his country, he hoped that he would have the courage to choose his friend. The ties of country, for many liberal-minded persons, are professedly weak, though one wonders in that case why they find it so important to expose and correct their country's misdeeds. But we do not have to consider special cases to recognize that the sense of belonging of which I have spoken can vary enormously from person to person, age to age, group to group. In times of war, as Bradley said in his rhetorical way, "the heart of a nation rises high and beats in the breast of each one of her citizens"; in times of peace, particularly prolonged peace, things can be very different, though this does not mean that in these conditions every kind of group solidarity will be lost. Again, external circumstances obviously affect the situation profoundly. A group like the Jews or the French Canadians which feels that its continued existence as a separate

W. H. Walsh, "Pride, Shame and Responsibility", *The Philosophical Quarterly*, vol. 20, no. 78, January 1970. Reprinted by permission.

unit is menaced by the actions of others will naturally react strongly to criticism, including criticism of the deeds of its former members; a group like the English which has never had to face that sort of challenge and has enjoyed unrestricted self-expression for many years will have far less sense of national self-identity and will accordingly be less sensitive to this sort of pressure. Yet it would surely be rash to claim that even the English have managed to dissociate themselves from their past entirely. Englishmen who live in foreign countries are certainly not allowed by their hosts to do so.

My concern now is not with the details of this situation but rather with its overall look. I take it to be a fact that there are people who, to turn to another sort of example, are ashamed of their humble origins or proud of their distinguished connections, whether this is a matter of family ties or of something wider. I take it to be a further fact that the sense of belonging of which I have spoken is something perfectly real, however much it may vary in particular cases; which means, if I am not mistaken, that there are circumstances in which men regard themselves as answerable for deeds which they did not do themselves. If the word 'answerable' is disputed here, on the ground that it implies a formal acceptance of responsibility of which there is no direct evidence, I can point to circumstances which nevertheless justify its use, for example to the fact that, in the situations described, men clearly see criticism of their forbears as reflecting in some way on themselves. But I shall not attempt to delineate the facts more carefully or more exactly at this point. Instead, I want to turn to the question what we are to make of them as philosophers.

Perhaps the most common contemporary way of dealing with the facts I have mentioned would be to admit their existence, but argue that they arise from misapprehension. Let it be agreed (we are told on this way of thinking) that there are people who are ashamed of their parents or uneasy about the actions of their countrymen in the past. The fact remains that neither in the one case nor in the other is there any reason for them to take up this position. Pride, shame and responsibility are properly in question only when those who manifest them have brought something about by their own efforts or their own neglect; for these terms to be used significantly the person to whom they are ascribed must have been in the position of an agent in the relevant matters. But clearly no-one acted as an agent in the matter of his own conception; no-one chose his parents, and so no-one can properly pride himself on his birth or has any reason to feel ashamed of it. If my father committed some particularly obnoxious crime before my birth, or in my childhood, that is a matter which calls for regret, or perhaps distress, on my part, but in no sense for shame. Since I obviously could have done nothing to alter my father's action in the circumstances described, I can clearly not be held in any way accountable for it. And what holds in this case holds equally in the other, though popular misapprehension on the subject is here perhaps more widespread. Whatever wrongs were committed by Englishmen in the past against the unoffending Scots, the unfortunate American colonists or the defenceless Irish, have nothing to do with me as a present-day Englishman. I did not do the deeds in question, and so cannot be asked to answer for them. If the Irish and Scots think otherwise—if they persist in suggesting that the actions of my ancestors are my concern too—they reveal themselves as subject to the most elementary philosophical confusion. . . .

Is there any reason why we should *not* accept this account? There are two sets of consideration which make me hesitate to accept it. First, it is clear that we can do so only if we are prepared to tell plain men, in what one must presume is a relatively familiar type of situation, that they are guilty of a gross misuse of language; their thought on the whole issue is confused. I see no reason in principle why plain men should not be guilty of confused thinking where complicated technical questions are concerned, but it is scarcely plausible to describe the present issue as technical. In the circumstances the least that can be asked for is a more careful and detailed description of the issues, to find out just what is being assumed and so to make clear at what point or points plain men can be said to be making unfounded claims. But I have a second and more serious reason for rejecting, or at least doubting, the above account. The argument it involves rests on the principle that a man is accountable only for what he has done himself or might have done himself, and here it is assumed that no difficulties arise in separating what I do as an individual from what others with whom I am associated do or have done. In other words, the thesis rests on a certain doctrine about the nature of the individual in thought and action: it sees him as being, in an important way, self-contained and self-subsistent. Widely as this doctrine is accepted today (for example, in much current talk about choice and decision in morals), I am not persuaded either that its implications have been made clear or that they would, if clarified, be able to stand up to critical scrutiny.

I shall now try to develop and defend these two lines of thought. To deal with the first it will be useful to imagine a series of conversations. (A) A man says to me gravely: "The career of Genghis Khan was deplorable", and I agree rather uneasily. He then adds: "It is something of which we should both be ashamed". What am I to say at this point? I might take him to be reminding me of the common humanity the two of us share with Genghis, and to be urging that the latter's barbarities implicate us too. But I might equally be wise to discontinue the conversation, on the ground that my interlocutor simply did not know what he was talking about, for, after all, what had Genghis Khan to do with me or him? (B) I encounter another troublesome companion, who says to me meaningfully: "Look at what the Athenians did at Melos; that is something you must agree reflects on you". In what way could it properly be said to reflect on *me?* Well, we all know that the fifth-century Athenians are among the great heroes of liberals, and I am (let us suppose) a passionate and notorious liberal. My companion is here trying to pin on me a measure of guilt by association, and the question is whether I can repudiate the association without abandoning the cause to which I am committed. I might manage to do so if, for example, I could show that it had all along been a mistake to regard the Athenians as interested in freedom for anyone else than themselves. Failing anything of that kind, however, I must in the circumstances described admit that the remark has its point: I should feel uncomfortable in these conditions, and for the reason that I cannot deny that the reputation of a cause I regard as mine is at stake. Things would of course be entirely different if I were, for instance, General Franco or Mao Tse-Tung; I could then say, as in case (A), that the Athenians had nothing to do with me.

(C) The problem of Scotland is once again under discussion, and as the only Englishman present I am being saddled with responsibility for the sins of my countrymen. At first the talk is all about discrimination by Whitehall and the failure of the government to spend a proper share of public money in Scotland today; later we move from the present to the past, and ancient wrongs of many kinds are brought up and thrown in my face. It is said, for instance, that the English mistreated the Scots shamefully over the Darien scheme. Must the shame rub off on me? Of course I could get out of it if I made out that my antecedents were Irish and so admitted that I am not really English at all. But if I want to stick to being English, can I dissociate myself altogether from the activities of the English in the past? Whatever I try to say, it seems pretty clear that my critics will scarcely allow me to do so.

The point of my three examples is to offer a series of different cases showing that the common man is perhaps not so naive about these matters as some philosophers might be ready to suggest. It is not true that the defence that "it has nothing to do with me" is everywhere repudiated. If I am saddled with the barbarities of Genghis I can very well invoke it, and the likelihood is that no-one will press the point any further. If someone brings up the misdeeds of the Athenians against me it is again open to me to invoke the defence, though it is far from clear that I could do so in all circumstances. Finally, when I am asked as an Englishman to accept a share of responsibility for what my forbears did I must either show that they did nothing discreditable or admit that part of the discredit must fall on me too. For the fact is that I stand in a special relationship to them, belonging with them to a wider unit covering more generations than one, a unit whose fortunes, past and present, reflect on all who fall within it.

But how is this apparently mystical doctrine to be justified? To see its necessity we must return to the criticisms voiced a page or two back.

Pride, shame and responsibility, according to most contemporary thinkers, are *really* in point only where a person's own actions are concerned. And the assumption is that there are no difficulties, practical or theoretical, in determining which of a man's ostensible actions are his own. The test is a simple one: we need to ask only if the act (or failure to act) issued from his will. Those actions are mine which I do willingly, or at least not unwillingly; those actions are mine which I choose or decide to do, or perhaps would not repudiate if someone subsequently ascribed them to me. It is already apparent that the notion of a responsible action is less clear than might at first appear; the circumstances in which a man expresses himself in action need careful investigation. It is not my purpose, however, to pursue this question here, but rather to turn to the related question of the nature of the self which he is supposed on these occasions to express.

Moral philosophers often write as if all human action took place on a single level, the level of private personal relationships. I do not, of course, deny that we do act at this level and that our actions there are often of importance, above all to ourselves. I suspect, however, that we tend to exaggerate the extent to which, even at this level, what we do is done by each of us in his individual capacity. Take the choice of a wife or husband, for example. We all know that there are societies where marriage is not a matter of personal choice, and most of us are glad that we do not live in such a society. Yet how true is it to say that in our society a person brings nothing but himself to this all-important decision? How many people make it with minds which are in no way coloured by attitudes which they have tacitly taken over from others? I do not mean here to imply that a person's thinking on this subject must simply reflect the preferences of his particular group or social class about the qualities desirable in a spouse; obviously people can and sometimes do make a stand against these as mistaken, in part if not as a whole. The point is, however, that when an individual rebels against his social background in this way, the likelihood is that he does it in the belief in a different set of principles, practised by a different group and no more of his own exclusive fashioning than the "conventions" he is wishing to discard. A person who cleared his mind of all extraneous thought on the subject and chose for himself alone might well end up with very peculiar results.

Nor is this all. I have taken the situation where two people agree to marry as an example of a private and personal act, and tried to show that more is involved than their individual decisions. But if whether A is to marry B is, in our society, ideally a matter only for the two of them, the decision is all the same not a purely private undertaking. This is because marriage itself is a social institution, part of a structure which individuals inherit and are powerless to alter except in minor ways. If I ask someone to be my wife and she agrees we may be committing ourselves to more than we have bargained for, not just because life is full of surprises, but also because the institution within which we are working may well have complications on which we have never reflected. Once we have taken the initial step we are bound by the rules of the institution, some of them legally, others socially, enforced, whether or not we have fully realized what they are. And though of course these rules are all man-made, they do not result from the choice of single individuals. A powerful person may perhaps introduce amendments in them, just as a powerful person can set a new fashion. But in each case whether he succeeds does not depend on himself alone: others have to acquiesce before accepted ways of behaving can be said to have changed.

If this argument is correct, there are aspects even of what are commonly taken as strictly private acts which cannot be ascribed to the purely personal choice of the individuals concerned. No doubt these individuals have the last word, but they choose in a situation which is by no means all of their own making, and their choice commits them to acts and attitudes which they inherit from others rather than fashion for themselves. You cannot marry without taking on yourself the obligations of marriage, however little you have considered them and however much you would like to repudiate them once you find out what they are. Equally, you cannot marry without involving yourself in the fortunes of another family, whose reputation from now on will be thought to reflect on you just as it does on its other members. Most of us, no doubt, would like to make our contracts on our own terms, but in the case of this particular contract, as indeed in most others, the terms tend to be fixed for us, apart from our individual volition. To insist on the fact that the choice is ultimately ours is to direct attention to the formalities of the situation rather than to its centre. For, after all, we are not, as individuals, in a position to alter this institution significantly; if we enter it at all, we enter it as a going concern.

I realize, of course, that there is much more to say on this point, but must defer further consideration of it and glance briefly at a different range of cases. I took the example of two people deciding to marry to illustrate what, in our society, is considered to be a matter for individuals only. But there are, of course, many acts which we undertake not as private individuals but in capacities which are, in one degree or another, public. Wherever a man has an office, in however small and unimportant an institution, he acts not just as himself but as a representative of the body in question, and the decisions he makes reflect that fact. The secretary of an Allotments Association protests to the Town Council not as plain Mr. Smith but in his corporate capacity; he perhaps voices indignation which he does not feel himself, and quite often he may be led to do things which he would not do as a private individual. Nor can it be said that his decisions are entirely his own, for on accepting office he takes over certain standing commitments and certain standing long-term aims, over some of which he may well be personally unenthusiastic; he must do what he can to further the interests of his members in circumstances whose complexity he may not have appreciated before taking up the appointment, and this may on occasion lead him to engage in actions which fall into the class Aristotle described as "non-voluntary". If this happens only rarely with minor officials of the kind I have mentioned, it may well be much more frequent with important persons who find themselves in positions of authority. Those of us who are quick to condemn ministers of the crown for failure to live up to professions they made before taking office should pause to reflect on these facts.

A member of the government, a director of a public company, a trade union leader, a military commander, a university official—these are a few of the enormous group of persons whose public actions are their own only in a significantly restricted sense. I am not thinking in this connection of the fact that many such people act under instructions and in so far as they do so can disclaim ultimate responsibility; the point I have to make covers principals as well as subordinates. What I want to stress is that even the former find themselves acting in situations where both the objectives to be pursued and the methods of pursuing them are largely determined for them. Because their position requires them to pursue the long-term interests of the body they represent, the actions open to them are often far more circumscribed than they might have hoped; because again they are engaged in activities which call for a wide range of skills they will naturally not be disposed to rely on their own untutored thoughts, but will draw on accumulated wisdom and well-tried experience to the maximum possible extent. The mind which manifests itself in the resulting actions is in consequence their mind only to a minor degree. It used to be said in the 'thirties that locutions such as 'Britain declared war on Germany' were profoundly misleading, since states were after all no more than logical constructions out of individual men and women. This doctrine is, I suggest, palpably untrue, despite the fact that all the actions of states or other groups have to be carried out by individuals. The point is that the persons concerned *(a)* appear not as their private selves but in a public capacity—as member of the government, ambassador, official messenger, etc.—and *(b)* that in any case their thinking, and hence their decision, in the situation tends to be of a collective rather than an individual character. Some particular person may have the last word in a given case, as the President of the United States has the last word about dropping the bomb. But we all know that any President who is confronted with the necessity for taking this decision will do so as the representative of a vast and continuing organization and that the considerations he brings to bear on the issue will be his own to a minor degree, if at all. Nor are these remarks meant to reflect on the competence or character of Presidents of the United States in particular; their predicament in this respect is shared by their political opponents, as well as by many persons whose activities are not political at all. Indeed, it is a feature of the modern world, which has witnessed the growth of organizations to an unprecedented extent and so seen men able to take ever-increasing advantage of the achievements of their predecessors, that the share of individuals in this sort of decision has steadily diminished. Things may have been different in more primitive times, when knowledge was scarce and kings and generals had to rely largely on themselves. But in modern conditions at least it is truer to say that organizations take decisions than that individuals do, where the decisions concerned are of the kind we have considered.

To speak of the acts and decisions of a nation, a business organization, a trade union, a university is thus, in my view, fully justified; it is not inaccurate or a mere piece of regrettable shorthand. Critics of Idealism made things altogether too easy for themselves when they assumed that the only conditions in which an entity of this sort could properly be said to act or suffer were those in which it was identifiable as a separate existent; conditions which they rightly believed could never be satisfied. But we do not have to think that England is something over and above English men and women to make sense of statements which have 'England' as their subject. To talk about what England did or does is to talk about what Englishmen did or do, but not just to speak of the doings of a number of separate persons. As I hope I have shown, it is naive to suppose that human beings act in total isolation from their fellows, or to think that they bring virgin minds to their actions, minds which in no sense bear the impress of their associations with other men. The truth is rather that, even in their personal actions, men's minds are penetrated by ideas which they share with others, and that, so far from its being true that collective action is but an amalgam of personal actions, collective action is *sui generis* and distinct. The difficulty, indeed, is to find clear criteria by which to mark off those actions which are done by persons in their private and individual capacity; in some societies of a primitive type, where individuality as we know it scarcely exists, it may well be impossible to locate them at all. But even in advanced societies it seems clear that collective action of the kind referred to above is the norm rather than the exception; we act in conjunction with others far more often and far more importantly than we act by ourselves alone.

The paradoxical character of the view I have expressed has, I hope, been lessened in recent years. . . . But it would not be surprising, even so, to find resistance to the main conclusions about responsibility persisting. To suggest that we are each of us less independent, less self-contained, than we imagined, is one thing; to draw the conclusion that we are therefore implicated with others in ways we had not suspected, quite another. The first we can tolerate as a realistic, if unwelcome, recognition of fact; the second seems to involve a value judgment which, to many people today, must necessarily appear wholly inequitable. For even if it turns out that I am what I am not as myself alone, but in virtue of my membership in some larger whole or wholes, how can I reasonably be expected to take responsibility for what these bodies do in circumstances where I could have no conceivable influence on their actions? Or if I am told that I must answer for organizations with which I have once formally identified myself, say a political party or a religious communion, how is that to apply to institutions of the kind from which this discussion set out, such as the state or the family? There is no time at which, in normal circumstances, a citizen of Britain is asked to declare his adherence to his country: a native of Great Britain is born a British citizen, and thus finds himself involved in an organization to which he has not chosen to belong. Similarly with a family, membership of which is a matter of brute fact rather than will. If my children or my contemporaries perpetrate shameful deeds I can perhaps be saddled with some share of the blame, since it is at least possible that I might have taken steps to prevent their acting in that way. But what action of mine could have altered my great-grandfather's regrettable addiction to the bottle, or prevented the Opium War with China in the early 1840s?

I do not pretend to have easy answers to these difficulties, but I think even so that they should not be accepted as decisive. One thing that encourages me in this attitude is the obvious relationship between the problem posed by my view and the classical problem of political obligation. That men have obligations to their country is something which is taken for granted whenever the authorities issue an income-tax demand or a call-up form; that they have these obligations as a result of an act of will on their part is far from obvious. If I ask what forces me to pay taxes or submit myself to the miseries of military service, the answer may be that I have no practical choice; the power of the law is such that I cannot escape. But not everyone is in the unhappy position of being literally forced to undertake these disagreeable duties; there are persons, odd as it may seem, who recognize the state's right to impose them. Yet how can it have a right over persons who are born into a certain condition, namely that of being (in the British case) subjects of the Crown? Naturalized citizens can be required in equity to pay their taxes or undertake military service, since they have formally accepted the obligations of citizenship. But the rest of us have never done so, and yet would feel uneasy if it were suggested that, in consequence, the state has no moral claim on us whatsoever. . . .

I should make clear that in all this I have not been advocating a species of Hitlerian *Gleichschaltung:* I am not saying that it is only as a member of a single community that a man is real. We are born members of a political community, but we are also born members of a family; we are British or English or Scots, but we are also Europeans and white men, and we are or can become, amongst other things, Christians or Moral Rearmers or Nuclear Disarmers. I see no reason why all these should be collapsed into one, and it seems to me obvious that human life would be impoverished if they were. But equally I argue that the fact that men belong to these larger wholes is vital to the understanding of what they are, and at the same time is sadly neglected in contemporary ethical theory.

If it is asked what has caused this neglect, I suggest that one answer may just be that we like to think of ourselves as masters of our own destinies, independent of tradition and of the bonds of nature, and frame our moral philosophy accordingly. Sartre makes great play with the contrast between the world of man, which is, or can be, free and self-created, and the realm of the physical, which is ruled by necessity and must be taken as it is. I suggest that this contrast is overdrawn, since, at least as far as we are concerned as individuals, there is much in the world of man also which has to be accepted as sheerly given. We might begin a more realistic appraisal of the contrast by recognizing this fact and acknowledging that it has a bearing on our practical imputations of responsibility. But moral philosophers may be prevented from reaching any such result not only because of their faulty metaphysics, but also because their notions of responsibility have, from Aristotle onwards, been dominated by legal conceptions. In law we seek to correct certain deviant members of society and for this purpose employ the principle that a man is answerable only for what in some degree issues from his will. To behave otherwise would be practically impossible, for though one can sue a corporation in the person of its officials, one cannot bring a legal indictment against a whole family or a whole nation. It does not, however, follow that the legal notion of responsibility must be carried over entire into the moral sphere, and my contention is that it is not. The criminal who is caught brings punishment upon himself, but he also brings shame and obloquy on his family and friends, who thus are saddled with the consequences of deeds they did not do themselves. There are persons today who say that this amounts to persecution of the innocent and would like, in consequence, to make radical alterations in our ways of dealing with offenders. I think that they ought to reflect on the function of law and morality before they proceed to any such conclusion. Law provides only a first line of defence against malefactors; it discourages anti-social conduct by the threat of definite penalties, which can, however, in most cases be paid off once and for all. Morals supplements law by bringing softer and subtler pressures to bear, pressures which affect a man not just in his personal capacity but also through his relatives, friends and associates, pressures which, again, are not always released when a prisoner completes his sentence or pays his fine. That things work out in this way may strike us as unfair; what I am concerned to stress now is only that this is how things are. The exercise of moral pressure in the way indicated is part of an elaborate system by which society tries to protect itself against undesirable forms of behaviour, and the man who proposes to sweep it away, or alter it radically, must tell us what he thinks could be put in its place. To insist on the principle of limited liability in morals as well as in law may have the unwelcome effect of destroying the possibility of stable society. But whether it does so or not, we should not make the change without being clearly aware of what it involves.

My Station and Its Duties

F. H. Bradley

I

The good will (for morality) is meaningless, if, whatever else it be, it be not the will of living human beings. . . . It is an organism and a moral organism; and it is conscious self-realization, because only by the will of its self-conscious members can the moral organism give itself reality. It is the self-realization of the whole body, because it is one and the same will which lives and acts in the life and action of each. It is the self-realization of each member, because each member can not find the function, which makes him himself, apart from the whole to which he belongs; to be himself he must go beyond himself, to live his life he must live a life which is not *merely* his own,

F. H. Bradley, *Ethical Studies,* Introduction by Ralph Ross. © 1951, The Bobbs Merrill Company, Inc. Reprinted by permission.

but which, none the less, but on the contrary all the more, is intensely and emphatically his own individuality. . . . It is real, and real for me. It is in its affirmation that I affirm myself, for I am but as a 'heart-beat in its system.' And I am real in it; for, when I give myself to it, it gives me the fruition of my own personal activity, the accomplished ideal of my life which is happiness. In the realized idea which, superior to me, and yet here and now in and by me, affirms itself in a continuous process, we have found the end, we have found self-realization, duty, and happiness in one;— yes, we have found ourselves, when we have found our station and its duties, our function as an organ in the social organism.

'Mere rhetoric,' we shall be told, 'a bad metaphysical dream, a stale old story once more warmed up, which can not hold its own against the logic of facts. That the state was prior to the individual, that the whole was sometimes more than the sum of the parts, was an illusion which preyed on the thinkers of Greece. But that illusion has been traced to its source and dispelled, and is in plain words exploded. The family, society, the state, and generally every community of men, consists of individuals, and there is nothing in them real except the individuals. Individuals have made them, and make them, by placing themselves and by standing in certain relations. . . . The whole is the mere sum of the parts, and the parts are as real away from the whole as they are within the whole. Do you really suppose that the individual would perish if every form of community were destroyed? . . . To put the matter shortly, the community is the sum of its parts, is made by the addition of parts; and the parts are as real before the addition as after; the relations they stand in do not make them what they are, but are accidental not essential to their being; and, as to the whole, if it is not a name for the individuals that compose it, is a name of nothing actual. . . .

A discussion that would go to the bottom of the question, What is an individual? is certainly wanted. . . . But we are not going to enter on a metaphysical question to which we are not equal; we meet the metaphysical assertion of the 'individualist' with a mere denial; and, turning to facts, we will try to show that they lead us in another direction. To the assertion, then, that selves are 'individual' in the sense of exclusive of other selves, we oppose the (equally justified) assertion, that this is a mere fancy. We say that, out of theory, no such individual men exist; and we will try to show from fact that, in fact, what we call an individual man is what he is because of and by virtue of community, and that communities are thus not mere names but something real, and can be regarded (if we mean to keep to facts) only as the one in the many.

And to confine the subject, and to keep to what is familiar, we will not call to our aid the life of animals, nor early societies, nor the course of history, but we will take men as they are now; we will take ourselves, and endeavour to keep wholly to the teaching of experience.

Let us take a man, an Englishman as he is now, and try to point out that, apart from what he has in common with others, apart from his sameness with others, he is not an Englishman—nor a man at all; that if you take him as something by himself, he is not what he is. Of course we do not mean to say that he can not go out of England without disappearing, nor, even if all the rest of the nation perished, that he would not survive. What we mean to say is, that he is what he is because he is a born and educated social being, and a member of an individual social organism; that if you make abstraction of all this, which is the same in him and in others, what you have left is not an Englishman, nor a man, but some I know not what residuum, which never has existed by itself, and does not so exist. If we suppose the world of relations, in which he was born and bred, never to have been, then we suppose the very essence of him not to be; if we take that away, we have taken him away; and hence he now is not an individual, in the sense of owing nothing to the sphere of relations in which he finds himself, but does contain those relations within himself as belonging to his very being; he is what he is, in brief, so far as he is what others also are. . . .

The 'individual' man, the man into whose essence his community with others does not enter, who does not include relation to others in his very being, is, we say, a fiction, and in the light of facts we have to examine him. Let us take him in the shape of an English child as soon as he is born; for I suppose we ought not to go further back. Let us take him as soon as he is separated from his mother, and occupies a space clear and exclusive of all other human beings. At this time, education and custom will, I imagine, be allowed to have not as yet operated on him or lessened his 'individuality.' But is he now a mere 'individual,' in the sense of not implying in his being identity with others? . . . The child is not fallen from heaven. He is born of certain parents who come of certain families, and he has in him the qualities of his parents, and, as breeders would say, of the strains from both sides. Much of it we can see, and more we believe to be latent, and, given certain (possible or impossible) conditions, ready to come to light. On the descent of mental qualities modern investigation and popular experience, as expressed in uneducated vulgar opinion, altogether, I believe, support one another, and we need not linger here. . . .

But the child is not merely the member of a family; he is born into other spheres, and (passing over the subordinate wholes, which nevertheless do in many cases qualify him) he is born a member of the English nation. . . .

Thus the child is at birth; and he is born not into a desert, but into a living world, a whole which has a true individuality of its own, and into a system and order which it is difficult to look at as anything else than an organism, and which, even in England, we are now beginning to call by that name. . . . He learns, or already perhaps has learnt, to speak, and here he appropriates the common heritage of his race, the tongue that he makes his own is his country's language, it is (or it should be) the same that others speak, and it carries into his mind the ideas and sentiments of the race (over this I need not stay); and stamps them in indelibly. He grows up in an atmosphere of example and general custom, his life widens out from one little world to other and higher worlds, and he apprehends through successive stations the whole in which he lives, and in which he has lived. Is he now to try and develop his 'individuality,' his self which is not the same as other selves? Where is it? What is it? Where can he find it? The soul within him is saturated, is filled, is qualified by, it has assimilated, has got its substance, has built itself up from, it *is* one and the same life with the universal life, and if he turns against this he turns against himself; if he thrusts it from him, he tears his own vitals; if he attacks it, he sets his weapon against his own heart. He has found his life in the life of the whole, he lives that in himself, 'he is a pulsebeat of the whole system, and himself the whole system.' . . .

So far, I think, without aid from metaphysics, we have seen that the 'individual' apart from the community is an abstraction. It is not anything real, and hence not anything that we can realize, however much we may wish to do so. We have seen that I am myself by sharing with others, by including in my essence relations to them, the relations of the social state. If I wish to realize my true being, I must therefore realize something beyond my being as a mere this or that; for my true being has in it a life which is not the life of any mere particular, and so must be called an universal life.

What is it then that I am to realize? We have said it in 'my station and its duties.' To know what a man is (as we have seen) you must not take him in isolation. He is one of a people, he was born in a family, he lives in a certain society, in a certain state. What he has to do depends on what his place is, what his function is, and that all comes from his station in the organism. Are there then such organisms in which he lives, and if so, what is their nature? Here we come to questions which must be answered in full by any complete system of Ethics, but which we can not enter on. We must content ourselves by pointing out that there are such facts as the family, then in a middle position a man's own profession and society, and, over all, the larger community of the state. Leaving out of sight the question of a society wider than the state, we must say that a man's life with its moral duties is in the main filled up by his station in that system of wholes which the state is, and that this, partly by its laws and institutions, and still more by its spirit, gives him the life which he does live and ought to live. . . . In short, man is a social being; he is real only because he is social, and can realize himself only because it is as social that he realizes himself. The mere individual is a delusion of theory; and the attempt to realize it in practice is the starvation and mutilation of human nature, with total sterility or the production of monstrosities. . . .

II

. . . 'my station and its duties' teaches us to identify others and ourselves with the station we fill; to consider that as good, and by virtue of that to consider others and ourselves good too. It teaches us that a man who does his work in the world is good, notwithstanding his faults, if his faults do not prevent him from fulfilling his station. It tells us that the heart is an idle abstraction; we are not to think of it, nor must we look at our insides, but at our work and our life, and say to ourselves, Am I fulfilling my appointed function or not? Fulfil it we can, if we will: what we have to do is not so much better than the world that we can not do it; the world is there waiting for it; my duties are my rights. On the one hand, I am not likely to be much better than the world asks me to be; on the other hand, if I can take my place in the world I ought not to be discontented. . . .

There is nothing better than my station and its duties, nor anything higher or more truly beautiful. It holds and will hold its own against the worship of the 'individual,' whatever form that may take. It is strong against frantic theories and vehement passions, and in the end it triumphs over the fact and can smile at the literature, even of sentimentalism, however fulsome in its impulsive setting out, or sour in its disappointed end. It laughs at its frenzied apotheosis of the yet unsatisfied passion it calls love; and at that embitterment too which has lost its illusions, and yet can not let them go—with its kindness for the genius too clever in general to do anything in particular, and its adoration of stargazing virgins with souls above their spheres, whose wish to be something in the world takes the form of wanting to do something with it, and who in the end do badly what they might have done in the beginning well; and, worse than all, its cynical contempt for what deserves only pity, sacrifice of a life for work to the best of one's lights, a sacrifice despised not simply because it has failed, but because it is stupid, and uninteresting, and altogether unsentimental. . . .

Loyalty to Loyalty

Josiah Royce

A cause, is a possible object of loyalty only in case it is such as to join many persons into the unity of a single life. Such a cause must therefore be at once personal, and, for one who defines personality from a purely human point of view, superpersonal. . . . All stable social relations may give rise to causes that may call forth loyalty.

Now, it is obvious that nobody can be equally and directly loyal to all of the countless actual social causes that exist. It is obvious also that many causes which conform to our general definition of a possible cause may appear to any given person to be hateful and evil causes, to which he is justly opposed. A robber band, a family engaged in a murderous feud, a pirate crew, a savage tribe, a Highland robber clan of the old days—these might constitute causes to which somebody has been, or is, profoundly loyal. Men have loved such causes devotedly, have served them for a lifetime. Yet most of us would easily agree in thinking such causes unworthy of anybody's loyalty. Moreover, different loyalties may obviously stand in mutual conflict, whenever their causes are opposed. Family feuds are embittered by the very strength of the loyalty of both sides. My country, if I am the patriot inflamed by the war-spirit, seems an absolutely worthy cause; but my enemy's country usually seems hateful to me just because of my own loyalty; and therefore even my individual enemy may be hated because of the supposed baseness of his cause. War-songs call the individual enemy evil names just because he possesses the very personal qualities that, in our own loyal fellow-countrymen, we most admire. . . .

Let us next note that all the complications which we just reported are obviously due, in the main, to the fact that, as loyal men at present are, their various causes, and so their various loyalties, are viewed by them as standing in mutual, sometimes in deadly conflict. In general, as is plain if somebody's loyalty to a given cause, as for instance to a family, or to a state, so expresses itself as to involve a feud with a neighbor's family, or a warlike assault upon a foreign state, the result is obviously an evil; and at least part of the reason why it is an evil is that, by reason of the feud or the war, a certain good, namely, the enemy's loyalty, together with the enemy's opportunity to be loyal, is assailed, is thwarted, is endangered, is, perhaps, altogether destroyed. If the loyalty of A is a good for him, and if the loyalty of B is a good for him, then a feud between A and B, founded upon a mutual conflict between the causes that they serve, obviously involves this evil, namely, that each of the combatants assails, and perhaps may altogether destroy, precisely what we have seen to be the best spiritual possession of the other, namely, his chance to have a cause and to be loyal to a cause. The militant loyalty, indeed, also assails, in such a case, the enemy's physical comfort and well-being, his property, his life; and herein, of course, militant loyalty does evil to the enemy. But if each man's having and serving a cause is his best good, the worst of the evils of a feud is the resulting attack, not upon the enemy's comfort or his health or his property or his life, but upon the most precious of his possessions, his loyalty itself.

If loyalty is a supreme good, the mutually destructive conflict of loyalties is in general a supreme evil. If loyalty is a good for all sorts and conditions of men, the war of man against man has been especially mischievous, not so much because it has hurt, maimed, impoverished, or slain men, as because it has so often robbed the defeated of their causes, of their opportunities to be loyal, and sometimes of their very spirit of loyalty.

If, then, we look over the field of human life to see where good and evil have most clustered, we see that the best in human life is its loyalty; while the worst is whatever has tended to make loyalty impossible, or to destroy it when present, or to rob it of its own while it still survives. And of all things that thus have warred with loyalty, the bitterest woe of humanity has been that so often it is the loyal themselves who have thus blindly and eagerly gone about to wound and to slay the loyalty of their brethren. The spirit of loyalty has been misused to make men commit sin against this very spirit, holy as it is. For such a sin is precisely what any wanton conflict of loyalties means. Where such a conflict occurs, the best, namely, loyalty, is used as an instrument in order to compass the worst, namely, the destruction of loyalty.

It is true, then, that some causes are good, while some are evil. But the test of good and evil in the causes to which men are loyal is now definable in terms which we can greatly simplify in view of the foregoing considerations.

If, namely, I find a cause, and this cause fascinates me, and I give myself over to its service, I in so far attain what, for me, if my loyalty is complete, is a supreme good. But my cause, by our own definition, is a social cause, which binds many into the unity of one service. My cause, therefore, gives me, of necessity, fellow-servants, who with me share this loyalty, and to whom this loyalty, if complete, is also a supreme good. So far, then, in being loyal myself, I not only get but give good; for I help to sustain, in each of my fellow-servants, his own loyalty, and so I help him to secure his own supreme good. In so far, then, my loyalty to my cause is also a loyalty to my fellows' loyalty. But now suppose that my cause, like the family in a feud, or like the pirate ship, or like the aggressively warlike nation, lives by the destruction of the loyalty of other families, or of its own community, or of other communities. Then, indeed, I get a good for myself and for my fellow-servants by our common loyalty; but I war against this very spirit of loyalty as it appears in our opponent's loyalty to his own cause.

And so, a cause is good, not only for me, but for mankind, in so far as it is essentially a *loyalty to loyalty,* that is, is an aid and a furtherance of loyalty in my fellows. It is an evil cause in so far as, despite the loyalty that it arouses in me, it is destructive of loyalty in the world of my fellows. My cause is, indeed, always such as to involve some loyalty to loyalty; because, if I am loyal to any cause at all, I have fellow-servants whose loyalty mine supports. But in so far as my cause is a predatory cause, which lives by overthrowing the loyalties of others, it is an evil cause, because it involves disloyalty to the very cause of loyalty itself.

In view of these considerations, we are now able still further to simplify our problem by laying stress upon one more of those very features which seemed, but a moment since, to complicate the matter so hopelessly. Loyalty, as we have defined it, is the willing devotion of a self to a cause. In answering the ethical individualists, we have insisted that all of the higher types of loyalty involve autonomous choice. The cause that is to appeal to me at all must indeed have some elemental fascination for me. It must stir me, arouse me, please me, and in the end possess me. Moreover, it must, indeed, be set before me by my social order as a possible, a practically significant, a living cause, which binds many selves in the unity of one life. But, nevertheless, if I am really awake to the significance of my own moral choices, I must be in the position of accepting this cause. . . . My cause cannot be merely forced upon me. It is I who make it my own. It is I who willingly say: "I have no eyes to see nor tongue to speak save as this cause shall command." However much the cause may seem to be assigned to me by my social station, I must cooperate in the choice of the cause, before the act of loyalty is complete.

Since this is the case, since my loyalty never is my mere fate, but is always also my choice, I can of course determine my loyalty, at least to some extent, by the consideration of the actual good and ill which my proposed cause does to mankind. And since I now have the main criterion of the good and ill of causes before me, I can define a principle of choice which may so guide me that my loyalty shall become a good, not merely to myself, but to mankind.

This principle is now obvious. I may state it thus: In so far as it lies in your power, so choose your cause and so serve it, that, by reason of your choice and of your service, there shall be more loyalty in the world rather than less. And, in fact, so choose and so serve your individual cause as to secure thereby the greatest possible increase of loyalty amongst men. More briefly: *In choosing and in serving the cause to which you are to be loyal, be, in any case, loyal to loyalty.*

This precept, I say, will express how one should guide his choice of a cause, in so far as he considers not merely his own supreme good, but that of mankind. That such autonomous choice is possible, tends, as we now see, not to complicate, but to simplify our moral situation. For if you regard men's loyalty as their fate, if you think that a man must be loyal simply to the cause which tradition sets before him, without any power to direct his own moral attention, then indeed the conflict of loyalties seems an insoluble problem; so that, if men find themselves loyally involved in feuds, there is no way out. But if, indeed, choice plays a part,—a genuine even if limited part, in directing the individual's choice of the cause to which he is to be loyal, then indeed this choice may be so directed that loyalty to the universal loyalty of all mankind shall be furthered by the actual choices which each enlightened loyal person makes when he selects his cause. . . .

Loyalty is a good, a supreme good. . . . But this very good of loyalty is no peculiar privilege of mine; nor is it good only for me. It is an universally human good. For it is simply the finding of a harmony of the self and the world,—such a harmony as alone can content any human being. . . .

Loyalty, then, is a good for all men. And it is in any man just as much a true good as my loyalty could be in me. And so, then, if indeed I seek a cause, a worthy cause, what cause could be more worthy than the cause of loyalty to loyalty; that is, the cause of making loyalty prosper amongst men? If I could serve that cause in a sustained and effective life, if some practical work for the furtherance of universal human loyalty could become to me what the House was to the Speaker, then indeed my own life-task would be found; and I could then be assured at every instant of the worth of my cause by virtue of the very good that I personally found in its service. . . .

Our question therefore becomes this: Is there a practical way of serving the universal human cause of loyalty to loyalty? And if there is such a way, what is it? Can we see how personally so to act that we bring loyalty on earth to a fuller fruition, to a wider range of efficacy, to a more effective sovereignty over the lives of men? . . .

I answer at once that the individual man, with his limited powers, can indeed serve the cause of universal loyalty only by limiting his undertakings to some decidedly definite personal range. He must have his own special and personal cause. But this cause of his can indeed be chosen and determined so as to constitute a deliberate effort to further universal loyalty. When I begin to show you how this may be, I shall at once pass from what may have seemed to you a very unpractical scheme of life, to a realm of familiar and commonplace virtuous activities. The only worth of my general scheme will then lie in the fact that, in the light of this scheme, we can, as it were, see the commonplace virtues transfigured and glorified by their relation to the one highest cause of all. My thesis is *that all the commonplace virtues, in so far as they are indeed defensible and effective, are special forms of loyalty to loyalty,* and are to be justified, centralized, inspired, by the one supreme effort to do good, namely, the effort to make loyalty triumphant in the lives of all men.

The first consideration which I shall here insist upon is this: Loyalty, as we have all along seen, depends upon a very characteristic and subtle union of natural interest, and of free choice. Nobody who merely follows his natural impulses as they come is loyal. Yet nobody can be loyal without depending upon and using his natural impulses. If I am to be loyal, my cause must from moment to moment fascinate me, awaken my muscular vigor, stir me with some eagerness for work, even if this be painful work. I cannot be loyal to barren abstractions. I can only be loyal to what my life can interpret in bodily deeds. Loyalty has its elemental appeal to my whole organism. My cause must become one with my human life. Yet all this must occur not without my willing choice. I must control my devotion. It will possess me, but not without my voluntary complicity; for I shall accept the possession. . . .

In order to be loyal, then, to loyalty, I must indeed first choose forms of loyal conduct which appeal to my own nature. This means that, upon one side of my life, I shall have to behave much as the most unenlightened of the loyal do. I shall serve causes such as my natural temperament and my social opportunities suggest to me. I shall choose friends whom I like. My family, my community, my country, will be served partly because I find it interesting to be loyal to them.

Nevertheless, upon another side, all these my more natural and, so to speak, accidental loyalties, will be controlled and unified by a deliberate use of the principle that, whatever my cause, it ought to be such as to further, so far as in me lies, the cause of universal loyalty. . . .

Yet herewith we have only begun to indicate how the cause of loyalty to loyalty may be made a cause that one can practically, efficaciously, and constantly serve. Loyalty, namely, is not a matter merely of to-day or of yesterday. The loyal have existed since civilization began. And, even so, loyalty to loyalty is not a novel undertaking. It began to be effective from the time when first people could make and keep a temporary truce during a war, and when first strangers were regarded as protected by the gods, and when first the duties of hospitality were recognized. The way to be loyal to loyalty is therefore laid down in precisely the rational portion of the conventional morality which human experience has worked out. . . .

My thesis is that *all those duties which we have learned to recognize as the fundamental duties of the civilized man, the duties that every man owes to every man, are to be rightly interpreted as special instances of loyalty to loyalty*. In other words, all the recognized virtues can be defined in terms of our concept of loyalty. And this is why I assert that, when rightly interpreted, loyalty is the whole duty of man.

For consider the best-known facts as to the indirect influence of certain forms of loyal conduct. When I speak the truth, my act is directly an act of loyalty to the personal tie which then and there binds me to the man to whom I consent to speak. My special cause is, in such a case, constituted by this tie. My fellow and I are linked in a certain unity,—the unity of some transaction which involves our speech one to another. To be ready to speak the truth to my fellow is to have, just then, no eye to see and no tongue to speak save as this willingly accepted tie demands. In so far, then, speaking the truth is a special instance of loyalty. But whoever speaks the truth, thereby does what he then can do to help everybody to speak the truth. For he acts so as to further the general confidence of man in man. How far such indirect influence may extend, no man can predict.

Precisely so, in the commercial world, honesty in business is a service, not merely and not mainly to the others who are parties to the single transaction in which at any one time this faithfulness is shown. The single act of business fidelity is an act of loyalty to that general confidence of man in man upon which the whole fabric of business rests. On the contrary, the unfaithful financier whose disloyalty is the final deed that lets loose the avalanche of a panic, has done far more harm to general public confidence than he could possibly do to those whom his act directly assails. Honesty, then, is owed not merely and not even mainly to those with whom we directly deal when we do honest acts; it is owed to mankind at large, and it benefits the community and the general cause of commercial loyalty.

Such a remark is in itself a commonplace; but it serves to make concrete my general thesis that every form of dutiful action is a case of loyalty to loyalty. For what holds thus of truthfulness and of commercial honesty holds, I assert, of every form of dutiful action. Each such form is a special means for being, by a concrete deed, loyal to loyalty.

We have sought for the worthy cause; and we have found it. This simplest possible of considerations serves to turn the chaotic mass of separate precepts of which our ordinary conventional moral code consists into a system unified by the one spirit of universal loyalty. By your individual deed you indeed cannot save the world, but you can at any moment do what in you lies to further the cause which both for you and for the human world constitutes the supreme good, namely, the cause of universal loyalty. Herein consists your entire duty. . . .

Ethical Responsibilities of Engineers in Large Organizations: The Pinto Case

Richard T. De George

The myth that ethics has no place in engineering has been attacked, and at least in some corners of the engineering profession has been put to rest.[1] Another myth, however, is emerging to take its place—the myth of the engineer as moral hero. A litany of engineering saints is slowly taking form. The saints of the field are whistle blowers, especially those who have sacrificed all for their moral convictions. The zeal of some preachers, however, has gone too far, piling moral responsibility upon moral responsibility on the shoulders of the engineer. This emphasis, I believe, is misplaced. Though engineers are members of a profession that holds public safety paramount,[2] we cannot reasonably expect engineers to be willing to sacrifice their jobs each day for principle and to have a whistle ever by their sides ready to blow if their firm strays from what they perceive to be the morally right course of action. If this is too much to ask, however, what then is the actual ethical responsibility of engineers in a large organization?

I shall approach this question through a discussion of what has become known as the Pinto case, i.e., the trial that took place in Winamac, Indiana, and that was decided by a jury on March 16, 1980.

In August 1978 near Goshen, Indiana, three girls died of burns in a 1973 Pinto that was rammed in traffic by a van. The rear-end collapsed "like an accordian,"[3] and the gas tank erupted in flames. It was not the first such accident with the Pinto. The Pinto was introduced in 1971 and its gas tank housing was not changed until the 1977 model. Between 1971 and 1978 about fifty suits were brought against Ford in connection with rear-end accidents in the Pinto.

What made the Winamac case different from the fifty others was the fact that the

Business and Professional Ethics Journal, vol. 1, no. 1, Fall 1981. © Richard T. De George. Reprinted by permission.

State prosecutor charged Ford with three (originally four, but one was dropped) counts of reckless homicide, a *criminal* offense, under a 1977 Indiana law that made it possible to bring such criminal charges against a corporation. The penalty, if found guilty, was a maximum fine of $10,000 for each count, for a total of $30,000. The case was closely watched, since it was the first time in recent history that a corporation was charged with this criminal offense. Ford spent almost a million dollars in its defense.

With the advantage of hindsight I believe the case raised the right issue at the wrong time.

The prosecution had to show that Ford was reckless in placing the gas tank where and how it did. In order to show this the prosecution had to prove that Ford consciously disregarded harm it might cause and the disregard, according to the statutory definition of "reckless," had to involve "substantial deviation from acceptable standards of conduct."[4]

The prosecution produced seven witnesses who testified that the Pinto was moving at speeds judged to be between 15 and 35 mph when it was hit. Harly Copp, once a high ranking Ford engineer, claimed that the Pinto did not have a balanced design and that for cost reasons the gas tank could withstand only a 20 mph impact without leaking and exploding. The prosecutor, Michael Cosentino, tried to introduce evidence that Ford knew the defects of the gas tank, that its executives knew that a $6.65 part would have made the car considerably safer, and that they decided against the change in order to increase their profits.

Federal safety standards for gas tanks were not introduced until 1977. Once introduced, the National Highway Traffic Safety Administration (NHTSA) claimed a safety defect existed in the gas tanks of Pintos produced from 1971 to 1976. It ordered that Ford recall 1.9 million Pintos. Ford contested the order. Then, without ever admitting that the fuel tank was unsafe, it "voluntarily" ordered a recall. It claimed the recall was not for safety but for "reputational" reasons.[5] Agreeing to a recall in June, its first proposed modifications failed the safety standards tests, and it added a second protective shield to meet safety standards. It did not send out recall notices until August 22. The accident in question took place on August 10. The prosecutor claimed that Ford knew its fuel tank was dangerous as early as 1971 and that it did not make any changes until the 1977 model. It also knew in June of 1978 that its fuel tank did not meet federal safety standards; yet it did nothing to warn owners of this fact. Hence, the prosecution contended, Ford was guilty of reckless homicide.

The defense was led by James F. Neal who had achieved national prominence in the Watergate hearings. He produced testimony from two witnesses who were crucial to the case. They were hospital attendants who had spoken with the driver of the Pinto at the hospital before she died. They claimed she had stated that she had just had her car filled with gas. She had been in a hurry and had left the gas station without replacing the cap on her gas tank. It fell off the top of her car as she drove down the highway. She noticed this and stopped to turn around to pick it up. While stopped, her car was hit by the van. The testimony indicated that the car was stopped. If the car was hit by a van going 50 mph, then the rupture of the gas tank was to be expected. If the cap was off the fuel tank, leakage would be more than otherwise. No small vehicle was made to withstand such impact. Hence, Ford claimed, there was no recklessness involved. Neal went on to produce films of tests that indicated that the amount of damage the Pinto suffered meant that the impact must have been caused by the van's going at least 50 mph. He further argued that the Pinto gas tank was at least as safe as the gas tanks on the 1973 American Motors Gremlin, the Chevrolet Vega, the Dodge Colt, and the Toyota Corolla, all of which suffered comparable damage when hit from the rear at 50 mph. Since no federal safety standards were in effect in 1973, Ford was not reckless if its safety standards were comparable to those of similar cars made by competitors; that standard represented the state of the art at that time, and it would be inappropriate to apply 1977 standards to a 1973 car.[6]

The jury deliberated for four days and finally came up with a verdict of not guilty. When the verdict was announced at a meeting of the Ford Board of Directors then taking place, the members broke out in a cheer.[7]

These are the facts of the case. I do not wish to second-guess the jury. Based on my reading of the case, I think they arrived at a proper decision, given the evidence. Nor do I wish to comment adversely on the judge's ruling that prevented the prosecution from introducing about 40% of his case because the evidence referred to 1971 and 1972 models of the Pinto and not the 1973 model.[8]

The issue of Ford's being guilty of acting recklessly can, I think, be made plausible, as I shall indicate shortly. But the successful strategy argued by the defense in this case hinged on the Pinto in question being hit by a van at 50 mph. At that speed, the defense successfully argued, the gas tank of any subcompact would rupture. Hence that accident did not show that the Pinto was less safe than other subcompacts or that Ford acted recklessly. To show that would require an accident that took place at no more than 20 mph.

The contents of the Ford documents that Prosecutor Cosentino was not allowed to present in court were published in the *Chicago Tribune* on October 13, 1979. If they are accurate, they tend to show grounds for the charge of recklessness.

Ford had produced a safe gas tank mounted over the rear axle in its 1969 Capri in Europe. It tested that tank in the Capri. In its over-the-axle position, it withstood impacts of up to 30 mph. Mounted behind the axle, it was punctured by projecting bolts when hit from the rear at 20 mph. A $6.65 part would help make the tank safer. In its 1971 Pinto, Ford chose to place the gas tank behind the rear axle without the extra part. A Ford memo indicates that in this position the Pinto has more trunk space, and that production costs would be less than in the over-the-axle position. These considerations won out.[9]

The Pinto was first tested it seems in 1971, after the 1971 model was produced, for rear-end crash tolerance. It was found that the tank ruptured when hit from the rear at 20 mph. This should have been no surprise, since the Capri tank in that position had ruptured at 20 mph. A memo recommends that rather than making any changes Ford should wait until 1976 when the government was expected to introduce fuel tank standards. By delaying making any change, Ford could save $20.9 million, since the change would average about $10 per car.[10]

In the Winamac case Ford claimed correctly that there were no federal safety standards in 1973. But it defended itself against recklessness by claiming its car was comparable to other subcompacts at that time. All the defense showed, however, was that all the subcompacts were unsafe when hit at 50 mph. Since the other subcompacts were not forced to recall their cars in 1978, there is *prima facie* evidence that Ford's Pinto gas tank mounting was substandard. The Ford documents tend to show Ford knew the danger it was inflicting on Ford owners; yet it did nothing, for profit reasons. How short-sighted those reasons were is demonstrated by the fact that the Pinto thus far in litigation and recalls alone has cost Ford $50 million. Some forty suits are still to be settled. And these figures do not take into account the loss of sales due to bad publicity.

Given these facts, what are we to say about the Ford engineers? Where were they when all this was going on, and what is their responsibility for the Pinto? The answer, I suggest, is that they were where they were supposed to be, doing what they were supposed to be doing. They were performing tests, designing the Pinto, making reports. But do they have no moral responsibility for the products they design? What after all is the moral responsibility of engineers in a large corporation? By way of reply, let me emphasize that no engineer can morally do what is immoral. If commanded to do what he should not morally do, he must resist and refuse. But in the Ford Pinto situation no engineer was told to produce a gas tank that would explode and kill people. The engineers were not instructed to make an unsafe car. They were morally responsible for knowing the state of the art, including that connected with placing and mounting gas tanks. We can assume that the Ford engineers were cognizant of the state of the art in producing the model they did. When tests were made in 1970 and 1971, and a memo was written stating that a $6.65 modification could make the gas tank safer,[11] that was an engineering assessment. Whichever engineer proposed the modification and initiated the memo acted ethically in doing so. The next step, the administrative decision not to make the modification was, with hindsight, a poor one in almost every way. It ended up costing Ford a great deal more not to put in the part than it would have cost to put it in. Ford still claims today that its gas tank was as safe as the accepted standards of the industry at that time.[12] It must say so, otherwise the suits pending against it will skyrocket. That it was not as safe seems borne out by the fact that only the Pinto of all the subcompacts failed to pass the 30 mph rear impact NHTSA test.

But the question of wrongdoing or of malicious intent or of recklessness is not so easily solved. Suppose the ordinary person were told when buying a Pinto that if he paid an extra $6.65 he could increase the safety of the vehicle so that it could withstand a 30 mph rear-end impact rather than a 20 mph impact, and that the odds of suffering a rear-end impact of between 20 and 30 mph was 1 in 250,000. Would we call him or her reckless if he or she declined to pay the extra $6.65? I am not sure how to answer that question. Was it reckless of Ford to wish to save the $6.65 per car and increase the risk for the consumer? Here I am inclined to be clearer in my own mind. If I choose to take a risk to save $6.65, it is my risk and my $6.65. But if Ford saves the $6.65 and I take the risk, then I clearly lose. Does Ford have the right to do that without informing me, if the going standard of safety of subcompacts is safety in a rear-end collision up to 30 mph? I think not. I admit, however, that the case is not clear-cut, even if we add that during 1976 and 1977 Pintos suffered 13 fiery fatal rear-end collisions, more than double that of other U.S. comparable cars. The VW Rabbit and Toyota Corolla suffered none.[13]

Yet, if we are to morally fault anyone for the decision not to add the part, we would censure not the Ford engineers but the Ford executives, because it was not an engineering but an executive decision.

My reason for taking this view is that an engineer cannot be expected and cannot have the responsibility to second-guess managerial decisions. He is responsible for bringing the facts to the attention of those who need them to make decisions. But the input of engineers is only one of many factors that go to make up managerial decisions. During the trial, the defense called as a witness Francis Olsen, the assistant chief engineer in charge of design at Ford, who testified that he bought a 1973 Pinto for his eighteen-year-old daughter, kept it a year, and then traded it in for a 1974 Pinto which he kept two years.[14] His testimony and his actions were presented as an indication that the Ford engineers had confidence in the Pinto's safety. At least this one had enough confidence in it to give it to his daughter. Some engineers at Ford may have felt that the car could have been safer. But this is true of almost every automobile. Engineers in large firms have an ethical responsibility to do their jobs as best they can, to report their observations about safety and improvement of safety to management. But they do not have the obligation to insist that their perceptions or their standards be accepted. They are not paid to do that, they are not expected to do that, and they have no moral or ethical obligation to do that.

In addition to doing their jobs, engineers can plausibly be said to have an obligation of loyalty to their employers, and firms have a right to a certain amount of confidentiality concerning their internal operations. At the same time engineers are required by their professional ethical codes to hold the safety of the public paramount. Where these obligations conflict, the need for and justification of whistle blowing arises.[15] If we admit the obligations on both sides, I would suggest as a rule of thumb that engineers and other workers in a large corporation are morally *permitted* to go public with information about the safety of a product if the following conditions are met:

1 if the harm that will be done by the product to the public is serious and considerable;

2 if they make their concerns known to their superiors; and

3 if, getting no satisfaction from their immediate superiors, they exhaust the channels available within the corporation, including going to the board of directors.

If they still get no action, I believe they are morally *permitted* to make public their views; but they are not morally *obliged* to do so. Harly Copp, a former Ford executive and engineer, in fact did criticize the Pinto from the start and testified for the prosecution against Ford at the Winamac trial,[16] He left the company and voiced his criticism. The criticism was taken up by Ralph Nader and others. In the long run it led to the Winamac trial and probably helped in a number of other suits filed against Ford. Though I admire Mr. Copp for his actions, assuming they were done from moral motives, I do not think such action was morally required, nor do I think the other engineers at Ford were morally deficient in not doing likewise.

For an engineer to have a moral *obligation* to bring his case for safety to the public, I think two other conditions have to be fulfilled, in addition to the three mentioned above.[17]

4 He must have documented evidence that would convince a reasonable, impartial observer that his view of the situation is correct and the company policy wrong.

Such evidence is obviously very difficult to obtain and produce. Such evidence, however, takes an engineer's concern out of the realm of the subjective and precludes that concern from being simply one person's opinion based on a limited point of view. Unless such evidence is available, there is little likelihood that the concerned engineer's view will win the day simply by public exposure. If the testimony of Francis Olsen is accurate, then even among the engineers at Ford there was disagreement about the safety of the Pinto.

5 There must be strong evidence that making the information public will in fact prevent the threatened serious harm.

This means both that before going public the engineer should know what source (government, newspaper, columnist, TV reporter) will make use of his evidence and how it will be handled. He should also have good reason to believe that it will result in the kind of change or result that he believes is morally appropriate. None of this was the case in the Pinto situation. After much public discussion, five model years, and failure to pass national safety standards tests, Ford plausibly defends its original claim that the gas tank was acceptably safe. If there is little likelihood of his success, there is no moral obligation for the engineer to go public. For the harm he or she personally incurs is not offset by the good such action achieves.[18]

My first substantive conclusion is that Ford engineers had no moral *obligation* to do more than they did in this case.

My second claim is that though engineers in large organizations should have a say in setting safety standards and producing cost-benefit analyses, they need not have the last word. My reasons are two. First, while the degree of risk, e.g., in a car, is an engineering problem, the acceptability of risk is not. Second, an engineering cost-benefit analysis does not include all the factors appropriate in making a policy decision, either on the corporate or the social level. Safety is one factor in an engineering design. Yet clearly it is only one factor. A Mercedes-Benz 280 is presumably safer than a Ford Pinto. But the difference in price is considerable. To make a Pinto as safe as a Mercedes it would probably have to cost a comparable amount. In making cars as in making many other objects some balance has to be reached between safety and cost. The final decision on where to draw the balance is not only an engineering decision. It is also a managerial decision, and probably even more appropriately a social decision.

The difficulty of setting standards raises two pertinent issues. The first concerns federal safety standards. The second concerns cost-benefit analysis. The state of the art of engineering technology determines a floor below which no manufacturer should ethically go. Whether the Pinto fell below that floor, we have already seen, is a controverted question. If the cost of achieving greater safety is considerable—and I do not think $6.65 is considerable—there is a built-in temptation for a producer to skimp more than he should and more than he might like. The best way to remove that temptation is for there to be a national set of standards. Engineers can determine what the state of the art is, what is possible, and what the cost of producing safety is. A panel of informed people, not necessarily engineers, should decide what is acceptable risk and hence what acceptable minimum standards are. Both the minimum standards and the standards attained by a given car should be a matter of record that goes with each car. A safer car may well cost more. But unless a customer knows how much safety he is buying for his money, he may not know which car he wants to buy. This information, I believe, is information a car buyer is entitled to have.

In 1978, after the publicity that Ford received with the Pinto and the controversy surrounding it, the sales of Pintos fell dramatically. This was an indication that consumers preferred a safer car for comparable money, and they went to the competition. The state of Oregon took all its Pintos out of its fleet and sold them off. To the surprise of one dealer involved in selling turned-in Pintos, they went for between $1000 and $1800.[19] The conclusion we correctly draw is that there was a market for a car with a dubious safety record even though the price was much lower than for safer cars and lower than Ford's manufacturing price.

The second issue is the way cost-benefit analyses are produced and used. I have already mentioned one cost-benefit analysis used by Ford, namely, the projection that by not adding a part and by placing the gas tank in the rear the company could save $20.9 million. The projection, I noted, was grossly mistaken for it did not consider litigation, recalls, and bad publicity which have already cost Ford over $50 million. A second type of cost-benefit analysis sometimes estimates the number and costs of suits that will have to be paid, adds to it fines, and deducts that total amount from the total saved by a particular practice. If the figure is positive, it is more profitable not to make a safety change than to make it.

A third type of cost-benefit analysis, which Ford and other auto companies produce, estimates the cost and benefits of specific changes in their automobiles. One study, for instance, deals with the cost-benefit analysis relating to fuel leakage associated with static rollover. The unit cost of the part is $11. If that is included in 12.5 million cars, the total cost is $137 million. That part will prevent 180 burn deaths, 180 serious burn injuries and 2100 burned vehicles. Assigning a cost of $200,000 per death, $67,000 per major injury, and $700 per vehicle, the benefit is $49.5 million. The cost-benefit ratio is slightly over 3–1.[20]

If this analysis is compared with a similar cost-benefit analysis for a rear-end collision, it is possible to see how much safety is achieved per dollar spent. This use is legitimate and helpful. But the procedure is open to very serious criticism if used not in a comparative but in an absolute manner.

The analysis ignores many factors, such as the human suffering of the victim and of his or her family. It equates human life to $200,000, which is based on average lost future wages. Any figure here is questionable, except for comparative purposes, in which case as long as the same figure is used it does not change the information as to relative benefit per dollar. The ratio, however, has no *absolute* meaning, and no decision can properly be based on the fact that the resulting ratio of cost to benefit in the above example is 3 to 1. Even more important, how can this figure or ratio be compared with the cost of styling? Should the $11 per unit to reduce death and injury from roll-over be weighed against a comparable $11 in rear-end collision or $11 in changed styling? Who decides how much more to put into safety and how much more to put into styling? What is the rationale for the decision?

In the past consumers have not been given an opportunity to vote on the matter. The automobile industry has decided what will sell and what will not, and has decided how much to put on safety. American car dealers have not typically put much emphasis on safety features in selling their cars. The assumption that American drivers are more interested in styling than safety is a decision that has been made for them, not by them. Engineers can and do play an important role in making cost-benefit analyses. They are better equipped than anyone else to figure risks and cost. But they are not better equipped to figure the acceptability of risk, or the amount that people should be willing to pay to eliminate such risk. Neither, however, are the managers of automobile corporations. The amount of acceptable risk is a public decision that can and should be made by representatives of the public or by the public itself.

Since cost-benefit analyses of the types I have mentioned are typical of those used in the auto industry, and since they are inadequate ways of judging the safety a car should have, given the state of the art, it is clear that the automobile companies should not have the last word or the exclusive word in how much safety to provide. There must be national standards set and enforced. The National Highway Traffic Administration was established in 1966 to set standards. Thus far only two major standards have been established and implemented: the 1972 side impact standard and the 1977 gasoline tank safety standard. Rather than dictate standards, however, in which process it is subject to lobbying, it can mandate minimum standards and also require auto manufacturers to inform the public about the safety quotient of each car, just as it now requires each car to specify the miles per gallon it is capable of achieving. Such an approach would put the onus for basic safety on the manufacturers, but it would also make additional safety a feature of consumer interest and competition.

Engineers in large corporations have an important role to play. That role, however, is not usually to set policy or to decide on the acceptability of risk. Their knowledge and expertise are important both to the companies for which they work and to the public. But they are not morally responsible for policies and decisions beyond their competence and control. Does this view, however, let engineers off the moral hook too easily?

To return briefly to the Pinto story once more, Ford wanted a subcompact to fend off the competition of Japanese imports. The order came down to produce a car of 2,000 pounds or less that would cost $2000 or less in time for the 1971 model. This allowed only 25 months instead of the usual 43 months for design and production of a new car.[21] The engineers were squeezed from the start. Perhaps this is why they did not test the gas tank for rear-end collision impact until the car was produced.

Should the engineers have refused the order to produce the car in 25 months? Should they have resigned, or leaked the story to the newspapers? Should they have refused to speed up their usual routine? Should they have complained to their professional society that they were being asked to do the impossible—if it were to be done right? I am not in a position to say what they should have done. But with the advantage of hindsight, I suggest we should ask not only what they should have done. We should especially ask what changes can be made to prevent engineers from being squeezed in this way in the future.

Engineering ethics should not take as its goal the producing of moral heroes. Rather it should consider what forces operate to encourage engineers to act as they feel they should not; what structural or other features of a large corporation squeeze them until their consciences hurt? Those features should then be examined, evaluated, and changes proposed and made. Lobbying by engineering organizations would be appropriate, and legislation should be passed if necessary. In general I tend to favor voluntary means where possible. But where that is utopian, then legislation is a necessary alternative.

The need for whistle blowing in a firm indicates that a change is necessary. How can we preclude the necessity for blowing the whistle?

The Winamac Pinto case suggests some external and internal modifications. It was the first case to be tried under a 1977 Indiana law making it possible to try corporations as well as individuals for the criminal offenses of reckless homicide. In bringing the charges against Ford, Prosecutor Michael Cosentino acted courageously, even if it turned out to have been a poor case for such precedent-setting trial. But the law concerning reckless homicide, for instance, which was the charge in question, had not been rewritten with the corporation in mind. The penalty, since corporations cannot go to jail, was the maximum fine of $10,000 per count—hardly a significant amount when contrasted with the 1977 income of Ford International which was $11.1 billion in revenues and $750 million in profits. What Mr. Cosentino did *not* do was file charges against individuals in the Ford Company who were responsible for the decisions he claimed were reckless. Had highly placed officials been charged, the message would have gotten through to management across the country that individuals cannot hide behind corporate shields in their decisions if they are indeed reckless, put too low a price on life and human suffering, and sacrifice it too cheaply for profits.

A bill was recently proposed in Congress requiring managers to disclose the existence of life-threatening defects to the appropriate Federal agency.[22] Failure to do so and attempts to conceal defects could result in fines of $50,000 or imprisonment for a minimum of two years, or both. The fine in corporate terms is negligible. But imprisonment for members of management is not.

Some argue that increased litigation for product liability is the way to get results in safety. Heavy damages yield quicker changes than criminal proceedings. Ford agreed to the Pinto recall shortly after a California jury awarded damages of $127.8 million after a youth was burned over 95% of his body. Later the sum was reduced, on appeal, to $6.3 million.[23] But criminal proceedings make the litigation easier, which is why Ford spent $1,000,000 in its defense to avoid paying $30,000 in fines.[24] The possibility of going to jail for one's actions, however, should have a salutary effect. If someone, the president of a company in default of anyone else, were to be charged in criminal suit, presidents would soon know whom they can and should hold responsible below them. One of the difficulties in a large corporation is knowing who is responsible for particular decisions. If the president were held responsible, outside pressure would build to reorganize the corporation so that responsibility was assigned and assumed.

If a corporation wishes to be moral or if society or engineers wish to apply pressure for organizational changes such that the corporation acts morally and responds to the moral conscience of engineers and others within the organization, then changes must be made. Unless those at the top set a moral tone, unless they insist on moral conduct, unless they punish immoral conduct and reward moral conduct, the corporation will function without considering the morality of questions and of corporate actions. It may by accident rather than by intent avoid immoral actions, though in the long run this is unlikely.

Ford's management was interested only in meeting federal standards and having these as low as possible. Individual federal standards should be both developed and enforced. Federal fines for violations should not be token but comparable to damages paid in civil suits and should be paid to all those suffering damage from violations.[25]

Independent engineers or engineering societies—if the latter are not co-opted by auto manufacturers—can play a significant role in supplying information on the state of the art and the level of technical feasibility available. They can also develop the safety index I suggested earlier, which would represent the relative and comparative safety of an automobile. Competition has worked successfully in many areas. Why not in the area of safety? Engineers who work for auto manufacturers will then have to make and report the results of standard tests such as the ability to withstand rear-end impact. If such information is required data for a safety index to be affixed to the windshield of each new car, engineers will not be squeezed by management in the area of safety.

The means by which engineers with ethical concerns can get a fair hearing without endangering their jobs or blowing the whistle must be made part of a corporation's organizational structure. An outside board member with primary responsibility for investigating and responding to such ethical concerns might be legally required. When this is joined with the legislation pending in Congress which I mentioned, the dynamics for ethics in the organization will be significantly improved. Another way of achieving a similar end is by providing an inspector general for all corporations with an annual net income of over $1 billion. An independent committee of an engineering association might be formed to investigate charges made by engineers concerning the safety of a product on which they are working;[26] a company that did not allow an appropriate investigation of employee charges would become subject to cover-up proceedings. Those in the engineering industry can suggest and work to implement other ideas. I have elsewhere outlined a set of ten such changes for the ethical corporation.[27]

In addition to asking how an engineer should respond to moral quandaries and dilemmas, and rather than asking how to educate or train engineers to be moral heroes, those in engineering ethics should ask how large organizations can be changed so that they do not squeeze engineers in moral dilemmas, place them in the position of facing moral quandaries, and make them feel that they must blow the whistle.

The time has come to go beyond sensitizing students to moral issues and solving and resolving the old, standard cases. The next and very important questions to be asked as we discuss each case is how organizational structures can be changed so that no engineer will ever again have to face *that* case.

Many of the issues of engineering ethics within a corporate setting concern the ethics of organizational structure, questions of public policy, and so questions that frequently are amenable to solution only on a scale larger than the individual—on the scale of organization and law. The ethical responsibilities of the engineer in a large organization have as much to do with the organization as with the engineer. They can be most fruitfully approached by considering from a moral point of view not only the individual engineer but the framework within which he or she works. We not only need moral people. Even more importantly we need moral structures and organizations. Only by paying more attention to these can we adequately resolve the questions of the ethical responsibility of engineers in large organizations.

NOTES

1 The body of literature on engineering ethics is now substantive and impressive. See, *A Selected Annotated Bibliography of Professional Ethics and Social Responsibility in Engineering*, compiled by Robert F. Ladenson, James Choromokos, Ernest d'Anjou, Martin Pimsler, and Howard Rosen (Chicago: Center for the Study of Ethics in the Professions, Illinois Institute of Technology, 1980). A useful two-volume collection of readings and cases is also available: Robert J. Baum and Albert Flores, *Ethical Problems in Engineering,* 2nd edition (Troy, N.Y.: Rensselaer Polytechnic Institute, Center for the Study of the Human Dimensions of Science and Technology, 1980. See also Robert J. Baum's *Ethics and Engineering Curricula* (Hastings-on-Hudson, N.Y.: Hastings Center, 1980).

2 See, for example, the first canon of the 1974 Engineers Council for Professional Development Code, the first canon of the National Council of Engineering Examiners Code, and the draft (by A. Oldenquist and E. Slowter) of a "Code of Ethics for the Engineering Profession" (all reprinted in Baum and Flores, *Ethical Problems in Engineering*.

3 Details of the incident presented in this paper are based on testimony at the trial. Accounts of the trial as well as background reports were carried by both the *New York Times* and the *Chicago Tribune*.

4 *New York Times,* February 17, 1980, IV, p. 9.

5 *New York Times,* February 21, 1980, p. A6. *Fortune,* September 11, 1978, p. 42.

6 *New York Times,* March 14, 1980, p. 1.

7 *Time,* March 24, 1980, p. 24.

8 *New York Times,* January 16, 1980, p. 16; February 7, 1980, p. 16.

9 *Chicago Tribune,* October 13, 1979, p. 1, and Section 2, p. 12.

10 *Chicago Tribune,* October 13, 1979, p. 1; *New York Times,* October 14, 1979, p. 26.

11 *New York Times,* February 4, 1980, p. 12.

12 *New York Times,* June 10, 1978, p. 1; *Chicago Tribune,* October 13, 1979, p. 1, and Section 2, p. 12. The continuous claim has been that the Pinto poses "No serious hazards."

13 *New York Times,* October 26, 1978, p. 103.

14 *New York Times,* February 20, 1980, p. A16.

15 For a discussion of the conflict, see, Sissela Bok, "Whistleblowing and Professional Responsibility," *New York University Educational Quarterly,* pp. 2–10. For detailed case studies see, Ralph Nader, Peter J. Petkas, and Kate Blackwell, *Whistle Blowing* (New York: Grossman Publishers, 1972); Charles Peters and Taylor Branch, *Blowing the Whistle: Dissent in the Public Interest* (New York: Praeger Publishers, 1972); and Robert M. Anderson, Robert Perrucci, Dan E. Schendel and Leon E. Trachtman, *Divided Loyalties: Whistle-Blowing at BART* (West Lafayette, Indiana: Purdue University, 1980).

16 *New York Times,* February 4, 1980, p. 12.

17 The position I present here is developed more fully in my book *Business Ethics* (New York: Macmillan, 1982, pp. 157–164). It differs somewhat from the dominant view expressed in the existing literature in that I consider whistle blowing an extreme measure that is morally obligatory only if the stringent conditions set forth are satisfied. Cf. Kenneth D. Walters, "Your Employees' Right to Blow the Whistle," *Harvard Business Review,* July–August, 1975.

18 On the dangers incurred by whistle blowers, see Gene James, "Whistle-Blowing: Its Nature and Justification," *Philosophy in Context,* 10 (1980), pp. 99–117, which examines the legal context of whistle blowing; Peter Raven-Hansen, "Dos and Don'ts for Whistleblowers: Planning for Trouble," *Technology Review,* May 1980, pp. 34–44, which suggests how to blow the whistle; Helen Dudar, "The Price of Blowing the Whistle," *The New York Times Magazine,* 30 October, 1977, which examines the results for whistleblowers; David W. Ewing, "Canning Directions," *Harpers,* August, 1979, pp. 17–22, which indicates "how the government rids itself of troublemakers" and how legislation protecting whistleblowers can be circumvented; and Report by the U.S. General Accounting Office, "The Office of the Special Counsel Can Improve Its Management of Whistleblower Cases," December 30, 1980 (FPCD-81-10).

19 *New York Times,* April 21, 1978, IV, p. 1, 18.

20 See Mark Dowie, "Pinto Madness," *Mother Jones,* September/October, 1977, pp. 24–28.

21 *Chicago Tribune,* October 13, 1979, Section 2, p. 12.

22 *New York Times,* March 16, 1980, IV, p. 20.

23 *New York Times,* February 8, 1978, p. 8.

24 *New York Times,* February 17, 1980, IV, p. 9; January 6, 1980, p. 24; *Time,* March 24, 1980, p. 24.

25 *The Wall Street Journal,* August 7, 1980, p. 7, reported that the Ford Motor Company "agreed to pay a total of $22,500 to the families of three Indiana teen-age girls killed in the crash of a Ford Pinto nearly two years ago. . . . A Ford spokesman said the settlement was made without any admission of liability. He speculated that the relatively small settlement may have been influenced by certain Indiana laws which severely restrict the amount of damages victims or their families can recover in civil cases alleging wrongful death."

26 A number of engineers have been arguing for a more active role by engineering societies in backing up individual engineers in their attempts to act responsibly. See, Edwin Layton, *Revolt of the Engineers* (Cleveland: Case Western Reserve, 1971); Stephen H. Unger, "Engineering Societies and the Responsible Engineer," *Annals of the New York Academy of Sciences,* 196 (1973), pp. 433–37 (reprinted in Baum and Flores, *Ethical Problems in Engineering,* pp. 56–59); and Robert Perrucci and Joel Gerstl, *Profession Without Community: Engineers in American Society* (New York: Random House, 1969).

27 Richard T. De George, "Responding to the Mandate for Social Responsibility," *Guidelines for Business When Societal Demands Conflict* (Washington, D.C.: Council for Better Business Bureaus, 1978), pp. 60–80.

SELECTED
BIBLIOGRAPHY

CHAPTER 1

Baier, Kurt: "Good Reasons," *Philosophical Studies,* vol. 4, 1953, pp. 1–15.

Bradley, F. H.: "Why Should I Be Moral?", *Ethical Studies,* Oxford University Press, London, 1927, Essay II, pp. 53–74.

Brock, Dan: "The Justification of Morality," *American Philosophical Quarterly,* vol. 14, no. 1, January 1977, pp. 71–78.

Butler, Joseph: *Five Sermons,* Stuart M. Brown, Jr. (ed.), Bobbs-Merrill, Indianapolis, 1950.

Carlson, George R.: "Ethical Egoism Reconsidered," *American Philosophical Quarterly,* January 1973, pp. 25–33.

Gauthier, David P.: "Morality and Advantage," *Philosophical Review,* vol. LXXVI, 1967, pp. 460–475.

Gewirth, Alan: "Moral Rationality," in John Bricke (ed.), *Freedom and Morality,* University of Kansas Press, Lawrence, 1976, pp. 113–150.

Kalin, Jesse: "Two Kinds of Moral Reasoning: Ethical Egoism as a Moral Theory," *Canadian Journal of Philosophy,* vol. 5, no. 3, November 1975, pp. 323–356.

MacIntyre, Alasdair: "Egoism and Altruism," in Paul Edwards (ed.), *The Encyclopedia of Philosophy,* Macmillan and Free Press, New York, 1967, vol. 2, pp. 462–466.

Milo, Ronald (ed.): *Egoism and Altruism,* Wadsworth, Belmont, Calif., 1973.

Nagel, Thomas: *The Possibility of Altruism,* Clarendon Press, Oxford, 1970.

Olson, Robert G.: *The Morality of Self-Interest,* Harcourt Brace Jovanovich, New York, 1965.

Pritchard, H. A.: "Does Moral Philosophy Rest on a Mistake?", *Mind,* vol. 21, 1912, pp. 487–499.

Slote, Michael Anthony: "An Empirical Basis for Psychological Egoism," *Journal of Philosophy,* vol. 61, no. 18, October 1, 1964, pp. 530–537.

Trigg, Roger: *Reason and Commitment,* Cambridge University Press, Cambridge, 1973.

CHAPTER 2

Benedict, Ruth: *Patterns of Culture,* Houghton Mifflin, Boston, 1934, chaps. 1–3.

Brandt, R. B.: "Ethical Relativism," in Paul Edwards (ed.), *The Encyclopedia of Philosophy,* Macmillan and Free Press, New York, 1967, vol. 3, pp. 75–78.

Coburn, Robert: "Relativism and the Basis of Morality," *Philosophical Review,* vol. LXXXV, January 1976, pp. 87–93.

Cohen, Brenda: "Three Ethical Fallacies," *Mind,* vol. LXXXVI, January 1977, pp. 78–87.

Garnett, A. C.: "Relativism and Absolutism in Ethics," *Ethics,* vol. 54, 1943–44, pp. 186–199.

Harman, Gilbert: "Moral Relativism Defended," *Philosophical Review,* vol. 84, 1975, pp. 3–22.

James, Edward W.: "A Reasoned Ethical Incoherence," *Ethics,* vol. 89, no. 3, April 1979, pp. 240–253.

Kluckhohn, Clyde: "Ethical Relativity," *Journal of Philosophy,* vol. 52, 1955, pp. 663–677.

Ladd, John (ed.): *Ethical Relativism,* Wadsworth, Belmont, Calif., 1973.

Lean, Martin E.: "Aren't Moral Judgments 'Factual'?", *Personalist*, vol. 51, no. 3, Summer 1970, pp. 259–285.

Mabbott, J. D.: "Is Anthropology Relevant to Ethics," *Proceedings of the Aristotelian Society, Supplementary Series 20*, 1946, pp. 85–93.

Meiland, Jack W., and Michael Krausz (eds.): *Relativism: Cognitive and Moral*, Notre Dame University Press, Notre Dame, Ind., 1984.

Sumner, W. G.: *Folkways*, Ginn, Boston, 1907.

Taylor, Paul W.: "Four Types of Ethical Relativism," *Philosophical Review*, vol. 63, 1954, pp. 500–516.

———: "Social Science and Ethical Relativism," *Journal of Philosophy*, vol. 55, 1958, pp. 32–44.

CHAPTER 3

Audi, Robert: "Moral Responsibility, Freedom, and Compulsion," *American Philosophical Quarterly*, vol. 11, no. 1, January 1974, pp. 1–14.

Beardsley, Elizabeth L.: "Determinism and Moral Perspectives," *Philosophy and Phenomenological Research*, vol. XXI, 1960, pp. 1–20.

Campbell, C. A.: "Is Freewill a Pseudo-Problem?", *Mind*, vol. 60, 1951, pp. 441–465.

Chisholm, Roderick M.: "Human Freedom and the Self," in John Bricke (ed.), *Freedom and Morality*, University of Kansas Press, Lawrence, 1976, pp. 23–35.

Duggan, Timothy, and Bernard Gert: "Voluntary Abilities," *American Philosophical Quarterly*, vol. IV, no. 2, 1967, pp. 127–135.

Fingarette, Herbert: "Responsibility," *Mind*, vol. 75, 1966, pp. 58–74.

Hampshire, Stuart: "Freedom of Mind," in John Bricke (ed.), *Freedom and Morality*, University of Kansas Press, Lawrence, 1976, pp. 37–51.

Hospers, John: "Meaning and Free Will," *Philosophy and Phenomenological Research*, vol. X, 1950, pp. 307–330.

James, William: "The Dilemma of Determinism," in *Essays on Faith and Morals*, World, Cleveland, 1962, pp. 145–183.

Ladenson, Robert F.: "A Theory of Personal Autonomy," *Ethics*, vol. 86, no. 1, October 1975, pp. 30–48.

Mandelbaum, Maurice: "Determinism and Moral Responsibility," *Ethics*, vol. 70, 1959–60, pp. 204–219.

Matson, Wallace I.: "The Irrelevance of Free Will to Moral Responsibility," *Mind*, vol. 65, 1956, pp. 489–497.

Morris, Herbert: "Persons and Punishment," *Monist*, vol. 52, 1968, pp. 475 *et seq*.

Pap, Arthur: "Determinism and Moral Responsibility," *Journal of Philosophy*, vol. 43, 1946, pp. 318–237.

Skinner, B. F.: *Walden Two*, Macmillan, New York, 1962.

Taylor, Richard: *Action and Purpose*, Prentice-Hall, Englewood Cliffs, N.J., 1966.

CHAPTER 4

Aquinas, St. Thomas: *Summa Theologica*, Prima Secundae, chap. 28, "Law" (Ia2ae. 90–7).

Austin, John: *The Province of Jurisprudence Determined*, Curwen, Plaistow, Great Britain, 1954, lecture V, pp. 118–191.

Devlin, Patrick: *The Enforcement of Morals*, Oxford University Press, Oxford, 1970.

Frankena, William K.: "Love and Principle in Christian Ethics," in *Faith and Philosophy*, Eerdmans, Grand Rapids, Mich., 1964, pp. 203–225.

Fuller, Lon: *The Morality of Law*, Yale, New Haven, 1964.

Gustafson, James M.: *Can Ethics Be Christian?*, University of Chicago Press, Chicago, 1975.

————: *Ethics from a Theocentric Perspective*, vol. 1: *Theology and Ethics*, University of Chicago Press, Chicago, 1981.

Hart, H. L. A.: "Legal and Moral Obligation," in A. I. Melden (ed.), *Essays in Moral Philosophy*, University of Washington Press, Seattle, 1958, pp. 82–107.

Hepburn, Ronald W.: "Secular Ethics and Moral Seriousness," in *Christianity and Paradox*, Humanities Press, New York, 1958, pp. 128–154.

Hick, John: "Belief and Life: The Fundamental Nature of Christian Ethics," *Encounter*, vol. XX, Fall 1959, pp. 494–516.

Nielsen, Kai: "Some Remarks on the Independence of Morality from Religion," *Mind*, vol. LXX, 1961, pp. 175–186.

Phillips, D. Z.: "Moral and Religious Conceptions of Duty: An Analysis," *Mind*, vol. LXXIII, 1964, pp. 406–412.

Ress, D. A.: "The Ethics of Divine Commands," *Proceedings of the Aristotelian Society*, vol. 57, 1956–57, pp. 83–106.

Stone, Christopher: *Where the Law Ends*, Harper & Row, New York, 1975.

Wasserstrom, Richard A. (ed.): *Morality and the Law*, Wadsworth, Belmont, Calif., 1971.

CHAPTER 5

Care, Norman S.: "Career Choice," *Ethics*, October 1983, pp. 283–302.

Chisholm, Roderick: "Supererogation and Offence: A Conceptual Scheme for Ethics," *Ratio*, vol. 5, 1963, pp. 1–14.

Falk, W. D.: "Morality, Self, and Others," in H. Castaneda and G. Nakhnikian (eds.), *Morality and Language of Conduct*, Wayne State University, Detroit, 1963, pp. 25–68.

Feinberg, Joel: "Supererogation and Rules," *International Journal of Ethics*, vol. 71, 1961, pp. 276–288.

Gass, William H.: "The Care of the Obliging Stranger," *Philosophical Review*, vol. 66, 1957, pp. 193–204.

Gert, Bernard: "Moral Ideals," in *The Moral Rules*, Harper & Row, New York, 1966, chap. 7, pp. 128–149.

Heyd, David: *Supererogation: Its Status in Ethical Theory*, Cambridge University Press, Cambridge, 1982.

Simon, John G., Charles W. Powers, and Jon P. Gunnemann: *The Ethical Investor: Universities and Corporate Responsibility*, Yale, New Haven, 1972.

Singer, Marcus: "On Duties to Oneself," *Ethics*, vol. 69, 1959, pp. 202–205.

Urmson, J. O.: "Saints and Heroes," in A. I. Melden (ed.), *Essays in Moral Philosophy*, University of Washington Press, Seattle, 1958.

CHAPTER 6

Anscombe, G. E. M.: "Modern Moral Philosophy," *Philosophy*, vol. 33, 1958, pp. 1–19.

Bok, Sissela: *Lying: Moral Choice in Public and Private Life*, Pantheon, New York, 1978.

Carritt, E. F.: *The Theory of Morals*, Clarendon Press, Oxford, 1928.

Diggs, B. J.: "Rules and Utilitarianism," *American Philosophical Quarterly,* vol. 1, 1964, pp. 32–44.

Fletcher, Joseph: *Situation Ethics: The New Morality,* Westminster, Philadelphia, 1966.

Gert, Bernard: *The Moral Rules,* Harper & Row, New York, 1966.

Kant, Immanuel: "On a Supposed Right to Lie from Benevolent Motives," in *The Critique of Practical Reason and Other Writings in Moral Philosophy,* Lewis White Beck (ed. and trans.), University of Chicago Press, Chicago, 1949, pp. 346–350.

Nowell-Smith, P. H.: "The Purpose of Moral Rules," in *Ethics,* Penguin, Baltimore, 1954, chap. 16.

Ramsey, Paul: *Deeds and Rules in Christian Ethics,* Scribner's, New York, 1967.

Ross, W. D.: *The Right and the Good,* Clarendon Press, Oxford, 1930.

Singer, Marcus G.: "The Golden Rule," *Philosophy,* vol. 38, 1963, pp. 293–314.

Singer, Peter: *The Expanding Circle,* Farrar, Staus, & Giroux, New York, 1981.

Taylor, Richard: *Good and Evil,* Macmillan, New York, 1970, chaps. 2 & 13.

CHAPTER 7

Beauchamp, Tom L., and James F. Childress: "The Principle of Autonomy," in *Principles of Biomedical Ethics,* Oxford University Press, New York, 1979, chap. 3.

Cranor, Carl: "Toward a Theory of Respect for Persons," *American Philosophical Quarterly,* vol. 12, October 1975, pp. 303–319.

Darwall, Stephen L.: "Two Kinds of Respect," *Ethics,* vol. 88, 1977, pp. 36–49.

Downie, Robert S., and Elizabeth Telfer: *Respect for Persons,* George Allen & Unwin, London, 1969.

Dworkin, Gerald: "Moral Autonomy," in H. T. Engelhardt, Jr., and Daniel Callahan (eds.), *Morals, Science, and Sociality,* Hastings Center, Hastings-on-Hudson, N.Y., 1978.

Haezraki, Pepita: "The Concept of Man as End-in-Himself," in *Kant: A Collection of Critical Essays,* Anchor Books, Garden City, N.Y., 1967.

Massey, Stephen J.: "Is Self-Respect a Moral or a Psychological Concept," *Ethics,* vol. 93, no. 2, January 1983, pp. 246–261.

Rawls, John: *A Theory of Justice,* Harvard, Cambridge, Mass., 1971.

Willard, Duane: "Aesthetic Discrimination Against Persons," *Dialogue,* vol. XVI, no. 4, 1977, pp. 676–692.

Williams, Bernard: "The Idea of Equality," in Joel Feinberg (ed.), *Moral Concepts,* Oxford University Press, Oxford, 1970, pp. 158–161.

CHAPTER 8

Benn, S. I.: "Rights," in Paul Edwards (ed.), *The Encyclopedia of Philosophy,* Macmillan and Free Press, New York, 1967, vol. 7, pp. 191–195.

Dworkin, Ronald: *Taking Rights Seriously,* Harvard, Cambridge, Mass., 1977.

Ethics, vol. 92, October 1981. This entire issue is devoted to rights.

Flathman, Richard: *The Practice of Rights,* Harvard, Cambridge, Mass., 1976.

Golding, Martin P.: "Towards a Theory of Human Rights," *Monist,* vol. 52, 1968, pp. 521–549.

Hart, H. L. A.: "Are There Any Natural Rights?" *Philosophical Review,* vol. 64, 1955, pp. 175–191.

Hohfeld, Wesley: *Fundamental Legal Conceptions,* Yale, New Haven, 1923.

Lyons, David: "Human Rights and the General Welfare," *Philosophy and Public Affairs,* vol. 6, 1977, pp. 113–129.

McCloskey, H. J.: "Human Needs, Rights and Political Values," *American Philosophical Quarterly,* vol. 13, 1976, pp. 1–11.

————: "Rights—Some Conceptual Issues," *Australasian Journal of Philosophy,* vol. 54, 1976, pp. 99–115.

Macdonald, Margaret: "Natural Rights," *Proceedings of the Aristotelian Society,* vol. 47, 1946–47, pp. 225–250.

Macklin, Ruth: "Moral Concerns and Appeals to Rights and Duties," *Hastings Center Report,* vol. 6, 1976, pp. 31–38.

Melden, Abraham I.: *Rights and Persons,* University of California Press, Berkeley, 1977.

Nickel, James W.: "Are Human Rights Utopian?" *Philosophy and Public Affairs,* vol. 11, no. 3, Summer 1982, pp. 246–264.

Singer, Marcus G.: "The Basis of Rights and Duties," *Philosophical Studies,* vol. 23, 1972, pp. 43–57.

CHAPTER 9

Becker, Lawrence C.: "The Neglect of Virtue," *Ethics,* vol. 85, 1975, pp. 110–122.

Brandt, Richard: "Traits of Character: A Conceptual Analysis," *American Philosophical Quarterly,* vol. 7, 1970, pp. 23–37.

Burnyeat, Myles: "Virtues in Action," in Gregory Vlastos (ed.), *The Philosophy of Socrates,* Doubleday, Garden City, N.Y., 1971, pp. 209–234.

Epictetus: *The Enchiridion,* T. W. Higginson, (trans.), Bobbs Merrill, Indianapolis, 1955.

Foot, Philippa: *Virtues and Vices and Other Essays in Moral Philosophy,* University of California Press, Berkeley, 1978.

Frankena, William K.: "Prichard and the Ethics of Virtue," *Monist,* vol. 54, 1970, pp. 1–17.

Gert, Bernard: "Virtue and Vices," in *The Moral Rules,* Harper & Row, New York, 1966, chap. 8, pp. 150–171.

Hauerwas, Stanley: *A Community of Character,* University of Notre Dame Press, Notre Dame, Ind., 1981, chap. 6.

Hudson, S.: "Character Traits and Desires," *Ethics,* vol. 90, 1980, pp. 539–549.

Hudson, Stephen D.: "Taking Virtues Seriously," *Australasian Journal of Philosophy,* vol. 59, no. 2, June 1981, pp. 189–202.

Pincoffs, Edmund: "Quandary Ethics," *Mind,* vol. LXXX, 1971, pp. 552–571.

Slote, Michael: *Goods and Virtues,* Clarendon Press, Oxford, 1983.

Urmson, J. O.: "Aristotle's Doctrine of the Mean," *American Philosophical Quarterly,* vol. 10, 1973, pp. 223–230.

Wallace, James D.: "Excellences and Merit," *Philosophical Review,* vol. 83, no. 2, April 1974, pp. 182–199.

Warnock, G. J.: *The Object of Morality,* Methuen, London, 1971, chap. 6.

CHAPTER 10

Ackerman, Bruce A.: *Social Justice in the Liberal State,* Yale, New Haven, 1980.

Ake, Christopher: "Justice as Equality," *Philosophy and Public Affairs,* vol. 5, no. 1, Fall 1975.

Arneson, Richard J.: "The Principle of Fairness and Free-Rider Problems," *Ethics,* vol. 92, no. 4, July 1982, pp. 616–633.

Becker, Lawrence C.: "Economic Justice: Three Problems," *Ethics*, vol. 89, no. 4, July 1979, pp. 385–393.

Benn, Stanley I.: "Egalitarianism and the Equal Consideration of Interests," *Equality*, Nomos IX, Atherton, New York, 1967, pp. 61–78.

Berlin, Isaiah: "Equality," *Proceedings of the Aristotelian Society*, vol. 56, 1955–56, pp. 301–326.

Bowie, Norman E.: "Equality and Distributive Justice," *Philosophy*, vol. XLV, no. 172, April 1970, pp. 140–148.

Dworkin, Ronald: "What Is Equality," Part I, "Equality of Welfare," *Philosophy and Public Affairs*, vol. 10, no. 3, Summer 1981, pp. 185–246.

Fishkin, James S.: *Justice, Equal Opportunity, and the Family*, Yale, New Haven, 1983.

Frankena, William K.: "Some Beliefs About Justice," in John Bricke (ed.), *Freedom and Morality*, University of Kansas Press, Lawrence, 1976.

Rawls, John: *A Theory of Justice*, Harvard, Cambridge, Mass., 1971.

Rescher, Nicholas: *Distributive Justice*, Bobbs-Merrill, New York, 1966.

Schaar, John H.: "Equality of Opportunity and Beyond," *Equality*, Nomos IX, Atherton, New York, 1967, pp. 228–249.

Sher, George: "Effort, Ability and Personal Desert," *Philosophy and Public Affairs*, vol. 8, no. 4, Summer 1979, pp. 361–376.

Simon, Robert: "An Indirect Defense of the Merit Principle," *Philosophical Forum*, vol. 10, nos. 2–4, 1978–79, pp. 224–240.

CHAPTER 11

Braybrooke, David: *Three Tests for Democracy: Personal Rights, Human Welfare, and Collective Preference*, Random House, New York, 1968.

Ewing, Alfred C.: "Utilitarianism," *Ethics*, vol. 58, 1948, pp. 100–111.

Hare, R. M.: *Moral Thinking: Its Levels, Method and Point*, Oxford University Press, New York, 1981.

Harrison, J.: "Utilitarianism, Universalization and Our Duty to Be Just," *Proceedings of the Aristotelian Society*, vol. LIII, 1952–53, pp. 105–134.

Haslett, D. W.: *Moral Rightness*, Martinus Nijhoff, The Hague, 1974.

Hodgson, I. H.: *Consequences of Utilitarianism*, Oxford University Press, London, 1967.

Lyons, David: *The Forms and Limits of Utilitarianism*, Oxford University Press, London, 1965.

Moore, George Edward: *Ethics*, Oxford University Press, London, 1961.

Narveson, Jan: *Morality and Utility*, Johns Hopkins, Baltimore, 1967.

Rosen, Bernard: *Strategies of Ethics*, Houghton Mifflin, Boston, 1978.

Sartorius, Rolf: *Individual Conduct and Social Norms*, Dickenson, Encino, Calif., 1975.

Sidgwick, Henry: *Methods of Ethics*, Macmillan, London, 1962.

Singer, M. G.: *Generalization in Ethics*, Knopf, New York, 1961.

Sobel, J. H.: "Utilitarianism, Simple and General," *Inquiry*, vol. 13, 1970, pp. 394–449.

Williams, Bernard: "A Critique of Utilitarianism," in *Utilitarianism For and Against*, Cambridge University Press, Cambridge, 1973, pp. 75–155.

CHAPTER 12

Downie, R. S.: "Can Governments Be Held Morally Responsible?" *Philosophical Quarterly*, vol. 11, 1961, pp. 328–334.

————: *Roles and Values: An Introduction to Social Ethics*, Methuen, London, 1971.

Emmet, D.: *Rules, Roles and Relations*, Beacon, Boston, 1966.

English, Jane: "What Do Grown Children Owe Their Parents?" in Onora O'Neill and William Ruddick (eds.), *Having Children: Philosophical and Legal Reflection on Parenthood*, Oxford University Press, New York, 1979, pp. 351–356.

Freedman, Benjamin: "A Meta-Ethics for Professional Morality," *Ethics*, vol. 89, no. 1, October 1978, pp. 1–19.

French, Peter: "What Is Hamlet to McDonnell-Douglas: DC-10," *Business and Professional Ethics Journal*, vol. 1, no. 2, Winter 1982, pp. 1–13.

Goldman, Alan H.: *The Moral Foundations of Professional Ethics*, Rowman & Littlefield, Totowa, N.J., 1980.

Held, Virginia: *The Public Interest and Individual Interests*, Basic Books, New York, 1970.

Lemmon, John: "Moral Dilemmas," *Philosophical Review*, vol. LXXI, 1962, pp. 139–158.

Murphy, C. P.: "The Moral Situation in Nursing," in E. Bandman and B. Bandman (eds.), *Bioethics and Human Rights*, Little, Brown, Boston, 1978, pp. 313–320.

O'Neill, Onora: "Begetting, Bearing and Rearing," in Onora O'Neill and William Ruddick (eds.), *Having Children: Philosophical and Legal Reflections on Parenthood*, Oxford University Press, New York, 1979, pp. 25–38.

Rousseau, Jean Jacques: *The Social Contract*, Charles Frankel (ed.), Hafner, New York, 1947.

Thompson, Dennis: "Ascribing Responsibility to Advisers in Government," *Ethics*, vol. 93, April 1983, pp. 546–560.

Walzer, Michael: "Political Action: The Problem of Dirty Hands," *Philosophy and Public Affairs*, vol. 2, 1973, pp. 160–180.

Wasserstrom, Richard: "Lawyers as Professionals: Some Moral Issues," *Human Rights*, vol. 5, 1975, pp. 1–24.